Landscapes in Early Childhood Education

Rethinking Childhood

Joe L. Kincheloe and Janice A. Jipson
General Editors

Vol. 4

PETER LANG
New York • Washington, D.C./Baltimore • Boston • Bern
Frankfurt am Main • Berlin • Brussels • Vienna • Canterbury

Landscapes in Early Childhood Education

Cross-National Perspectives on Empowerment— A Guide for the New Millennium

EDITED BY
Jacqueline Hayden

PETER LANG
New York • Washington, D.C./Baltimore • Boston • Bern
Frankfurt am Main • Berlin • Brussels • Vienna • Canterbury

LIBRARY OF CONGRESS CATALOGING-IN-PUBLICATION DATA

Landscapes in early childhood education: cross-national perspectives on
empowerment, a guide for the new millennium / edited by Jacqueline Hayden.
p. cm. — (Rethinking childhood; vol. 4)
Includes bibliographical references.
1. Early childhood education—Cross-cultural studies.
I. Hayden, Jacqueline. II. Series.
LB1139.23.L26   372.21—dc21   99-052000
ISBN 0-8204-3735-2
ISSN 1086-7155

DIE DEUTSCHE BIBLIOTHEK-CIP-EINHEITSAUFNAHME

Landscapes in early childhood education: cross-national perspectives on
empowerment; a guide for the new millennium / ed. by: Jacqueline Hayden.
—New York; Washington, D.C./Baltimore; Boston; Bern; Frankfurt am Main;
Berlin; Brussels; Vienna; Canterbury: Lang.
(Rethinking childhood; Vol. 4)
ISBN 0-8204-3735-2

Cover design by Lisa Dillon

The paper in this book meets the guidelines for permanence and durability
of the Committee on Production Guidelines for Book Longevity
of the Council of Library Resources.

© 2000 Peter Lang Publishing, Inc., New York

All rights reserved.
Reprint or reproduction, even partially, in all forms such as microfilm, xerography,
microfiche, microcard, and offset strictly prohibited.

Printed in the United States of America

In memory of Felicien Nytakyamana, who is one of the hundreds of thousands of victims of a holocaust that continues without respite in Rwanda, the Congo, and other areas of Central Africa, and who, for me, remains forever an example of the ability of the human spirit to rise above any circumstance with dignity, generosity, wisdom, and hope.

This book is dedicated to Sonya and Christine who, for twenty-two years, have filled my landscape with challenge, adventure, fun, and awe.

Contents

Foreword xiii

Acknowledgments xvii

Introduction 1
1 Early Childhood Education: Multiple Perspectives 3
2 Early Childhood Landscapes: A Framework for Analysis 19

The Big Picture 31
3 Childcare and the Growth of Love:
   Preparing for an Unknown Future 33

National Landscapes 47
4 Policy Development and Change on the
   Australian Landscape: A Historical Perspective 49
5 Early Childhood Education on the
   Canadian Policy Landscape 69
6 The Early Childhood Landscape in New Zealand 83
7 Hong Kong's Early Childhood Landscape:
   Division, Diversity, and Dilemmas 95

The Landscape of Policy and Practice 113
8 Hitting the Wall: Early Childhood Education in the
   Primary and Tertiary Sectors—An Australian Case Study 115
9 Choosing Childcare for Infants: Social, Cultural, and
   Demographic Influences and Outcomes 133
10 Empowering Children to Learn and Grow—*Te Whāriki*:
   The New Zealand Early Childhood National Curriculum 153

11	Landscapes of Intimacy, Sensuality, and Care in Early Childhood Settings	171
12	The Social Policy Context of Day Care in Four Canadian Provinces	187
13	Empowerment and Entrapment: Women Workers in Home-Based and Center-Based Settings	205
14	Exploring Parental Involvement in Canada: An Ideological Maze	219
15	Immigrant Families in Early Childhood Centers: Diverse Expectations	239

The Professional Landscape   **251**

16	Preparing the Early Childhood Profession: An Australian Analysis	253
17	When Does a Teacher Teach? The Queensland Early Childhood Profession on Trial	271
18	The Politics of Restructuring and Professional Accountability: A Case Study of Curriculum Choice for Early Childhood Programs	291
19	The Emergent Professional: Training and Credentialing Early Childhood Teachers—An Australian Case Study	307
20	Early Childhood Services in Rural and Remote Areas: Four Case Studies	317
21	Implementing the Australian Early Childhood Association Code of Ethics: A Constitutional Strategy	331
22	Empowering the Migrant Worker: The Childcare Assessment and Bridging Project	341

The Classroom/Curricular Landscape   **353**

23	Family Literacy: Challenges for Early Education	355
24	Literacy in the Preschool: An Australian Case Study	375
25	Effects of Sociocultural Contexts and Discourses on Science and Technology Teaching in Early Childhood Education	393
26	The Kindergarten Landscape	409

The Way Forward   **425**

27	British Columbia's Ministry for Children and Families: A Case Study in Progress	427

Afterword **443**

28 Early Childhood Education: An Empowering Force
    for the Twenty-First Century?   445

Glossary of Terms   459

The Contributors   463

Foreword

Ivan Snook

At the beginning of his book, *The Pedagogy of Hope,* the celebrated educator Paulo Freire writes: "This book is written in rage and love, without which there is no hope" (1995, p. 10). Dr. Hayden's collection reveals starkly that there is much to rage about in the field of early childhood. But it reveals just as forcibly the love that the contributors have for the field, for those who work in it, and for those they serve. It is a book of hope.

Hope is not to be confused with optimism, a state of mind that may be irrational and ineffective. Those who are hopeful, on the other hand, are realistic: they examine the situation clearly and face it honestly. Then they commit themselves to the action needed to bring about the hoped-for future. As Freire puts it: "The future of which we Dream is not inexorable. We have to make it, produce it, or else it will not come in the form we would more or less wish it to. We have to make it out of the concrete reality and more as a project, a Dream, for which we struggle" (p. 101).

For 200 years, early childhood workers have lived by a passionate belief in the inherent capacities of the young child. Rousseau and Froebel based this on metaphysical views: Rousseau on a view of human nature (the child is naturally good) and Froebel on a view of the divine (the child is literally part of God). Dewey, the secular philosopher, endorsed their educational principles but grounded them not in the abstract world of metaphysics but in the concrete demands of social life. In the twentieth century, he argued, the values of early childhood educators are identical to those needed by adults in a democratic society. The progressive spirit that focuses on the child as an autonomous person is also the spirit of democracy. In both cases, however, the social is just as important: we must, he says: "train children in cooperative and mutually helpful living; to foster in them the consciousness of mutual interdependence; and to help them practically in making the adjustments that will carry this spirit into overt deeds" (1956, p. 117).

The papers in this volume relate early childhood to the wider social scene. They reveal the enormous influence that politics, self-interest, and ideology have had on every sphere of education including early childhood education. These influences have now become part of the reality that educators have to recognize clearly, criticize trenchantly, and work to subvert. It is no longer appropriate to retain a Romantic view of childhood as if there is an essence which is noble and innocent. In many Third World countries children are enslaved and exploited, and in the developed world (as it is called) they are now "children of the market", soaking up the selfish values that contemporary ideology has made respectable.

It is well known that in the eighteenth century children were not clearly distinguished from adults. They were portrayed, dressed, and treated as "miniature adults". Progressive educators campaigned against this. (As a slogan for those looking after the very young, Rousseau's "Let childhood ripen in your children" cannot be improved). In the mid-twentieth century many began to argue that childhood itself is a recent social invention in the Western world. Several books in the 1980s took this further by arguing that just as childhood was created, it is now being demolished. Suransky (*The Erosion of Childhood*) lays the blame for this on the increasing involvement of "the market" in childcare. In the search for profit, the physical, emotional, and cognitive needs of the child are forgotten: a child is not a person but merely another unit carrying dollars for entrepreneurs. She speaks of children as "incarcerated in early childhood institutions across the country" (1982, p. 133) and says "if childhood, as a life phase, is a 'becoming at home in the world', the *homelessness* of the children in these hostile and unfriendly institutions is sad testimony to the erosion of childhood" (p. 187).

Postman (*The Disappearance of Childhood*) blames the mass media for breaking down the distinctions between childhood and adulthood. In the media children are again depicted as miniature adults. Their fashions in clothes, their entertainment, their values, and their opinions are seen as little different from those of adults. Alcoholism, drug use, crime, and sexual activity are increasingly features of young as well as old. He believes that the boundaries between child and adult are being broken down, and childhood is being systematically destroyed. In the foreword to the 1994 edition, Postman says that, much as he would like to have been wrong, the contemporary situation provides no reason for him to change his mind. He is, however, impressed by the number of children who have disputed his views and insisted that they are still children. He concludes: "I will stand by the theme of the book: American culture is hostile to the idea of childhood. But it is a comforting, even exhilarating thought that the children are not" (1994, p. ix).

The task of early childhood educators is not simply to sustain childhood but to create it and re-create it. For this to happen many of the images of the age and the institutional and technological pressures on young children will have to be resolutely challenged. As Dr. Hayden puts it in her introduction: "The need for a new vision for the early childhood profession is implicit in every case study and every point raised in this book."

Most of the papers, hopeful as they are, recognize the enormity of the task of today's early childhood educators. The restraints—of resources, policies, ideologies, interests, politics—are very real and must be acknowledged and analyzed. Then begins the struggle to overcome them.

Ivan Snook
Emeritus Professor of Education
Massey University

References

Dewey, J. (1956). *The child and the curriculum and the school and society*. Chicago: University of Chicago Press.

Freire, P. (1995). *Pedagogy of hope*. New York: Continuum.

Postman, N. (1982,1994). *The disappearance of childhood*. New York: Vintage.

Suransky, V. (1982). *The erosion of childhood*. Chicago: University of Chicago Press.

Acknowledgments

The pleasure of reading and reviewing each chapter in this book has been, perhaps, the most rewarding aspect of a diverse and fulfilling career in the field of early childhood education. I am extremely grateful to all the contributors who shared their notions, problems, interests, and issues and who struggled to articulate these within the chosen framework.

My deepest appreciation to the inspiring faculty members at Ryerson University, Toronto, where the concept for the book was conceived; to Joe Kincheloe and Christopher Myers of Peter Lang Publishing for running with it; to Professor Ivan Snook for his unremitting attempts to mould my development as a scholar and thinker; to my colleagues at University of Western Sydney, Nepean, for their constant support, with special thanks to Professor Trevor Cairney, Pro Vice Chancellor, for generous financial support.

Others who deserve special mention are Margaret Knowlden for putting up with those late night visits, and once more meeting impossible timelines; Margaret Heathers for her fine eye; Professor John Macdonald for his encouragement; and the members of the School of Learning, Development and Early Education—Alison Elliott, Ross Elliott, Linda Newman, Denise Fraser, Jean Ashton, Carol Burgess—who helped me out in myriad ways.

Finally, to my family, both here and in Canada—Bernie, Christine, Sonya, all of the Haydens, Georges, Hunters, Kings, Milfords, Nygrens—and, especially, to Mum—who put up with my erratic appearances and disappearances, strange working hours, preoccupation, forgetfulness, and obsessions as though this were all normal and acceptable behavior: for your generosity and good humor, heartfelt thanks.

Jacqueline Hayden
Sydney, Australia.

Introduction

Chapter 1

Early Childhood Education: Multiple Perspectives

Jacqueline Hayden

Introduction

My purpose in presenting the case studies and essays in this book has reflected a work in progress. I started with the intention of exposing the parallels among the early childhood landscapes that I experienced in my work and travels around Canada, Australia, New Zealand, and other places. I thought that analyses of issues would illuminate similarities and encourage us to work together toward solutions.

As my discussions with the researchers, social and policy analysts, practitioners, and others who have contributed to this volume progressed, I took on a different perspective. The book would be about salient issues that professionals need to face as they confront a new era of early childhood education in the new millennium. The book would help to sort the macro, global issues, from the micro issues. By raising awareness of the big picture, I would be assisting in forwarding the profession toward more *constitutional* solutions.[1]

Finally, as chapters rolled in, I saw a different book emerge. The book would still incorporate analyses of similarities and differences (but mostly similarities) that form a global early childhood landscape. It would still be about current and future issues which have macro, universal significance, and it would still illuminate how early childhood issues reflect, respond to, and also influence socio/cultural/economic/political movements—but beyond this it became an expression of optimism in difficult times. As the title suggests, the purpose of this book goes beyond raised awareness and presentation of areas for action. It is to provide new perspectives and to re-situate early childhood education within changing frameworks.

The case studies described in this book reveal our collectivity. They show how, across the globe, we have addressed similar issues, confronted constraints and supports, and struggled to deal with common problems. They show how we are united in our understandings and our goals—and in our commitment to meet those goals.

The Book as Guidepost

The first essay in the book comes from Philip Gammage. In this powerful commentary Gammage describes not only what early childhood education is or should be—but what childhood is and should be. There is not, in current times, a great deal of distinction. Most children in Canada, Australia, New Zealand, and similar nations attend early childhood programs. It is part of childhood, and thus will soon be part of our collective unconscious. As Gammage shows in his harrowing overview of social conditions throughout much of the world, the distribution of more money or the securing of a higher status for professionals is not in itself of particular importance. These may represent some means, but they are not ends. What is important is a consolidated effort, on all fronts, to work toward a humane and just society—and to reflect this love and commitment in our provision for children. As Gammage points out, time is not on our side, and there is no rehearsal.

The last case study in the book—the *dénouement* of what and how early childhood services can achieve—is described by Alan Pence and Allison Benner. Their chapter paints a vision of how early childhood issues can be addressed from a policy perspective within large and relatively decentralized national political frameworks such as those of Canada and Australia. According to Pence and Benner, the answer lies in recognition of the *fourth discourse*—"early childhood services as institutions of cultural, social, and economic significance; community resources that should be multifunctional to meet a variety of needs, including care, education, socialization, health, and family support, and that should be available to all families irrespective of parents employment status."

In between these chapters there are few aspects of the early childhood landscape that have been left unexamined—and few activities of early childhood professionals that are not confronted and explored.

The book is hard on the profession. It presents case studies that exemplify poor judgment, erroneous practices, and lost opportunities. It shows how earnest but misguided early childhood professionals have lobbied for distributions instead of constitutional allotments, have accepted poor decision making, and have submitted to unjust and iniquitous policies and to naive or uncaring policymakers. It shows also how, among other things, early childhood teachers, at times, go out of their way not to teach (Raban & Ure), eschew the richness of the technological classroom (Elliott), give in to moral panic and do not fight for the right to touch (Johnson), have been unable to articulate their activities in a way that reflects their professionalism and skills (Burton and Lyons), and how (as Doxey describes in a most unusual way) teachers who deny their early childhood orientation can diminish the voice of children and families.

The purpose of this book, however, is not to berate the profession but just the opposite—to illustrate that early childhood issues and problems cannot be addressed in isolation. Thus it is the broader sociocultural, political, and economic landscape which needs to be analyzed as we prepare to further our professional goals and outcomes—so that the voices of early childhood are not drowned out by the louder cries of social/political change. The interface between the field of early childhood education and other macro and micro trends is illustrated in every case study presented in this volume.

The majority of case studies have been written to raise awareness of impasses in the landscape—areas where concerted attention is needed to remedy issues that have not been appropriately or adequately addressed in the field of early childhood education. These problems will not be solved with dollars, or by those policies (distributions) that emanate from external sources. They need deeper, constitutional resolutions.

Thus while this volume exposes mistakes that have been allowed, it simultaneously provides a signpost for proactive, positive development. Some chapters celebrate the victories of collaboration, consultation, and progress. May and Carr, for example, describe the success of a national curriculum, *Te Whāriki*, in New Zealand. Pence and Benner tell about the newly created Ministry of Children in British Columbia. Ferguson and Prentice describe how some Canadian provinces have attempted structured, regulated approaches to parental involvement which maximize shared decision making/ and control. Cairney describes an Australian community-based literacy program that has demonstrated positive outcomes for all stakeholders—children, families, and schools. And there are many other examples of excellence and progress.

One step toward improvements in the field, and a sub-theme of many chapters, is the need to unpackage what early childhood education is. Studies of early childhood education encompass a huge array of factors within at least five categories—human development, pedagogy, philosophy, curriculum, and policy studies. Each category can be subdivided into myriad specializations. Whereas early childhood professionals tend to band together to distinguish themselves from other specialists within the fields of education, psychology, and policy studies, their focus is not as monolithic or as homogeneous as the term implies. Hayden argues that a confusion over the diverse use of the term "early childhood" constrains the ability of decision makers outside of the field to address issues appropriately. She offers a number of definitions to help clarify the situation. And, Pence and Benner, and Lero show how not one, but no less than four discourses are incorporated into the notion of early childhood education in developed and majority world nations.

What This Book Covers: The Case Studies

Introduction
The introductory chapters in this book describe the purpose and the framework for analyses of the early childhood landscape for current times, and into the next millennium.

The Big Picture
Philip Gammage reviews the critical nature of childrearing in several nations to remind us of the "big picture" and of the role of early childhood services and professionals in creating that picture.

National Landscapes
This section contains case studies which apply historical, social, economic, and political perspectives to an analysis of the development and delivery of early childhood services in four nations.

Jacqueline Hayden describes three trends that have underlined developments in early childhood education in Australia. The role of women in society, the shift toward economic rationalism, and the public image of the early childhood profession, she argues, have played a critical role in the way that the field has been resourced, supported and/or marginalized. Martha Friendly describes how early childhood issues and approaches reflect the issues within the very social fabric of Canada, and Ann Meade uses the case study of New Zealand to show how politics have interacted with early childhood education to create a system whose goals (at least) reflect those deeply embedded principles of the nation—social justice, equality, and equal access to goods and services.

One of the most astounding chapters in this volume, and one that could only be written in 1999, is Elizabeth Mellor's case study of Hong

Kong. In the late 1990s few societies could boast more radical developments than could Hong Kong. Amid the furor of political, economic, social, and cultural debates that have grabbed world attention, early childhood services in Hong Kong grope for a structure, a system, and an articulated purpose within the changing context. In this chapter Mellor shows how early childhood services are a microcosm for social development, being both influenced by, and reflective of, the changing context. More importantly, early childhood services are an indicator of success. If China can get this right, that is, find a way through a formal early education and care system to "reunify," embrace some diversity, integrate rather than alienate, and provide equity in accessibility and standards of service delivery to its youngest citizens, then there is hope for the nation. If not, the disruption may proceed for generations.

Not surprisingly, some of the broader issues uncovered by Mellor are similar to, or have parallels in, those of more stable political nations such as Canada, Australia, and New Zealand. Western oriented service providers and organizations will do well to watch, reflect upon, and learn from developments unfolding in Hong Kong.

The Landscape of Policy and Practice

In this section, nine case studies demonstrate how organizational structures, social mores, national policy, and other variables extrinsic to the early childhood field have a direct impact upon policies and practices at the micro level.

Hayden shows how structural developments in two related educational domains (primary and tertiary) are influencing the early childhood field. Despite some positive distributions in terms of rhetoric and increased training opportunities, early childhood education is hitting a wall—being obstructed by decentralization and amalgamation trends that are taking place in other sectors. These movements result in the devolution of responsibility to decision makers who may have little or no orientation to the goals and outcomes of early childhood philosophy and pedagogy. Interviews with key players reveal how naiveté on the part of decision makers may, without deliberate intent, be causing a systematic corrosion of early childhood programs.

Margaret McKim presents an unusual piece of research. Her topic is parental choices for infant care. In a startling revelation she shows how what goes on *inside* childcare settings is less influential to parental decision making than are external variables such as family demographics, and social and cultural issues. The findings from this study show how the provision and use of childcare are correlated to physical, geographical, political, and economic factors; and that internal family dynamics also play a major role in the demand, use of, and satisfaction with childcare services. Divisions between internal, external, micro, and macro landscapes are, McKim reveals, increasingly blurred. We should not, and cannot, examine any one activity/phenomenon in the field of early childhood without being aware of the ecological balance between that factor and myriad others.

An encouraging case study is presented by Helen May and Margaret Carr in their analyses of the development and use of *Te Whāriki*—the groundbreaking national curriculum document recently launched by the New Zealand Government. Their chapter, perhaps more than any other, captures the theme of this book. May and Carr, in a fascinating section on politics, tell how the redrafting of the *Te Whāriki* document was subject to various raids by "pens that were not early childhood"—either in focus or in sympathy. Despite this, a collaborative and consultative approach within the field succeeded in gaining unified support from all organizations and constituent groups and overcoming political resistance. This case study typifies the interaction of the landscape of early childhood with the broader national landscape. The authors emphasize that while approval of *Te Whāriki* represents a great success in the history of New Zealand early childhood developments, this event cannot transcend the political and educational context in which it is situated. Funding, regulations, accountability, and training policies are also part of the fabric—and success is dependent upon a concomitant, appropriate infrastructure.

As has been shown regarding developments in Australia and Canada, policy decisions (distributions) that lack structural fabric (constitutional allotments) can actually hinder progress because they provide an appearance of support that rationalizes government activity and appeases pressure groups (see Hayden, 1993, 1994, 1997). The chapter by May and Carr provides an optimistic and in-depth analysis of what can be done with a unified approach—but also what needs to be watched in order to consolidate any victory. Early childhood professionals, it seems, cannot become complacent.

The temptation to simply follow the social flow is strong, as Richard Johnson demonstrates in his chapter on intimacy, sensuality, and care in early childhood settings. In a personal and courageous way, Johnson examines how a misguided social trend and an accompanying moral panic has beset the educational field—and made us all fearful of expressing touch, warmth, and affection. The very essence of early childhood education is being affected by variables that are in opposition to our goals and responsibilities.

Continuing the theme of external influences, Mary Lyon and Patricia Canning report on their investigation of day care centers in Atlantic Canada. Their findings add another dimension to McKim's analyses of the myriad variables affecting choice of infant care by families. Lyon and Canning reveal the relationship between center auspice, provincial regulations, geographical location, teacher characteristics, and adult working conditions, family socioeconomic status, and quality and child development in day care centers. The diversity and breadth of their study allows them to present a macro view about policy shifts that are needed in order to ensure a universally high-quality system of services to children and families.

Andrea Petrie and Judith Burton foreshadow some concerns that are highlighted in later chapters. Their analyzes of the way in which social structures shape the experiences of those who work in early childhood education, especially those in home-based and center-based care, reveal inherent issues of empowerment and entrapment for women workers. Much work needs to be done to challenge existing assumptions and frameworks for childcare professionals. Subsequent chapters take up this challenge.

The role of parental involvement in the early childhood landscape is reviewed in two unique studies. Evelyn Ferguson and Susan Prentice reveal how "parent involvement" reflects deeply embedded values about the role of families, the role of the state, the role of professionals, social entitlement and to an extent our very concept of modern pluralistic democracy. The authors' analyses of Canadian provinces/territories reveal a continuum of approaches to parental involvement which range from "silence" to "full control." Each approach incorporates economic (market based) and social/cultural biases and demonstrates how parental involvement serves as a mirror for—and victim of—regional, national, and international political/economic trends.

The work of Marjory Ebbeck and Anne Glover enhances the Prentice and Ferguson study. Ebbeck and Glover surveyed/interviewed 100 immigrant families, from five nations, who were accessing childcare services in Australia and found that immigrants cannot be considered a monolithic grouping. Attitudes about childcare services were shown to differ according to country of origin, and also to differ significantly from those of the Australian early childhood teachers. While home-center articulation remains a vital aspect of quality delivery, early childhood specialists cannot assume that their notion of parental involvement is appropriate in all situations. Teachers need to examine their own attitudes and expectations in order to ensure that cultural sensitivity, over and above current concepts of "best practice", is driving their interactions with all families.

The Professional Landscape

This section addresses the issues involved in training and preparing early childhood teachers for a changing and increasingly complex role.

Collette Tayler summarizes the professional landscape by applying an ecological framework to the issues involved in training early childhood professionals. There is a pressing need to address change theory and to apply socially critical frameworks if professionals are to function effectively in the context of the new millennium. This need, however, is thwarted by traditional approaches to teacher training and by a climate of fiscal constraint and other distributional reductions. Tayler shows how changes in child and family demographics have wide reaching effects. She calls upon a mobilization of the collective power of early childhood specialists in order to solidify constitutional issues and to meet the challenge of the next stage of development for the early childhood profession.

One such challenge is the recent ruling by the industrial relations tribunal of Queensland, Australia, that teachers in day care centers do not teach, and thus do not warrant teaching salaries. This ruling was made in the face of the fact that the day care teachers had tertiary training deemed to be equivalent to that of primary teachers. Judith Burton and Michael Lyons analyze the issues inherent in this decision and identify the importance of constitutional approaches to early childhood education. This chapter may be the most important piece of current research in the field of early childhood education in Australia or elsewhere. The astonishing ruling, and the evidence which was collected to support it, reflects some of the labyrinthine obstacles within the field—and may provide an explanation for the roller coaster scenario of accomplishments and disasters over the past three decades. If early childhood practitioners cannot articulate and demonstrate their professionalism, they will be assigned neither professional status nor associated professional allotments by the community/society. But when society does not value the work of those who care for young children because of gender, ideological, historical, or philosophical reasons, the push for professionalism can be seen as a threat to prevailing mores. Again, the acute symbiosis of early childhood issues with the prevailing sociocultural zeitgeist is revealed.

Corrie provides another example of particular challenges for early childhood teachers in her case study about the purchase and statewide promotion of a curriculum package. The package garnered widespread demand from principals, parents, and even from early childhood teachers despite the fact that it did not reflect appropriate early childhood practice. The need to meet financial, structural, and space requirements is shown to powerfully influence curriculum choices.

Veale uses the case study of South Australia to present a history of the emerging profession of early childhood education. Her description illuminates how a care versus education dichotomy has been reinforced by structural and systemic forces which reflect social and economic trends. While development in tertiary training for early childhood professionals is reflecting the wider base of responsibility for early childhood specialists (supporting their role as community leaders—the fourth discourse), this same development may be serving to exacerbate differences between the education and childcare sectors. Students who gain credentials through the less expensive, more accessible community college (TAFE) system in South Australia could become "stuck" in the childcare sector while their more privileged colleagues are receiving increasingly prestigious qualifications at university, and increasingly more leadership based positions. Articulation of the two training vehicles is a positive way to overcome the potential "ghetto-fication" of the childcare sector and those who work in it.

The chapter by Jan White and Tracey Simpson reflects a universal dilemma. The four case studies described within this chapter show what can happen when urban solutions are applied to rural problems. Simpson and White make two important points. First, they show how the context of early childhood education in remote/rural areas is heterogeneous—so that one issue which arises in one remote/rural area may be as different from that in another remote/rural area as it is from urban concerns. Second, the authors demonstrate that the goal for standardized practice and common regulations, as a way to develop and maintain professional standards in early childhood education, can be carried too far. A lack of flexibility in policy implementation can have devastating effects for the field. Of all the case studies presented in this volume, the events described in this chapter may be the most tragic. Under the guise of national standards, good early childhood programs have been damaged, and good and needed early childhood professionals have been lost to the field. The need for attention to constitutional aspects—empowerment to those who have relevant knowledge and expertise—has never been more graphically revealed.

Newman describes why and how a distinct form of ethical reasoning can be integrated into preservice training programs for (often young) graduates who find themselves in positions of significant influence over families and children. Codes of Ethics, she argues, need to be more than posters on the wall; they need to be addressed, confronted, debated, and activated by teachers during their preservice, formative years.

Vicki Greive and Carmel Maloney describe an innovative initiative from Western Australia. The undersupply of trained early childhood teachers prompted an experiment whereby new migrants with diverse but related credentials or experiences were trained and recruited into the field. The result was a richer, more socially and culturally representative profession. Financial and immigration policies are sadly reducing the effects of this positive development, but seeds may have been sown for a revised professional profile.

The Classroom/Curricular Landscape
The chapters in this section explore how the teaching and learning activity that takes place within the walls of the "classroom" reflect broader social goals and mores.

Trevor Cairney reviews the concept of family literacy and describes the benefits when teachers embrace and reflect the diverse literacies of the families and cultures which are represented in their centers/classrooms. He offers an inspirational case study. The parent-centered, community/school-based program, which he designed to increase the articulation of literacy between home and educational settings has been successful in meeting a number of goals. Cairney shows that despite the difficulty in transforming traditional, embedded educational structures and systems, social evolutionary development *is* possible when true partnerships are formed among institutions, communities, and the families/children they serve.

Bridie Raban and Christine Ure provide a different micro perspective on literacy learning. Their chapter focuses on the articulation between professionals in terms of literacy-related activities within preschool classrooms. Based on their research findings, the authors demonstrate how a constitutional deficiency—a clear articulation of the purpose and function of early childhood education—has resulted in misunderstandings by early childhood teachers, and, in some cases, in a paucity of challenging opportunities for preschool children. The study reported in this chapter reveals that some early childhood professionals associated literacy teaching with didactic (primary) strategies which they deemed to be nondevelopmentally appropriate. Children, it was felt, needed to be protected as long as possible from the pressure and outcome-orientation of the school curriculum. Meanwhile, primary teachers did not want their preschool colleagues to "do their job." The authors argue that a misunderstanding of roles, responsibilities and of the discourses of primary schools and preschool staff may be preventing children from capitalizing on the most opportune learning time of their lives. While the authors indicate stark "non- alignment of policy and practice with well established theoretical perpectives", they also offer some encouraging solutions. One outcome of the research process was an increased awareness of roles and of avenues for mutual support and collaboration between preschool and primary teachers. This coalition of colleagues from different sectors represents a constitutional dimension that increases the voices of both groups. As Raban and Ure make clear, society as a whole benefits when early childhood specialists receive both the distributional and constitutional support necessary to ensure maximum use of their knowledge and skills.

Alison Elliott investigates conceptions and outcomes of the use of science and technology curricula in early childhood settings. She shows that, while support for the integration of science and technology as part of modern living has dominated educational rhetoric and policy for most of the 1990s, this support has not been reflected by an increase in opportunities for preschool and early school-aged children. The gulf between rhetoric and reality is a result of much more than poor resourcing or lack of knowledge, and skills, and the recalcitrant attitudes of teachers and consultants/administrators. These are symptoms, rather than causes of pedagogical *nonpractice*. It is the constitutional issues—the sociocultural context, the gendering of experiences, the use of an early childhood pedagogical discourse (which juxtaposes notions of play against the more cognitive and scientific conception of technology) which are defining and restricting growth within the arena. In her sweeping and thorough analyses, Elliott proves that technology can (must) be used to foster deeper level thinking skills, and that early childhood settings are the most appropriate places to confront outmoded attitudes and to integrate science and technology within the *evolving social/cultural landscape.*

Isabel Doxey offers an unusual analysis of kindergarten from the perspective of the kindergartener. This perspective illuminates a multitude of issues which, she states, are too easily lost among the fiscal and political forces that drive kindergarten delivery. Her stories of three children who struggle to make meaning in their world reinforce the need to address critical issues. These include: a) that quality service delivery needs to be measured in a way that incorporates the child's perspective; b) that parents must be acknowledged as key players and that teachers need to hear what they are saying; and c) that policymakers should ensure that teacher reports rather than statistics drive decision making about curriculum and programming (especially in light of research which has shown that teachers are as accurate in their assessment of children's socializing, problem solving abilities, and academic potential, as are normed tests). Finally, Doxey uses children's voices to show how school readiness needs to concentrate on making schools ready for children, not vice versa, and echoes Cairney in her argument that articulation with home, culture, and the child's own (real) world needs to be at the forefront of the kindergarten landscape.

Conclusion: The Way Forward
The concluding chapter by Alan Pence and Allison Benner brings the analyses of early childhood to a new level. The authors describe the creation in British Columbia of a Ministry for Families which could be the first step in meeting the macro goals of social/political integration for early childhood professionals.

Finally, Donna Lero presents a sweeping overview in her Afterword. She unpackages the four early childhood discourses and concludes that there are means and ways to move forward toward that fourth, comprehensive, collaborative discourse for early childhood education.

Conclusion

Early childhood professionals are not particularly valued in current times. Our knowledge base, practices, and contributions may be seen as soft and inexpert in an era that is obsessed with cost benefit analyses, fiscal restraint, consumer sovereignty, and measurable outcomes. Teaching young children, not just for a future outcome, but for the pleasure of learning in the here and now; modeling compassion at a time when compassion is not revered; lobbying for smallness—small groups, small ratios, small, daily goals—instead of embracing economies of scale, comprehensive, multipurpose systems and structures, makes us seem anachronistic at best, and irrelevant at worst.

But this book has proved the opposite. Not only are we important players in human development, we may be the most important players within an increasingly disengaging society—a society whose future is unknown.

The need for a new vision for the early childhood profession is implicit in every case study and every point raised in this book. As early childhood specialists we can no longer be classroom-oriented pedagogues concerned with the presentation of content and the manipulation of experiences for groups of children during established hours. We need to do much more than this; to be ambassadors for better practice, and forgers of a more advanced approach to discovery and learning; that is, we must embrace the *fourth discourse.*

We need also to be aware that we cannot expect support for our mission from external sources unless we ourselves create a changed landscape. Recent studies have revealed how, at every level of industry and the professions, workers claim to have the knowledge and the ability to improve their job output and to improve the efficiency and effectiveness of their organizations. Often, they state, they are simply not asked, nor given opportunities to do so (Boyatzis & Skelly, 1991).

The authors in this volume are reminding us what can be done to increase the quality of early childhood education on a personal, structural, policy-wide, and global basis. The answer lies in confronting the true (constitutional) obstacles. Rather than waiting to be asked, we must determine the directions, invent the opportunities.

We have the knowledge, the skill, the means, and the power to create a better place and time for children. This book shows both the worst and the best of what is happening in the field of early childhood education today—and it shows the active role that professionals can take in shaping that field. More than anything else this book proves that we *can* mold the future, we *can* take control, and we *can* make things better for young children and their families.

Note

1. The notions of *distributional* and *constitutional* aspects of the field of early childhood education are central to the theme of this book. These are explained in Chapter 2.

References

Boyatzis, R., & Skelly, F. (1991). The impact of changing values on organizational life. In R. Kolb, I. Rubin, & J. Osland (Eds.). *The Organizational Behavior Reader.* (pp. 1–16) Englewood Cliffs, NJ: Prentice Hall.

Hayden, J. (1993). The childcare chimera: Policymaking and the hidden agenda. In J. Mason (Ed.). *Child Welfare: Critical Australian Perspectives* (pp.183-197). Sydney: Hale and Iremonger.

Hayden, J. (1994). Half full or half empty? Children's services policy and the missing bits. In E. Mellor & K. Coombe (Eds.). *Issues in Early Childhood Services.* Australian Perspectives. (pp. 11–25). New York: WCB.

Hayden, J. (1997). *Neo Conservatism and child and childcare services in Alberta: A case study.* Occasional Paper 9. Center for Childcare Research and Resources, Toronto: University of Toronto.

Chapter 2

Early Childhood Landscapes: A Framework for Analysis

Jacqueline Hayden

Abstract

This chapter provides an overview of policy analysis methodology and presents an inclusionary model that accommodates the diversity of theory and issues prevalent in the field of early childhood education. The model, in distinguishing distributional allotments to the field (those relating to service delivery) from constitutional outcomes (those relating to empowerment of the profession), contributes a framework for investigating past, current, and future trends in the development of early childhood education.

Introduction

This book analyzes current trends and issues that comprise the *landscape* of early childhood education in three nations—Canada, Australia and New Zealand.[1] The analyses incorporate the interaction between developments in the early childhood field and the broader socio/political/economic context.

The movement in Canada, Australia, and New Zealand toward right wing politics, and the concomitant policy shift toward market economics, minimal intervention, privatization, outcome accountability for tax dollars, cutbacks, and program dissolution has influenced the delivery of early childhood services in diverse ways. Recent case studies are used to explore the interaction between these aspects of the political/social landscape and the policy area of early childhood education. A major purpose is to analyze the influence and power mechanisms that are driving policy reform and practice and to identify the role of the early childhood professional[2] and advocate in terms of the changing context.

The analyses of current events and issues are used to raise awareness in professionals of their influence upon the creation of the early childhood policy field and of the political landscape with which it interacts. The case studies serve also as guideposts for those concerned with future directions for early childhood education.

Ecological studies, or those which relate specific policy areas to the larger social/political context, are becoming increasingly significant in the analysis of policy development and reform. The new millennium marks a crossroad for the field of early childhood education on an international scale. In some nations early childhood education is being heralded as a vital aspect of educational and social reform. In others, programs that encompass early childhood education have been the first to feel the sting of fiscal restraint and government cutbacks.

The demise or prominence of early childhood education reflects the interaction of *political developments and social issues* (such as the expansion of workfare programs, fiscal restraint, an ideological shift toward individualism that incorporates government reassessments of child and family oriented policies, and debates on public versus private responsibilities for the complete range of social services) with *educational* issues such as downsizing exercises in universities and school boards, reevaluation of the role of teachers and of the goals for compulsory and pre-/post- compulsory education, reviews of educational priorities; and with *professional issues* such as the recognition of a need for specialized skills, the self-concept of early childhood professionals, accountability for service delivery, credentializing, and research dissemination.

The interaction of these developments upon the field of early childhood education, upon early childhood professionals, and upon society in general is the focus of this book.

A Cross-National Approach to the Topic: Canada/Australia/New Zealand

The significance of cross-national studies of social policy development has been noted by Baker (1995) and Lubeck (1995) among others. While defending cross-national research as "an important intellectual exercise in itself" (p. 11), Baker argues that an interchange in policy solutions between countries with similar cultural backgrounds is becoming more crucial due to increasing travel, communication, trade, and economic/political agreements. Most importantly, she adds:

> A more thorough understanding of social policies in industrialized counties, including the ways in which they are shaped by cultural and political differences,

can contribute to our knowledge and repertoire of alternatives. Without an understanding of policy alternatives, it is difficult to recognize government- or employer-initiated ideologies about the range of possible solutions to social problems. (Baker, 1995: p. 12)

Lubeck echoes this notion in her declaration of the importance of cross-national studies for suggesting "potential constraints and mitigating factors that make it difficult (or easier) within a given social and historical context to move public policy in a particular direction" (Lubeck, 1995, p. 470). In other words, cross-national studies are needed to provide a broader knowledge base of options from which to determine feasibility of, and advocate for, effective and appropriate program developments which are based upon evidence and experience over ideologies and dogma, and upon a sound understanding of the variance and influence of the social/political/historical context in which each program develops.

This need has been recognized by a growing number of publications that provide overviews of early childhood education and childcare programs in a variety of regions and nations. While comparative studies of early childhood education,[3] and particularly those with an ecological perspective[4] are increasing, studies which present a cross-national analysis of the influences upon policy development and of the interaction of policy outcome in terms of the social/political/economic climate are less common. Indeed, in her review of cross-national studies of childcare and early childhood education, Lubeck concludes that "little work to date has been done to compare . . . policies and programs in some systemic way" (Lubeck, 1995, p. 474). Parallels between Canadian policy developments in social services and those of Australia have been noted by several researchers (see Foster, 1995, Baker, 1995), as have the similarities in approaches to childcare policy developments (see Jones, 1984; Hayden 1993, 1995, 1995a). New Zealand has been included because its unique and radical approach to social policy reform in the 1990s calls for careful assessment. Hong Kong presents a unique opportunity to review developments in early childhood education during a time of political/social transformation.

The last five years, in all four nations, have seen the flourishing of childcare policy developments that are unmatched for intensity, speed or magnitude in any other era. Initiatives in all segments—funding, regulatory reform, standard development, monitoring, and sponsorship—have resulted in a radically changed profile of childcare service delivery. This has been especially apparent in Australia. The 1992 amendment of the Childcare Act, which allowed government funds to be diverted into for-profit organizations, caused succeeding waves of macro changes in the childcare system, including the development of national childcare standards, concomitant State regulatory reforms, the development and implementation of a national accreditation system, and extreme changes in the demands and expectations of the childcare workforce. Meanwhile, changes in government-defined priorities, funding guidelines, and patterns of support have impacted upon the development, delivery, accessibility, and quality of childcare programs, as well as the use, training needs, and diversity demanded of childcare providers.

In Canada and New Zealand, early childhood services are being subjected to similar reformulation. In Canada, a political shift toward conservatism in some provinces has resulted in sweeping reconstruction and, in some cases, destruction of some components of early childhood service delivery. Examples include the removal of funds for junior kindergartens in Ontario and the 50% decrease for funding of early childhood services in Alberta. Childcare budgets have also been slashed.

The field, across nations, has been subject to increased demand for specialized forms of care, and to unprecedented support for privatization of service provision. These changes have not been matched with research into the consequences. The pace of change has militated against sustained, incremental progress based on rigorous evaluation and assessment of the new undertakings. Nor has there been any attempt to investigate the extent to which recent policy developments have altered the need for, behavior of, and/or demands upon childcare providers and professionals, or how these changes have improved or decreased the quality of care. This book is intended to fill this gap in the current knowledge base and literature.

A Framework for Analysis

In their review of the processes involved with policy analysis, Hoggwood and Gunn distinguish between studies that reflect a broad (holistic) approach and those that present a narrow view (one that focuses upon a particular aspect of the policy area). The former group includes researches of policy content, policy process, policy output, and policy evaluation. Narrow studies focus on analyses of policy information dissemination, policy process advocacy, and policy advocacy (Hoggwood & Gunn, 1981). The authors suggest that much policy research targets a specific purpose (advocacy) and thus tends to present the narrow (or partial) view.

In her review of comparative policy studies, Chrichton refers to this distinction between the analysis of a policy field as a whole and analyses of smaller bites (the narrow view), and describes the limitations of each

(Chrichton, 1995). Holistic policy analyses have been criticized for their insufficient use of theory, while small bite analyses may have limited generalizability. Chrichton promotes the necessity of situating policy analysis within a solid disciplinary base, but, as she questions 'what should be that base?' Limitation to an historical, sociological, economic, and/or social welfare disciplinary approach to policy analysis will illuminate that aspect of the system only (Chrichton, 1995, p. 61). As Chrichton implies, a multidisciplinary approach to policy analysis is needed.

Penn provides an example of a multidisciplinary approach in her review of the development of early childhood policy and services in Strathfield, Scotland. She analyzes the conflicts that characterized the process in terms of divergent perspectives, including a feminist perspective, a social diversity perspective, a social context perspective, a political perspective, and an educational perspective. Penn concludes that it is impossible to uphold a values-free and context-less definition of goals (policy) for early childhood services. Divergent perspectives—a lack of common goals and even common zeitgeist among stakeholders—mean that analyses of early childhood policy and of policy outcomes must, by their very nature, take into account multiple perspectives.

While not referring specifically to policy analysis, the findings of Moss and Pence reinforce this conclusion. In searching for a definition of quality for early childhood services (i.e., a policy goal), the authors conclude that there is a need for a new *inclusionary paradigm*—in which services must be viewed in terms relative to the culture and practices of the context and must be subject to continuous evaluation and research. The authors identify the importance of incorporating analyses of *who* participates (in the process of policymaking), *the nature of that participation* (conflict versus cooperation), the *extent of participants' involvement* (full versus marginal) and the *inclusion of many levels* (the extent of participation in policymaking at various political levels) (Moss and Pence, 1994).

Elsewhere I have argued the importance of including two further components in the analysis of early childhood policies. These are the review of policy content (the specific issues which have been addressed by policy developments) and the review of *non policies* (the issues which were ignored or neglected by policy developments and/or which were "addressed to death"—sabotaged in implementation and/or through other power mechanisms) (Hayden, 1993; 1994; 1997).

In summary, analyses of early childhood policy need to take into account:

1. the goal(s) of the analyses,
2. multiple perspectives,
3. an investigation of players,
4. historical and current social/political/cultural contexts, and
5. developments and *nondevelopments*.

These components are accommodated within the distributional versus constitutional model of analysis which is used throughout this book.

Distributional Allotments Versus Constitutional Outcomes

A distributional versus constitutional framework for policy analysis incorporates the components described above. This framework divides policy developments into two dimensions. The distributional dimension describes concrete allotments to the policy field—what is given or not given. The constitutional dimension is more complex to describe and to analyze. It defines not what is given in a concrete sense, but what structures and frameworks exist and/or develop which result in empowerment of the policy field.

These two components of policy are explained by Tuohy as follows:

> The distributional dimension of policy relates to the allotment of the tangible benefits across various interests in society. The constitutional dimension relates to the allocation of positions of influence in the making and implementation of policy. (Tuohy, 1994: p. 249)

Distributional allotments tend to be ephemeral. Constitutional dimensions are more deeply embedded. An increase in distributional allotments gives the appearance of progress within a policy field (such as increased political debate and/or increased funding for programs), but if the increase in political activity does not incorporate the constitutional dimension, the "progress" is precarious—as easily retracted as it was allocated.

This framework fits with the analytical model presented by Hoggwood and Gunn. The distributive aspects of the policy process deal with the policy *per se* can be analyzed (evaluated) according to content, the process for implementing that content, and/or the result, or output of that content. Analyses of the constitutional component of policies will reveal how and why policies come to contain that content, and/or to be processed in such a way.

Incorporating the constitutional dimension in early childhood education policy analyses allows for the multidisciplinary and historical perspectives suggested by Chrichton. Constitutional factors reflect the broad political/social/economic context with which each policy area interacts. Tuohy calls this the *political landscape,* which she compares to the *policy landscape* (in this case, the policy landscape means ideas and practices within the field of early childhood education).

The political landscape represents the "window of opportunity" for policy developments. That window opens onto the landscape of particular policy ideas (e.g., early childhood education). The policy idea landscape is dynamic and evolutionary. It is based on research, stakeholder advocacy, and current issues. The way in which this *policy* landscape is absorbed and translated depends upon the existing *political* landscape.

Constitutional changes, thus, take place from the episodic intersection of factors in the policy field with the prevailing political landscape. This explains why both the wider context and the particularities of the field need to be included in policy analyses.

Tuohy gives an example of the necessity of including a constitutional dimension in policy analyses. In her review of health care programs, she describes how different nations developed different schemes of public health according to the time period and the political/economic context in which the decision was made. For example, Canada developed a national system of Medicare one decade later than Britain. That decade was one of relative economic prosperity in Canada during which generous private and state level funding was available for medical services. Thus, when the Federal Medicare system was implemented in Canada, expectations were high and demands were for a level of service that mirrored the current delivery systems. In Britain, because of a lack of precedent, the public accepted a lower level of service. The expectations that had arisen from a generous system in Canada colored the parameters of the new federal system and produced a low public tolerance toward necessary refinements during later periods of fiscal restraint.

Analyzing Constitutional Allotments

Constitutional dimensions of policy developments exist in macro and micro form. On the *macro* level constitutional allotments incorporate the *zeitgeist* or context in which the program exists (such as whether the economic cycle is high or low) and the social/cultural context. Analyses of the Australian macro context in the past decade would include trends such as the growth of economic rationalism, fiscal restraint, an aging population, the devaluing of children, increased migration, a revision of female roles in society, changes in patterns of marriage, and other social and demographic concerns (see Gammage, this volume).

The constitutional dimension provides an explanation for the onset of public responsibility for childcare in Australia, Canada, and New Zealand, and elsewhere. The program could not have developed during the pronatal, parochial, and patriarchal culture of the 1950s, but was well suited to the social reform movement of the mid 1960s to late 1970s (coinciding with the women's liberation movement as well as with an extraordinary outpouring of research findings about human/child development) (see Hayden, 1994). In the same vein, regressive arguments that are currently being put forth to remove affirmative action programs for some disadvantaged groups (such as girls' strategies in schools) blend well with the constitutional framework that incorporates a move toward neo-conservatism (Hayden, 1997).

Thus, if the constitutional context is ripe, it will mesh with the demands/needs from the prevailing policy landscape and result in constitutional change. If the constitutional field is hostile, change at this level will not occur, although there may be some dissemination of distributional "goodies" to appease lobbyists and pressure groups, and/or to buy public favor (especially around election times).

The *micro* level of the constitutional dimension refers to the political and structural components of the policy field. These incorporate the influence of professionals and others involved with the field; the structural and systemic supports to the field; and the empowerment of the field within the wider social/economic/political context. Analyses of the following components provide an indication of the state of the micro constitutional dimension of early childhood education and other fields:

1. clearly articulated goals, principles, and terms of reference for the field;
2. clearly identified avenues for advocacy;
3. identifiable leaders/spokespersons;
4. professional bodies, associations with wide representation;
5. containable content area, clear parameters of responsibility;
6. system whereby the field self-monitors and self-perpetuates.

Conclusion: Applying the Framework

Australia provides an example of the way in which distributions have affected the early childhood landscape. When distributions only are reviewed, developments in the field appear to be positive and progressive. Thus, the response to demand for early childhood distributions from the Australian Commonwealth government has been, from one perspective, remarkably successful. The progression from no funding in the early 1970s to over $1.3 billion by the mid 1990s[6] heralds unmitigated success for advocates of early childhood education.

Distributions to early childhood services have also moved beyond budget allocations. Between 1990 and 1995 there was a large increase in the number of funded spaces for preschool-aged children under a variety of auspices. A national system of quality control (QIAS) was implemented. In 1994 a new childcare rebate program pumped $90 million into the childcare field. The amalgamation of teachers colleges with faculties of education gave higher status to teachers of early childhood education. Looser controls (over ownership) resulted in a large increase of (private) childcare operators, organizations, associations, and consultants. The past few years have seen increasing numbers of early childhood graduates with higher degrees, more demand for high level credentials, and more jobs at all levels. The report entitled *Childcare Workers* (Commonwealth of Australia, 1995) gives historical data that shows that many aspects of working conditions in the field of early childhood education have undergone vast improvements. These include in-service training opportunities, better qualified staff, increased job opportunities, and higher wages.

Thus, despite a reduced government presence in nearly all aspects of Australian society, early childhood services, from a quantitative perspective and a qualitative perspective (due to the national accreditation system), have flourished.

Analyses of the constitutional dimension of early childhood services in Australia reveal a different picture from that of distributional allotments. Constitutional developments such as deregulation and reductions in accountability; the introduction of national standards which are below those of some states; divisive industrial awards and increasing competition amongst early childhood professionals—private versus nonprofit advocates, college versus university-trained specialists, preschool versus childcare supporters reflect regressive trends in the field. These developments have a far greater impact than do funding fluctuations or other distributions (see Hayden, this volume, Chapter 8).

The way in which constitutional components (both macro and micro) have interacted with developments in all aspects of early childhood education in Canada, Australia, New Zealand, and elsewhere constitutes the essence of this book. Its purpose is to show how professionals in early childhood education have confronted and dealt with the constitutional dimension of the field—in order to reshape the landscape for the challenge of the new millennium.

Notes

1. A case study of early childhood developments in Hong Kong has also been included.

2. See Glossary for an explanation of the way in which the term " early childhood professional" is being used in this book.

3. See the chapter in Woodill, G., Bernhard, J., & Prochner, L. (1992) entitled *Comparative early childhood education—An English bibliography* which lists over 280 references on this topic.

4. See Moss & Pence (1994), Melhuish & Moss (1991); Tobin, Wu, & Davidson (1990); Olmstead & Weikart (1989), (pp. 401–406); Werner (1988).

5. A notable exception to Lubeck's observation is Moss and Pence (1994), which provides an excellent model of systemic comparative early childhood education.

6. Cited in *Future childcare in Australia 1994–1995*. Economic Policy Advisory Commission, Childcare Task Force, Canberra. Commonwealth of Australia (p. 28).

7. This progression and the struggle for government distributions to early childhood services are particularly well documented by Brennan (1994). See also Hayden (1994, 1995).

References

Baker, M. (1995). *Canadian family policies: Cross-national comparisons.* Toronto: University of Toronto Press.

Brennan, D. (1994). *The politics of Australian childcare.* Cambridge: Cambridge University Press.

Creighton, A. (1995). Health Care in Canada and Australia: The development of a comparative analytical framework. *Australian Canadian Studies,* 13(2): 59–71.

Foster, L. (1995). ACSANZ 1995 conference report. *The Association for Canadian Studies in Australia and New Zealand Journal* (ACSANZ), 24: 1–3.

Hayden, J. (1993). The childcare chimera: Policymaking and the hidden agenda. In J. Mason (Ed.). *Child Welfare: Critical Australian Perspectives.* (pp. 183–197) Sydney: Hale and Iremonger.

Hayden, J. (1993a). *Childcare in Canada and abroad: Who really benefits?* Paper presented at the Canadian Childcare Federation (CCCF) Conference, Toronto (unpublished).

Hayden, J. (1994). Half full or half empty? Children's services policy and the missing bits. In E. Mellor & K. Coombe (Eds.). *Issues in Early Childhood Services. Australian Perspectives* (pp. 11–25) New York: WCB.

Hayden, J. (1995). *Confronting the "big" issues in early childhood care and education A global perspective.* International Year of Tolerance Conference, Sydney Day Nursery and Kindergarten Union, Sydney, November (unpublished).

Hayden, J. (1995a). *Training, quality care, and the administration of childcare centers: An international comparison.* Paper presented at the Association for Childhood Education International (ACEI) Conference, Washington, DC (unpublished).

Hayden, J. (1997). *Neo Conservatism and child and childcare services in Alberta: A case study.* Occasional Paper 9. Center for Childcare Research and Resources. Toronto: University of Toronto.

Hoggwood, B., & Gunn, L. (1988). *Policy analysis for the real world.* New York: Oxford University Press.

Jones, A. (1984). Comparing Canadian and Australian social policies: The case of day care. *Australian Canadian Studies,* 2: 59–73.

Lubeck, S. (1995). Nation as context: Comparing childcare systems across nations. *Teacher's College Record* 96(3): 467–491.

Melhuish, E., & Moss, P. (Eds.). (1991). *Day care for young children: International perspectives.* London: Routledge.

Moss, P., & Pence, A. (Eds.). (1994). *Valuing quality in early childhood services.* New York: Teachers College Press.

Olmstead, P., & Weikart, D. (Eds.). (1989). *How nations serve young children.* Yipsilanti, Michigan: High/Scope Press.

Tobin, J., Wu, D., & Davidson, D. (1989). *Preschool in three cultures: Japan, China, and the United States.* New Haven: Yale University Press.

Tuohy, C. (1994). Response to the Clinton proposal: A comparative perspective. *Journal of Health Politics, Policy and Law* 19(1): 249–254.

Werner, E. (1988). A cross cultural perspective on infancy. *Journal of Cross Cultural Psychology,* 19(1): 96–113.

The Big Picture

Chapter 3

Childcare and the Growth of Love: Preparing for an Unknown Future

Philip Gammage

Let it be hoped, then, that all over the world men and women in public life will recognize the relation of mental health to maternal care, and will seize their opportunities for promoting courageous and far reaching reforms. (Bowlby, 1965 rev. ed., p. 241)

Abstract

This chapter takes John Bowlby's famous title and, half a century after the original text was written, summarizes the current context of childrearing and early childhood education and the likely needs in the future.

The writer revisits the areas affecting the love and care of our children and advocates the unification of care and educational policy and of carefully planned provision from birth, emphasizing the importance of providing good professionally staffed institutions, accessible to all who need them. Circumstances such as changing economic forces, uptake of women in the workforce throughout the world, and the changing patterns of family life, of divorce, and child experiences are demanding increased and rigorous investment and commitment to our young children. The problem is urgent. Future societal cohesion and well-being depend upon it.

Introduction

It is now over 50 years since John Bowlby's influential book, *Childcare and the Growth of Love* was published. Bowlby argued there was no substitute for mother love and that close parenting was a necessity for a sane adult life and for a cohesive society. Half a century later, while we may acknowledge the pioneering work of Bowlby, of Spitz, or of Rutter and others, we are also much more aware that attachment comes in many guises and that still relatively little is known about precisely what it is in our childhood that may make us function for good or ill as adults. We know that some people are surprisingly resilient. We also know that many are not and that longterm delinquency may be predicted with some accuracy in boys, by the age of three or so (Silver, 1997), though here the interplay between nature and nurture raises serious, as yet, unresolved, issues. There is no doubt that Bowlby in some aspects was misunderstood and (to some extent) used by politicians and others who wished to see segregated roles sustained and women kept at home. But Bowlby's advocacy was much more a focus on the *quality* of attachment, and his concerns for affectionate parenting were extremely timely and had an immensely positive effect upon many childcare institutions throughout the world. He can, therefore, with a certain amount of warmth, be regarded as right on function and (probably) wrong on structures, though of course we have the benefit of hindsight; and all ideas have to be considered in their context. Bowlby was an eclectic psychologist. He drew on many aspects of biology and medicine to propound his theories on interpersonal relationships and emotional development. People suffer, he said, from inadequate parenting, and we need to be aware of it. And adults do suffer from having been wrongly handled and nurtured, of that there is no doubt; and the timing of key events seems critical.

Damage to self-esteem does seem to follow disturbed attachment, and as Holmes (1993) said in his assessment of Bowlby, there is no really good argument against providing high-quality care and protection during childhood. Countless longitudinal studies, countless psychodynamic accounts, countless criminal lawyers, and countless teachers and carers would testify to the wisdom of Bowlby's message!

At the turn of the millennium, therefore, where are we in our understanding of the importance of early nurture and learning, and what are the implications for the future? Are our children well provided for, cared for, nurtured with more sympathy and understanding than half a century ago? Are we approaching deeper insight into the nature of childrearing, the crucial importance of early learning? Can we see a future that secures children so lovingly and appropriately that our own societies benefit and flourish? Do we understand the balance necessary between societal/economic needs and the individual creative forces that make for a humanizing culture, and can we get that balance right?

This chapter attempts to draw upon my 37 years of work in education and care, experience in other countries, of having taught young children in a variety of settings and then of melding all those varied (and sometimes conflicting) experiences with my interests as a researcher and psychologist.

Current Context

Taking a broadly ecological view (Bronfenbrenner, 1979), what may we perceive in the countries of OECD (29 richest), in the European Union, and (increasingly) in the developing world?

First, one would be extremely blind if one did not see within the overall context the long march of women. The Second World War is often cited as a catalyst to the process of gradual emancipation. But in reality the whole century of rapid social and medical change, the accelerating advance in technology, especially of communications technology, and the concomitant speed of consciousness-raising, are probably of far greater significance. Add the freedom of choice attributed to the use of more efficient contraception; add the more recent gradual demise of heavy industry and one begins to see how potent is the mix and how inevitable its course. Indeed, many of us (men and women alike) delight in the changes taking place, see the domination of social and political systems by men as a temporary, "unholy" and disagreeable feature of certain periods of history. While there are many miles yet to travel and many social systems to improve, ascertain, and understand and, while greater equality of the sexes should surely enrich and stabilize this world in a far more fitting manner than any other major political upheaval hitherto, within such a crude overview lie many complexities.

Some schools of thought see the socialization of children as largely the right of the mother, and thus any weakening or amelioration of that role as an attack on women's expertise and power; others see the exact opposite and expect men to operate across more dimensions of nurturance than they have traditionally in the past. Still others remind us that the nuclear family is often far from perfect and sometimes a hotbed of crushing emotional mismanagement and potentially lethal psychological modeling.

Whatever position one takes (and there are many more), one inevitably returns to the changed roles of women in modern societies and to the fact that mobility, economics, and changing needs have largely destroyed the extended family as well. When one adds the patterns of divorce to it all, one begins to see that early childhood care and education are in need of reassessment, and they may have to be provided by collective responsibility, will, and concern, rather than by haphazard adoption of market forces, private negotiation, or any return to those mythical "family values" so beloved by many policymakers!

After "the long march" (in reality, alongside it) comes the changing concept of marriage. In many countries divorce laws have slowly relaxed, religious strictures weakened, tax laws altered, and financial penalties ameliorated. These last have not necessarily always been intended; it has sometimes been more to do with the shift in economic needs, rather than resulting from direct legislation. But it means that many, many more people are able to contemplate divorce and that many actually act on that contemplation (currently about a third of all Australian and Canadian marriages end in divorce).

Predictions of future patterns are difficult, but it does seem likely that the proportion will go on increasing. Already this means that approximately 40% of children in these countries under 10 years of age will have experienced the divorce of their parents. It means that more children live in single parent families, cohabiting households or with step families. This alters the dynamics of relationships as well as the traditional lifestyle once associated with childrearing. In short, what has been described as "serial monogamy" is now a reality for many persons in our societies.

Third, we should note that our children are not the same from generation to generation. In many respects they are more mature and more sophisticated, particularly in relation to technology and to access of social and technological information. By contrast, in many of the postindustrial countries, the child's access to unsupervised play activities out of doors has markedly diminished. Thus, while children are heavier and more mature, they will also be more vulnerable to quite different life stressors from those of their parents. The secular trend in decline of age at menarche ensures that most western girls reach physical maturity by age twelve. This means that many primary children will be physically mature; a feature not anticipated by the founders of elementary education one or two centuries ago. Our children will also have surprisingly sedentary lives in much of North America and Australia, such that obesity is a minor but serious issue among children.

Overall, in Australia and Canada, as in Scandinavia and the U.S., there are signs of greater acceptance of childbearing outside marriage and of different forms of relationship other than conventional marriage. Additionally, even many traditionally strong Catholic countries have made the process of divorce easier and less likely to carry stigma.

Trends

How might one explain some of these trends and what are the implications for us as professional carers and educators? One might assert the following:

1. Longer life expectancy has prolonged the possibility of being in a relationship for a very long time. Among other things this means that as people grow and change they may find that increasingly intolerable incompatibilities emerge. Moreover, people are encouraged to stay fitter, sexually active, and younger looking; all of which can affect adult perceptions in later life. Retraining and reeducation are encouraged and these too can change perspectives and necessitate a change of location.
2. Employed and employable women are more inclined to react unfavorably to bad marriages. There is evidence that women sue for divorce at three times the rate of men. Satisfaction in marriage and satisfaction in bed are no longer things merely hinted at. These aspects are discussed openly in many modern magazines (e.g., *Cosmopolitan*), in newspapers, and on television.
3. Increasingly women are being taken into the workforce, not for "extra money," but as essential elements in a diverse economy. They accept jobs in service industries, but also increasingly in technology and medicine. There are areas of Canada, U.S., and the U.K. where proportionally more women are employed than men, and this is especially true in geographical areas where the employment of unskilled male labor has declined. In the U.K., graduate women are less likely to be unemployed six months after graduation than are the corresponding cohort of men. Such changes may alter the "power relationship" in a way unpalatable to either sex. Certainly role-specific tasks are no longer usually appropriate, though there is plenty of evidence that women still perform many household tasks, even when in fulltime employment. Also, one should in no way assume that women are in equal positions of power. In a recent BBC broadcast (10 December 1997) it was stated that, in the U.K., women held only 2.5% of top managerial posts.
4. In North America and Australia, the average "working" woman is increasingly likely to be back at work (either full or parttime) within a year of the birth of her child. Thus, almost every child needs some provision early on in life.
5. Mobility and geographical separation have become almost a way of life (especially in countries such as Canada and Australia, where families will move 3,000 miles to change jobs and will leave grandparents and other members of the family behind).
6. In the majority of the OECD countries, the size of the family has reduced drastically. Currently the average number of children per adult couple is around two in Australia, slightly less in Canada. However, migrant groups and socioeconomic status cause some

perturbations in the overall figures, with a tendency for families to be somewhat larger as you move down the socioeconomic scale.
7. Throughout any discussion on human development, we should constantly be aware that human institutions are "socially constructed," invested with importance that often relies on tradition and hearsay, on values and upon custom. Their reality is sometimes contained more in the ideology than the substance. Terms like "family" and "childhood" are invested with meanings drawn from the mores of the time. Consequently, it is important to recall that childhood itself is a "moving target." It will mean different things in different groups at different times and in different contexts (Tudge, Shanahan & Valsiner, 1997). Moreover, adults define childhood from the vantage point of power and old age. They may, therefore, be out of date and inappropriate in what they think they perceive. And, the media have become especially potent in the debate in almost every country. Children have little real political power, except perhaps in Scandinavia, where their rights are taken more seriously than elsewhere, even being enshrined in part in the Swedish Education Act.
8. Even at the end of the 20 century the majority of the world's children can be legitimately classed as "poor": and poverty results in poor living conditions, chronic disease and death—and in some countries—excessive exploitation and long hours of child labor. The richer countries are not always better since, though poverty is defined as relative to the average income within a country, recent UNICEF reports have clearly indicted Canada and Australia, along with the U.S. and U.K., as nations still displaying surprising inequalities in respect of care and provision of their young (Hewlett, 1993).
9. If one looks to both "developed" and "developing" countries one is immediately aware that the subjective and interpersonal burden is still one largely carried by women. The so-called "objective" interests (which for the most part align with power and money) are still mainly the province of men. Men frequently define the political, and hence the social and family arena. (The debate about abortion in Eire was largely controlled, if not conducted, by men.)

Prime Constraints

No one would deny that the child clearly brings a cluster of inherited features to this world of ours. Some psychologists think that even certain traits (like irritability) may well be inherited (Silver, 1997). Whatever the case, many researchers have pointed out that learning begins at birth (if not before), and that children are tuned to imitate and absorb in a frighteningly fast manner. The acceleration of neuron-synapse connections is immense and the learning accomplished as a result, particularly in respect of language, is clearly preprogrammed such that in normal children much of their basic learning is complete before they ever attend primary school.

The prime constraints (or facilitators) of learning are family (including siblings if any), the media, peers, and preschool/care group carer. It is not to be assumed that any of these are necessarily benign in their influence on the growing child, but it becomes clear that each of our children may experience many more socializing influences than might have been the case a generation ago. Patchwork arrangements and multiple caretakers is the norm for even the youngest of infants. Often children do not have any forewarning of pending change, such as when parents need to accommodate to a regular carer being ill, or a grandparent not coping, or a change of location, or a modification to expense. Indeed a feature of all our children's lives now must surely be the haphazard and multiple nature of their caring and modeling experiences; unless they are lucky enough to be born into very secure circumstances, or into a country (such as Finland or Denmark) where provision from birth is seen as a public responsibility and taken seriously.

The principle in part espoused by Bowlby is that parents, if they are "good" offer what might be termed as *unreasonable care,* that is, that parents are committed over and above what is reasonable to expect. They are, as a rule, on the child's side in a way which it is difficult for a professional to be. The parent nearly always sees the swan, not the goose!! Yet, as Tizard and Rees pointed out some years ago, in an ideal world the professional early childhood worker is *free to plan her interactions so that the parenting impulses necessary for really good work can be brought into play at the appropriate time* (Tizard & Rees, 1975). Too much bureaucracy stultifies such judgement. It often prevents children's care outside the family from becoming "unreasonable" in the important way that Bowlby meant. This is a problem we have to address in an era of increasing bureaucracy and over-reliance on instruments of accountability.

Surprisingly, children are generally least safe in their own homes and most safe in school, nursery, preschool or care. While many of us are aware that the streets may no longer be the ideal location for play and we have, perhaps, been alerted to certain sorts of abuse which has taken place in institutions, few of us seem to be aware that homes are often the most unsafe environments and that sometimes parents are the most subtle and devious of abusers! It is generally not considered ethical to remove children from their parents' care, unless there are signs of crushing neglect. Even then bureaucracy and the legitimate "need to be certain" usually demand such a weight of evidence that in some terrible cases the child has been dead before intervention can be achieved.

Whilst poor parenting is *not* a correlation of poverty, certain things like extreme youth or psychological inadequacy do seem to be (Hudson and Ineichen, 1994). Under such circumstances intervention, or supplementary support structures which include help, group support and advice are surely features which a modern society might well want to ensure. Some noted research, intervention and action projects exist in this respect. Two examples are the PEEP Project (Peers Early Education Project) at Oxford, England, which works with all children born in a certain part of Oxford and recruits the parents from the time of the birth of the child; it has a prime aim of providing a better environment for literacy and self-esteem (Roberts, 1997) and the Bright Futures Project at Peoria, Illinois, U.S., which involves crèche facilities, parenting "lessons" and also attempts to ensure better skill training (for eventual jobs) for parents without employment prospects (Bradley University). There are many more throughout the world. Most focus on the belief that parenting is not a "natural" skill, that parents can be lonely and insecure, that a good early start for children in terms of understanding play, talk and social-emotional development can be extremely beneficial for the rest of life. Such schemes do not replace good preschool care and education; they *supplement* them by emphasizing that the child is a learner from birth and that some parents are fully aware how best to support this.

Of prime importance nowadays are the *media.* Their socializing power is immense. We are all operating nowadays in a context of values expressed by them. Such contexts generate messages of greater salience than does home itself (or preschool or care; and frequently those messages are presented in packages of such sophistication, attraction and slickness that no mere parent or carer can counter the fashion or the thought. As early as the 1970s both Illich and Reimer were concerned by the domination of American life by technology. They asked the question about who might profit from it and whether the mores thus ensured by its domination were desirable or appropriate (Reimer, 1971). More recently, Saachi and Saachi estimated that British children influenced £31 billion worth of consumer sales! (BBC Broadcast, December 15, 1997). A common thread throughout this debate has been the likelihood of a "common denominator" being profit and poor taste. Such views still concern those worried by the impact of TV and video violence on children. We know that children as young as three years watch up to twenty hours of TV per week; we know that video systems are all-pervasive and often used to "amuse" or "mind" the child when the parent is harassed, pre-occupied or even absent. We know how common it is nowadays for "The Rambo family of images (to form) part of a complex cultural reality" (Grixti, 1989 p. 180). We are also well aware that, with a few notable exceptions, the media are in a unique position to cultivate basic assumptions about the nature of society, to provide stereotypes of almost lasting endurance in which, for instance, women may well be demeaned, violence applauded or subtly affirmed, and status inevitably assigned largely to men (Bum, 1996). In a recent Australian study, Hayden revealed how the portrayal of nonmaternal childcare in television, video, and film media was categorized as unprofessional, frightening or evil (Hayden, 1996). Thus while the teaching/learning possibilities of all the media are well-recognized and often used wisely, it may be that the forces of *laissez-faire* capitalism (and of the lowest common denominator in taste?) are not the best ways to ensure a tranquil future for our children (see Zigler, Kagan & Hall, 1996).

The Social Context

Humankind is undoubtedly social. Most of our learning is social. Indeed *in extremis* it is hard to identify learning that is not, in some part, socially constructed. We know that the baby is a good imitator of its carer and seeks actively to interact with him or her. It is therefore very important that every child has lots of rich social experience from other children. Learning to share, to copy, to communicate are all essential elements of our survival. Such elements also enrich our lives immeasurably. As Gordon Allport was reputed to have said, "You can't have a personality in a desert." This means our children need that social interaction fairly soon on in life. They benefit from it enormously. It is the stuff of early learning, to accommodate, to manage oneself, to assimilate, negotiate and so on. The obverse is that, whereas once psychologists seemed to write of the peer group as though it were a phenomenon of adolescence, now they note its salience to even the very young (ably supported no doubt by the influence of TV). Moreover, manufacturers know how powerful fashion and social norms can be, even for three-year-olds. They are fully aware that toys are sold when "every one" in the group talks of them. In short, we now recognize the power of the group for attitude formation in even the very young. This complicates interactions and learning. It makes disentangling nature and nurture even more difficult; it offers intriguing glimpses into sex-role behavior; it underscores the wisdom of feminist-post structuralism, because it gives us insight into how adult relationships are in part formed from a "system" of discourse which may be embedded in the life of the very young.

Implications

Where does all this leave care and education? Where does it leave us in terms of the growth of love? It surely means the following, with its "good" implications and its "bad" implications:

1. We have to recognize that care and education are interwoven to such an extent that it no longer make sense to see them as anything but thoroughly interdependent. We need to deploy the same energy and zeal for early childhood provision that our forefathers brought to the establishment of elementary education. This societal "need" is at least as important as other *major* national issues, like banking or defense. These children are not just our intellectual and economic capital. Indeed, to view them as solely that demeans the notion of childhood, devalues any concepts of human development, and dangerously plays into the hands of instrumental, "ends justify means" approaches to childhood. These are not little economic investments waiting to mature. They are bundles of attitudes and feelings which, more than knowledge of math or technology, will shape the whole future of our society and possibly of our planet. The evidence that love, respect, and responsibility are learned early in life is overwhelming. The evidence that there are members of our societies who are at risk, crippled by lack of the former, not necessarily through any fault of their own, is well-documented. Is it that we suffer from "mural dyslexia", as someone once called it, that we can't see the writing on the wall? Some of our children will need good institutions from birth. Some families will need support and advice. Some parents will want to stay at home initially with their newborn children. Within any institutions we provide, however, must be care and love and learning of the highest order. Our professionals will need to be of both sexes, well-trained, and frequently given opportunities for further learning. They will need to be professionally responsible, but also given room for their own judgement, not anxiously "hedged in" by facile or over-bureaucratic notions of accountability.

2. Parallel with the provision of good institutions must go *effective* parental support. This means supporting parents at home (as in some of the Scandinavian and French systems). It means providing support systems where there are known risks (as in "deprived" inner-city or rural areas). It implies sensitivity and respect for different perspectives and it means that the effects of poverty should not constantly be glossed over, ignored, or assigned to a system of blame. No matter who else is to blame, the children clearly are not! To neglect inadequacy of parenting is to establish a minefield of societal breakdown in the future.

Yet, within all this are real dangers. Loving and socializing our children are frightening prospects if they were to be entirely institutionalized. How do we ensure consistency of love? Does that come solely from professionals? How do we provide that "unreasonable care" deemed so essential in good parenting? Who is going to be on the child's side? These are the challenges for our society, for policymakers, for reformers, for those who care about human warmth, love, and concern and who know them to be the best bulwark against an unknown future. None of this is easy; and to provide inadequate, haphazard, or unloving institutions would be to fall into the very abyss outlined by Bowlby.

Lastly, we should recall, as the OECD does:

> The leaders of single parent families are *usually* women and the poverty that can exist in such circumstances is therefore largely a feminine issue. Women work, often of necessity and with the expectation that they will be able to continue their working lives as soon as their children can be adequately cared for outside the home—an expectation engendered and supported by equity in education. The care of young children is, then, a pressing issue. The signal importance of the early years has been demonstrated (Evans, 1995, p. 140).

Preparing for an Unknown Future

Bowlby believed in the central importance of helping families. In terms of broad psychological theory, he has not been discredited. Our children need love and care. It is the question that won't go away. No one advocates that love and care of children should only take place in large groups (least of all Bowlby), nor that they should be solely the woman's responsibility. Nowadays we can surely recognize the importance of support from good quality staff and from ratios of adult to child which ensure the sensitivity and match of the professional decision which intervenes, which goes over and above mere "minding."

The challenge for us all, therefore, is to ensure the melding of care and education into a secure profession. This is not about special pleading for money and high status. It is about the way that we can best provide the childcare and the growth of love that ensure a humane and just society. I think time is not on our side. We have to persuade lots of male policymakers, among other things. We must do it now, but we have to do it in ways that reflect the essential messages from social science and from medicine, from law and from education, since these are the objective things to which men may be more likely to respond. This is an aspect which challenges our ability to advocate, to marshal argument, and to employ theory and empirical finding to good effect. Such challenges are about deep issues, about the balance between autonomy, mutuality, and responsibility, about what it is to be a sentient human being. There is only one life for us, or our children: no rehearsal!

From the first
tentative scratch on the wall
To the final
unfinished, hurried scrawl:
One poem.

Roger McGough

References

Bowlby, J. (1965). (rev. ed.). *Childcare and the growth of love.* Harmondsworth: Penguin.

Bronfenbrenner, U. (1979). *The ecology of human development: Experiments by nature and design.* Cambridge, MA: Harvard University Press.

Bum, S.M. (1996). *The social psychology of gender.* New York: McGraw Hill.

Evans, P. (1995). *Our children at risk.* Paris: OECD/CERI.

Grixti, J. (1989). *Terrors of uncertainty.* London: Routledge.

Hayden, J. (1996). Beyond Mr. Bubbles: Images of early childhood care and education In *Australian Research in Early Childhood Education.* Vol.1. 65–77.

Hewlett, S.A. (1993). *Child neglect in rich nations.* New York: UNICEF.

Holmes, J. (1993). *John Bowlby and attachment theory.* London: Routledge.

Hudson, F., & Ineichen, B. (1994). *Taking it lying down.* London: Routledge.

Reimer, E. (1971). *School is dead: Alternatives in education.* New York: Doubleday.

Roberts, R. (1997). PEEP Annual Report. Oxford: Peers School.

Silver, P. (1997). (Ed.). *From child to adult: The Dunedin multidisciplinary health and development study.* Oxford: Oxford University Press.

Tizard, B., & Rees, J. (1975). Effects of early institutional rearing on the behavior problems and affectional relationships of four-year-old children. In *Journal of Child Psychology and Psychiatry,* 16. 61–73.

Tudge, J., Shanahan, M.J., & Valsiner, J. (1997). *Comparisons in human development: Understanding time and context.* Cambridge: Cambridge University Press.

Zigler, E.F., Kagan, S.L., & Hall, N.W. (1996). *Children, families, and government.* Cambridge: Cambridge University Press.

National Landscapes

Chapter 4

Policy Development and Change on the Australian Landscape: A Historical Perspective[1]

Jacqueline Hayden

Abstract

In this chapter the early childhood landscape in Australia is described in terms of three trends: a) notions about motherhood, gender equality, and childcare responsibility; b) the move from social justice to an economic rationalist approach to social services; and c) the public image of childcare services. Changes for improved services need to be aware of these influences and need to target constitutional issues in order to move toward the development of a new discourse, a new vision, a new era for early childhood education in Australia.

Introduction

This chapter describes how ideological, economic, and media trends in Australia have reflected and influenced the landscape of early childhood education especially in terms of distributions to childcare programs. The specific issues that have affected historical and current developments in early childhood services in Australia are: a) notions about motherhood, gender equality, and childcare responsibility; b) the move from a social justice to an increasingly economic rationalist approach to social services in the nation; and c) the public image of childcare services.

Motherhood, Gender Equality, and Childcare Responsibility

The Ideology of Motherhood
There is a fundamental ambivalence in Australia and many other nations (such as Canada, U.S., New Zealand, UK) toward the provision of state

(government) assisted childcare.[2] The ambivalence stems from an embedded belief that the care of young children is the responsibility of the family, particularly the mother (O'Connor, 1995; Gammage, this volume). This "ideology of motherhood" reflects the collective perception of women, and of their role in society. There is reason to believe that the traditional belief in the sanctity and reverence of motherhood has not significantly changed since the Industrial Revolution and that this ideology represents the fundamental barrier to the development of a universal system of childcare.

Mother responsibility for childcare is related to the relatively recent notion of childhood as a prolonged stage of dependence, separation, protection, and delayed responsibility for children (Aries, 1962). This concept of the dependence and concomitant need for "care" of children became entrenched during the era of industrialization. Children in agrarian societies were viewed as productive units, contributing to the family economy. With the separation of work from home during the industrial era, children eventually lost their value as workers, and became instead dependents—begging the question of where the responsibility for these dependent agents lay. Historians commonly associate this era with the emergence of the ideology that prescribed the family with the responsibility and autonomy for childrearing (Edgar & Ochiltree, 1983).

This movement from an agricultural to industrial society, the concomitant geographical separation of work from home, increased affluence allowing for the emergence of a specialized nonwage role for women, and the segregation and lengthy period of dependency of children culminated in a division of spheres of influence—women and children in the home and men in the world of commerce, industry, and production (Kessler-Harris, 1982). Thus did the ideology of motherhood take hold throughout the Western World, despite the fact that there is little empirical support for it (O'Connor, 1990).

According to Margaret Mead, exclusive care of children by their mothers is neither a universal nor a natural condition, and is "only possible under highly artificial, urban conditions" (Mead, 1966, p. 248). Indeed, Whiting and Whiting (1975) have reported that the *lack* of the role specialization for mothers is correlated with a "healthier development pattern in children." Recent research findings have also concluded that children develop better when their mothers work (Hoffman, 1979; Gottfried & Gottfried, 1988), and that mothers who are in the workforce are more physically healthy and less prone to depression (Harris & Brown, 1975).

These studies do not seem to have altered deeply embedded beliefs, and the notion of state intervention in childcare strongly conflicts with the entrenched vision whereby mother-care represents the basis of family and social functioning. In this context, state assistance for childcare, in any form, is seen as either welfare for mothers who are not capable of fulfilling their "natural" role; or as an aberration that absolves mothers from meeting their "true" responsibilities.

In Australia, as in other nations, the state took on some childcare responsibility during a crisis situation—the critical labor shortage that occurred while men were overseas during the Second World War. During this employment crisis the Commonwealth government in Australia, through the Department of Labor and National Service, made unprecedented grants available for the expansion of services to various Kindergarten Union and Day Nursery Associations, encouraging mothers to go off to work. After the war, however, men needed their jobs back. Grants for childcare were arbitrarily withdrawn, despite strong lobbying efforts to retain them (see Brennan & O'Donnell, 1986, p. 20).

The postwar need to move women out of the workforce and to shift childcare responsibility back into the home was advanced by the newly developed sciences of psychoanalysis and cognitive psychology. Studies of abandoned war children were used to provide empirical support of the importance of the motherhood role during early childhood. Mothers in the 1950s were shown to be singularly responsible for the healthy development of children. Research findings claimed that a child deprived of mothering was most unlikely to "remain normal"; that effects were lifelong; and that damage from early maternal deprivation was irreversible (Spitz, 1945; Bowlby, 1951). The following statement from the popular British psychologist and psychoanalyst, D.W. Winnicott, summarizes the ethos of the times:

> What is much needed at the present time is to give moral support to the ordinary good mother, educated or uneducated, clever or limited, rich or poor and to protect her from everyone and everything that gets between her baby and herself (Winnicott, 1957, p. 144).

Despite this type of powerful propaganda promoting a traditional image of the family, and of the role of the wife/mother within it, the wartime experiences of women in the workforce and the (albeit, brief) period of state provision of childcare had sown the seeds of change by inaugurating a modified perspective on the position of women in modern society.

Gender Equality

Female workforce participation during the world wars gave birth to a change in attitudes, primarily those of childcare consumers—women who were unwilling to give up their new found independence—and to the emergence of numerous other stakeholders with divergent reasons for demanding state intervention in childcare provision.

Providers came to reflect the growing professionalism in the field of childcare. This newly-formed body of experts, prompted by their discovery of positive outcomes for children in care and/or by employment prospects, became a powerful advocacy group for public childcare provision. Similarly, some employers were reluctant to give up a now trained and experienced female workforce, and many families may have discovered the benefits of two incomes (the need for which was promoted through the advance of television with its consumer orientation). The proliferation and marketing of labor-saving devices for homemakers, medical advances that prolonged life, and the availability of contraception (which prevented and/or delayed birth) resulted in the tasks of homemaking and childrearing demanding a much smaller percentage of a woman's life (Simons & Vella, 1984; Midgley & Hughes, 1983). These factors, combined with the emergence of articulate spokespeople such as Germaine Greer (1970), Kate Millet (1971), and Betty Freidan (1971), created a climate in which mothercare could be questioned, and prompted the onset of the Women's Liberation Movement.

Meanwhile, the research findings of the 1950s suggesting long-term debilitating effects for children separated from mothers, were replaced by a second generation of studies emphasizing the positive outcomes of out-of-home-care (see Belsky & Steinberg, 1978). At the same time popular ideas about childcare stressed the adaptability of the babies and the suggestion that the mother's rights could, to some extent, supersede those of the child. The best selling *Baby and Childcare* by Dr. Benjamin Spock counseled parents to follow their instincts—"Trust yourself . . . what you feel like doing for your baby is probably best" (Spock, 1953, pp. 3–4).

The reduction of state-supported childcare services after the Second World War created a reactive lobby from both providers and users of the care whose satisfactory arrangements were suddenly withdrawn. The introduction of labor-saving household devices, the recognition that work need not be differentiated by gender, increased rates of divorce and of single parenthood, demands for increased income, and feminist rhetoric culminated in increased demands for state support for childcare. The demands were couched within a doctrine of gender equality.

Growing out of the women's liberation movement, spurred by the influence of behaviorism, and strengthened by equal rights legislation for minority groups, this new ideology espoused the idea that the social differences between men and women are environmentally caused—and that these differences can be eliminated by redefining roles and breaking down stereotypes. Proponents of this belief system call for state action to counteract discrimination by legislating equal rights and privileges to women, including access to opportunities for training and workforce participation. In response to these demands, and reflecting worldwide trends in this direction, legislation was passed in Australia that addressed the elimination of work-related discrimination against women, focusing primarily on job-related and maternity benefits. The *Australian Commonwealth Sex Discrimination Act of 1984* made unlawful acts of discrimination on the grounds of gender, marital status, or pregnancy in employment and other areas. It gave effect to some provisions of the *UN Convention on the Elimination of All Forms of Discrimination Against Women*, ratified by Australia in July 1983, and it promoted recognition and acceptance within the community of the principle of equality between men and women. Australian states have also enacted legislation. In New South Wales, for example, the 1980 amendment to the *Anti-Discrimination Act of 1976* requires certain employing authorities to develop equal employment opportunity management plans and to adopt affirmative action programs.

Resistance to a Changed Ideology

While women's options, expectations, and role in society have undergone drastic change since the 1950s, the ideology of motherhood lingers and continues to provide rationale for reducing or marginalizing childcare service delivery in Australia.

Resistance to an alternative to the motherhood ethic is reflected in many ways. Empirical findings have become available to support a renewed emphasis on the importance of mothercare, reiterating older research studies which pointed to the deleterious effects of out-of-home care (see, for instance, Belsky, 1988). The role of the media in influencing prevailing attitudes is significant as well (Connell, 1977). Into the 1990s, images of traditional motherhood roles continue to outweigh new female images on television and in films and magazines (Faludi, 1991; Hayden, 1996). Meanwhile, research findings that indicate that center-reared infants exhibit poor attachment to mothers have been reported in the popular press without the concomitant reservations regarding methodology and other factors which temper these conclusions. The ensuing collective vision associates the provision and use of institutionalized childcare with inhumane, destructive practices at worst, or with individual selfishness at best.

Some believe that perceived changes in the role of mothers and women in society have instigated a backlash (Faludi, 1991). In the 1990s a wave of neo-traditionalists have emerged and are thriving within powerful political and social spheres. Traditionalists work to recreate a mythical "correct" society which is based on specific gender roles. Within this vision, institutionalized childcare becomes the antithesis of sound "family values," and social changes such as increased rates of divorce and of working mothers with infants are seen as symbols of a declining morality. In Australia, the election of the conservative Coalition government in the late 1990s is a case in point. Prime Minister John Howard promotes traditional notions about women and private responsibility for childcare. Funding cuts of over $8 million in the first two years of his government reflect this viewpoint.

But politicians do not necessarily create beliefs—they also reflect public opinion. Australia's childcare policies are an outcome, not only of misguided economic and political trends, but of widespread ambivalence about what Australians really believe, and really desire (see Hayden, 1992). In the 1990s, only a small minority of children under 12 years of age are cared for full time by their mothers. Despite this fact, surveys have shown that the belief in motherhood as the sacred, natural, and best role for women, and in mother care as the best child rearing technique, permeates all levels of society and socioeconomic groupings in Australia and elsewhere (Wearing, 1984; O'Connor, 1995).

Early childhood professionals themselves may be contributing to the collective vision of childcare as a *necessary evil*. In a survey of graduating early childhood teachers, not one stated that he or she would make use of a childcare center for their own young baby. They did not believe in the value of the services they had been trained to deliver, develop, and lead (Ashton & Elliott, 1995).

From Social Justice to Economic Rationalism

Childcare entered the political arena in Australia in the early 1970s, during an era characterized by policies which aimed at the creation of a "just society." Since the 1980s early childhood services in this country have mostly reflected the principles of economic rationalism.

Childcare in Australia has become a means to other ends such as equal employment opportunities which address feminist interests; an enlarged pool of labor, and improved productivity which meet the needs of employers; small business development; reduced welfare payments; and a host of other economically rational goals. This latter phase has been marked by support to long day care over preschools and by regulatory reforms which address costs of service provision over and above quality care.

The Social Justice Era of Childcare in Australia

Government support for childcare in Australia can be traced back to the launching of a Russian space satellite in 1957. This example of superior technological know-how in the Soviet Union caused panic in the U.S. and other Western countries. Politicians blamed the educational systems for failing to develop the minds and talents of its citizens. The launching of *Sputnik* came to symbolize the complacency of the West. Attention focused on the wastage rates and high percentage of school dropouts. Public education, it was declared, had failed to advance the educational or social achievements of vast numbers of low income students and families. In fact, the public school system was actually seen to be perpetuating inequality of opportunity and mitigating against any break in the cyclical patterns of poverty (see, for instance, Coleman, 1966; Holt, 1969, 1970; Postman, 1969; Illich, 1971). This notion helped to secure a re-focus of government spending priorities. The development of human capital became a major goal and nations began to experiment with a *bubble up* economic strategy—shifting economic resources directly to the poor in the form of nutrition, health, employment, and educational programs (Ebrahim, 1982; Seigel, 1985).

Compensatory Education

These economic developments coincided with a paradigmatic shift in our understanding of human development. The early 1960s produced a proliferation of child development studies that provided astonishing evidence that experiences during the first years of life are significantly related to later functioning. Based on the principles of imprinting, chances for appropriate development of the human mind and personality were shown to exist at particular stages, with little chance of reparation if the correct timing was missed. The first four years of life were shown to be a crucial time for irrevocable cognitive, emotional, social, physical and even psychosexual development (Bowlby, 1951; Bloom, 1964; Harlow, 1966; Kagan, 1971), and the preschool years were touted as a critical period for intervention, not only to meet educational and other socialization goals, but in order to maximize human potential!

It was a short step from these findings to those that subsequently proved that the provision of certain experiences to "culturally deprived" preschool aged children would significantly alter their performance during the first years of primary schooling. Language, cognitive skills, and intelligence quotient were shown to improve markedly in children who were given a few hours of targeted instruction, whose parents were made aware of certain child developmental needs and appropriate practices, and who were exposed to early health screening and nutritional programs. Experiences during early childhood were seen to dictate later school (and life) success, and thus, exposure of deprived groups to certain developmental activities would equalize educational opportunity (Frost, 1973). The concept of compensatory education for children from disadvantaged backgrounds emerged.

Compensatory education—programs targeted at "deprived" groups, especially very young children—became the *cure all* for the 1970s. Millions of dollars were raised to research, develop, and implement a variety of preschool "miracle" programs. Much controversy arose over which experiences were most beneficial and/or most "equalizing." Some of these well-resourced, university-based programs concentrated on language and cognitive cramming. Others focused on emotional and self-esteem building. The results were inconclusive, but all agreed that young children from impoverished homes (monetary hardship and cultural deprivation were somehow deemed to be synonymous) benefited immensely from exposure to certain experiences which were provided in group settings by people other than parents and relatives.

Equality of Opportunity as a National Goal

Escalating the educational levels of the population was seen as a critical means for national advancement in an increasingly technological world. The education system became the panacea for correcting both social injustice and the need for increased competence and technical know-how.

The goal of maximizing the potential of citizens, reducing wastage, and improving the social and economic conditions of the poor, not only justified, but compelled state intervention in preschool years under the guise of "equality of educational opportunity." This is the root of government involvement with preschool aged children. Demands for civil rights and equality were translated into a theory of individual responsibility (individuals, not systems, were to blame for social diseases). Thus salvation from poverty and racism, as well as the alleviation of crime and urban disorder, would be achieved, not through structural changes in society, but by improved usage of the public school system, and particularly by the more equitable distribution of preschool experiences. The foundational principle of state intervention in the care of young children was to ensure that impoverished citizens learned proper attitudes and work habits during their formative years so that they could be more precisely assimilated into mainstream society.

In Australia, the notion of state responsibility for "compensating" selected groups of citizens was reflected in a number of commissioned reports, inquiries, and legislation. Most notable are the *Karmel Report* (1973), which initiated the redistribution of educational resources to "disadvantaged schools," and the *Childcare and Protection Act of Australia* (1972), which heralded Commonwealth support for children's services.

Meanwhile a group of childcare stakeholders had emerged. The livelihood and status of a number of professionals came to depend upon acceptance of the notion that certain early childhood experiences are beneficial, necessary, even critical to normal development, that the state had responsibility for ensuring equal access to these experiences, and/or that early childhood education became a legitimate arm of the public education system.

These stakeholders include university specialists, other trainers, and trained providers of care with interests in universal availability of children's services, as well as high standards of care. Their demands focus upon the need for a child-centered, quality basis for policy decision making. Recent reports such as the *Review of New South Wales Schools* (Carrick, 1989) reflect these demands. One section is titled *The particular importance of early childhood education* (p. 83) and others refer to a state role in parental education as a means of meeting the needs of children below the age of three (pp. 79–90).

The Phase of Economic Rationalism

In the 1980s early childhood education programs came to incorporate a childcare component. The increase in distributions at this time were targeted at work incentive programs for parents—not educational programs for children. This transformation of childcare from its compensatory/social justice beginnings to a system that provides government support for the care of young children while their parent or parents work, look for work, and/or attend classes has changed the face of early child service delivery in Australia.

The transformation from calls for preschool programs to equalize educational opportunity, to a demand for universal childcare to increase the labor force, was paralleled by the appearance on the scene of new stakeholders. Feminists, entrepreneurs, employers, and influential government economists have jumped on the childcare band wagon; each group promoting its own interests and pursuing diverse goals.

Childcare is Linked to Employment Opportunity: Feminists Become Stakeholders

The association of childcare to increased labor force participation was the initial catalyst for state intervention in the area and took place long before the social justice programs of the 1960s and 1970s. As mentioned above, the Commonwealth of Australia gave grants and other support to provide childcare for women who were working in "essential war services" during World War II. Despite the fact that these services were withdrawn as soon as the war ended, the brief period of state provision of childcare sowed some significant and irrevocable seeds. The provision of state-run day nurseries (regardless of standards) demonstrated how shared responsibility for childcare could have positive effects on labor force participation, on the economy, and on expanded opportunities for women, and it incited the demand for the elimination of gender discrimination in the workforce.

The availability of childcare services was seen to be a critical strategy in the pursuit of equality of employment and of economic opportunities for women. Thus the rationale for childcare support switched from children, and from impoverished and special needs families, to feminists. Demand grew dramatically. Throughout the 1970s, 1980s and 1990s women with children represented the fastest growing segment of the labor force. In Australia, 70% of children below the age of five years are presently in some form of nonparental care. The demand for care is estimated to grow by 15% over the next 15 decades (Economic Planning Advisory Commission, 1996).

Feminists have frequently been named as the most dominant group of childcare stakeholders in Australia (Brennan, 1994). Certainly, they have been the most vociferous. Although some would argue that childcare is a society-wide, rather than a women's issue, there remains a solid connection between public childcare and the aroused awareness of women's rights. In Australia, the Women's Electoral Lobby is credited with having made a powerful contribution to the Labor victory of 1972, and with the passing of the progressive Commonwealth Childcare Bill (*The Childcare and Protection Act, 1972*). Feminist demands for increased support for the program do not focus upon childcare because of its role in equalizing educational opportunity for children, but target increased availability in order to ensure maximum life options for all adults.

Childcare Becomes an "Industry": Entrepreneurs Become Stakeholders

The temporary emergence of childcare delivery services during the Second World War, and their subsequent abrupt termination, created a market demand, and a new group of stakeholders emerged to meet it. Private childcare operators grew out of the discrepancy between the limited amount of publicly funded childcare and the increasing demands for service. There has always been a substantial number of for-profit childcare centers in Australia. Since 1990 when the Commonwealth extended fee relief to families using for profit centers, the percentage of commercial operations has risen to 70% of all childcare services.

Stakeholders within the category of entrepreneurs, include equipment distributors, real estate agents, architects and others who gain financially from an expanded childcare industry. These business people are not primarily concerned with *accessibility* and *quality* of childcare, nor are they demanding increases in (competitive) government-provided care. The demand from childcare entrepreneurs is for financial support (in the form of incentives and user subsidies) that promotes increased usage of out-of-home childcare. That is, they want more quantity, less emphasis on quality. Under these auspices, childcare has changed from a "service" to a "business," stimulating consumer spending and economic growth. In the recession-ridden 1990s, this "production" orientation has met the goals of policymakers. Entrepreneur stakeholders generate revenue, reduce obstacles to employment, provide a highly demanded service, and generally boost the economy. Their very existence takes the pressure off governments for increased public provision of childcare. Not surprisingly, this group tends to be highly influential in the development of government policies (or lack thereof) (see Hayden, 1994). Childcare entrepreneurs in the U.S. have been credited with preventing the development of national childcare standards (Phillips, 1986). In Australia these stakeholders have been successful in their campaigns to prevent more rigorous childcare regulations, increased monitoring and enforcement of regulations, an extension of the national system of accreditation, and supplemental funding for nonprofit childcare operations.

Employers Become Stakeholders

Employer benefits from childcare are seen in terms of increasing the pool of potential workers, maintaining the services of women who have been trained, and maximizing worker productivity through the reduction of childcare related stress. This latter characteristic has received much public attention. Childcare provision has been associated with reduced tardiness and absenteeism, reduced use of sick days, lower turnover rates, increased post-maternity retention, even decreased non-work-related telephone usage and less office "pilfering" (Burad, 1984). These arguments are used increasingly to devolve responsibility for childcare from the state onto employers—with the justification that "those who benefit the most should carry the cost."

Employers thus have many reasons to support childcare availability. Like commercial operators of childcare centers, their interests lie in enhanced government responsibility (funding, and/or incentives) for the program and in increased childcare availability to support workforce needs. Standards of care and quality service delivery are not the main focus of their advocacy.

Government Support for Childcare

By the 1980s, *bubble up* was abandoned as a cure-all for social and economic depression, and fiscal policy embraced trickling down with more gusto than ever before. The fact that compensatory—or the more ideologically correct, *special programs for disadvantaged areas*—has had a rocky road during recession years in many nations is not surprising. Because there was now a welfare state to dismantle, the trickle-down philosophy has had to be promulgated with new commitment and childcare has been caught up in the rhetoric and the practices.

During the 1980s, budgets for equity oriented programs were consistently reduced while the "user-pays" creed, free market principles, and economic rationalism became new icons. Resources were directed toward corporate and business interests and away from educational and social programs. Public support for childcare thus needed to be (and was) rationalized according to economic rather than child development needs. A plethora of cost/benefit and efficiency studies were conducted. They revealed that the loss of tax revenues from non-working mothers is significant (Sylva, 1988), that expenses for the education and training of females are recoupable when women remain for longer periods in the workforce (Anstie, R., Gregory, R., & Dorovich, S., 1988), and that welfare payments are more costly than childcare subsidization—especially when minimally or nonrelated regulated (cheap) care is provided.

Thus childcare policymaking took on a new dimension. Policies were developed that supported (in some cases *forced*) increased female workforce participation while those relating to standards were redesigned (in some cases dismantled) with the aim of keeping the costs down.

Currently some regulations are being severely curtailed as a means of increasing private entrepreneurial operations. In Australia, despite the promises of a national, government-supported accreditation system for childcare standards, the recent declaration of National Standards for Childcare has cleared the way for lower standards of care (and lower delivery costs). In New South Wales, for example, regulatory reforms have downgraded the qualifications of a "trained teacher/authorized supervisor" and are threatening to reduce crucial staff-to-child ratios. In most states personnel in social service departments have been cut to such an extent that whatever legislation exists is rendered meaningless by inadequate, token enforcement.

Most of the chapters in this volume describe the outcome of current economic rationalist approaches to childcare and other aspects of early childhood education services. While the landscape is not inspiring, there are pockets of hope and triumph. Some case studies show clearly that there are pathways (through constitutional measures) which lead to adequate, even improved services despite current economic and political constraints.

The Public Image of Childcare

The public image of childcare both reflects and influences the trends described above. The public image of early childhood education, and especially of the childcare component of this program, influences the attitude toward, and thus public support for, government funding decisions, the status of early childhood workers, the ability to attract people into the profession, and many other constitutional issues.

For reasons outlined above, the perception that out-of-home, group care cannot be as good as *mother care* has prevailed in Australia and other Western nations. Despite the reality, the perception of childcare as a *poor* product has been highly resistant to change. No matter what the reality of high-quality care is, parents and the public, who are funding services through tax payments, have for many years held onto the conviction that institutionalized childcare is not quality care (O'Connor,1995).

Research into the Public Image of Childcare in Australia

In 1988 a preschool operator in Sydney was accused of sexually assaulting his charges during "bath time". "Mr. Bubbles" (named after the bath time activities) garnered sensational headlines for many years. He became the archetype of potentially evil childcare personnel—performing satanic rites and unspeakable deeds, exploiting parent trust and children's innocence, pervading the profession, lurking at each childcare center. Six years later, there remained evidence that *Mr. Bubbles* (later vindicated of charges) still represented the public image of childcare in Australia. A Sydney-based study investigated the public image of childcare and the way in which that image has influenced community perceptions of early childhood care and education services (Hayden, 1996a). The research examined how the concept of childcare was reflected in the popular culture and involved the analysis of newspaper and magazine items, video and film productions, and of prime time television programs.

The findings revealed that childcare was underrepresented as a function of normal family life on television and in films. When it *was* addressed, childcare was shown to have negative or frightening outcomes. In the news media, childcare was most frequently portrayed as an employment-related issue with an economic rationale. The benefits of early childhood care and education for children and the social justice goals of childcare were shown to be significantly underrepresented in all segments of the popular media. A survey of the public-at-large demonstrated how these media representations were reflected in common misconceptions about childcare programs and those who worked within them.[3] Sixty eight per cent of respondents expressed negative views about the need for tertiary qualifications for those who work in the early childhood field. eighty percent of respondents did not believe that early childhood specialists should be classified as "professionals". Fifty-three percent of respondents stated that they would not use the formal system of childcare for their own child (Hayden, 1994a, 1996a).

Summary of Results

In the study cited above, the majority of respondents were not aware of the positive attributes of a quality childcare program, preferred not to use out-of-home childcare if it could be avoided, and did not think that training (certainly not university training) was necessary for childcare teachers. Many respondents associated childcare publicity with the *Mr. Bubbles* affair. Amazingly, this 1988 case was still making headlines in 1994. *Mr. Bubbles Sensation* screamed the front page headlines of the *Sydney Telegraph*, on March 2, 1994—six years after the event! Although the text of this article was positive, indicating that the incident had not been as horrific as originally portrayed, the headlines and picture of the accused perpetrator, looking decidedly evil, served as a reminder of the fact that in childcare centers these types of things could and do take place (see Johnson, this volume, on the issue of moral panic in childcare centers).

Conclusion

This chapter has described some of the salient trends which contribute to the landscape of early childhood services in Australia, especially the childcare sector.

Childcare emerged during a political and economic era that heralded a more equal, socially just society. The newly emerged field of child psychology identified the importance of early experiences upon later learning and healthy development, and trained professionals were seen to be the most appropriate vehicle by which *all* children, regardless of race, background, and economic standing, could be guaranteed access to positive, developmental experiences in their formative years. The political winds shifted however, and with them, the support and perceived value of a child-centered system of early childhood education. Despite gains in terms of policies, numbers, dollars, and other aspects of a well-developed system of public childcare, an ideology of motherhood has guided, and continues to underlie, the delivery of childcare services in Australia. The ideology is reflected in a public image that highlights negative aspects and downplays the benefits of other-than-mother care. Childcare does have more presence on the political agenda than it did 20 or even 10 years ago. But being on the agenda does not always mean that issues are being addressed. As Stonehouse noted:

> There is a non-trivial distinction between issues related to children being on the political agenda, and children being on the political agenda. The former has been achieved but not the latter (Stonehouse, 1992, p. 162).

Indeed as Faludi points out, the more perceived gains from the promoters of childcare (she said *feminism*), the more ardent is the opposition. The onus is on early childhood professionals to seek out and develop long-term constitutional improvements which can transcend embedded notions and which will move toward the development of a new discourse, a new vision, a new era for early childhood education in Australia and elsewhere.

The chapters that follow in this volume describe and analyze current efforts to address these goals for early childhood education in Australia, Canada, New Zealand, and elsewhere.

Notes

1. Parts of this chapter have appeared in a previous publication by the author: Hayden, 1996.
2. For a detailed account of the political developments and outcomes in Australian early childhood education, and particularly the politics of the childcare system, see Brennan, 1994; Hayden, 1994; Mellor 1990.
3. One hundred survey questionnaires were distributed to a random selection of the public. Survey questions were asked orally to individuals at shopping malls, at bus stops, and train stations. Some survey questionnaires were handed out at a nonrelated workplace. Respondents ranged in age from 14 years to 74 years of age; 48 males and 52 females were included in the study. No other characteristics were noted.

   The questionnaire consisted of four questions:

   1. What do you think of when I mention the term childcare? (Image of childcare)
   2. What do you think early childhood training involves? Do you think early childhood educators are professionals?
   3. Comment on the way childcare is portrayed in the media?
   4. Do you or would you use childcare for your own child? Why or why not?

   The findings from this study are reported in more detail in Hayden, 1996a.

References

Anstie, R., Gregory, R., & Dorovich, S. (1988). *Government spending on work related childcare: Some economic issues.* Center for Economic Policy Research, ANU, Discussion Paper 191.

Aries, P. (1962). *Centuries of Childhood.* London: Jonathan Cape.

Ashton, J., & Elliott, A. 1995. Students teacher perceptions of early childhood care and education issues. Paper presented at the Australian Association for Research in Education Annual Conference, Hobart, 27–30 November.

Belsky, J. (1988). *The effects of infant day care reconsidered.* Washington: National Institute of Child Health and Human Development.

Belsky, J., & Steinberg, L. (1978). The effects of day care: A critical review. In *Child Development* 49: 929–949.

Bloom, B. (1964). *Stability and change in human characteristics.* New York: Wiley.

Bowlby, J. (1951). *Maternal care and mental health.* Geneva: World Health Organization.

Brennan, D. (1994). *The politics of Australian childcare.* Cambridge: Cambridge University Press.

Brennan, D., & O'Donnell, C. (1986). *Caring for Australia's children.* Sydney: Allen and Unwin.

Burad, S. (1984). *Employer supported childcare: Investing in human resources.* New York: Auburn House.

Carrick, J. (1989). *Report of the committee of review of New South Wales schools.* Sydney: Government of New South Wales.

Coleman, J. (1966). *Equality of educational opportunity.* Washington, DC: US Dept of Health, Education and Welfare, Office of Education.

Connell, W. (1977). *Ruling class, ruling culture.* Cambridge: Cambridge University Press.

Ebrahim, G. (1982). *Child health in a changing environment.* London: MacMillan Press.

Edgar, D., & Ochiltree, G. (1983). *Family change—early childhood development*. Discussion Paper Number 6, Melbourne: Australian Institute of Family Studies.

Faludi, S. (1991). *Backlash. The undeclared war against American Women*. New York: Anchor Books.

Freidan, B. (1971). *The feminine mystique*. London: Gollan.

Frost, J. (Ed.). (1973). *Revisiting early childhood education*. New York: Holt, Rhinehart and Winston.

Gottfried, A., & Gottfried, A. (1988). *Maternal employment and children's development*. New York: Plenum Press.

Greer, G. (1970). *The Female Eunuch*. London: Palladin.

Harlow, A. (1966). Learning to love. *American Scientist* 54: 244–272.

Harris, T., & Brown, G. (1975). Social class and psychiatric disturbance among women in urban population. *Sociology*. 9: 225–245.

Hayden, J. (1992). Available, accessible, high-quality childcare in Australia; Why we haven't moved very far. *Children Australia*. 17(1):10–16.

Hayden, J. (1994). Half full or half empty? Childcare policy and the missing bits. In E. Mellor & K. Coombes *Issues in Early Childhood: Australian Perspectives*. New York: WCB.

Hayden, J. (1994a). The public image of childcare. *Every Child* Spring 1: 14–16.

Hayden, J. (1996). *Management of early childhood services—an Australian perspective*. Sydney: Social Science Press.

Hayden, J. (1996a). Beyond Mr. Bubbles: An analysis of the public image of early childhood care and education in Western Sydney. *Journal of Australian Research in Early Childhood Education*. Vol. 1: 65–77.

Hoffman, L. (1979). Maternal employment. *The American Psychologist* 34: 859–865, October.

Holt, J. (1969). *The underachieving school*. New York: Pitman.

Holt, J. (1970). *How children fail*. New York: Dell.

Illich, I. (1971). *De-schooling society*. New York: Harper and Row.

Kagan, J. (1971). *Change and continuity in infancy.* New York: John Wiley.

Karmel, P. (1973). *Schools in Australia—Report of the interim committee of the Australian Schools Commission.* Canberra: Government of Australia.

Kessler-Harris, A. (1982). *A history of wage earning women in the United States.* New York: Oxford University Press.

Mead, M. (1966). A cultural anthropologist's approach to maternal deprivation. In A. Ainsworth, R. Andry, R. Harlow, M. Lebovici, M. Mead, D. Prugh, and B. Wootton. *Deprivation of maternal care: A reassessment of its effects.* New York: Schoken Books.

Mellor, E. (1990). *Stepping stones: The development of early childhood services in Australia.* Sydney: Harcourt, Brace, Jovanovich.

Midgley, & Hughes. (1983). *Women's choices.* London: Weidenfeld and Nicolson.

Millet, K. (1971). *Sexual politics.* London: Rupert Hart-Davis.

Mintern, O., & Lambert, W. (1964). *Mothers of six cultures: Antecedents of childrearing.* New York: Wiley.

O'Connor, S. (1990). Rationales for the institutionalization of programs for young children. *American Journal of Education.* Feb. vol: 114–146.

O'Connor, S. (1995). Mothering in public. *Early Childhood Research Quarterly* 10(1): 63–80.

Phillips, D. (1986). The federal model of childcare standards act of 1985: Step in right direction or hollow gesture? *American Journal of Orthopsychiatry* 56(1): 56–64.

Postman, N. (1969). *Teaching as a subversive activity.* Hammondsworth: Penguin Books.

Seigal, M. (1985). *Children, parenthood, and social welfare in the context of developmental psychology.* Oxford: Clarendon Press.

Simons, F., & Vella, P. (1984). Why childcare has become an industrial issue. *Australian Journal of Early Childhood* 9 December (4).

Spitz, R. (1945). Hospitalism: An inquiry into the genesis of psychiatric conditions in early childhood. *Psychoanalytical Study of the Child* 1: 53–74.

Spock, B. (1953). *Baby and childcare.* New York: Pocket Books.

Stonehouse, A. (1992). Early childhood grows up. In B. Lambert (Ed.). *Changing Faces: The early childhood profession in Australia.* Canberra: Australian Early Childhood Association

Sylva, A. (1988). *Competence and coping in children.* Paper presented at the Australian Early Childhood Association Conference, Canberra, September.

Wearing, B. (1984). *The ideology of motherhood.* Sydney: George Allen and Unwin.

Whiting, B., & Whiting, J. (1975). *Children of six cultures: A psychocultural analysis.* Cambridge: Harvard University Press.

Winnicott, D. (1957). *The child and the family.* London: Tavistock Publications.

Chapter 5

Early Childhood Education on the Canadian Policy Landscape[1]

Martha Friendly
Mab Oloman

Abstract

This chapter describes the social policy landscape of early childhood education in Canada focusing on the childcare sector and on two major considerations. The first consideration addresses the fundamental question: "is childcare a matter of public concern, or is it a private family responsibility?" The second major consideration revolves around the issue of "what (and who) is childcare for?"

Introduction: The Historical Context

Childcare first appeared on Canada's policy landscape before the turn of the last century. It wasn't until the mid 1960s, however, when major development of Canada's social safety net was well underway, that the federal government began to accept some limited financial and policy responsibility for childcare through national welfare legislation. Although in the 1970s provincial and territorial governments began to assume a primary role in childcare by providing regulation, funding, and training, the federal government, through a policy framework of conditional costsharing, maintained an interest in childcare policy and services.[2] In this way, not only did the supply, variety, and quality of services grow across the country but childcare remained high on the political agenda.

In the 1990s, however, this trend reversed. The childcare situation deteriorated in almost every region (Doherty, Friendly, & Oloman, 1998). In the 1990s, the circumscribed role assumed by the federal government in the preceding 30 years dwindled even further. Several attempts to develop national childcare policy—in 1984, 1987, and finally in 1994—failed. Finally, in the mid 1990s, the involvement of the government of Canada in childcare was withdrawn.

As federal retreat from childcare (and other social programs) accelerated in the 1990s, the funding and regulation commitments of provincial governments began to dwindle as well. Thus, a key characteristic of Canada's current childcare situation is that responsibility for childcare has been dispersed not only to provincial/territorial governments, but to the local level, and to parents. Regional disparity and service delivery fragmentation—always a key characteristic of early childhood education and childcare provision in Canada—has increased. Indeed it can be argued that the single most important factor that has influenced the development of Canadian early childhood education and childcare has been the *absence* of a coherent national early childhood education and childcare policy!

This policy vacuum is associated with the political, social, and economic considerations and pressures that have affected Canada throughout its history. Early childhood education and childcare programs across Canada demonstrate considerable variety in the range of services offered, funding, requirements for the provision of care, monitoring, and enforcement of requirements. Although it is sometimes suggested that this disparity is a suitable response to regional diversity in community needs, the outcome remains services that have developed inconsistently rather than coherently (Friendly & Oloman, 1996). While each province and territory hosts a tangle of early childhood education and childcare programs, few children and families have access to the services they need.

Canada, like its sister nations Australia and New Zealand, can be categorized as belonging to the Anglo-American cluster of countries (Bronfenbrenner, 1992; Hewlett, 1993; Girard 1995). Historically, early childhood education and childcare programs in the three nations have been poorly developed (Sims, 1994), at least when compared to the more coherent public service systems for young children in nations like France, Italy, and the Nordic countries (European Commission Network on Childcare, 1996). Indeed, both Bronfenbrenner's observation that the United States, Great Britain, and Canada all approach childcare "in an Anglo-Saxon mode," and Hewlett's discussion of "neglected children in rich (Anglo-American) nations" can both be applied to early childhood education and childcare in all three countries.

In the past decade, Canada has undergone a major rightward political shift. This shift has been characterized by a focus on government deficit reduction; concomitant cutbacks in government spending (especially social spending); dispersion of responsibility for social programs to provincial and local governments, religious and voluntary institutions, and families; decentralization of government operation; privatization of public services; and downsizing of the public sector. The shift has been accompanied by rhetoric about the value of self-reliance and individual responsibility. This neo-conservative approach to social issues has become a concrete impediment to maturation of an adequate system of early childhood education and childcare for Canadians (see Hayden, 1997).

During the era of Canadian federal leadership in shaping national social programs like Medicare, social welfare, pensions, and unemployment insurance (1940s through the 1980s) childcare was not on the public agenda. It wasn't until the 1980s that the benefits of early childhood education and childcare programs to young children's development began to be widely acknowledged in Canada, or that mothers of young children were in the paid workforce in sufficient numbers to constitute a political force. By the time that childcare gained a spot on the national political agenda in Canada, fiscal and political factors had begun to mitigate against introduction of a potentially expensive social program, or introduction of a new national program of any variety (Doherty et al., 1998). One could say that childcare, still in its infancy as a social program, had failed to "catch the wave" of social policy development.

Social Policy in the 1990s

Two issues had enormous influence on social policy developments that followed in Canada in the 1990s. The first of these was the fiscal tensions generated by the deficit and debt; the second was apprehension about the possible separation of Québec from Canada.

The new decade began with a federally imposed cap on cost-sharing through the Canada Assistance Plan in the three wealthiest provinces—Ontario, British Columbia, and Alberta.

A severe recession stimulated the preoccupation of both federal and provincial governments with fiscal issues, encouraging almost all provincial governments to embrace deficit-reducing neo-conservative agendas. The advances that childcare had made in the 1980s began to fade. For the first time in a decade, the increase in new regulated childcare spaces slowed down. Provinces that had initiated programs of direct operating funding and wage enhancement grants to raise staff wages began to freeze, reduce, or even eliminate them; by 1995, nine of the twelve jurisdictions had taken one of these three steps (Childcare Resource and Research Unit, 1997).

At the same time, the historical tension between Québec and the rest of Canada was growing. In the conservative era before 1993, two efforts at rewriting the Canadian Constitution to secure Québec's participation failed. Québec's constant threat to separate fueled the decentralist aspirations of the other provinces. These calls for increased provincial sovereignty were exacerbated by the unilateral decision to cap the Canada Assistance Plan in 1990 and shrinking federal transfer payments for health care (Doherty, et al., 1998). A key domain in which the provinces wanted more autonomy was social policy.

In 1995, the government of Canada announced that it was eliminating the Canada Assistance Plan, with its conditional, open-ended cost-sharing, thus eradicating (along with the national welfare program) the mechanism for existing federal spending on regulated childcare. The 1996 Speech from the Throne confirmed that the federal government intended to draw back from sharing responsibility for shaping social programs, an ominous message for childcare. It stated that:

> The government (of Canada) will not use its spending power to create new shared-cost programs in areas of exclusive provincial jurisdiction without the consent of a majority of the provinces. (Speech from the Throne, 1996).

The Speech from the Throne signaled a massive restructuring of Canadian federal/provincial jurisdictional arrangements that would be known as "the new social union" (Doherty, Friendly, & Oloman, 1998).

Today the childcare situation in many provinces has become increasingly precarious. The jurisdictional shifts known as "the new social union" and the funding shifts support the primacy of provincial decision making in social policy. Although provincial governments have argued throughout the 1990s for more authority for social programs vis-a-vis the federal government, their enthusiasm appears to have diminished as well (Doherty, et al., 1998). As the new millennium arrives, reductions in federal funding and federal withdrawal from social policy, together with provincial downsizing and deregulation, have induced a new childcare crisis. In this last decade, childcare is no longer making gains; it is, instead, losing ground.

Two Themes Driving Policy

There are two main themes that are integral to an overview of Canadian early childhood education and childcare. The first theme is concerned with a fundamental question: "Is childcare a matter of public concern, or is it a private family responsibility?" The response to this question determines whether childcare is treated as a private commodity within a market model or as a public service within the framework of social policy. This is a fundamental point because whether childcare is considered a private responsibility or a "public good" is central to the design of childcare policy and, ultimately, to service delivery.

The second main theme is also concerned with a question: "What (and who) is childcare for?" The answer to "what is childcare?" ranges from "healthy child development" and "readiness to learn" to "a tool to support parental employability," from "equality for women" to "reduction of reliance on social assistance" to "early intervention for children at risk"; the answer to "who is childcare for?" varies from "children" to "parents", from "families" to "women".

Public and Private Responsibility

Conceptions about responsibility for childcare in Canada have experienced two shifts. The first occurred when governments began to assume a greater role in funding, development, and maintenance of childcare beginning in the 1960s, and increasing through the 1980s. The second shift occurred in the 1990s when governments moved away from responsibility.

The evolution of Canadian childcare has been consistent with Canada's approaches to social programs generally. In the nineteenth century, health and education were considered to be within the private sphere while social welfare had not yet developed as an issue. When there was a need for assistance outside the nuclear and extended family, it was usually churches that stepped in; nonreligious charitable institutions also assumed the role of aiding the poor.

The first change in this conception was from the idea of individualistic, family-centered, or charitable responsibility to one of a more collective, societal obligation. This first shift occurred between post-World War II and the early 1970s when Canada's main social programs—health care, unemployment insurance, pensions, and social welfare—emerged. During this period, both federal and provincial governments assumed major responsibility for these functions. The federal government assumed a policy-shaping role while the role of service deliverer and program manager fell to the provinces.

Under Canadian constitutional arrangements, the federal government has no direct jurisdiction over education, health, or social welfare. Although social welfare as we know it today did not exist in the early days of the Canadian Federation, the courts later allotted responsibility for education, health, and social welfare programs to the provinces. In the years following World War II when these programs were maturing, it became apparent that the provinces did not have the financial resources to meet this responsibility. Funding programs were established to allow the federal government to provide the provinces with the funds required. Thus, Canadian health care and social welfare programs were developed by the provinces using both provincial and federal funds.

It was through the "federal spending power" that the federal government had a role in shaping these areas. Programs under provincial jurisdiction like health care or welfare services would use federal funds given to the provinces under specified conditions. Throughout the 1980s and the first half of the 1990s, it was assumed by federal and provincial governments that the federal government would have a role in shaping childcare policy as it has shaped the national health care program (Cooke, London, Edwards, & Rose-Lizeé, 1986; Government of Canada, 1987; Human Resources Development Canada, 1994).

Most Canadian health, educational, and social programs emerged as universal programs. Medicare, the national health care program, is a good example of a program that has defined its target group as all Canadians, rather than the poor or needy. Canadian postsecondary, elementary and secondary education, and Canada Pension and Unemployment Insurance also were conceived as universal programs. In contrast, the Canada Assistance Plan was designed not as a universal but as a "residual" or targeted program. The CAP's provisions for general welfare or social assistance, child welfare, and childcare through public funding were restricted to those defined as "needy" or "likely to become needy", reflecting CAP's conception of social welfare as "alleviating or preventing of poverty."

The Canada Health and Social Transfer (CHST), introduced by the federal government in 1996, exemplifies the second shift in responsibility for social programs, this time away from federal leadership and responsibility to the provincial domain; in some regions, devolution went further to the local or individual sphere (Bach & Phillips, 1997). The CHST replaced the Canada Assistance Plan and federal funds for postsecondary education and health care with an amalgamated block fund bound by few conditions. The change devolved federal policy-shaping to the provinces, formalized the federal government's withdrawal from cost-shared social services, and ended the traditional federal role of shaping programs under provincial jurisdiction through its use of the "spending power". This mammoth shift—the "new social union" is having a major impact on existing social programs like Medicare (Kent, 1997) as well as future possibilities for national social programs like childcare (Battle & Torjman, 1995).

At the same time, almost all provincial and territorial governments have retreated from the affirmative role in improving accessibility and quality in childcare that many of them adopted in the late 1980s (Friendly & Oloman, 1995). As the shifts occurred in federal/provincial authority and the federal government has reduced its funding, more and more of the provinces have been either unwilling or unable to finance expansion or even maintenance of childcare services. Thus, many of the provinces have retreated toward targeted and market-driven childcare. In Ontario, the largest province, for example, responsibility for childcare has been further dispersed to the municipal level and, ultimately, with reductions in funding and reduced regulation, to individual families.

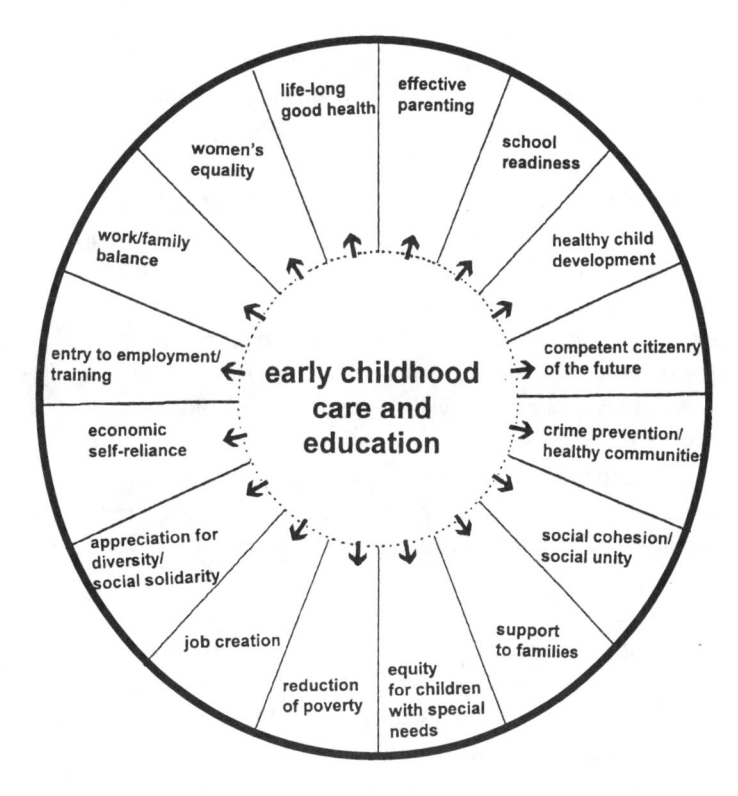

Figure 1
Child Care at the Center
Child Care Research and Resource Unit, 1996

What is Childcare?

Fragmentation has long been a second main theme in Canadian early childhood education and childcare. Historically, these services have resembled what has been called a "patchwork quilt" characterized both by regional disparity and discontinuous service provision. Without a coherent policy, Canada has no mechanism to answer the questions "What is childcare?" and "Who is it for?" Canadian early childhood education and childcare programs may be directed at the "high risk child", "the welfare mom", "aboriginal children on reserve", "aboriginal children off-reserve", "affluent families who want early childhood education for their child", "employability", or "a business expense".

In the policy vacuum that prevails, an assortment of discrete early childhood education and childcare services and programs has evolved arbitrarily, each with its own goals, objectives and funding arrangements. These include regulated childcare (centers, family day care, nursery schools), parenting programs, family resource centers, kindergarten, targeted services for "at-risk children" (sometimes called "Head Start"), and demand-side subsidies to parents (dependent care allowances and tax deductions). The assortment of programs is rarely coordinated. From the perspective of the children and families who are the users, appropriate services are not sufficiently available in most region, services are often too costly for ordinary parents, have restrictive eligibility requirements, or are inappropriate from a scheduling point of view; or the quality of what is available is inadequate to support children's healthy development.

Early childhood education and childcare are at the center of a range of multiple goals with interconnected purposes. If a system of early childhood education and care is well-designed and of high-quality, it has the capacity to meet a range of needs simultaneously: it can be part of a strategy to enhance all children's healthy development, a support to families whether they are in the labor force or not, be part of a comprehensive approach to the alleviation of poverty, and a key to women's equality.

Ironically, in a time of rhetoric about fiscal accountability, the array of early childhood education and care services and programs is devised in such a way that Canadians get the "least bang for the buck" (Rose, 1997). While fragmentation has historically prevailed in childcare, the inability to resolve the key questions as well as increased targeting to low income and at-risk children and parents has maintained and even accelerated the proliferation of disjunctive early childhood education and care programs in the 1990s.

Who is it For?
It has been suggested that at least part of the reason for the current situation is that childcare has never found a stable policy "home" (Friendly & Oloman, 1996). As this chapter's analysis of the current fragmented, discontinuous provision of programs demonstrates, this homelessness is with reference both to jurisdictions (social welfare, education, health) and federal/provincial jurisdiction. There has been both a historical and persistent lack of consistency about how governments view the purpose(s) of early childhood education and childcare and about who is willing to take responsibility for it. It has been treated at various times as a service to care for the children of indigent parents, as a welfare service for the needy, as a way of encouraging women to work in industries essential for the war effort, as a tool for reducing women's reliance on social assistance, as essential to women's equality, as a means to ensure that children considered to be "at risk" are "ready to learn", as a business expense, as a tool to support parent employability, and as early childhood education for all children. Different early childhood education and care services have, variously, been treated as a private, and a public, responsibility. Regulated childcare, reliant on user fees for its operating revenue, has been developed and delivered primarily by voluntary community-based groups with limited support from a fragmented set of federal and provincial/territorial programs whereas kindergarten, though publicly funded and available to all children, is provided part-time, part-year, and/or for only one segment of preschool-age children—five-year-olds.

Conclusion: The Future

It has been increasingly evident that high-quality early childhood education and childcare are crucial components of a wide array of strategies that address broad national policy objectives. These objectives include promoting the optimal development of all children, reducing the incidence of child poverty, developing a healthy economy, and promoting women's economic and social equality. It provides collective, as well as individual benefits, to communities and the society at large as well as parents and children. Thus, the availability of affordable, quality childcare is in the public interest, and public expenditures for childcare may be seen as a public investment, not merely a public cost (see Hero, this volume).

In the 1990s, Canadian governments have embarked on a massive restructuring of social roles and responsibilities. This restructuring, the "new social union," has vast implications for children and their families.

A social union involves certain expectations of the rights, obligations, and relationships between citizens and their governments and, in a federation such as Canada, between and among the federal and the provincial/territorial governments. As a recent policy study points out, it has yet to be determined whether the new political arrangements that are emerging in Canada will "work" (Doherty, et al., 1998). Developing a plan of action for early childhood education and childcare that works for children, women, families, employers, communities, and society at large would be a worthy challenge.

Notes

1. Portions of this chapter are based on work carried out by the authors and Gillian Doherty for a policy research study funded by Status of Women Canada.

2. Regulated childcare services in Canada historically relied on a combination of full parent fees and income-tested fee subsidies for low income parents; there was no funding for funding the operational costs of services. This funding arrangement meant that the cost of high-quality childcare for fee-paying parents was usually too high for ordinary families. Québec provided the first funding directly to services to contribute to the operating costs of services in 1979. It took years before other provinces followed suit. By the end of the 1980s, almost all provinces/territories were providing "operating grants" or "salary grants" to approved (and in some jurisdictions, only to not-for-profit) childcare services. These were different from fee subsidies because they were not tied to the economic circumstances of the user-parents; in essence they were Canadian childcare's first "universal" funding.

References

Bach, S., & Phillips, S.D. (1997). Constructing a new social union: Childcare beyond infancy? In Swimmer, Gene (Ed.). *How Ottawa Spends 1997–98. Seeing Red: A Liberal Report Card* (pp. 235–258). Ottawa: Carleton University Press.

Biggs, M. (1997). *Building blocks for Canada's new social union.* Unpublished working paper. Ottawa: Canadian Policy Research Networks.

Blain, C. (1985). *Government spending on childcare in Canada.* Task Force on Childcare. Ottawa: Status of Women Canada.

Bronfenbrenner, U. (1979). *The Ecology of Human Development.* Cambridge, MA: Harvard University Press

Bronfenbrenner, U. (1992). Childcare in the Anglo-Saxon mode. In M. Lamb, K. Sternberg, C. Hwang, and A. Broberg, (Eds.). *Childcare in Context: Cross-cultural Perspectives:* (pp. 281–291). Hillsboro, NJ: Lawrence Erlbaum Associates.

Childcare Resource and Research Unit. (1997). *Childcare in Canada: Provinces and territories.* Toronto: Center for Urban and Community Studies, University of Toronto.

Cooke, K., London., J., Edwards., R., & Rose-Lizée, R. (1986). *Report of the Task Force on Childcare.* Ottawa: Status of Women Canada.

Doherty, G., Friendly, M., & Oloman, M. *Women's support: Women's work: Childcare in an era of deficit reduction, devolution, downsizing and deregulation.* Status of Women Canada. Ottawa: Status of Women Canada.

Doherty G., Rose, R., Friendly, M., Lero, D.S. & Irwin, S. (1995). *Childcare: Canada can't work without it.* Occasional Paper No. 5. Toronto: Childcare Resource and Research Unit, Center for Urban and Community Studies. University of Toronto.

European Commission Network on Childcare. (1996). *A review of services for young children in the European Union 1990–1995.* Brussels: European Commission Directorate General V (Employment, Industrial Relations and Social Affairs) Equal Opportunities Unit.

Friendly, M. (1997). What is the public interest in childcare? *Policy Options.* 18(1): 3-6. Montreal: Institute for Research on Public Policy.

Friendly, M. (1994). *Childcare policy in Canada: Putting the pieces together.* Don Mills, Ontario: Addison Wesley Pub. Ltd.

Girard, P. (1995). *Why Canada has no family policy: Lessons from France and Italy.* Osgoode Hall Law School Journal, Vol. 32, No. 3:581-611.

Goelman, H., Pence, A.R., Lero, D.S., Brockman, L.M., Glick, N., & Berkowitz, J. (1993). *Where are the children? An overview of childcare arrangements in Canada.* Canadian National Childcare Study. Ottawa: Statistics Canada.

Government of Canada. (1996). *Speech from the Throne to open the second session of the thirty-fifth Parliament of Canada, 7.* Ottawa: Author.

Hayden, J. (1997) *Neo Conservatism and Childcare in Alberta: A Case Study.* Occasional Paper No. 9, Center for Urban and Community Studies, Toronto: University of Toronto

Hewlett, S.A. (1993). *Child neglect in rich nations.* New York: United Nations Children's Educational Fund (UNICEF).

Krashinsky, M., & Cleveland, G. (1997). Rethinking the rationale for public funding of childcare. *Policy Options.* 18(1): 16-19. Montreal: Institute for Research on Public Policy.

Lamb, M.E., (1997). Nonparental childcare: Context, quality, correlates, and consequences. In I.E. Sigel & K.A. Renninger (Eds.). *Child psychology in practice.* W. Damon (Gen. Ed.). *Handbook of Child Psychology* (4th ed.). New York: John Wiley and Sons.

Liberal Party of Canada. (1993). *Creating opportunity: The Liberal plan for Canada.* Ottawa: Author.

Moss, P. (1997). Early childhood services in Europe. *Policy Options.* 18(1): 27-30. Montreal: Institute for Research on Public Policy.

National Forum on Health. (1997). *Canada health action: Building on the legacy—Vol. I. Final report of the national forum on health. Vol. II. Canada Health Action: Building on the legacy. Synthesis reports and issues reports.* Ottawa: Health Canada, National Forum on Health.

Rose, R. (1997). For direct public funding of childcare. *Policy Options*. 18 (1): 31-33. Montreal: Institute for Research on Public Policy.

Sims, M. (1994). Education and care: Revisiting the dichotomy. *Early Childhood Development and Care*. Vol. 103:15-26.

Torjman, S., & Battle, K. (1995). *The dangers of block funding*. Ottawa: Caledon Institute on Social Policy.

Chapter 6

The Early Childhood Landscape in New Zealand

Anne Meade

Abstract

In New Zealand in the late 1980s, a shared vision and collective action contributed to policy changes which were in harmony with research findings and constituency goals for quality early childhood education. A balance between, and full integration of, care and education was achieved. Many distributional and some constitutional gains occurred. Although there have been losses relating to the current conservative political context, this chapter shows how constitutional items such as collective action and a shared discourse have had mitigating effects.

Introduction

In 1989, at the time of the major reforms to the administrative system for education in New Zealand, approximately 90% of four-year-olds, 61% of three-year-olds, and 40% of all children under the age of five attended an early childhood program. Most enjoyed some government support for the early education. Places were not targeted for any one group, such as children from low socioeconomic status families.

At that date, the largest proportion of children aged three to five were enrolled in free kindergartens run by community-based committees and staffed by college of education-trained teachers. The other main services in New Zealand were *kohanga reo* (Maori language nests), playcenters, private kindergartens, childcare centers, Pacific Island language nests, and family day care. In total, in 1989 there were over 20 types of early childhood organizations receiving government support via 26 different funding formulas. The amount of expenditure per child-space varied by service and ranged from $190 to $1,000 according to the Treasury briefing papers to the incoming government (1987). Parents' fees ranged from a nominal donation to free kindergartens to over NZ$100 per week for full-day care, more for infants.

Less than a decade later, nearly all four-year-olds and over 80% of three-year-olds were enrolled in some form of early childhood education. It is estimated that over half of New Zealand children aged 0 to 5 years were enrolled. Childcare centers became the dominant service. Enrollments were concentrated in center-based childcare (36%), kindergartens (29%), and playcenters (11%).

A wide range of early childhood organizations continue to be subsidized, but the amount of government expenditure per child-space per hour has been standardized (except for infants and toddlers who attract more funds). The expenditure per child-space varies depending on the hours per week each child attends. Fees are much the same as the late 1980s, which indicates a possible decline in costs to parents in real terms. There remains no targeting of places.

There are markedly different political and policy contexts presently than those of 10 years ago. There has been a change from a Labor government to a National (conservative) government and then to a National and New Zealand First Coalition government since the education reforms. Arguably, the most significant changes in policy occurred when Labor was in power. It changed the basis of the relationship between early childhood providers and the government, as well as many policies. (These will be described later.) However, the introduction of an official early childhood curriculum, *Te Whāriki*, came under the national government. The policy context within some of the early childhood organizations now differs as well, sometimes as a consequence of government policy changes.

Early Childhood Services in New Zealand

The majority of early childhood services in New Zealand are community-based, run by voluntary movements. Some are run for profit by private enterprise individuals or companies. A few are associated with private schools or with tertiary institutions. Government provision is the exception. Since the beginning of 1993, the Correspondence School has been the only service owned by central government, although kindergartens were covered by the State Sector Act (1988) until 1997.

In general, much of the diversity of services has resulted from already established services not adapting to changing needs of women and young children in earlier decades. The government has never directly intervened, for example, to fill gaps, except for remote rural areas. For each new type of service, establishment was followed by a long slow road to negotiating reasonable funding levels from the government.

New Zealand families have expected the government to give reasonable levels of grants-in-aid. At the time of the 1989 education reforms, this expectation was met for kindergartens and playcenters (which operate as parent cooperatives); while childcare centers—whether community-based or private—were in receipt of fees subsidies for low income families, along with a trained staff grant. The lobbyists had been consistent in seeking government grants to go to service providers rather than to families via such mechanisms as tax rebates, fees subsidies, or some sort of voucher.

All early childhood services in New Zealand—including center-based and home-based childcare—were placed under one government department, the Department of Education, from 1986. This was the first of a series of significant policy changes that changed the landscape of early childhood education markedly. The second change was the introduction of three-year, integrated, early childhood training for kindergarten teachers and childcare staff in colleges of education, beginning in 1988. All graduates receive a Diploma of Teaching. The distinguishing features of New Zealand early childhood services and policies at the time of the 1989 reforms were:

1. next to no direct Government provision of early childhood services;
2. community-based provision, and some private sector provision, with minimal government ownership;
3. diversity of service providers—both center-based and home-based;
4. diverse funding formulae—each type of early childhood service received different levels of funding from the government, based on different formulae;
5. all services under one government department: education;
6. private childcare centers treated no differently from community-based centers;
7. government funding of service providers, with a minimum amount going to users (directly or indirectly via fees subsidies);
8. state colleges of education provision of integrated training courses for early childhood teachers (with no distinction between those destined for kindergarten or childcare work).

Policy Reforms

In February 1988, Cabinet established a working group on early childhood care and education, primarily as part of its social equity program—not because of the school reform plans. In part, the working group was a response to political promises made in the Labor Party manifesto during the 1987 election campaign. It turned out to be imperative that this working group (which I chaired) attended to the impending school reforms in order to plan alternative infrastructural supports from 1989. We gathered together the collective wisdom of over a decade of conferences and reports, formulated recommendations, and produced a green paper, *Education to Be More* (Meade, 1988). This received widespread support within government and from the community.

In early 1989, the early childhood reforming policies in *Before Five* were released, cementing most Meade working party recommendations into policy, but without any funding announcements.

"Before Five"

The elements of the new policy platform were:

1. bulk grants for services which are licensed and chartered, based on a standard per hour per child formula, and capped at 30 hours per child per week, paid by the Ministry of Education;
2. higher per hour-per child rate for infants and toddlers;
3. fees subsidies for low income families using childcare;
4. discretionary grants to help nonprofit services start up;
5. charters, to be drawn up in consultation with parents, and endorsed by them;
6. non-chartered services must still be licensed;
7. the Education Review Office to check standards and other accountability measures annually;
8. the Early Childhood Development Unit established to help with development, advisory, and coordination activities;
9. the Special Education Service to extend its services to young children not yet at school; and
10. the Teacher Registration Board to register early childhood teachers.

In mid-1989, after intense lobbying by a very large and diverse number of people and groups from early childhood organizations, education unions, and women's groups, a staged plan for increased funding levels was announced by the government.

The next significant policy change was that the government confirmed the Diploma of Teaching as the benchmark qualification for supervisors and Head Teachers needed for charters in almost all types of early childhood services by 1994, with another staged plan for increased numbers of staff needing the Diploma from 1994 onward.

All these policies continued the pattern of minimizing the distinction between care and education. How have the policies shaped up over the 1990s?

Current Policies and Services—What Has Happened?

Funding

Funding for New Zealand early childhood places is demand-driven, unlike many other countries, and demand has increased dramatically. There have been large increases in government expenditure. In 1988, it totaled $82 million; a decade later it was $280 million. One result of the new funding formula, and the demand-driven policy, has been significant growth in places. Total enrollments were over 160,000 by 1996, and still increasing. The 1996 budget estimated a further 32% increase in expenditure in the next three years, mostly because of growth in the number of places.

However, bulk funding levels have remained nearly the same since their inauguration at the beginning of 1990. Soon after coming to power in late 1990, the national government stopped the staged plan to increase funding levels. Subsidies for infants and toddlers were reduced by approximately one-third in 1992. This had an uneven influence on services, with childcare, *kohanga reo*, and family day care bearing the brunt of it. The "savings" were used for more targeted fees subsidies and to start a new program, Parents as First Teachers. As the effect for government was fiscally neutral, some politicians thought the effect on services was neutral. It was not. Staff numbers and conditions declined, and the number of infant places decreased.

As a consequence, services became far more vigilant about advising families to apply for fees subsidies because they could no longer underwrite low income families. In no time at all, Government expenditure on fees subsidies had blown out. The next step was the government decision to cap the fees subsidy (later this was eased).

In 1996, "quality funding" was introduced. Services with better than minimum standards with regard to staff qualifications and staff to child ratios now receive a higher per child grant. As well, there was a small across-the-board increase in 1997.

As government's bulk funding levels for early childhood services were found to be increasingly inadequate (e.g., Wylie, 1993), resulting in some service-providers changing their policies; for example, one policy adopted by kindergarten associations was to increase enrollment to an unprecedented 45 children in the morning, and 45 in the afternoon, where demand is high.

Equity of Access
One of the goals of the changes to policy recommended in the green paper, "Education to be more" (Meade, 1988), was to improve equity of access. The increases in enrollments of Maori children (296%) and Pacific Island children (332%) over the decade have been far greater than the average percentage increase for other groups (76%). Credit has to be given to the various communities for their work to establish culturally appropriate services. Until they did, Maori and Pacific Island children were underrepresented in early childhood services. Notice the difference in proportions of Maori children enrolled from 1989 when *kohanga reo* were included in education statistics.

However, an inequitable situation exists for Pacific Island families. Most are enrolled in government-funded playgroups, which receive lower per-child funding because they have not attained charter status. A variety of factors act against these playgroups getting charters and moving to a higher level of funding, which explains the fairly static pattern of enrollments in Pacific Island language groups in recent years despite the large increase in Pacific Island children's enrollments.

Another feature of early childhood services in New Zealand is that the majority of children with special/developmental needs are enrolled in regular rather than segregated early childhood services. In 1996, the number of children with individual development plans (indicating some extra resourcing) on regular rolls was 2,277 (1.4% of total enrollments).

Increase in Enrollments
The number of enrollments in early childhood services has almost doubled in the last decade. However, the increases have not been evenly spread across types of service. The greatest growth has been in playgroups (which receive support from the Early Childhood Development Unit, a government agency, and a lower rate of subsidy) and in center-based and home-based childcare services. Kindergarten has grown more slowly and is no longer the dominant service catering for the most children (29%, compared with 36% in childcare centers).

Charters

Generally, quality assurance is created through the mechanisms of regulations, advisers, and reviewers, and the provision of training for early childhood teachers. In New Zealand, we have all these. The 1990 revised regulations demonstrated the Labor Government's attention to quality features shown by research to benefit young children.

In addition, New Zealand has another mechanism for quality assurance: charters. To agree to a charter and receive higher funding, in the early days of the reforms, centers had to meet additional quality guidelines published in departmental circulars, a "Management Handbook" (1989), and a supplement entitled "Conditions for Receipt of the Early Childhood Bulk Grant" (1990). These quality conditions were soon superseded, however. In mid-December 1990, "A Statement of Desirable Objectives and Practices" was officially promulgated and replaced the other documents.

The Education Review Office's attention to charters keeps them in staff and management consciousness at least during review periods, *but* these reviews are now only happening every three to four years as a consequence of budget cuts, plus the growth in the number of centers. (see Hayden, 1992.) The 1997 budget restored some funding for a small increase in the frequency of reviews.

Training and Qualifications

State-funded colleges of education now train teachers for careers in kindergarten or childcare. They graduate with a Diploma of Teaching (Early Childhood Education) and usually complete part or all of a university degree concurrently.

This has been an important constitutional gain. Research shows that training matters (e.g., Meade, 1985; Whitebook, et al. 1989; Smith, 1997; Wylie, et al. 1996) if positive benefits are to flow from early childhood care and education (see Tayler, this volume).

Several decisions and developments since 1990 have led to the area of qualifications and training of early childhood staff becoming not only very confused but also a site of intense struggle. By not insisting that headteachers and supervisors hold a qualification and instead accepting a patchwork of courses, the next government bought a major problem for itself in 1991, and confused most people in the sector beyond belief. The kindergarten movement has taken a stand against this development and will only employ teachers who have a Diploma of Teaching.

The so-called pathways government policy did provide incentives to encourage staff to complete qualifications—focusing on partially trained early childhood staff gaining their Diploma of Teaching.

At the time of writing, however, an advisory committee to the New Zealand Qualifications Authority has recommended two-tier national qualifications for early childhood staff—a lower level certificate, as well as the Diploma of Teaching.

Changes in Government Agencies' Functioning

The 1988 *Before Five* set of policies also covered some central agencies and what they were to do for young children and their families (as well as focusing on early childhood education organizations).

The Education Review Office was to have monitored regulatory compliance and the quality of early childhood services every year. As its funding has been reduced and centers have proliferated, the frequency of reviews has lessened.

The Early Childhood Development Unit also suffered cutbacks in 1991. A significant proportion of its work—the advisory support function—was put out to tender from 1992. The result has been a division and multiplication of advisory services and a fragmentation of provision. There have been mixed educational results from this approach.

The Specialist Education Service has been operating under the shadow of contestability (i.e., tendering of services) being imposed for several years. Different models have been promulgated, but not fully implemented to date. For the most part, services to young children have not been mooted. The last five years have mostly produced good news for young children with special developmental needs and their families. The Specialist Education Service has progressively and markedly increased direct services to this group.

Conclusion: Progressive Developments

There are many recent initiatives that have "improve quality" as their goal. New Zealand is further ahead than it was a decade ago. However, as has been indicated, many of the *Before Five* and related policies have been diluted or changed. Unfortunately, in most cases the effects have been loss of quality, despite New Zealand research (see Wylie, et al., 1996) and overseas studies demonstrating clearly that high-quality early childhood education is needed if children are to benefit from their time in kindergartens, childcare centers, and other types of early childhood services.

In recent years, *nga kohanga reo*, childcare centers, and family day care have lost funding for quality infant care and education; all services have declined in real terms with bulk funding levels; and qualifications and training targets were fudged, which has undermined the standard of teaching in childcare in particular. Helen May (1996) argues that these erosions have allowed the care and education division to begin to re-emerge.

Nevertheless, the early childhood sector in New Zealand is still among the world leaders because of the integration of education and care in policies, administration, and training. All children have an equitable chance of attending services of a satisfactory level of quality (Wylie, et al., 1996).

There have been positive developments. First, *Te Kohanga Reo* now receives Ministry of Education funding for its training program. Second, a Code of Ethics' professional working group has produced a Code of Ethics for early childhood teachers, and some accompanying resources. Third, the Ministry of Education is sponsoring a significant longitudinal research project called "Competent Children: Influences of Early Childhood Experiences" (see Wylie, et al., 1996). Fourth, there were some increases to bulk funding levels in 1997.

Finally, the most significant change is New Zealand breaking new ground with its curriculum framework, contained in Te Whāriki (see May & Carr, this volume). These guidelines strand together curriculum principles and goals for infants, toddlers, and preschoolers. No other country in the world that I know of gives official recognition to a curriculum for infants and toddlers. Few other countries (if any) assume that an educational curriculum will be implemented equally well in childcare centers and kindergartens. Here is another positive off-shoot of New Zealand's integration of care and education under the auspices of the Ministry of Education.

Quality: A Shared Vision

Many key groups in the early childhood sector in New Zealand made a strategic decision to focus their shared endeavors on the aspiration of high-quality early childhood education. The groups were aware that collective action toward a shared vision had been instrumental in achieving many long-sought goals in the "Before Five" policies. They were also aware that collective action had dissipated soon thereafter. Discussions were held, and it was agreed that one central value, high-quality early childhood education, should be the focus of political action. When upheld, it ensures a balance between the interests of the child, of parents and caregivers, and of society.

This value has pervaded a variety of activities that involve individual services, or interorganizational, endeavors. It has been often stated in research, in submissions, in seminars, in codes of practice, in resources for parents and teachers, in working parties, *and* in government policies. The 1995 change to government policy was called "quality funding"; the politicians had picked up on the dominant discourse and capitalized on it!

The views of the majority in the sector, however, are not always taken into policy. Recently, the New Zealand Qualifications Authority has approved two tiers of national qualifications—a certificate and a diploma, with students being able to progress from one to the other. This was sought by the for-profit services, for reasons to do with teacher supply and teacher rewards (and, therefore, with profit).

The sector now awaits with interest to see whether the informed voice on the importance of highly qualified teachers being in charge of kindergartens and centers will be adopted in policy for licenses and charters.

References

Before Five: Early childhood care and education in New Zealand (1988). Wellington: Department of Education.

May, H. (1996). *Training, qualifications and quality: The costs of compromise*. A keynote address given at a national seminar. Children's Issues Center, 15–6 May, Wellington.

Meade, A. (1985). *The children can choose*. Wellington: New Zealand Council for Educational Research.

Meade, A. (1988). *Education to be more: Report of the working group on early childhood care and education*. Wellington: Department of Education.

Smith, A. B. (1997). Quality childcare and joint attention. A paper presented at the NZARE.

Te Whāriki: Curriculum framework for early childhood services (1996). Wellington: Ministry of Education.

Tomorrow's schools: The reform of education administration in New Zealand (1988). Wellington: Department of Education.

Whitebook, M., Howes, C., & Phillips, D. (1989). *Who cares? Childcare teachers and the quality of care in America*. Los Angeles: UCLA, Childcare Employee Project.

Wylie, C. (1993). *The impact of salary bulk funding on New Zealand kindergartens: Results of the second national survey*. Wellington: New Zealand Council for Educational Research.

Wylie, C., Thompson, J., & Kerslake Hendricks, A. (1996). *Children's competencies at age 5*. Report to the Ministry of Education. Wellington: New Zealand Council for Educational Research.

Chapter 7

Hong Kong's Early Childhood Landscape: Division, Diversity, and Dilemmas

Elizabeth J. Mellor

Abstract

There is no public preschool system in Hong Kong, yet almost all children between the ages of three and six attend some type of preschool service. Services include kindergartens, playgroups, nursery schools, and childcare centers. Within each of these types of services, there is a variety of providers, programs, and patterns of provision. Early childhood services in Hong Kong currently operate in a climate of considerable political, social, and economic change. This chapter commences with an overview of recent developments in Hong Kong's political, social, and economic landscapes and their possible implications for early childhood services. Current diversity and divisions within early childhood services are described and some of their major causes identified. Developments likely to promote cohesion within the early childhood field are discussed. The chapter concludes with some lessons to be learned from the early childhood landscape in Hong Kong.

Developments in the Political, Social, and Economic Landscapes

At midnight on June 30, 1997, amid the glare of international publicity, Hong Kong ceased to be a British colony and became a Special Administrative Region of China. Power was formally transferred from the British governor and elected Legislative Council to the Beijing-backed chief executive, Tung Chee Wah, and a Beijing-approved Provisional Legislature.

British armed forces in Hong Kong were replaced by members of the Peoples Liberation Army and Deng's policy of "One country, two systems" came into force. Under this policy Hong Kong has, at least initially, retained considerable autonomy over its local affairs and has, until recently, maintained a highly profitable capitalist economy. It has also become subject to Chinese Basic Law and foreign policy.

Dramatic as the formal transfer of power on June 30 may have seemed, in some respects, power and influence had been shifting for months. Governor Patten's views had ceased to be as important as those of Tung Chee Wah and his advisers, while the policies and laws of the Legislative Council became less important than those proposed by the Provisional Legislature. Even within the highly bureaucratized civil service, change had been occurring as the policy of appointing and promoting local rather than expatriate staff was implemented, and the exodus of British senior civil servants provided promotion opportunities for those likely to support the new regime.

Yet in spite of these shifts in power, Britain left a colony that exhibited a high degree of law, order, and stability. The new leadership was quick to reaffirm that it was "business as usual" in Hong Kong and that overseas observers, particularly investors, had nothing to fear from the change in power (July 2, 1997, *Hong Kong Standard*. Since reunification, it has become clear that Hong Kong is threatened more by the economic meltdown in Southeast Asia than by social and political upheaval.

The change in sovereignty has, however, posed a number of significant questions for the Hong Kong early childhood landscape. Such questions include the degree of importance the new administration will place on early childhood education and whether Tung's education policy will not only encompass the preschool years but also address some of the organizational difficulties the preschool sector has traditionally experienced. A vital question still remains as to the amount of freedom churches and religious organizations in Hong Kong will continue to enjoy as part of China. Religious organizations are major providers of preschool services, particularly kindergartens, and any diminution of their activities would seriously affect availability of services. There are also questions as to how much autonomy semi-government organizations such as the University Grants Commission and the Hong Kong Council for Academic Accreditation will continue to enjoy under the new regime. The former organization determines the academic profile of tertiary institutions while the latter is responsible for the accreditation of new courses. The policies and procedures of both organizations have a direct impact on the number of funded places and approved courses available for training early childhood staff. A longer term question is whether Hong Kong early childhood philosophy and practice will be expected to conform to that of mainland China.

Early publicity had labeled the historic change in sovereignty as "the hand-over." However as June 30 approached, the language changed and "hand-over" was replaced by "reunification." This was more than a change in rhetoric or a political ploy, it represented a very real change in emphasis intended to reaffirm the Chinese roots and culture of over 95% of Hong Kong's population, most of whom had come from the Cantonese speaking southern provinces of China.

The strength of Chinese influence is seen in Hong Kong's languages, festivals, and traditions. Although Hong Kong has three official languages, the major spoken language is Cantonese. Chinese festivals are included in the Hong Kong calendar, along with Christmas and Easter, while Chinese New Year is the major public holiday period. Chinese traditions, superstitions, and symbols permeate all aspects of life. The teachings of Chinese philosophers, particularly Confucius, are well known and are apparently widely accepted regardless of what religion may be practiced. As a result, there are widely held common values including the importance of hard work, achievement, and obligations to the family. These values are reflected in a need to succeed which dominates all levels of schooling, including preschool. Such values also help to explain the respect teachers have traditionally received, and parents' willingness to pay substantial preschool fees to improve their children's chance of success at school.

There have also been signs of economic change in Hong Kong that have implications for early childhood education. In recent years, Hong Kong's economy has shifted from a manufacturing base to a service industry base. Many industries have moved their operations over the border into mainland China where labor costs are lower. One consequence is increasing unemployment amongst the unskilled in Hong Kong. A related consequence is renewed concern to improve Hong Kong's education system so that children are better prepared for the new skills required by technology-based service industries. Education is seen as the key to longterm prosperity and as a means of combating social problems (Wong, 1996). Reforms and changes to the primary school curriculum directly influence on preschool curricula because preschool staff specifically prepare children for the Primary I curriculum, that is, for the first year of primary schooling.

Of increasing social concern is the number of mainland China families and children entering Hong Kong. In recent years there has been a steady flow of migrants, many of whom have subsequently had difficulties in finding employment in Hong Kong unless they could speak Cantonese, English, or had appropriate skills. As well as migrants who enter Hong Kong legally, there have been increasing numbers of "illegals" who are smuggled in by speed boats or under lorries. "Illegal" children are a particular problem. They are often smuggled into Hong Kong so that they can rejoin a family member already living there, or they overstay their visitor's visa. Many are the children of men who have families in both China and Hong Kong. On arrival in Hong Kong such children face an uncertain future. Some children are rejected by their Hong Kong-based family, others have great difficulties in coping with school if they lack the necessary language background. Under the Basic Law, tens of thousands of mainland Chinese children may well be eligible for right of abode in Hong Kong. Uncertainty as to how the Basic Law will be interpreted over right of abode, and a lack of confidence in the Education Department's assurances that schools will be able to cope with the influx, have made mainland children a source of deep concern (July 4, 1997, *Hong Kong Standard*). It is acknowledged that such children and their families have particular needs, but kindergartens have traditionally provided few support services for families, and their staff are ill-prepared to help families with such complex problems.

The Early Childhood Landscape

There are two major divisions within the Hong Kong early childhood landscape and both have organizational origins. The first is the division between preschool and school. In the Hong Kong landscape, any form of preschool is additional, optional, and normally paid for by parents. All preschool services are provided by the private sector—on either a profit-making or nonprofit-making basis. Primary schooling, however, is compulsory, free from tuition fees, and provided by the government through a system of government schools and aided schools run by the private sector.

The second major organizational division occurs between types of preschool (Opper, 1992). Kindergartens are registered with the Education Department and come under the Education Ordinance and Regulations, which describe kindergarten education as "education suitable for normal pupils who have attained the age of four years" (Hong Kong Government, 1994. p. 11). Childcare services, including day nurseries and play groups, are registered with the Social Welfare Department and come under the Childcare Centers Ordinance and related regulations which stipulate that their major functions are care and supervision. These regulations also provide standards for registration, operation, and inspection including the requirement that all childcare workers complete a recognized course of training within a year of entering service (Opper, 1993). A range of early intervention services also come within the ambit of the Social Welfare Department.

These structural divisions have been reinforced, at least until very recently, by staff training provisions. Kindergarten teacher training has been traditionally provided by the Education Department through its teachers' college system, and particularly the former Grantham Teachers College. Most kindergarten training courses are now provided by the Hong Kong Institute of Education, a new tertiary institution funded through the University Grants Committee. Kindergarten training programs are normally in-service part time courses ranging in length from three months to two-and-a-half years. A distance teaming Certificate in Pre-Primary Education has also been offered by the Hong Kong Polytechnic University (Hong Kong Government, 1996). Childcare training is provided primarily by the Hong Kong Polytechnic University, also funded through the University Grants Committee and the Lee Wai Lee Technical Institute (Opper, 1993).

Kindergartens

Kindergartens are the major form of preschool in Hong Kong and are attended by 80% of children aged between 3 and 5 (Wong, 1996), though some enroll children as young as two-and-a-half (Lam, 1997). Kindergartens are typically organized into three levels based on age: nursery classes cater to the youngest children, while the lower kindergarten and upper kindergarten levels cater for four-and five-year-olds respectively. Though some kindergartens date to the turn of the century, most were established during the 1970s, in order to prepare children for school entry tests. The focus on preparation for school has continued, as indicated in the general aim of the *Guide to the Kindergarten Curriculum* (Curriculum Development Council, 1993), and may help to explain the popularity of kindergarten as a form of preschool in a culture that places great store on school success (Opper, 1992). Significantly, kindergarten staff normally refer to their kindergartens as schools.

The *Guide to the Kindergarten Curriculum,* Hong Kong Government (1984a), also stipulates specific aims in relation to intellectual development, communicative development, social, and moral development, as well as personal, physical, and aesthetic development, and provides developmental guidelines, principles of curriculum planning, and suggested activities. It needs to be noted, however, that this publication, along with its predecessors, *Education Department Manual of Kindergarten Practice* (Hong Kong Government, 1984b) and the Education Department *Guidelines on Nursery Class Activities* (Hong Kong Government, 1987) are guides only and their recommendations cannot be enforced.

In the most recent survey, there were 706 kindergartens in Hong Kong (excluding those as part of English foundation schools and international schools). Two-thirds of these were run on a nonprofit-making basis and as such were eligible for tax exemptions and reimbursement of rents and rates from the Education Department (Hong Kong Government, 1996).

Notwithstanding such concessions, monthly kindergarten fees remain substantial, ranging from 1,000 to 3,000 Hong Kong dollars per month before obligatory extras such as uniforms, school bus costs, and contributions to the cost of birthday and other celebrations. A means-tested fee remission scheme operates, but nevertheless three years of kindergarten fees represent a substantial family investment in young children's education.

Kindergartens vary in many aspects of their operations. They vary in size from 50 children to over a thousand and they also vary in the number of staff they employ and the amount of training their staff have received. Currently, at least 40% of the staff in a kindergarten must be trained (Hong Kong Government, 1996). Although maximum pupil to teacher ratios are legislated at 20:1 in nursery grades, and 30:1 in the higher grades, class sizes also vary, with typically one or two teachers teaching a class of up to 40 children. These children are usually subdivided into groups of 7 to 10 which rotate around activities designed to follow up the theme taught by the teacher during "theme time" each session.

Kindergartens also vary markedly in the quality of their facilities and equipment. A few enjoy well-equipped, purpose-built facilities but more commonly they are located within churches, other public buildings or situated within high-rise apartment blocks. Space is at a premium and only around 70% have an outdoor play space. Those in high-rise housing estates often have particular space problems, including having to take the children in relays to use toilets located on other floors of the building and keeping the children indoors throughout sessions to avoid being struck by objects falling from above. Staff in kindergartens run as profit-making ventures frequently complain about owners' unwillingness to provide equipment or adequate supplies of consumables.

Patterns of program delivery also vary amongst kindergartens, with the most common being sessions of three to four hours' duration from

Monday to Friday. Some kindergartens offer Saturday sessions while a small number offer whole-day programs. Whole-day programs were intended as a form of childcare, but they have not proved popular as few have had adequate facilities (Opper, 1992).

There are common elements amongst this diversity. Kindergartens still typically devote the majority of their program to the development of preacademic skills such as reading and writing. Instruction is typically in Cantonese, with some English taught as a second language. Writing is taught using either the conventional approach or preparatory approach. The former is based on the premise that the more practice a child gets, the better will be the result. In kindergartens using this approach, children commence learning to write on entry to kindergarten. They are instructed how to make each part of a character and then practice until they have mastered it. In kindergartens using the preparatory approach, children are given prewriting activities such as drawing and coloring-in for six months until more formal teaching of writing is introduced (Chan, 1993).

Although kindergarten programs are typically structured and teacher-centered, most also include opportunities for group work and some free time at the end of sessions when children may do an activity of their choice. Art activities, storytelling, music, and movement are usually included in programs. Relatively little time is devoted to outdoor activities or gross motor activities other than games. Research by Olmsted and Lockhart (1995) found that gross motor development was a low priority for preschool staff and parents alike. Certain common practices persist in spite of recommendations to the contrary in the *Education Department Manual of Kindergarten Practice*. These include setting homework, tests and end-of-year examinations. A recent study found that some four- and five-year-olds did up to two hours of homework a night, and that the practice of setting homework was overwhelmingly supported by parents (Mellor, et al., 1996). Parents are expected to help their children with homework, and may also participate in special events such as outings and graduation celebrations. They are seldom, however, consulted over program matters and parent-teacher meetings are the exception rather than the rule.

Childcare

There is also both diversity as well as common features among preschool services registered with the Social Welfare Department. Major types of services include day nurseries, which offer both part-day and whole-day childcare, and playgroups for children aged 2 to 6. Services include profit-making ventures as well as those which are nonprofit-making and rely on considerable financial support from sources such as the Community Chest, the Hong Kong Jockey Club, and charitable foundations. Curriculum guidelines for day nurseries are included in the *Social Welfare Department Childcare Centers Advisory Inspectorate Code of Practice (1988a)* and the *Social Welfare Department Childcare Centers Advisory Inspectorate, Activity Guidelines for Day Nurseries* (Hong Kong Government, 1988b). The use of themes and activity approach is recommended while the aim of a day nursery curriculum is specified as being the development of the whole child. In summarizing the differences between kindergarten and day nurseries, Opper (1992) concluded that kindergartens were more likely to be sponsored by religious and profit-making organizations than nurseries which were more likely to be sponsored by voluntary and social ones. Kindergartens had higher enrollments and larger class sizes, but charged lower fees. Kindergarten teachers tended to be less trained, but have more teaching experience. Kindergarten programs for younger children were more academic though programs for older children were similar at both types of preschool. Nurseries offered more social work services and made more contacts with parents.

Early Intervention Services

In addition to day nurseries and play groups, the Department of Social Welfare subvents services run by voluntary organizations such as the Heep Hong Society for Handicapped Children. This organization, with additional funding from private sector sources, is a major provider of early intervention services. It currently operates seven Early Education and Training Centers for disabled children aged from birth to six and their families, as well as eight Special Childcare Centers and two Parent Resource Centers (Heep Hong Society for Handicapped Children, 1995). Working with the families of young disabled children through multidisciplinary staff teams is a particular feature of Heep Hong's work. Other early intervention services are provided by Education Department Special Education Service Centers, which offer a wide spectrum of assessment, education, and support services for preschool and school-age children; the Education Department also funds additional resource teachers for kindergartens participating in the integration of mildly handicapped preschoolers into normal kindergarten programs (Rehabilitation Division, 1996).

Divisions within the Early Childhood Landscape

Some of the divisions that currently occur within the Hong Kong early childhood landscape are the consequence of the division of services between the Education Department and the Social Welfare Department. As elsewhere, for example in Australia, similar organizational divisions have fostered a dichotomy between education and care and have tended to fragment services for families. Again as elsewhere, the division between education and care has been deepened by providing different training programs for kindergarten and childcare staff and offering them through different institutions. This has resulted in different aims and emphases in training programs and a lack of common purpose among those trained for childcare and kindergarten positions. Divisions between types of training are further complicated when, as is now the case in Hong Kong, training becomes the responsibility of tertiary institutions that have to compete with each other for the right to offer courses, and attract government-funded places. The complex relationship between education and care is then compounded by institutional rivalry and graduates' loyalties. It remains to be seen whether the recently developed "harmonized" course, designed to allow those who complete childcare training to undertake additional studies and meet the requirements for qualified kindergarten teacher status, and vice versa, will achieve its aim of overcoming some of the existing boundaries within the Hong Kong early childhood field.

Though the division of services between the Education Department and Social Welfare Department may explain the lack of cohesion between kindergartens and childcare services, it does not explain why there are so few links between primary school and preschool. One explanation may relate to training. Although kindergarten teachers have traditionally been trained within teachers colleges, they have undertaken different courses, have generally had a lower standard of secondary education than primary teachers, and have been paid at a lower rate. Until recently, the majority of kindergarten teachers were untrained, and so it could be argued that differences in professional status contribute to the division between primary and kindergarten schooling.

Another explanation for the division between primary school and preschool may be the lack of specialist junior primary teacher education programs. Primary teacher education programs in Hong Kong prepare students to be specialists in two to three subjects within the primary curriculum, rather than specialist teachers of a specific age group. Teachers who work in the lower primary grades are, therefore, unlikely to share a common pedagogy with their preschool counterparts. Although the "Activity Approach" is recommended for both childcare staff and for teachers of lower primary grades, it is seldom implemented in schools.

Another factor in the division between kindergarten and primary teachers may be the lack of common issues and concerns. Issues that have done much to stimulate professional dialogue between preschool and school staff elsewhere, such as what is an appropriate school entry age, how transition to school might be improved, and whether children should be taught to read and write prior to entering school, are not major issues in Hong Kong. Thus, apart from seminars run by the Education Department to which kindergarten and day nursery personnel are invited, there have been few attempts in the past to establish links between preschool and primary services (Opper, 1993).

Developing Cohesion within the Early Childhood Landscape

Yet amongst the divisions and diversity within the Hong Kong early childhood landscape, there are also developments that indicate a growing cohesion within the field. At a systemic level, the Board of Education, a government advisory group, has recommended unifying the services provided by the Education Department and the Social Welfare Department. It remains to be seen whether Tung Chee Wah will implement such recommendations. The Education and Manpower Branch, of which the Education Department is a part, recently reconstituted a Joint Working Party on Kindergarten Education with wide-ranging representation. This Working Party and its ad hoc groups have been responsible for developing a new *Guide to the Pre-primary Curriculum* (Curriculum Development Institute, 1996) for use in both kindergartens and childcare centers; a "harmonized", i.e., comparable pay scale for kindergarten teachers and childcare workers; and the "harmonized" training program for kindergarten and childcare staff referred to above (Wong, 1996). Organizations such as the Hong Kong Council for Social Services bring together representatives from nongovernment care and education services, particularly in relation to the provision of early childhood services for young children with special needs.

There have also been important professional initiatives from within the early childhood field which have helped to facilitate greater cohesion. One initiative has been the establishment of OMEP-Hong Kong, which has as its mission to strive for developmentally appropriate early education and care for every child. Besides hosting annual conferences that provide a forum for delegates from government and nongovernment schools, as well as kindergartens, childcare, and health services organizations, OMEP-Hong Kong recently developed a draft *Criteria for High-quality Programs of Early Childhood Education and Care in Hong Kong* (1996) based largely on the work of McCrea and Piscitelli in Australia.

Although as has been argued above, initial staff training provisions have tended to fragment the early childhood field, it can also be argued that early childhood postinitial and postgraduate programs are helping to provide some common professional opportunities and understandings. The Hong Kong University periodically offers a Masters in Early Childhood Education program, which attracts applicants from a variety of services and tertiary institutions. Members of the Hong Kong early childhood services and tertiary institutions also undertake overseas higher degrees programs, particularly in Australasia and North America, and these also help to foster a common early childhood pedagogy and understandings. These understandings are furthered through collaborative course development activities, in which Hong Kong tertiary institutions, without the resources to develop and staff their own early childhood programs, offer programs developed and accredited overseas. Alternatively, Hong Kong institutions with sufficient staff resources may jointly develop, accredit, and deliver an early childhood program in collaboration with an overseas partner. In either case, overseas institutions, particularly Australian universities, are having considerable input into the Hong Kong early childhood field at the graduate level.

Notwithstanding the increasing influence of western early childhood pedagogy and philosophy, Chinese culture and values continue to be a cohesive force in the Hong Kong early childhood landscape. Within Chinese culture, teachers are imparters of knowledge as well as moral preceptors (Contextual Analysis Research Team, 1997). The family is still, in theory if not in fact, the most important group in society, and its members, including children, are expected to put family interests above their own. Children have an obligation to do well at all levels of the school system in order to enhance the family's reputation. The family also has responsibilities to its members, which include caring for children while their parents work, or taking care of disabled members. Hong Kong families with problems are more likely to try to meet their needs within family resources than seek outside professional assistance. This tradition may help to explain why there is less need for childcare than would be expected in a society where frequently both parents work.

In a society where the Confucian values of hard work and effort predominate, the teaching and learning processes do not have to be enjoyable, or even interesting. Learning which requires application and effort is valued. Consequently, while inspectors and western-educated early childhood educators may deplore the custom of assigning even three-year-olds homework, the practice remains widespread. Children at kindergarten are rewarded with sweets, stamps, tokens, and praise for being good, that is, for being polite, obedient, kind, and successful. When a group of kindergarten principals was asked why children were seldom rewarded for improvement or effort, they replied that there was no need to reward children for doing their duty. Such a view about learning helps to explain why teacher-centered instruction, repetition, and practice remain widely accepted ways of teaching and learning in preschool services, and why children are expected to work hard in order to be successful.

Lessons from the Hong Kong Early Childhood Landscape

A major challenge facing the Hong Kong early childhood field is to determine what early childhood ideas and practices gleaned from overseas are appropriate to Hong Kong's cultural context. The lesson for early childhood educators elsewhere is the danger in trying to transpose concepts and their related practices from one culture to another without very careful consideration. Differences in language make such transpositions even more difficult. The concept of play as a major learning tool is a case in point. There is no consensus as to what constitutes play among western early childhood staff even though it is a key tenet in their credo. This lack of consensus is further compounded in Hong Kong because "play" has different connotations when translated into Cantonese, the main language of Hong Kong early childhood staff. In Cantonese, "play" has connotations of relaxation and recreation so that western early childhood axioms such as "play is the work of young children", are confusing. An example may illustrate this point. Following a discussion on caring for animals, a kindergarten teacher brought out a small turtle which each child was allowed to touch in turn. The teacher proudly explained that this activity was an example of how she was incorporating play into her program.

Another lesson to be learned is the contribution that professional bodies such as OMEP-Hong Kong can make to bridging systemic divisions and encouraging a sense of identity and cohesion. This organization has avoided becoming a platform for particular interest groups within the early childhood field. Overseas examples would suggest that when early childhood organizations shift their focus from broad-based professional goals to political, industrial, or specific interests groups, they foster division rather than cohesion within the early childhood field. The reasons for OMEP-Hong Kong's success are worth closer examination.

Possibly the most important lessons and issues which arise from the Hong Kong early childhood landscape relate to the impact of cultural expectations on early childhood practice. Some of these expectations challenge assumptions of western early childhood education. For example, by completion of preschool, Hong Kong children are expected to be able to write the alphabet in both upper and lower case, recognize and write Chinese characters, write their own name, and write a selection of English and Chinese words (Chow, 1993). This flies in the face of assumptions that young children are not "developmentally ready" to acquire such skills, and/or that the teaching of reading and writing is the domain of the primary school, as some preschool staff have claimed (Raban & Ure, this volume). Similarly at age five, Hong Kong kindergarten children are expected to add and subtract within 1 to 10, count by rote up to 100, and complete simple equations after only limited exposure to concrete materials for counting, sorting, and classifying. Current Hong Kong early childhood practice challenges the simplistic assumption that there is a "right way" of educating young children which can transcend national boundaries and cultural contexts. What constitutes acceptable practice and desirable outcomes in one country may well be irrelevant or inappropriate in another.

Conclusion

At present, countries like Australia consider education to be an important export commodity. Tertiary early childhood educators are being encouraged to export their courses and expertise in order to raise revenue for their cash-strapped universities. The challenge for the Hong Kong early childhood field will be to identify and incorporate those aspects of overseas early childhood practice that are culturally relevant. The challenge to early childhood educators in other national landscapes will be to review their own practices in light of their own cultural contexts, and to export their expertise with sensitivity and caution.

Though the Hong Kong early childhood landscape is moving toward greater cohesiveness, it faces uncertainties and restraints arising from changes in the political, economic, and social landscapes. Until now, most children have been able to access preschool services because their families have been able to pay all or part of the fees required, and the private sector has been able to provide sufficient places with some financial incentives, regulation, and advisory support from government. It remains to be seen whether the current means of providing preschool places will be adequate to cope with the influx of children expected under Right of Abode legislation. It also remains to be seen whether the private sector will continue to provide sufficient places if government decides to respond to mounting pressure for increased registration requirements and quality control measures in order to improve the quality of preschooling. Higher costs may reduce the number of places provided on a profit-making basis. How to maintain a workable balance between private sector provision and government regulation and assistance will remain an important dilemma in Hong Kong while there is no system of public-sector preschools to offset any major changes in private sector provision. Whether Tung Chee Wah and his government intend to change the extent and nature of government involvement in preschooling will be announced shortly. In Hong Kong as elsewhere, government rhetoric about the importance of preschool has not been matched with financial support.

Notes

1. The term "early childhood services" is used throughout this chapter to refer to services for children from birth to age eight. "Preschool" is used as a general term for services for children prior to commencing school, while "kindergarten" refers to specific educational programs for children aged three to six. "Childcare services" is used in a general way to refer to preschool services which have the care and supervision of young children as their primary function. "Early intervention services" is used to refer to a range of services for young children with special needs.

References

Chan, G. Y-y (1993). Development of writing skills in preschool children. In S. Opper (Ed.) *Early Childhood Education in Hong Kong. Education Paper 16.* Hong Kong: University of Hong Kong Faculty of Education.

Chow, H.Y-m (1993). Hong Kong kindergarten and primary school teachers' expectations of school readiness skills in young children. In S. Opper (Ed.). *Early Childhood Education in Hong Kong. Education paper 16.* Hong Kong: University of Hong Kong Faculty of Education.

Contextual Analysis Research Team. (1997). *Contextual analysis for program development.* Hong Kong: Hong Kong Institute of Education.

Curriculum Development Council. (1993). *Guide to the kindergarten curriculum.* Hong Kong: Government Printer.

Curriculum Development Institute. (1996). *Guide to the pre-primary curriculum.* Hong Kong: Government Printer.

Heep Hong Society for Handicapped Children. (1995). *Annual report 1993/4.* Hong Kong: Heep Hong Society.

Hong Kong Government. (1996). *Education Department teacher survey 1995.* Hong Kong: Government Printer.

Hong Kong Government. (1994). *Education and manpower branch. A guide to education and training in Hong Kong.* Hong Kong: Government Printer.

Hong Kong Government. (1984a). *Education Department guide to the kindergarten curriculum.* Hong Kong: Government Printer.

Hong Kong Government. (1984b). *Education Department manual of kindergarten practice.* Hong Kong: Government Printer.

Hong Kong Government. (1987). *Education Department guidelines on nursery class activities.* Hong Kong: Government Printer.

Hong Kong Government. (1988a). *Social Welfare Department, childcare centers advisory inspectorate, Code of Practice.* Hong Kong: Government Printer.

Hong Kong Government. (1988b). *Social Welfare Department, childcare centers advisory inspectorate, activity guidelines for day nurseries.* Hong Kong: Government Printer.

Lam, H. M-y (1993). Effects of physical education on gross motor performance of preschool children. In S. Opper (Ed.). *Early Childhood Education in Hong Kong. Education paper 16.* Hong Kong: University of Hong Kong Faculty of Education.

Lam, H. M-y (1997). *A study of Hong Kong parents' views on kindergarten education.* Unpublished manuscript.

Mellor, E. (1996). *Why homework is set in Hong Kong kindergartens.* Unpublished paper presented at the OMEP-Hong Kong Annual Conference. Hong Kong.

Olmsted, P.P., & Lockhart, S. (1995). *Do parents and teachers agree? What should young children be learning?* High/Scope ReSource Winter (reprint).

OMEP-Hong Kong (1996). *The criteria for high-quality programs of early childhood education and care in Hong Kong.* Causeway Bay: OMEP-Hong Kong.

Opper, S. (1992). *Hong Kong's young children. Their preschools and families.* Hong Kong: University of Hong Kong Press.

Opper, S. (1993). (Ed.). *Early childhood education in Hong Kong. Education Paper 16.* Hong Kong: University of Hong Kong Faculty of Education.

Opper, S. (1996). *Hong Kong's young children. Their early development and learning.* Hong Kong: University of Hong Kong Press.

Rehabilitation Division. (1996). *Hong Kong review of rehabilitation program plan* (1995–1998/9). Hong Kong: Government Printer.

Wong, J.W.P. (1996). *The 1996 policy address. Education policy commitments.* Hong Kong: Government Printer.

Working Party on Kindergarten Education. (1996). *Guide to the pre-primary curriculum.* Hong Kong: Curriculum Development Institute.

The Landscape of Policy and Practice

Chapter 8

Hitting the Wall: Early Childhood Education in the Primary and Tertiary Sectors— An Australian Case Study

Jacqueline Hayden

Abstract

This chapter describes findings from recent studies which show how administrative and structural changes in other educational sectors are having significant effects upon the early childhood landscape. The term "early childhood education" is unpackaged to reveal where gaps and misunderstandings may occur. While distributions to early childhood education are stable or increasing in primary and tertiary sectors in Australia, the constitutional dimension of the field is "hitting a wall"[1]—being obstructed by a variety of factors including generalized approaches to teacher training, and devolved decision making to those who may be unaware of the goals and benefits of early childhood education. Thus initiatives that appear to be positive and/or benign within the primary and tertiary sectors are, in fact, having corroding effects on early childhood professionals and practices.

Introduction

Early childhood services fall within three domains—the community sector (childcare and related services), the primary education sector (the early school years), and the tertiary training sector (universities, community colleges, and private institutions that provide training for early childhood specialists). This chapter shows how structural changes taking place in primary and tertiary institutions are affecting early childhood developments within these sectors.

Recent trends such as decentralization (within government departments of education) and amalgamation (of faculties in universities) are having a significant effect upon the field of early childhood education in Australia. Restructuring results in the devolution of decision making to new players. Meanwhile the need to economize by generalizing programs of delivery and training are making it increasingly difficult to break through the "wall"—and to secure a pedagogical and philosophical space for early childhood education in primary schools and tertiary institutions.

The need for clearly articulated principles and goals of early childhood education is critical as decision making structures change within the primary and tertiary sectors. With trends toward generalist directors, reduced consultative resources, and multiskilling in large organizations (departments of school education) and concomitant decentralization to smaller units (schools), program decision making is more likely to take place at middle management levels.

While this can have positive effects, devolved decision making places the onus on principals to be aware of the special needs and particular issues of programs for which they may have little background or experience, and for which advice and support resources are reduced. The result is a lag in the knowledge base of decision makers who are having increased influence over early childhood service delivery (see Corrie, this volume).

In tertiary settings, the trend toward larger faculties in order to exploit economies of scale is similarly resulting in deans and others whose "pens will direct early childhood programs" but who may not have experience with, and/or awareness of, the particularities of the early childhood field. As studies reported later in this chapter show, the notion that teaching very young children commands some specialist knowledge/training is not always recognized by those outside of the early childhood field.

In some cases, confusion over what the term *early childhood education* means exacerbates misunderstandings between those who are early childhood specialists and those who are not. Thus the first step toward increased constitutional allotments for early childhood professionals, as they try to influence and/or to become players within larger arenas, is to clarify parameters and unpackage the terminology. A deconstruction of the term "early childhood education" is offered below.[2]

Clarification of the Term Early Childhood Education

The term "early childhood/early childhood education" can refer to one of four discrete concepts (see Glossary, this volume). These are:

1. Early childhood as a chronological age and/or a developmental stage of human beings;
2. Early childhood education as a philosophical approach to teaching and learning;
3. Early childhood education as a pedagogical term describing a particular set of teaching strategies;
4. Early childhood as a political ideology that addresses the role of the state in the care and education of children prior to the onset of compulsory schooling.

Early Childhood as a Chronological Age and/or a Developmental Stage of Human Beings

Early childhood describes a stage of development from birth to mid-primary years. According to Piaget and others, the stage of early childhood officially ends when a child is capable of performing tasks involving mental representation, conservation, class inclusion, serialization, and similar concepts. At this point the child is ready to deal with higher order formal operations, or abstract thought, usually around the age of 8 years.

Early Childhood Education as a Philosophical Approach to Teaching and Learning

The philosophy of early childhood education is grounded in the work of Froebel, Pestalozzii, Rousseau, and Montessori. These theorists viewed the developing child as having within her the seed of healthy and productive adulthood. Teaching the young child really meant nurturing her inner drives, as one nurtures a plant (thus "kindergarten"). Thus there is no standard or knowledge base upon which a child is compared, and concomitantly, no failure. Further, because of the integrative concept of child development/learning, no one developmental area (cognition) is more important for teachers to address than is any other area (social/emotional/physical).

Early Childhood Education as a Pedagogical Term Describing Teaching Strategies

During the early years, cognitive and other areas of development rely upon the ability of the child to experience and experiment with concrete operations in order to assimilate and accommodate thought strategies. The success with these concrete operations forms the foundation for cognition, physical progress, self-esteem, creativity, social effectiveness, and general approaches to learning and living.

Traditional early childhood pedagogy reflects theories forwarded by Piaget. Piaget was instrumental in revealing how children are intrinsically motivated, active players in their learning outcomes. Thus the role of the teacher is not to disseminate information but to create an environment whereby self-learning occurs (child-centered approach to learning). Currently the work of Vygotsky and others have modified this approach. The Vygotskian approach incorporates the teacher's role as being more directive, leading rather than following the development of the child. The teacher does this by capitalizing on the *zone of proximal development* whereby a number of teaching strategies are employed to enable the child to complete tasks that would otherwise be beyond his or her immediate capabilities. These strategies are referred to as "scaffolding" and include modeling behavior, offering prompts, cues, answers, questions, and suggestions that will guide the child toward successful task completion and concomitant restructuring of cognition (Elliott, 1995).

The early childhood curriculum incorporates goals for supporting gross motor and fine motor development; social, cognitive, and emotional development; and the traditional "academic" goals for literacy, numeracy, creativity, collaborative skills, and skills for planning, gathering, and organizing ideas and learning (Queensland School Curriculum Council, 1997). Early childhood teachers rely on observation and other strategies to determine individualized goals which ensure that each child is challenged to move along his/her own developmental path toward his/her maximum potential.

Teaching strategies are informed in the early childhood years by child development theory and an approach to learning which incorporates "play." The use of the term play is frequently misunderstood by those outside of the field. In lay terms "play" can imply engagement in intrinsically determined, open-ended, purposeless activities that are not necessarily enhanced by adult intervention. However, in the discourse of early childhood education, the term "play" refers to a process of extending children's understanding of their world, teaching communication skills, encouraging reflection and articulation, and integrating numeracy, literacy and other aspects of the curricula. The subtleties of the role of the adult in children's play can result in misconceptions about the scaffolding and teaching activity that it entails (see Burton and Lyons, this volume).

The Differences Between an Early Childhood and a Primary Pedagogy

Early childhood teacher training programs in New South Wales incorporate components that are not included in the training of primary teachers (see Veale, this volume, for analyses of teacher training programs in other states). Early childhood courses tend to emphasize analyses of, and strategies for, working with parents/families and the community; strategies for developing individualized goals based on observations; and the development and implementation of a curriculum designed to meet individual as well as group needs/goals. Other topics that are unique to courses for early childhood teachers in many Australian universities include business management, and administration issues; policy development; the politics and economics of early childhood education; and advocacy.

Early Childhood Is a Political Ideology. It Refers To a Philosophy Of State Intervention.

Universally, the age of compulsory schooling starts around seven years of age which coincides with what Piaget identified as the stage of formal operations. Early childhood education is generally considered to encompass care and educational provision which takes place prior to, and does not have, compulsory school status. Since the 1970s, in many developed nations, early childhood education has been recognized as a means to improve the efficacy of the school system and has become valued and universal, if not compulsory, for that reason.[3]

Since the 1970s, the term early childhood education has come to incorporate a notion which goes beyond formal education for young children, to include the concept of substitute parenting. The benefits of an increased labor force, female equity programs, and reduced welfare expenditures underlay burgeoning state interest in childcare. The availability of early childhood education has, in this way, become embroiled in debates about public versus private responsibilities for children (residual versus universal approach to social services). In this sense early childhood education, and the support which it receives, can be seen to represent a political ideology (see Gammage, this volume).

Breaking Through the Wall: Why Early Childhood Education is Important in Primary Settings

Those outside of the field may not be aware that the term "early childhood education" refers to a complex integration of philosophy, pedagogy, and even politics, or that the developmental progression from age 0–8 years falls within the early childhood realm. A common argument is to abandon early childhood approaches to teaching, when children "hit the wall" of a changed system and structure in the compulsory school system. This argument is often supported by parents who want children to "learn" not "play" when they get to school (Hoot, 1996), and by principals who are increasingly pressured to demonstrate performance outcomes (Goldstein, 1997).

Counter to these pressures is a growing body of research that identifies the correlation between exposure to early childhood education and later success in a number of variables (see Goldstein, 1997). Longitudinal studies are now showing that the myriad benefits accrued to preschool experiences are dependent upon a child-centered approach (early childhood pedagogy), and that the benefits are reduced when a teacher-directed approach is prevalent in the preschool and the early school years. This is especially true for children from disadvantaged areas (Schorr, 1988). Indeed experience in child directed programs in the early years is now known to be correlated to variables such as reduced juvenile delinquency, reduced need for academic remediation, reduced teenage pregnancy, joblessness, and other social diseases up to 27 years later (Schweinhart & Weikart, 1993)!

These findings were reflected in a recent Australian study. The purpose of the study was to analyze the relationship between entry age into primary school and reading age in later primary. It was shown that, for both disadvantaged and middleclass schools, there was no significant relationship between age of entry of pupils and reading age by year two. The differences in pupil outcome were significantly related, not to age of entry, but *to what happened once children had entered the classroom* (Rivers, 1996; see also Clyde, 1996). The following classroom/teacher attributes were found to correlate to successful student development. They reflect what is considered to be typical early childhood pedagogical strategies:

1. There is an emphasis by teachers on process skills and/or micro objectives that focus on meaningful learning.
2. Teachers celebrate the diversity of student talents and provide ample opportunity for social interaction.
3. The culture in the classroom encourages students to be active and critical instead of compliant.
4. The teacher/school embraces the inclusiveness of the parent/caregiver in the learning process.

Distributional and Constitutional Dimensions of Early Childhood Education

In Australia, in the past decade, the distributions to the field of early childhood education in primary and tertiary sectors have been substantial.

Distributions in the Tertiary Sector

In the tertiary sector, distributions are related to the amalgamation of colleges of education with university faculties which took place in Australia in 1989. Some of the outcomes of that movement include an increase in higher level university positions for early childhood specialists; there is increased demand for spaces by university students; and increased numbers of postgraduate scholars. While early childhood still lags behind other areas in the dissemination of large grants from traditional sources such as the prestigious Australian Research Council, there is visible growth in the research activity in this area.

Distributions in the Primary Sector

In the primary sector distributions to early childhood education can be measured by an increase in the rhetoric which incorporates an early childhood education approach toward teaching in the early school years. Over the past decade, in a number of significant reports released from the Department of School Education, New South Wales, the rhetoric of early childhood education/pedagogy and philosophy has been promoted as the means to improve successful outcomes for children. This statement, recently released by the New South Wales Minister for Education and Training articulates the official approach to an early childhood education oriented pedagogy:

> In the field of education, there is now an increased knowledge of child development and a recognition of the importance of early childhood experiences on later development. (In schools there is) a greater emphasis on catering for individual differences through developmentally appropriate programs. It is widely accepted that the best educational program for children in their first year of school is one which is integrated, developmental, and sufficiently flexible to cater for the individual needs of all children. Effective early learning is associated with the inclusion of parents in children's formal learning program, and the professional support of teachers (Aquilina, 1996: p. 2).

Early childhood-oriented statements such as this one have been used in several official documents and policy reports. The implication is that senior policymakers are articulating the need for teachers and principals to be supportive of early childhood philosophy and to be oriented to early childhood pedagogy—and that more early childhood specialists will be needed in school settings in order to implement these pedagogical directions.

Ironically, while the distributional allotments appear to be increasing, the constitutional dimension of early childhood education in both primary and tertiary sectors is diminishing. Some of the indicators of reduced constitutional allotments are described below.

Constitutional Trends within the Tertiary Sector

Cuts to higher education in universities and increased student fees in Australia are prompting potential students to consider alternative training options such as TAFE (community college level) courses. In the field of early childhood, two-year college trained childcare workers have not been visibly distinctive from three-year university trained teachers. The major differences have been structural—salary and regulated responsibilities. Differences are not articulated in professional terms such as distinct job descriptions and/or leadership roles. A high school leaver who is interested in working in the early childhood field may apply for the same position on graduation from TAFE as he or she would on graduation from a Faculty of Education course in early childhood. In some cases, the TAFE graduate is preferred by the employer (due to award issues).

A second trend in universities which is affecting early childhood education is the reduction of funding and concomitant increased need for rationalization and accountability. An offshoot of this is the need to rationalize staff positions. Since early childhood education is a relatively new component of university faculties (came within University auspices under the tertiary reforms of 1989), the number of senior, tenured positions in this field is relatively small. When staff cuts are made, the junior and/or less embedded positions are often the first to be considered.

Constitutional Trends within the Primary School Sector

There are indications of an increasing demand for a structured, subject-centered approach to education in the early school years. The demand comes from officials and parents who are concerned about accountability in the school system. This trend is demonstrated by a recent cross-national study of parents' views about what constitutes developmentally appropriate classroom practices for children aged 3–5 years. Parents reported that they were in favor of didactic teaching approaches, use of workbooks and textbooks for instruction, and weekly formal assessment (Hoot, 1996).

A further reflection of this trend is the increase in the demand for, and use of, standardized testing at early stages of schooling. Indeed there are indications that Australia is moving toward the British model of standardized assessment where externally set pencil and paper tests for 5-year-olds are currently in use. The use of such tests to monitor schools (and/or to assess teacher effectiveness) is contra-indicated for early childhood education where goals (performance outcomes) are developed from individual needs of each child (Clements, 1996). In Victoria there is a movement to accredit teachers according to numerically scaled personal performance targets. The focus upon external standards of progress in young children devalues the pedagogical approach that distinguishes early childhood teaching from primary teaching (Huggard, 1996, p. 2).

The studies described below were designed to test the implication of these trends and others. The goal was to ascertain the status, the perceived value of, and the commitment to an early childhood perspective within the primary and tertiary sectors.

Studies of Early Childhood Education in the Primary and Tertiary Sectors

Early Childhood Student-Teachers Are Wary of Primary School Culture

Hayden conducted a series of studies to gauge the perceptions of preservice early childhood trained and primary trained teachers and their university lecturers. Her findings include the following:

> Early childhood teachers report that there is a difference between the working climate in the community sector and the school sector (Hayden & Newman, 1996). The majority of early childhood trained teachers perceived that the following work related variables were more likely to be found in a childcare setting than in a primary school setting: autonomy, positive co-worker relations, positive supervisor relations (Hayden & Newman, 1996).
> Early childhood teachers covet early childhood trained supervisors. 43% of early childhood trained teachers reported that a supervisor with training similar to theirs was very important to them. (Only 13% of respondents reported that the background of their supervisor was not important to them.) (Hayden & Newman, 1996).

The perceptions of these preservice early childhood teachers were authenticated by a study that took place in Western Australia, described below (see also Corrie, this volume).

Early Childhood Teachers and Classrooms Receive Less Support from Principals

The Western Australia study analyzed principals' interactions with early childhood teachers. The classrooms of these teachers (called preprimary classes) were assessed as distinguishable from other classes in the same schools in the areas of curriculum, teaching style, classroom management, and evaluation. Other distinguishing features included the practices of situating children in small groups, resulting in continual movement (by teacher), and a focused attention to the individual needs of children (Stamopoulos, 1995, p. 24).

Principals reported providing less leadership to early childhood teachers than they provided to primary trained teachers. Interview data revealed that:

> Principals felt as though they lacked the necessary knowledge and experience to provide adequate leadership to early childhood teachers;
> Principals spent less time in preprimary classrooms;
> Principals perceived preprimary classes as being less critical than other primary classes;
> Principals felt that pre-primary classes warranted less accountability than did other primary classes.[4]

Principals May Not Value Early Childhood Specialists

Documents were reviewed and interviews were conducted with key planners/policymakers in one department of education in Australia. Findings revealed that staffing decisions rest with principals (Hayden, 1996). It follows that principals who are not aware/committed to early childhood pedagogy and philosophy will not seek, recruit, or create a demand for early childhood trained teachers.

University Lecturers Responsible for Training Primary Teachers May Not Promote the Benefits of an Early Childhood Pedagogical Approach for Children Aged 5–8 Years

Through interviews and surveys of university lecturers and graduating students in one faculty of education in New South Wales, the following was revealed:

1. Few lecturers who teach in courses that lead to degrees for primary teaching reported having training in early childhood education—although a number did have experience in teaching in the early school years;
2. Lecturers in the primary education course did not promote the need to implement an early childhood pedagogical approach when working with children below the age of eight;
3. Senior administrators in the faculty of education did not reflect an awareness of differences and/or the need to address differences in the training of primary versus early childhood teachers.

Attitudes of senior administrators fell into three categories:

Denial—a denial of pedagogical/philosophical differences between teaching young children and teaching older children—as reflected in the statement below:

> Separation between the fields (of early childhood and primary) is a social and institutional artefact rather than a reflection of children's lives and developmental experiences. It has as much to do with professional bureaucracies as anything else (Respondent A).

Nonprofessional—an antiprofessional approach reflecting the notion that some individuals are simply (born) more nurturing and thus better suited for teaching young children:

> Teachers (in the early school years) are in a sense born. They just adapt naturally and easily to that age level whereas other (primary teachers in training) find the whole task very difficult and never really adjust (Respondent B).

Supplemental—a notion that early childhood education is equivalent to a subject which some students might want to add onto their completed teacher training:

> I'd like (our students) to think of themselves as teachers first, and then maybe take on an area of specialization—math, science, or early childhood (Respondent C).

The outcome of the attitudes described above were reflected in a survey of students about to graduate with primary teaching credentials.[5]

The graduands reported being ambivalent about teaching in early school years but felt that they were capable of doing so. Sixty-eight percent of the primary graduands in the study stated that they would prefer to teach in the later school years or that they had no preference regarding teaching in the early or later school years. Thirty-two percent of graduands in the study stated that they preferred the early school years, but of these, thirty-five percent did not want to take on a kindergarten class[6] (Hayden & Newman, 1996).

Conclusion

The studies cited above indicate that early childhood teachers could feel alienated by the primary school culture that develops during preservice tertiary training. Early childhood graduands perceive that they will have less autonomy and poorer interpersonal relationships within the primary school sector than they will have in the community (childcare) sector. Their perceptions are correct. In an unrelated study, principals reported providing fewer supports to early childhood teachers than to primary trained teachers working in higher level grades. Meanwhile, graduands of primary teacher training programs did not reflect an awareness of the significant correlation between early childhood classroom strategies and outcome in terms of school success or that working with children at earlier stages of development warrants an early childhood approach in the pedagogical and philosophical meaning of that term.

The significant body of literature that shows the correlation of early childhood pedagogy to school and life success for children—especially to those who come from disadvantaged backgrounds—has not been integrated into the practices of primary and tertiary sectors. Despite distributional allotments in terms of rhetoric and increased training opportunities, early childhood education in primary and tertiary sectors is hitting a wall—being constrained by factors that militate against raised awareness and support for the particularities of early childhood education.

As May and Carr describe in another context, there is an increasing danger when decisions are being made by "pens which are not early childhood" (May & Carr, this volume). In this case, well-meaning individuals can inadvertently curtail early childhood programs and systems because they are unaware of the multiple issues, goals, and outcomes of the early childhood approach to teaching and learning (see Hayden, 1993). In the primary school sector, the increasing devolution of responsibility onto principals and the reduction of central office supports such as specialist consultants is eroding early childhood infrastructures. In the tertiary sector the amalgamation of faculties in universities results in dilution of early childhood courses. Meanwhile, newly graduated primary teachers were shown to remain mostly unaware of the benefits of a distinct early childhood pedagogy, and thus were likely to perpetuate the "mismatch between cultures in the [primary] school" (Goldstein, 1997, p. 6; see also Raban & Ure, this volume). Accordingly early childhood teacher graduates reported being wary of their role within school settings.

Ironically, Australia has boasted some of the best teacher training courses for early childhood in the world. Currently a number of Australian universities are continuing to offer degrees at all levels in the area of early childhood education—and are graduating highly specialized professionals for the field. In some cases early childhood education is receiving renewed and significant attention and resources by visionary university decision makers.[7] Indeed some states have enacted policies that decree that only those with early childhood training teach in the early school years.[8]

Despite these advances, a concerted and rigorous commitment is needed to develop, strengthen, and embed constitutional allotments. Without this, early childhood professionals will continue to "hit the wall"—and the benefits of early childhood approaches to educational outcomes will become increasingly less visible and less valued.

Notes

1. The terms distributions and constitutional allotments are defined as follows:

    The distributional dimension of policy relates to the allotment of the tangible benefits across various interests in society. The constitutional dimension relates to the allocation of positions of influence in the making and implementation of policy (Tuohy, 1994: p. 249).
    These terms are central to the theme of this book and are explained in detail in chapter 2.

2. See Pence & Benner and Lero (this volume) for their analyzes of the four discourses which define early childhood education.

3. The Commonwealth of Australia has designated a priority-of-access policy for four-year-olds. Children aged four or over must be given priority for placement in preschools/childcare centers. Nationwide, 57% of Australian children attend preschool prior to entering the public school system (Economic Planning Advisory Commission, 1996). This report was particularly adamant about the importance of early childhood as the foundation of education. Its recommendations articulated a commitment to early childhood pedagogy and curriculum and included strategies for increasing awareness of the distinctive needs of early childhood personnel in primary schools.)

4. Other findings from this study include:
    1. Sixty-five percent of principals in study claimed that they were unsure and/or gave poor or very poor support to early childhood teachers in the areas of curriculum development and implementation.
    2. Over 70% of principals claimed that they were unsure or gave poor or very poor leadership in the diagnosing of educational problems for early childhood teachers.
    3. Principals felt that they provided educational advice and leadership to a greater extent than the early childhood education teachers felt that they received advice and leadership from principals.
    4. Over 80% of principals nominated professional development in early childhood education as a medium or high priority for themselves.

5. In NSW these teachers are eligible to teach from kindergarten to year six (5–12 year-olds) with their Bachelor of Teaching (Primary) Degree. Early Childhood Teachers are trained to teach children from birth to Year Two (0–8 year-olds) but, because of Department of Education policy which does not distinguish specialities once in the school system, early childhood graduands are officially eligible to teach higher grades as well.

6. Reasons stated for preferring to teach in the later school years included:

    a. chances for advancement are higher;
    b. the status of teaching is greater in the later school years;

c. teaching in the early grades is too hard./ I am not skilled in this area. I am not ready for this kind of teaching;

d. there is less support from the curriculum in the early school years. Teaching in the early school years means too much work for the teacher.

7. The University of Western Sydney, Nepean, is one example. Their newly formed School of Learning, Development and Early Education has broken away from the faculty of education and offers undergraduate degrees, postgraduate diplomas, a Master of Teaching, Master of Education, and postgraduate research degrees such as Doctorate in Education (EdD) and Doctorate of Philosophy (PhD) with a strictly early childhood focus (see Hayden, 1997).

8. This has been addressed in a recent report by the Senate Employment, Education and Training Reference Committee, Commonwealth of Australia:

> The Committee recommends that State and Territory Education Ministers ensure that, where appropriately qualified early childhood trained teachers are available, they should be given priority over generalist teachers for appointments to position at the junior primary school level (Senate Employment, Education and Training References Committee, 1996, p. 87).

References

Acquilina, J. (1996). *Kindergarten entry age in New South Wales: Consultation paper*; New South Wales Ministry for Education and Training, Department of School Education.

Boston, K. (1994). *Opening address: Forward together: Partners in education.* Early Childhood Education Seminar, Department of School Education, Sydney, April 15.

Carrick, J. (1989). *Report of the Committee of Review of New South Wales School.* Sydney: Government of New South Wales.

Clements, K. (1996). Assessment. *Directions* 5(13):2.

Clyde, M (1996). "Early Childhood: No "Best Age." *Directions in Education* Vol. 5(13):1.

Creighton, A. (1995). Health care in Canada and Australia: The development of a comparative analytical framework. *Australian Canadian Studies* 13(2): 59–71.

Elliott, A. (1995). Scaffolding young children's learning in early childhood education settings. In M. Fleer (Ed.). *DAP Centrism: Challenging Developmentally Appropriate Practice.* (pp. 24–330). Canberra: Australia Early Childhood Association.

Economic Planning Advisory Commission. (1996). *Future childcare provision in Australia: Task force final report.* Canberra: Australian Government Publishing Service.

Goldstein, L. (1997). Between a rock and a hard place in the primary grades: The challenge of providing developmentally appropriate early childhood education in an elementary school setting. *Early Childhood Research Quarterly* 12(1): 3–27.

Hayden, J. (1993). The childcare chimera: Policymaking and the hidden agenda. In J. Mason (Ed.). (pp. 183–197). *Child Welfare: Critical Australian Perspectives.* Sydney: Hale and Iremonger.

Hayden J. (1996). *The use of early childhood trained teachers in primary schools.* University of Western Sydney, Nepean, unpublished paper.

Hayden, J. (1994). Half full or half empty? Children's services policy and the missing bits. In E. Mellor & K. Coombe (Eds.). (pp. 11–25). *Issues in Early Childhood Services. Australian Perspectives.* New York: WCB.

Hayden, J. (1997). Facing the future together: New programs in early childhood education at University of Western Sydney, Nepean, *Rattler* 44, Summer: 19–20.

Hayden, J., & Newman, S. (1996). *Perceptions of pre-service primary teacher and their trainers.* University of Western Sydney, Nepean, unpublished paper.

Hoot, J. (1996). Cross-national perspectives on developmentally appropriate practices for early childhood programs. *Journal of Research in Childhood Education* 10(2): 160–172.

Huggard, R. (1996). Assessment: Call for secondary LAP tests. *Directions* 5(8):2.

Leonard, D. (1996). Effective schools: A review of the literature. *Practicing Administrator* (3): 36–44.

Queensland School Curriculum Council. (1997). *Preschool Curriculum Guidelines Brisbane*: Queensland Government.

Rivers, J. (1996). *Ready if you are!* Unpublished paper presented at the Postgraduate Research Seminar, University of Western Sydney, Nepean, October 29.

Schweinhart, L., & Weikart, D. (1993). Success by empowerment: the High/Scope Perry preschool study through age 27. *Young Children*, 49(1): 54–58.

Senate Employment, Education and Training References Committee. (1996). *Childhood matters: The report on the inquiry into early childhood education.* Canberra: Commonwealth of Australia.

Stamopoulos, E. (1995). *The professional background and perceptions of principals on their leadership role in pre-primary.* Unpublished MEd Honors Thesis, Edith Cowan University.

Tuohy, C. (1994). Response to the Clinton proposal: A comparative perspective. *Journal of Health Politics, Policy and Law* 19(1): 249–254.

Chapter 9

Choosing Childcare for Infants: Social, Cultural, and Demographic Influences and Outcomes

Margaret K. McKim

Abstract

This study reveals that parental choice of their childcare setting is more likely to be related to family psychological and social characteristics than to what is going on inside the center. The findings show how the provision and use of childcare incorporates, but extends beyond, physical, geographical, political and/or economic factors. Internal family dynamics also play a major role in the demand, use, and satisfaction with childcare services. Division between the external and internal landscapes of infant care is becoming increasingly blurred.

Introduction

A majority of Canadian parents with infants and toddlers use out-of-home care arrangements (Statistics Canada, 1992), but little is known about the psychological or social characteristics of families choosing different types. How these familial factors interact with childcare characteristics to predict developmental outcomes such as mother-infant attachment security is only beginning to be addressed (see NICHD Early Childcare Research Network, 1997a). The research reported here had two purposes. First, we were interested in finding out whether families with different social, psychological, and health characteristics make different decisions about maternal employment, type of care arrangement chosen, age of entry into out-of-home care, and quality/stability of care selected. Second, to help clarify the controversial question of whether early and extensive use of infant out-of-home care is associated with increased risk of attachment insecurity, we evaluated the role of childcare characteristics (type, quality, amount, age of entry, and stability) as well as family/child characteristics and their interactions in predicting attachment security.

Factors Associated with Childcare Choice

Previous research examining factors associated with childcare choice have concentrated on demographic and economic indicators (e.g., Boyuk & Lochhead, 1993; Cleveland & Hyatt, 1993; Hofferth & Wissoker, 1992). These studies have been used by policy analysts to determine the impact of price, income, tax policy, or the availability of public subsidy on choice. Canadian research shows that family demographic characteristics are related to childcare decisions. Family income, family type (one versus two-parent) and child age have all been shown to influence the type of childcare arrangements parents of infants and toddlers in Canada choose and/or prefer (e.g., Boyuk & Lochhead, 1993; Ministry of Community & Social Services, Ontario, 1991, National Childcare Information Center, 1994; Statistics Canada, 1992; Symons & McLeod, 1993). These studies show that:

1. Low income families' choices are influenced by the availability of subsidy;
2. Mothers with more income potential start using alternate care sooner after childbirth and for longer hours;
3. Families with younger infants prefer and use parent care or care by a relative more often than families with older infants or toddlers;
4. More than 85% of families requiring childcare for their infants or toddlers use unlicensed family home care;
5. Employed single parents use and prefer center care over any other form of childcare.

In the present study, the role of family income and child age in discriminating between families making different childcare arrangements was examined.

In recent years measures of childcare quality have been included in equations designed to predict parental childcare decisions, with mixed results. Although staff/child ratio, caregiver education, group size, and other composite measures of childcare quality are not often found to influence choices (Hofferth & Wissoker, 1992; Waite, Leibowitz & Witzberger, 1991), a relationship has been found between quality of care chosen and socioeconomic status (SES) (Howes, Sakai, Shinn & Phillips, 1995; Schleicker, White & Jacobs, 1991; White, Parent, Change & Spindler, 1992). White, et al. (1992) reported that low SES parents using low-quality care were more likely than parents using higher quality care to cite low cost, convenient hours, and lack of a waiting list as factors influencing choice. The latter issues are not typically included in the primarily structural measures now used to define differences in childcare quality. Waite, et al. (1991) have suggested that the structural elements that are currently the focus of licensing are, in fact, largely irrelevant in terms of what parents demand from childcare (p. 47). White, et al. (1992) would not concur. Their data indicated that parents agree on what they are looking for in a childcare arrangement (i.e., "experienced qualified caregivers, supervision, safe and clean environments, nutritious food provided, warm and friendly caregivers, availability of materials" (p. 107). But when it comes to choosing one care arrangement over another, they suggest that other factors may be important. That is, individual family constraints, needs, and characteristics may play a significant role in the type of childcare selected as well as the quality and stability of that care.

Stability
With respect to stability, there is evidence to suggest that as many as 30% to 40% of very young children change care arrangements at least once over a one-year period (Moss & Brannen, 1987). Although Canadian data are not available, it is clear that infants and toddlers who are cared for by many temporary caregivers or who experience a series of losses relating to significant caregivers are at risk for later problems (Howes & Phillips, 1987). Raikes (1993) reported that infants and toddlers who had been with the same caregiver for a year were more likely to be secure in those relationships than those who were in less stable relationships. Similarly Howes and Hamilton (1992, 1993) and Barnas and Cummings (1994) have documented that stability of care is particularly important in promoting secure attachment patterns with children under 30 months. Despite the developmental significance of stable care and the associated stress and anxiety felt by parents and caregivers when arrangements fail, little is known about what circumstances precipitate the decision to terminate a care arrangement, whether some families are more likely than others to change care arrangements or whether changes are more common in, for example, center as opposed to family home care issues were explored in the present study.

Characteristics of Families/Mothers

Another objective was to find out whether families making different childcare decisions for their infants and toddlers have different health, psychological, or social needs before care begins. We cannot change family income, family type, or the ages of children in different care arrangements. But if families with different needs are choosing different types of care then parent support and childcare programs should address these issues.

Few Canadian studies have been reported on the health or psychosocial characteristics of families choosing different types of childcare before care begins, although Howe and Jacobs (1995) have identified a need for such research. Studies conducted both here and in other countries show that women who are returning to employment after childbirth are more likely to show higher career orientation and work commitment, stronger beliefs in sex role equality, less strong beliefs in the need for exclusive maternal care, and less dependence on others in decision making compared to those who elect to stay home and care for their infants (Hock, 1980; Morgan & Hock, 1984; Symons & McLeod, 1993, 1994; Vollig & Belsky, 1993). These attitudinal differences are reflected in different psychological needs. In a series of studies, Hock and colleagues have reported that the mental health of mothers with young children is related to both employment preference and status (Hock & DeMeis, 1990; Hock, DeMeis, & McBride, 1988; Hock, McBride, & Gnezda, 1989). Women who prefer to work but stay home experience higher levels of stress and are more depressed than those whose employment preference and status are consistent (home preference/at home or work preference/employed) or those who prefer to stay home but are employed. Mothers who prefer to care for their child at home but are working feel more anxious, sad, and guilty about being separated from their child. Women who experience increased anxiety related to their perception of separation effects on the child are more likely to use family home care than day care centers.

Although informative, most of these studies were conducted after mothers had started employment and their children had already been placed in an out-of-home care arrangement. Thus it is impossible to tell whether observed differences in maternal mental health were the cause or the result of having made different decisions. A recent exception to this design is the large prospective childcare study conducted at 10 sites across the United States (NICHD Early Childcare Research Network, 1997b). In that study, families were recruited when the infants were born, and the course of nonmaternal care over the first 15 months of children's lives was monitored. Results showed that those who believed more strongly in the benefits of alternate care and maternal employment at one month used more extensive and earlier nonmaternal care. However, neither maternal depression nor mother's separation anxiety measured at one month were related to age of entry, extent of nonmaternal care, or type of care selected. In the research reported in this chapter, characteristics of mothers who had made childcare decisions but had not yet either begun employment or placed their children in care were assessed in relation to employment decision (stay home or work) and preference (prefer to stay home or prefer to work) as well as type of care selected, age of entry, and quality of alternate care. Characteristics assessed included maternal depression, separation anxiety, health status, and parent stress. Given the discrepancy in findings between prospective and cross sectional studies, no specific predictions were made.

Child/Mother Interactions

Maternal characteristics are, of course, not the only factors that may influence childcare decisions. The relationship between infant characteristics or parent-child interaction patterns and childcare choice and developmental outcome is also not clear. Some studies have reported differences in infant temperament, parent-child and peer interaction patterns among infants and toddlers in different types of care while others have not (e.g., Belsky, 1988; Honig & Park, 1993; Melhuish, Moss, Mooney, & Martin, 1991). But once again, most studies reporting differences were conducted after mothers had returned to work and children had been in out-of-home care for some time. As Richters and Zahn-Waxler (1988) pointed out, it is impossible to tell whether the more difficult, insecure, noncompliant, and aggressive children found in some out-of-home care arrangements exhibited these attributes before they started care or because of their day care experience. Interestingly, in evaluating this hypothesis, the NICHD prospective study of early childcare found no significant main effects of childcare experience (quality, amount, age of entry, stability, or type of care) on mother-infant attachment security as measured by the strange situation (NICHD, 1997a). Maternal sensitivity alone and in interaction with childcare quality, amount, and stability were important predictors. That is, insensitive mothers had less secure children and insensitive mothers whose children were in low-quality, unstable, and extensive care had the most insecure infants at 15 months. Further, boys with extensive out-of-home care were at higher risk of insecurity.

Hypotheses

Given the controversy over the relationship between attachment security and early infant care, we designed our study to allow examination of the role of precare family and child characteristics in childcare decisions and attachment security and used an analysis plan modeled after that employed in the NICHD study as much as possible. Following the NICHD study (1997a), two types of hypotheses were tested with respect to attachment security. One hypothesis predicted that characteristics of out-of-home childcare (i.e., early, extensive, unstable, low-quality) would increase the risk of insecure mother-infant attachment independent of family or child characteristics. In addition, another hypothesis predicted that childcare variables would interact with either or both child and family characteristics. For example, high-quality care could reduce the risk of insecure infant-mother attachment security for difficult temperament, male children with insensitive mothers.

Description of the Study

Participants

Families with infants between 2 and 30 months of age (101 male, 88 female), who had experienced little or no previous out-of-home care at the time the study began, were included. Of the children 52.4% were first-born and 47.6% were later-born. Participating families were visited two to three weeks before starting full-time day care and followed throughout the first six months of care. Four types of care arrangements were studied: a) parent care, b) center care, c) licensed family home care, and d) care by an unlicensed babysitter, which we called independent home care. These four represent the full range of infant care options in Canada, with the exception of care by relatives or nannies in the child's own home. The latter groups were excluded since current quality of care measures were not designed for use in the infant's own home, and we could not control or easily measure the nature or extent of previous relative contact with the child.

Families in the Ottawa-Carleton region of Eastern Ontario, Canada, were recruited over an 18 month period. This geographic region was selected because the population was large enough to support the study, all types of care under study were available, and demographic characteristics of the area (e.g., ethnic origin, age distribution, income) parallel those for Canada as a whole. Data were collected from 1992 through 1994.

Of the 128 caregivers involved, 55 were employed at 25 different childcare centers, 34 worked in their own homes under the supervision of a licensed family day care agency and 39 worked independently, providing care in their own homes. Caregivers and parents were similar in educational background and SES. Both groups were, on average, well educated (completed high school, some university), and the sample as a whole represents a middle-class income group, although lower and upper income groups were represented. Forty-four families qualified for childcare subsidy. Mothers' ages ranged from 14 to 43 years (M = 30.6) and 16.9% of the sample were single parents. Caregivers' ages ranged from 22 to 58 years (M = 33.4), and 74.8 % of caregivers were married or living with a partner. Caregivers in licensed family home care were older, less educated, and worked longer hours than caregivers working in day care centers or providing independent family home care. Caregivers in centers were generally paid better than caregivers in other settings, but because they were also more likely to be single, household incomes across caregivers from different care settings were not significantly different. Complete attachment security data were available for 120 families.

Measurement and Analysis

Families were visited before out-of-home care was begun and then monitored for six months. The information reported on in this chapter was obtained at different times during the course of the study. First, a home visit occurred two to three weeks before out-of-home care was to begin. Parent care families were matched for age of child and SES as closely as possible and visited at the same times as those families using other forms of care. The measures obtained during the first home visit (before care) included maternal age, education, occupation, family income, employment preference ('If you had a choice of being employed or staying home, which would you choose?'), child age, birth order, sex, temperament (Infant Characteristics Questionnaire, ICQ; Bates, Freeland & Lounsbury, 1979; Bates & Bales, 1984; Frankel & Bates, 1990; Lee & Bates, 1985), maternal depression (Center for Epidemiologic Studies Depression Scale (CES-D); Radloff, 1977), maternal health status (General Measure of Illness (GMI); Michalos, 1978), maternal separation anxiety (Maternal Separation Anxiety Scale (MSAS); Hock, McBride, & Gnezda, 1989), parent stress (Parenting Stress Index (PSI); Abidin, 1990), maternal sensitivity (Parent-Infant Observation Under Stress (PIOUS); McKim, Stuart, & O'Connor, 1996), child reactivity (Parent-Infant Observation Under Stress (PIOUS); McKim, Stuart, & O'Connor, 1996), child health status (Child

General Measure of Illness, (CGMI); based on Michalos, 1978), child distress episodes (St James-Roberts & Halil, 1991), and night-waking.

Second, at one month after out-of-home care had begun or a new care arrangement started, childcare centers and family home care settings were visited and rated by an independent observer on either the Infant-Toddler Environment Rating Scale (ITERS; Harms, Cryer, & Clifford, 1990) or the Family Day Care Rating Scale (FDCRS; Harms & Clifford, 1989).

Third, if a change in care arrangement was made at any time during the six month period, parents and caregivers were interviewed independently by telephone about the change. All families were telephoned every two weeks. When parents or caregivers informed us of an impending or recent change in care arrangements, both parent and caregiver (for out-of-home care groups) participated in a structured interview independently to determine (a) who initiated the change; (b) why the change was initiated; (c) whether and how much advance notice was given; (d) what type of new childcare arrangement was made; and (e) how the parent/caregiver felt about the change. Finally, at six months after care had begun, attachment security was assessed by having mothers complete the Attachment Q-Set (AQS) for those infants who were at least 12-months old at the 6-month mark.

Two separate but related sets of analyses were conducted. First, using the information provided by families in the first home visit before out-of-home care, a series of analyses identified family and child characteristics related to childcare decisions (employment preference/decision, type of care, age of entry, quality of care, change in care).

The second set of analyses were designed to assess the relationships among childcare characteristics (type, quality, extent of care, stability, and age of entry), family/child characteristics, and infant-mother attachment security.

Findings and Discussion

To Work or Not to Work Outside the Home?
To determine the effects of conflict between employment preference and employment decision on childcare decisions, women were divided into four groups on the basis of their responses to questions during the first home visit (i.e., before any were employed): Group 1, Employment preference/employment decision (n = 53); Group 2, Employment preference/home decision (n = 14); Group 3, Home preference/employment decision (n = 63); Group 4, Home preference/home decision (n = 56).

A direct discriminant function analysis addressed whether employment decision and preference groups differed as a function of other family and child pre-care characteristics. Because Group 2 (employment preference/home decision) had such a small n (i.e., 14), the analysis was conducted with three groups only (Group 1, employment preference/employment decision; Group 3, home preference/employment decision; Group 4, home preference/home decision).

Mothers preferring and choosing to stay home (Group 4) were convinced that they "would resent their jobs if it meant they had to be separated from their children" and were more worried about the effects of separation on their children than mothers who had both decided to work and preferred to work outside the home (Group 1).

Maternal depression was the strongest predictor loading on the second function. Mothers who preferred to stay home but who had decided to work (Group 3) were significantly more depressed than those whose decision and preference to stay home were consistent (Group 4).

Interestingly, Group 2 (employment preference/home decision) appeared to be like Group 3 (home preference/employment decision) in that they seemed more depressed. However, Group 2 were like Group 1 (employment preference/employment decision), showing less separated anxiety than both home preference groups (groups 3 and 4).

Thus, in support of Hock's findings (Hock & DeMeis, 1990; Hock, et al., 1988, 1989), maternal separation anxiety and depression distinguished employment preference/decision groups. Those whose decision to work outside the home was complemented by their employment preference (i.e., Group 1, Employment preference/employed, Group 4, Home preference/home) appeared less depressed than those whose decisions and preferences were not complementary (i.e., Group 2, Employment preference/home; Group 3, Home preference/employed). Interestingly, Hock and DeMeis' (1990) Group 3 were not significantly more depressed than either Group 1 or 4. Our results suggest that it is complementarity of employment preference and decision that is critical in determining maternal mental health. Even though groups 1 and 4 differed in that they had different perspectives on motherhood (e.g., home preference/home mothers were more anxious about separation, more invested in the maternal role and less career-oriented than employment preference/employed mothers), they were similar in that their preference and investment in motherhood and career were consistent.

What Type of Care and When?

Discriminant function analyses were conducted to determine (a) whether family pre-care characteristics could predict type of childcare selected (day care center, licensed family home care, independent home care) and (b) whether pre-care family characteristics could distinguish those electing early (<12 months) from later (>12 months) entry to out-of-home care.

With respect to type of care, only one function accounting for 83% of between groups variance was significant. It separated those choosing center care from those selecting licensed or independent family home care. Parents using either type of family home care (licensed or independent) had higher household incomes and were observed to be more sensitive to their child's needs in a mildly stressful situation than parents choosing center care. For age of entry, household income and mother's depression had significant loadings on the discriminant function separating early (<12 months) from later entry (>12 months). These results are consistent with previous research in that low-income families were more likely to opt for center-based care where subsidies were more readily available and mothers in families with higher household income began using alternate care sooner after childbirth (e.g., National Childcare Information Center, 1994; Symons & McLeod, 1993).

Quality of Care
The Infant and Toddler Rating Scale (ITERS) mean total ratings ranged from 4.82 to 6.43, while the Family Day Care Rating Scale (FDCRS) mean total ratings ranged from 3.36 to 6.49. No center or family home care setting (licensed or independent) received a rating associated with "inadequate" quality. (Licensing standards are assumed to make it impossible for "inadequate" care arrangements to operate in Canada (Schleiker, White, & Jacobs, 1991). Ten centers (34.5%) were rated "good" and 19 centers (65.5%) were considered "excellent." Of the 30 licensed family homes, 3 (10%) were "minimal," 19 centers (63.33%) were "good" and 8 (26.67%) were "excellent." Among independent family home are arrangements, 2 (6.45%) were "minimal," 16 (51.6%) were "good" and 13 (41.9%) were rated "excellent."

Close inspection of the ITERS and the FDCRS revealed that, while the subscales have slightly different names, they are complementary. In this way our interest in determining whether family and child characteristics could predict differences in the quality of care chosen could be examined without being confounded by type of care (center, licensed or independent home selected). It is important to note that in this sample over 90% of all care arrangement received "good" or "excellent" quality ratings.

We did not find a relationship between family characteristics and quality of care selected. Whether this reflects relatively high licensing standards in Canada or simply that only high-quality programs agreed to participate in our study is not clear. Certainly these findings contrast those reported in the NICHD study (1997b). In that study, family income was positively associated with quality of care in family home care, and low- and high-income groups received higher quality care in day care centers than those from middle-income families. Further research would be needed to clarify this discrepancy since different measures of quality were used in the two studies. Interestingly, in our sample, unlicensed family home care, what we called independent care, was rated to be of no less quality than licensed programs. Clearly self-selection may have played a role here but these results do suggest that licensing *per se* is not necessarily a guarantee of higher quality care.

Who Changes Care Arrangements? Why? How?

We found that 25% of our total sample, or 39.5% of children who had started in out-of-home care arrangements, experienced a change in care during the six months of the study. Both parents and caregivers initiated changes in all care type groups. Children in Center Care were most likely to change to a new caregiver (38.6% of those in centers, whereas 31.4% of those in licensed family homes, 18.9% in independent family homes, and 2.9% using parent care changed primary caregivers). "Graduations" from one group to another within centers were common although many of these changes were not in response to licensing requirements (i.e., moving from "infant" to "toddler" rooms at 18 months of age). "Younger" infants moved to "slightly older" infant groups; and "younger" toddlers moved to "more advanced" toddler groups, leaving their first caregiver.

Excluding within-center moves, there were still 19% of the total sample or 30.8% of those who started in out-of-home arrangements who changed care, 52.8% initiated by parents and 47.2% initiated by caregivers. Parents' reasons for changes were mostly practical (the family moved, the new center or caregiver was closer to school or work, home parents started work, or a new arrangement was less expensive). However, 42% of parent-initiated changes were a result of dissatisfaction with the parent-caregiver relationship or concerns about chronic infections. In contrast, 94% of caregiver-initiated changes were caused by caregivers changing jobs, careers, or becoming ill. Whether initiated by parents or caregivers, 70% of all changes were not announced in advance (at least two days notice) to either the parents or caregiver, and 77% of children were neither told of the change before it happened nor prepared in any way (e.g., visiting new caregiver before the change). Parents received last minute phone calls, caregivers waited for children who just didn't arrive one day, and children did not have a chance to say "goodbye" or "hello". Both parents and caregivers reported strong emotions about the change. "Grief", "sadness", "betrayal", "anger", "guilt", "disappointment", "shock", and "frustration" were all mentioned frequently.

A t-test comparing the quality ratings of care arrangements that were changed to those which were stable for the six months was not significant. A separate comparison of quality ratings of care arrangements where parents as opposed to caregivers initiated changes was also not significant.

An examination of the relationship between maternal employment preference/employment decision groups and changes in care arrangements was carried out. Families where women were employed but preferred to stay at home (Group 3) were more likely to have changed care arrangements than any other group (57.45% of all those who changed). Three Group 3 families actually changed care arrangements twice during the six months of the study. Only one women who preferred parent care and had stayed home made a change. Depressed mothers of first-borns were more likely to have changed care arrangements in the first six months of care.

The Significance of Maternal/Psychological Characteristics

The finding that children of Group 3 mothers (home preference/employed) were more likely than any other group to change care arrangements during the six months of the study provides further support for the importance of addressing employment preference among those seeking out-of-home care for their children. Given that depressed mothers of first-borns who were employed but preferred to stay home were more likely to experience changes in care arrangements highlights the possibility that maternal psychological characteristics and not characteristics of care itself such as quality, convenience, and cost play a role in decisions to change care arrangements. Contrary to the NICHD study, household income was not related to stability of care. To the extent that these results are replicated, it appears that access to stable care is not linked to income. Certainly, whatever the underlying causes of changes in care arrangements, both caregivers and parents could do a much better job at easing the transition from one care arrangement to another than was evident in the present study.

Does Infant Care Jeopardize Infant-Mother Attachment Security?

A hierarchical regression analysis was performed to determine which characteristics (i.e., child, mother, or day care) significantly predicted attachment security among children receiving out-of-home care. The contribution of childcare variables was assessed by entering a block of four measures: quality of care (standardized ITERS or FDCRS total scores), stability of care (whether there had been a change in caregiver), extent of care (hours per week in out-of-home care), and age of entry (months). Both individually and as a set, these variables did not significantly predict attachment security. These findings are consistent with the NICHD study (1997a) in that neither type of care (parent care, center care, licensed family home care, independent family home care) nor childcare characteristics alone were associated with mother-infant attachment security.

Early (before 12 months), unstable, or lower quality care did not increase the probability of insecurity, and unstable, high-quality care did not contribute to secure mother-infant relationships. Others have reported strong relationships between stability of care and attachment security (Suwalsky, Zaslow, Klein, & Rabiovich, 1986) peer competence (Howes & Stewart, 1987) and behavior problems in preschool and kindergarten (Howes, 1988; Howes & Hamilton, 1993). But in these studies outcome measures were obtained at longer intervals than in the present study. It is an empirical question as to whether the children in this study will show problems later that are related to instable care-giving histories. While these results are different from earlier reports, the NICHD Early Childhood Research Network has argued that the population of families using infant care now is different from those who participated in those earlier studies. Use of infant care now involves a majority of the population and families may have adjusted expectations and family relationships to accommodate. The strength of these findings is further increased by the fact that, while our results are similar to those reported in the NICHD study, we used somewhat different measures as our measure of attachment security (i.e., maternal Q-Sort versus Ainsworth Strange Situation), and both were prospective studies.

After accounting for the influence of care characteristics, the relative contribution of both child characteristics (sex, temperament) and family characteristics (maternal sensitivity, depression, stress, health, and household income) to the prediction of attachment security was assessed in a stepwise procedure.

Only two variables significantly predicted attachment security, namely child temperament (i.e., difficult children were less secure) and maternal sensitivity (i.e., insensitive mothers had less secure children). It would appear that attachment security has more to do with *who* receives the care in place of *whom*, but not the *kind of care* received. Overall, then, these results provide clear support for the main effect and not compensatory effect of child and mother characteristics on attachment security.

An interactional analysis showed combinations of predictor variables on children's attachment security. Attachment security is lowest for children of less sensitive mothers who have more exposure to alternate care. This finding is consistent with that reported in the NICHD study (1997a), even though the two studies used different attachment security and maternal sensitivity measures. Perhaps more sensitive mothers need less time together with their infants to establish and maintain a secure relationship, as suggested by the NICHD Early Childhood Research Network. To the extent that inconsistency in responsiveness is a feature of maternal insensitivity, it may be that infants with somewhat less sensitive mothers are able to internalize more predictability of relationship with more time together.

The interaction between child temperament and extent of care was significant. Coupled with a significant main effect for child temperament, these results suggest that whereas insecure mother-infant relationships are more frequent for children with difficult temperaments, security is enhanced if these same children spend more time in out-of-home care arrangements.

Contrary to the NICHD report that boys in extensive out-of-home situations have a risk of insecure mother-infant relationships, we found no sex difference alone or in interaction with childcare variables when predicting attachment security.

Summary and Implications

The results of the present study provide strong support for the hypothesis that psychological and social characteristics of families play a significant role in childcare choice, stability of care and developmental outcome. In this prospective Canadian study, infants and toddlers in out-of-home care were no more likely than those who were reared at home to be secure in their relationship with their mother. Rather, maternal sensitivity and child temperament alone and in interaction with number of hours in out-of-home care were important predictors of mother-infant attachment security as measured six months after entry into care.

Low-income families were more likely to choose center-based care, where subsidies were more readily available, and mothers in families with higher household income began using alternate care sooner after childbirth. We did not find a relationship between family characteristics and quality of care selected although this may reflect relatively high licensing standards in Canada. As well, in our sample, unlicensed family home care was rated to be of no less quality than licensed programs. These results suggest that licensing is not necessarily a guarantee of higher quality care.

When it comes to maternal mental health and stability of care for infants and toddlers, complementarity of employment preference and decision is more important than family income or whether women decide to work outside the home. Women who were doing what they wanted to be doing (whether working or at home) were less depressed than women who are working and wanted to be at home. Unhappy employed mothers were more likely to be dissatisfied about care arrangements for their children and consequently made more frequent changes in care. Thus, maternal psychological characteristics and not characteristics of the care itself such as quality, convenience, and cost play a role in decisions to change care arrangements. Our results suggest the possibility that the negative consequences for children of unstable care may be ameliorated both by more sensitive transition policies (e.g., longer notice and termination policies that respect the practical and psychological needs of caregivers, parents, and children) as well as policies in day care centers that allow individual caregivers and children to stay together through the early childhood years from early infancy through to at least three years of age.

Neither type of care (parent care, center care, licensed family home care, independent family home care) nor childcare characteristics alone were associated with mother-infant attachment security. Early (before 12 months), unstable, or lower quality care did not increase the probability of insecurity, and stable, high-quality care did not contribute to secure mother-infant relationships. Less sensitive mothers in general, and particularly less sensitive mothers whose children were in more extensive out-of-home care, were less secure in their relationships six months after starting full-time care. Difficult temperament children were less secure in their relationships with their mothers generally, but difficult infants in extensive out-of-home care appeared to be buffered against this effect. This would suggest that both mothers and difficult children benefit when day care can provide respite. Potentially sensitive mothers may have their resources taxed beyond what they can provide with a highly demanding infant. Sensitive alternate caregivers may both allow such mothers to receive a much needed rest and establish a second secure relationship. Further research is needed to test these suppositions and replicate these effects.

The central conclusion emerging from this research is that child and family characteristics play an important role in determining childcare decisions and their associated developmental outcomes. While our results highlight the importance of prospective childcare research, further research is needed to explore in more detail the processes that are associated with different developmental pathways through the childcare experience.

References

Abidin, R.R. (1990). *Parenting Stress Index* (3 ed.). Charlottesville, VA: Pediatric Psychology Press.

Barnas, M.V., & Cummings, E.M. (1994). Caregiver stability and toddlers' attachment-related behavior toward caregivers in day care. *Infant Behavior and Development, 17(2)*: 141–147.

Bates, J.E., & Bales, K. (1984). Objective and subjective components in mother's perceptions of their children from age 6 months to 3 years. *Merrill-Palmer Quarterly 30*: 11–130.

Bates, J.E., Freeland, C.A.B. & Lounsbury, M.L. (1979) Measurement of infant difficultness. *Child Development, 50*: 794–803.

Belsky, J. (1988). The effects of infant day care reconsidered. *Early Childhood Research Quarterly, 3*: 235–272.

Boyuk, K., & Lochhead, C. (1993). *Childcare preferences of Canadian Families*. Canadian Council on Social Development, Center for International Statistics: Ottawa.

Cleveland, G., & Hyatt, D.E. (1993). *The effect of price on the choice of childcare arrangements*. Proceedings from the Childcare Policy & Research Symposium: Occasional Paper No. 2: 89–99.

Frankel, K.A., & Bates, J.E. (1990). Mother-toddler problem solving: Antecedents in attachment, home behavior and temperament. *Child Development, 61*: 810–819.

Harms, T., & Clifford, R.M. (1989). *Family day care rating scale*. New York: Teachers College Press.

Harms, T., Cryer, D., & Clifford, R.M. (1990). *Infant/Toddler environment rating scale*. New York: Teachers College Press.

Hock, E. (1980). Working and non-working mothers and their infants: A comparative study of maternal caregiving characteristics and infant social behavior. *Merrill-Palmer Quarterly, 26*: 79–101.

Hock, E., & DeMeis, D.K. (1990). Depression in mothers of infants: The role of maternal employment. *Developmental Psychology, 26(2)*: 285–291.

Hock, E., DeMeis, D.K., & McBride, S.L. (1988). Maternal separation anxiety: Its role in the balance of employment and motherhood in mothers of infants. In A. Gottfried & A. Gottfried (Eds.). (pp. 191–227) *Maternal employment and children's development: Longitudinal research.* New York: Plenum Press.

Hock, E., McBride, S.L., & Gnezda, M.T. (1989). Maternal separation anxiety: Mother-infant separation from the maternal perspective. *Child Development, 60*: 793–802.

Hofferth, S.L., & Wissoker, D.A. (1992). Price, quality and income in childcare choice. *The Journal of Human Resources, 27(l)*: 70–109.

Honig, A.S., & Park, K.J. (1993). Effects of daycare on preschool sex role development. *American Journal of Orthopsychiatry, 63(3)*: 481–486.

Howes, C. (1988). Can the age of entry into childcare and the quality of childcare predict adjustment in kindergarten? *Developmental Psychology, 26*: 292–303.

Howes, C., & Hamilton, C.E. (1992). Children's relationships with childcare teachers: Stability and concordance with parental attachments. *Child Development, 63(4)*: 867–878.

Howes, C., & Hamilton, C.E. (1993). The changing experience of childcare: Changes in teachers and in teacher-child relationships and children's social competence with peers. *Early Childhood Research Quarterly, 8*: 15–32.

Howes, C., & Phillips, D. (1987). Indicators of quality in childcare: Review of research. In D. Phillips (Ed.). *Quality in Early Childhood Programs: What Does Research Tell Us?* Washington, DC: NAEYC.

Howes, C., Sakai, L.M., Shinn, M., & Phillips, D. (1995). Race, social class and maternal working conditions as influences on children's development. *Journal of Applied Developmental Psychology, 16(1)*: 107–124.

Howes, C., & Stewart, P. (1987). Child's play with adults, peers, and toys. *Developmental Psychology*: 423–430.

Howes, N., & Jacobs, E. (1995). Childcare research: A case for Canadian National Standards. *Canadian Psychology,* 36: 131–148.

Lee, C.L., & Bates, J.E. (1985). Mother-child interaction at age two years and perceived difficult temperament. *Child Development, 56*: 1314–1325.

McKim, M.K., Stuart, B., & O'Connor, D.L. (1996). Infant care: Evaluation of pre-care differences hypotheses. *Early Education and Development 7(2)*: 107–119.

Melhuish, E.C., Moss, P., Mooney, A., & Martin, S. (1991). How similar are day care groups before the start of day care? *Journal of Applied developmental Psychology 12*: 331–346.

Michalos, A.C. (1978). *Life changes, illness and personal life satisfaction.* Guelph, ON: Rural Development Outreach Project.

Ministry of Community & Social Services, Ontario. (1991). *Current and preferred care arrangements: National Childcare Survey,* Ontario, 1988. Toronto, ON: Childcare Branch.

Morgan, K.C., & Hock, E. (1984). A longitudinal study of the psychosocial variables affecting the career patterns of women with young children. *Journal of Marriage and the Family, 46*: 383–390.

Moss, P., & Brannen, J. (1987). Discontinuity in daycare arrangements for very young children. *Early Child Development and Care, 29*: 435–449.

National Childcare Information Center. (1994). *Status of Day Care in Canada,* 1992. Ottawa, ON: Ministry of Supply and Services, Canada.

NICHD, Early Childcare Research Network. (1997a). The effects of infant childcare on infant-mother attachment security: Results of the NICHD study of early childcare. *Child Development, 68(5)*: 860–879.

NICHD, Early Childcare Research Network. (1997b). Familial factors associated with the characteristics of nonmaternal care for infants. *Journal of Marriage and the Family, 59*: 389–408.

Radloff, L.S. (1977). The CES-D Scale: A self-report depression scale for the general population. *Applied Psychological Measurement, 1*: 385–401.

Raikes, H. (1993). Relationship duration in infant care: Time with high-ability teacher and infant-teacher attachment. *Early Childhood Research Quarterly, 8(3)*: 309–325.

Richters, J.E., & Zahn-Waxler, C. (1988). The infant day care controversy: Current status and future directions. *Early Childhood Research Quarterly, 3*: 319–336.

Schliecker, E., White, D.R., & Jacobs, E. (1991). The role of day care quality In prediction of children's vocabulary. *Canadian Journal of Behavioral Science,* 23(1): 12–24.

Statistics Canada. (1992). *Canadian families and their childcare arrangements: The Canadian National Childcare Study.* Ottawa, ON: Statistics Canada.

St James-Roberts, I., & Halil, T. (1991). Infant crying patterns in the first year: Normal community and clinical findings. *Journal of Child Psychology and Psychiatry, 32(6)*: 951–968.

Suwalsky, J., Zaslow, M., Klein, R.P., & Rabiovich, B.A. (1986, September). *Continuity of substitute care in relation to Infant-mother attachment.* Paper presented at the meeting of the American Psychological Association, Washington, DC.

Symons, D.K., & McLeod, P.J. (1993). Maternal employment plans and outcomes after the birth of an infant in a Canadian sample. *Family Relations, 42*: 442–446.

Symons, D.K., & McLeod, P.J. (1994). Maternal, infant, and occupational characteristics that predict postpartum employment patterns. *Infant Behavior and Development, 17*: 71–82.

Vollig, B.L., & Belsky, J. (1993). Parent, infant, and contextual characteristics related to maternal employment decisions in the first year of infancy, *Family Relations, 42*: 109–124.

Waite, L., Leibowitz, A., & Witsberger, C. (1991). What parents pay for: Childcare characteristics, quality and costs. *Journal of Social Issues,* 47(2): 33–48.

White, D., Parent, M.B., Change, H., & Spindler, J. (1992). Parental selection of quality childcare. *Canadian Journal of Research in Early Childhood Education,* 3,(2): 101–108.

Chapter 10

Empowering Children to Learn and Grow—*Te Whāriki*: The New Zealand Early Childhood National Curriculum

Helen May
Margaret Carr

Abstract

This chapter appraises the development of the New Zealand early childhood national curriculum document *Te Whāriki* within the broader international context of governmental interest in curriculum across the education sectors. The philosophical framework, development process, and early implementation of *Te Whāriki* is outlined as a case study showing how the early childhood communities cooperated, firstly to protect early childhood from the downward inroads of a new national school curriculum, and secondly to articulate for the first time an inclusive national statement on early childhood curriculum. Whether this curriculum, which survived the political process "against the odds", is able to make a real difference for children is still dependent on a broader fabric of government support for early childhood services.

Introduction

In 1996, the Prime Minister of New Zealand launched the final version *of Te Whāriki, Early Childhood Curriculum* (Ministry of Education 1996a). Early childhood services are now required to demonstrate that their programs are operating according to the principles, strands and goals outlined in *Te Whāriki*. In 1991 the authors were contracted by the Ministry of Education to coordinate the development of a national early childhood curriculum that would firstly, embrace a diverse range of early childhood services and cultural perspectives; secondly, articulate a philosophy of quality early childhood practice; and thirdly, make connections with the new national curriculum for schools. *Te Whāriki* was released to early childhood centers in late 1993 (Ministry of Education, 1993a). There was an official process of trial and evaluation which indicated a high level of support within the early childhood community for the document. In 1994 the Ministry of Education contracted a range of professional development projects to support early childhood practitioners in coming to understand and work with the document. The Ministry is now funding two research projects to develop frameworks for evaluation and assessment based on the principles, strands, and goals outlined in *Te Whāriki*. There are, however, many issues for centers regarding the implementation of *Te Whāriki*. First, current low regulatory requirements and funding levels make it difficult for centers to meet the high expectations of quality outlined in *Te Whāriki*. Second, the holistic and bicultural approach to curriculum of *Te Whāriki*, which is inclusive of children from birth, is a challenge to practitioners who are more familiar with the traditional focus on play areas and activities for preschool-aged children in mainstream centers. Third, the current political climate of accountability makes more demands than previously on early childhood practitioners in relation to curriculum, assessment, and evaluation. Much of this is a new language for early childhood practitioners, some of whom (although not all) are volunteers, and/or are poorly paid and/or have low levels of training. There is so far little extra resourcing to support centers to manage the extra work that implementing a new curriculum involves.

The Broader Context

During the past decade Western governments have articulated more clearly the connections between the economic success of the nation and education. The intent has been to increase the skill base of the future workforce to ensure that the economy can benefit from sufficient workers who have a high level and flexibility of skills for work in the new technological era. Supporting this shift has been the impact of new right economic views, which have formulated the question of who benefits, and what are the benefits from government investment in education? Under attack have been so-called *laissez faire* progressive approaches to curriculum, which relied more on child and/or teacher interest and articulated ideals of individual growth and development. A number of countries have developed national curriculum statements that detail more specific content and skills, and usually require more rigorous approaches to assessment and evaluation. In the New Zealand school sector there was a dramatic shift in thinking between 1987 and 1991. The 1987 Curriculum Review (Department of Education, 1987) did not mention the economy, but emphasized aims for individual growth and development with learning how to learn seen as "an essential outcome" (p. 10). The draft National Curriculum of New Zealand (Ministry of Education, 1991), however, emphasized primarily the need to "define a range of understandings, skills and knowledge that will enable students to take their full place in society and to succeed in the modern competitive economy" (p. 1). It set out seven principles, three of which were explicitly to do with education needed for work or for the needs of the economy. These underpinned the later New Zealand Curriculum Framework (Ministry of Education, 1993b) which defined seven learning areas and eight domains of essential skills. It was amidst these initiatives that the government suddenly decided there would also be a national early childhood curriculum.

Governments had not previously been concerned with curriculum in the early childhood sector. Each of the different early childhood services (such as playcenter, kindergarten, childcare, *Kohanga Reo*, family daycare, Pacific Island language group etc) had their own approaches to curriculum, although the term curriculum itself was rarely used (Carr & May 1993a). In 1989 policy reforms established a common formula for funding, administration, and regulations across all early childhood services known as the Before Five policy. With government funding now reaching an average of 50% of operating costs of early childhood centers, alongside a new policy of a "seamless" education system from birth to tertiary (Ministry of Education, 1994), there was sufficient rationale for government to justify an interest in the early curriculum itself.

Early childhood organizations were originally wary of the idea of a national early childhood curriculum, concerned that it might constrain their independence and diversity. The alternative of not defining the early childhood curriculum was, however, a potentially dangerous one for the early childhood organizations: the national curriculum for schools might start a downward move, particularly as the government was introducing more systematic assessment during the school years. Our curriculum project at the University of Waikato, which won the contract with the Ministry of Education, was established in response to this latter concern.

Te Whāriki as a Curriculum

The development of *Te Whāriki* involved a broad consultative process with all the services and organizations. This was also the first development of a bicultural curriculum framework with a partnership in New Zealand. This was established at the onset with the Kohanga Reo Trust, which developed a curriculum for Maori immersion centers. The subsequent parallel framework of principles, strands, and goals were not translations of an another but revealed connected domains. The development process and the framework of *Te Whāriki* has been outlined more fully elsewhere (Carr & May, 1993b, 1994, 1996) but it will be useful to summarize its key features.

The Weaving Metaphor
The title *Te Whāriki* is a central metaphor. First, the early childhood curriculum is envisaged as a *whāriki*, a woven mat for all to stand on. The principles, strands and goals defined in the document provide the framework, which allows for different program perspectives to be woven into the fabric of the weaving. There are many possible patterns for this. This is a curriculum without "recipes" but more like a "dictionary" providing signposts for individuals and centers to develop their own curriculum weaving through a process of talk, reflection, planning, evaluation, and assessment. Second, it describes a "spider web" model of curriculum for children, in contrast to a "step" model (Eisner, 1985, p. 143). The "step" or "staircase" model conjures up the image of a series of independent steps that lead to a platform from which the child exits and at which point measurable outcomes can be identified. The *Te Whāriki* model views the curriculum for each child as more like a spider web or weaving, and emphasizes a model of knowledge and understanding for young children as being a "tapestry of increasing complexity and richness".

A Developmental Continuum
Te Whāriki defines three age groups (infants, toddlers, and the young child) but, consistent with the idea of the curriculum for each child as being more like a weaving than a flight of stairs, we do not see these as self-contained stages. We suggest that learning and growing during the early childhood years should be seen as part of a continuum linked to age but recognizing that development will vary for individual children in unpredictable ways. The direction and speed of development will fluctuate for each child on a daily basis. Where they are, who they are with, and what the children perceive as the agenda will all make a difference. *Te Whāriki* emphasizes that curriculum for the early childhood years must be able to embrace the everyday realities of rapid change, leaps and regressions, uneven development, and individual differences.

The Principles, Strands, and Goals

An early position paper from the project (Carr & May, 1991) described the process of choosing a theoretical framework or "guideposts" in terms of a metaphor of finding a tentative path through a forest. Coming to see that a national early childhood curriculum must be strongly grounded in the social and cultural context (Vygotsky 1978; Bruner Haste, 1987), and exploring the connections between this and notions of "development", became part of the journey. The 1993 draft of *Te Whāriki* detailed a number of sources of curriculum with the view that the early childhood curriculum is about experiences that are humanly, nationally, culturally, developmentally, individually, and educationally appropriate. The 1996 final document sets these within an ecological framework (Bronfenbrenner, 1979) with the sources of curriculum ranging out from the individual child as a learner, within their particular environment, to be finally shaped by a nation's beliefs and values about children.

We looked at early childhood curriculum documents from other countries and found another "forest" of possibilities. In the event *Te Whāriki* was a curriculum structured around aims (in the 1996 version these became strands) and goals for children in New Zealand. This was a model grounded in our own New Zealand social and cultural contexts, but where current knowledge about child development and learning shapes the principles, processes, and practices for realizing these aims and goals (Carr & May, 1993a, 1994). The theme of empowering children to learn and grow was established early in the curriculum development process and incorporates both the developmental and social/cultural contexts of the curriculum. This became a foundation principle. Three further guiding principles were established: that the curriculum should (a) reflect the holistic way children learn and grow, (b) enable children to learn through responsive and reciprocal relationships with people places and things, and (c) include the wider world of family, *whanau* and community.

A dual set of parallel strands in Maori and English were developed. They are not translations of one another but the domains of empowerment they describe are seen as equivalent in both cultures.

Mana Atua	Well-Being
Mana Whenua	Belonging
Mana Tangata	Contribution
Mana Reo	Communication
Mana Ao Turoa	Exploration

The conceptualization of an early childhood curriculum around these strands takes a different approach to the more traditional developmental curriculum map of physical, intellectual, emotional, and social (PIES) skills. Instead, the strands integrate all aspects of development by defining the major interests of infants, toddlers, and young children: emotional and physical *well-being,* a feeling that they *belong* here, making a *contribution* and being recognized as an individual, an interest in *communicating* through language and symbols and a capacity to *explore* and make sense of the environment. Each strand has been elaborated into goals for learning and development which were further expanded to illustrate what they might mean in practice in a variety of contexts: Maori immersion programs, including children with special needs, Home-based programs, and *Tagata Pasefika* programs. The 1993 document also included the implications of the framework for adults and management. In the final document this contextual elaboration was considerably reduced, with government favoring a more integrated approach. We regretted this.

Implementing *Te Whāriki* to Make a Difference for Children

Transforming a national curriculum into practice to make a difference for children in early childhood programs is the challenge and, like the weaving metaphor of *Te Whāriki*, the process is a complex crisscross of connecting threads. There is still a long journey to turn adult words into realities for children. This next section addresses the possibilities, problems, and pathways of this process.

The Ministry of Education's division of curriculum implementation coordinates the development and implementation of the new national curricula for early childhood programs and schools. For all documents there is a similar process of consultation and development, trialing, professional development, redrafting, and regulatory ratification and resource development. The difference, however, has been in the amount of resources that has been apportioned to support the two national curriculum documents. The early childhood share has been minuscule by comparison.

The Trialing, Appraisal, and Critique

The document, its philosophy and framework, has been well received (Murrow, 1995), although in the first instance some of the acclaim might have been a sense of relief that *Te Whāriki* was no "takeover" by the school national curriculum; that it respected the existing diversity; that it affirmed some firmly held beliefs about early childhood practice; that it was very much a New Zealand statement and not another import from abroad. On the other hand, it soon became apparent that the document was complex, partly because it resisted telling practitioners what to do by "forcing" each program to "weave" its own curriculum pattern. As Nuttall and Mulheron (1993) wrote:

> With the introduction of *Te Whāriki* many early childhood practitioners are going to be thrown headlong into a major learning curve. Although the principles of Belonging, Communication, Exploration, Well-being and Contribution have long been accepted in early childhood, the way they have been defined and, if you like packaged, will be new. It is a challenge for centers now to try them out. *Te Whāriki* resists the temptation to provide specific "recipes" for centers. (p. 1)

In *Te Whāriki* there are reflective questions linked to each goal to encourage practitioners to debate the issues. We were mindful of the research linking quality with debate and discussion (Penn, 1991), but we were also aware that many early childhood programs find such debate difficult if not dangerous.

The Ministry commissioned a survey of early childhood practitioners from centers (Murrow, 1995) as well as inviting responses from anyone who had read *Te Whāriki*. The summary report from the center survey concluded that:

> Support for *Te Whāriki* as a whole was very high, with the vast majority of the respondents supporting the document in principle or without reservation. Comments made were often highly supportive of the document. Reservations expressed by respondents tended to focus on physical aspects such as wording, presentation and binding, however, some respondents were concerned with philosophical or practical difficulties of implementation. (p. 28)

Two research trials with groups of centers were also commissioned (Dunedin College of Education, 1994). These trials confirmed a high degree of support but revealed some disquiet at center level regarding the process of implementing something new and conceptually different. A lack of time and resources put pressures on staff, and a new curriculum requiring considerable debate was an added burden. These trials made it clear that for *Te Whāriki* to really make a difference for children there would need to be a considerable level of ongoing professional development in a sector that still had large numbers of untrained or poorly trained staff. Similarly, it was apparent that government funding levels affecting such issues as staff turnover, ratios, group size, and qualifications were a significant factor in implementing *Te Whāriki*.

Te Whāriki has been in the public domain for three-and-a-half years during which time academic support was also strong but, given the assurances that Te Whāriki is likely to survive the rocky political process, it is timely for some more rigorous theoretical critique from academia. Joy Cullen has begun such an appraisal (Cullen, 1996). She highlights the tensions between the developmental and sociocultural perspectives inherent in Te Whāriki and expresses concern that much of the current professional development and training is being conducted by educators unfamiliar with the theoretical underpinnings of the latter. To Cullen the issue of training is a crucial one, and "for the busy practitioner, implementation of Te Whāriki is likely to be constrained by a superficial understanding of its rationale and implications for practice." Underlying Cullen's concern is the difficulty in achieving a balance between rigor and accountability for children's learning and the realities of an under-resourced and ill-trained sector that has historically been more *laissez-faire* in its approach. Cullen is uncertain whether what she perceives as perhaps the "soft" approach of Te Whāriki can deliver on the former (quality provision) given the realities of the latter (resources and training).

There has been considerable international interest, particularly in Europe and Britain, in the philosophy and structure of Te Whāriki as a national curriculum statement. Cathy Nutbrown (1996) highlights the emphasis in Te Whāriki on children's rights as a source of curriculum and also the respect for children as learners, which acknowledges the importance of emotional and social development as contributing to intellectual growth. The Early Childhood Forum in the United Kingdom, following the model of Te Whāriki, developed its own curriculum framework which it calls "foundations for early learning" (Early Childhood Forum 1997). This project was designed to counter the British government's own national document *Nursery Education Desirable Outcomes for Children's Learning on Entering Compulsory Education* (SCAA, 1996) which was prescriptive, content focused and skill based. Tina Bruce has urged her British colleagues to speak out and clarify for the politicians, "What we want for our children in early childhood. This has been done in New Zealand the radicals have been allowed to speak" (1996, p. 11).

Professional Development

During the development phase, the authors coordinated seminar workshops with practitioners and trialed ways of working with Te Whāriki in order to begin the process of each organization and/or center and/or teacher/worker "weaving" a curriculum that was appropriate to their particular situation using the principles, strands, and goals. Many people working in early childhood have not had much experience in articulating why they do things or what they do.

Since 1994, the Ministry of Education has let contracts for professional development to a range of organizations to mount a variety of programs (Nally, 1995). Within the short term constraints of the contracts, some innovative work has been done, which has facilitated debate in a sector where issues of curriculum, quality, program planning, evaluation, and assessment were often given scant attention. Implementing *Te Whāriki*, however, is a long-term process, and with the rapid changes in staff in early childhood programs and the high levels of voluntary and untrained staff, professional development will need to be ongoing, involve the whole center and be multilayered in terms of complexity and focus i.e., in relation to parents, management, supervisors/head teachers, and trained and untrained staff. At present the government investment in professional development is insufficient.

Training

A number of the major training institutions have begun using *Te Whāriki* as a framework and a resource. At the University of Waikato the early childhood curriculum courses have for some years been matched up with the five strands, and there is also a progression of courses that build upon each other in the professional strand of the degree:

1. Learning through exploration and play
2. Growth and well-being
3. Language and communication
4. *Belonging* and *contribution:* the social development of young children
5. Making sense of the world

In the third and fourth years, students move toward integrating the strands into programs

1. Integrating the arts
2. Planning and evaluating programs for infants toddlers and young children
3. Inclusive programs
4. Bicultural programs
5. Transition to school

In most of these courses, students spend time working with children in centers; coming to understand the child development knowledge and research as it applies to the respective strands; learning to plan programs using the principles, strands and goals; thus coming to understand the links between practice and theory, curriculum and research. In 1998 a new joint degree at Victoria University of Wellington and the Wellington College of Education started. Like Waikato, the curriculum papers are also structured around the framework of *Te Whāriki*.

Research

From the beginning we were concerned to ensure a clear alignment between research and curriculum in *Te Whāriki* and believed that research must be a powerful tool for "making a difference." There were two aspects to this focus: a) research on the various aspects of child development and learning, and b) research on the well-being and development of children in group situations.

In relation to (a) the draft document *Te Whāriki* included extensive footnotes and a bibliography. During its development and trialing phase we wanted to show that the ideas and suggestions had a research base that provided sound arguments to support *Te Whāriki* through a complex political process. We also wanted to provide practitioners with a rationale for why certain curriculum principles and practices were important for the well-being and development of children. In relation to (b) it was important to ensure that current research on quality was evident in the document (Howes 1987; Whitebook, Howes, & Phillips, 1989; Ball, 1994). For example, the sections for the Management and Organization of the Environment in the 1993 document drew strongly on research on the structural indicators of quality: i.e., staff ratios, group size, training, parent involvement, and staff stability.

The philosophy and framework of *Te Whāriki* is, however, both new and unique and it will be important that New Zealand-based research is supported; research that will evaluate and critique *Te Whāriki*; research on new approaches to training and professional development; and research that will develop for example, new ways of planning, evaluating and assessing programs using the Principles Strands and Goals of *Te Whāriki*.

The Early School Years

The government has a vision for a seamless education system from early childhood through to tertiary (Ministry of Education, 1994). The early childhood curriculum development is seen as an important part of achieving this process. As a consequence, it became important for the early childhood document to clearly articulate why and how the early childhood curriculum must be organized differently from the seven subject-based learning areas outlined in the New Zealand Curriculum for Schools (Ministry of Education, 1993b). It was also important to show how the integrated approach of *Te Whāriki* connected with the early school years. *Te Whāriki* outlines these connections as words in a document, but in reality there is a mismatch and disruption for children at age five as they move from early childhood programs into the early school years. "Developmental" play-based programs in new entrant classes appear to be a historic relic from the past as school teachers seem less able to articulate the value of play, or see play as a fill-in between the subject-based areas of the new curriculum. While these new learning areas of the school curriculum can be taught holistically and through play, many school teachers are finding the complexities and requirements of measuring objectives and assessment for each child for each learning area as a reason for a more timetabled and subject-driven approach. It is a dilemma for teachers in school, and the demands of the more content-based school curriculum may override (and run counter to) the demands of a curriculum like *Te Whāriki* that focuses on learning strategies and dispositions. Both are necessary.

Assessment and Evaluation

Evaluation and assessment guidelines for *Te Whāriki* have not yet been written. The research literature on assessment in early childhood is enormous, much of it spearheaded by researchers in the UK (e.g., Blenkin & Kelly, 1992; Drummond, 1993; Pascal, et al., 1994). A New Zealand Ministerial Working Party on *Assessment for Better Learning* (1990 p. 8) set some guidelines: "The primary purpose of assessment should be to provide information which can be used to identify strengths and guide improvement." Given a curriculum model that sees learning as the development of more complex and useful understanding knowledge and skill attached to cultural and purposeful contexts rather than as a staircase of individually acquired skills, the assessment and evaluation of children and programs becomes a complex matter. Finely focused "snapshot" assessments are inappropriate, and unreliable for the majority of young children (Barnett, et al., 1992). Given, too, a curriculum where knowledge skills and attitudes often coalesce into learning strategies, attitudes and dispositions, traditional assessments of observable skills become problematic. The idea of the individual assessment of children (often perceived as formal and written) is viewed with alarm by many early childhood practitioners. We regarded with interest the UK, SCAA (1995) *Draft Desirable Outcomes for Preschool Education* document, which stated (p. 7) that evaluation of quality will be based on a judgment "about the extent to which the quality of the provision is appropriate to the desirable outcomes, rather than on the achievement of the outcomes themselves by individual children." Observations of children will presumably be part of quality provision, and (although we have a framework of very different, and ongoing, learning outcomes that might encourage formative rather than summative procedures) this would be a useful guideline for New Zealand too. Assessment and evaluation procedures for the new early childhood curriculum will need to be carefully researched and discussed. In 1992, *Desirable Objectives and Practices* (Ministry of Education, 1992) were published by the government as requirements for funded centers. These indicated that planning and evaluation procedures must be specified, and provision must be made to discuss children's "progress" and daily program with parents and families. The revised and newly published *Statement of Desirable Objectives and Practices* (Ministry of Education, 1996b) state that evaluation and assessment practices must be in accordance with the four principles of *Te Whāriki*. This is a positive move. There are now two Ministry of Education-funded research projects looking at formative approaches to evaluation and assessment "in tune" with the principles and strands of *Te Whāriki*. Margaret Carr is coordinating the Assessment Project at Waikato, and Helen May and Val Podmore (from the New Zealand Council of Education Research) are coordinating a parallel but very new project on evaluation. These interconnected projects are, however, long-term and it is hoped that government has the patience to wait and get it right rather than impose inappropriate measures in this climate of increasing accountability.

Interest in the idea of assessing new entrants on their arrival at school is, however, of concern. The Ministry has recently released a *School Entry Assessment* kit (*Education Gazette*, March 10, 1997) on literacy, language, and numeracy with the content of the school curriculum in mind, and with what appears to be little reference to the *Te Whāriki* framework. If schools establish assessment criteria for new entrants that are significantly different from the learning goals of *Te Whāriki*, these will dictate a new curriculum for four-year-olds. It would be a pity if New Zealand started to move in the direction of four-year-olds either in reality or in effect being in a school classroom, coming under a national curriculum for schools. We should learn from the UK experience (Pascal, Bertram, & Ramsden, 1994). It will be important that the interface between early childhood and early school years be responsive to early childhood philosophy.

The Politics

The redrafting of *Te Whāriki* into its final version was undertaken by the Ministry of Education with only limited consultation within the early childhood field. Early on, however, the Ministry expressed an intention to retain the philosophy and framework of the 1993 draft, which had been so well received. Key aspects of the document such as the principles, aims (renamed Strands), and Goals were retained, but the Ministry's redrafting was subject to various "raids" with considerable relocation, removal, and a changing emphasis coming from pens that were not early childhood. One of the key features of the final version was a list of outcomes for children associated with each of the goals, although there is no expectation that they will be assessed against all of these separately. There was also an increased focus on the relationship between the national early childhood and school curriculum documents to demonstrate the ways in which *Te Whāriki* supported the learning areas and essential skills of the school document. A loss in the final version, as mentioned earlier, was the lesser emphasis on specialist curriculum contexts such as home-based curriculum, Pacific Island contexts, and children with special needs. In an attempt to integrate difference, the strength of these sections in the earlier drafts was much watered down. On the other hand, the early childhood community was relieved and somewhat surprised that the integral philosophy and framework of *Te Whāriki* survived such a complex political process. A collaborative and consultative process was a key to gaining unified support for the document from all organizations and constituent groups. This overcame initial political resistance because *Te Whāriki* didn't "look like" a curriculum. The Minister of Education would not allow the first draft of *Te Whāriki* to be called a "curriculum" because it looked so different from the national school curriculum document. The final version of *Te Whāriki* is a "curriculum".

Curriculum developments such as *Te Whāriki* sit in a wider political and educational context for achieving quality experiences for children. Issues such as funding, regulations, accountability, and training policies are also part of the fabric. *Te Whāriki* was developed on the assumption that early childhood centers would have the funding and the trained staff to operate quality programs. It will not be possible for the Strands and Goals to work for children in a satisfactory way under current levels of funding and minimal regulatory and accountability requirements. The early trials of *Te Whāriki* have highlighted this issue. The original Early Childhood Charter developed with the *Before Five* policy required centers receiving government funding to demonstrate how they were moving toward defined quality measures. These measures have since disappeared. Since the national government took office in 1990 there has been a gradual erosion of the *Before Five* policies (May 1992; Dalli, 1993). Most devastating was the halting of a four-year staged funding plan after one year, which left most centers unable to balance the equation of low fees, reasonable wages, and quality for children. The 1995 budget, however, introduced a new tier of funding for early childhood programs again using quality criteria as the basis (Ministry of Education, 1995). In 1997 further small increases in funding were announced for early childhood centers, but the overall amount of the "reward" is not large enough for centers to sufficiently address quality. In summary, "making a difference" for children through curriculum will depend a lot on the commitment and energy of staff and management in centers and programs. But unless the structural fabric is in place (adequate funding levels, quality staffing, and training requirements) *Te Whāriki* will be left high and dry and remain a document only. That structural fabric is the responsibility of the government, not of staff and management in centers. Without it, the new curriculum will not make the difference for children that was intended. Getting a national statement that protected early childhood from inappropriate curriculum expectations was only a beginning.

References

Ball, Sir C. (1994). *Start right: The importance of early learning*. Report for the Royal Society for the encouragement of arts, manufactures and commerce. London: The RSA.

Barnett, D. W., Macmann, G.M., & Carey, K.T. (1992). Early intervention and the assessment of developmental skills: Challenges and directions. *Topics in Early Childhood Special Education* 12,1: 21–43.

Blenkin, G.M., & Kelly, A.V. (Eds.). (1992). *Assessment in early childhood education*. London: Chapman.

Bronfenbrenner, U. (1979). *The ecology of human development*, Cambridge: Harvard University Press.

Bruce, T. (1996). Weaving links between New Zealand and the United Kingdom. At *The beyond desirable objectives seminar*, Pen Green Research, Development and Training Base, November.

Bruner, J., & Haste, H. (1987). *Making sense: The child's construction of the world*. London: Methuen.

Carr, M., & May, H. (1993a). *The role of government in early childhood curriculum*. In NZCER Invitational Seminar: What is the government role in early childhood education. Wellington.

Carr, M., & May, H. (1993b). Choosing a model: Reflecting on the development process of Te Whāriki, National Early Childhood Curriculum Guidelines in New Zealand. *International Journal of Early Years Education,* Vol. 1, No 3: 7–22.

Carr, M., & May, H. (1994). Weaving patterns: Developing national early childhood curriculum guidelines in Aotearoa-New Zealand. *Australian Journal of Early Childhood Education,* Vol. 19, No.1: 25–33.

Carr, M., & May, H. (1996). Te Whāriki: making a difference for the under fives? *The New National Early Childhood Curriculum,* Delta Vol. 48, Issue 1: 101–112.

Cullen, J. (1996). The challenge of Te Whāriki for future development in early childhood education. *Delta* Vol. 48, Issue 1: 113–125.

Drummond, M. J. (1993). *Assessing children's learning.* London: Fulton.

Dunedin College of Education (1994). *Te Whāriki Curriculum Trial.* Wellington: Ministry of Education.

Early Childhood Forum (1997). *Quality in diversity in early learning, a framework for practitioners* (draft version). National Children's Bureau, Goldsmith College.

Eisner, E. (1985). *The educational imagination: On the design and evaluation of school programs.* New York: Macmillan.

Howes, C. (1987). *Quality indicators in infant and toddler care: The Los Angeles study.* In D. Phillips (Ed.) Quality in Childcare: What Does the Research Tell Us? Washington: NAEYC.

Ministry of Education (1992). *Early childhood charter guidelines: a statement of desirable objectives and practices.* Wellington: Government of New Zealand.

Ministry of Education (1993a). *Te Whāriki: Draft guidelines for developmentally appropriate programs in early childhood services.* Wellington: Learning Media.

Ministry of Education. (1993b). *The New Zealand curriculum framework,* Wellington: Learning Media.

Ministry of Education. (1994). *Education for the 21 Century,* Wellington: Learning Media.

Ministry of Education. (1996a). *Te Whāriki: Early Childhood Curriculum,* Wellington: Learning Media.

Ministry of Education (1996b). Statement of Desirable Objectives and Practices. Wellington: Government of New Zealand.

Murrow, K. (1995). *Early childhood workers' opinion on the draft document Te Whāriki,* Research Section Report Series No.5, Ministry of Education, New Zealand.

Nally, P. (1995). *Professional development for the implementation of new curriculum in the early childhood sector.* Paper presented to the Sixth Early Childhood Convention, Auckland.

Nuttall, J., & Mulheron, S. (1993). *What's for Pudding? Curriculum and change for staff of childcare centers in Aotearoa-New*

Zealand. Paper presented to the CECUA Early Childhood Curriculum Conference, Christchurch.

Pascal, C., Bertram, A., & Ramsden, F. (1994). *Effective early learning: an action plan for change.* Worcester College of Higher Education: Amber Publishing.

School Curriculum and Assessment Authority (1995). *Preschool education consultation: Desirable outcomes for children's learning and guidance for providers.* SCAA Autumn.

The School Curriculum and Assessment Authority. (1996). *Nursery education desirable outcomes for children's learning on entering compulsory education.*

Vygotsky, L. S. (1978). *Mind in society: The development of psychological processes.* Cambridge: Cambridge University Press.

Whitebook, M., Howes, C., & Phillips, D. (1989). *Who cares? Childcare teachers and the quality of care in America, Final Report. National Childcare Staffing Study.* Oakland, CA: Childcare Employee Project.

Chapter 11

Landscapes of Intimacy, Sensuality, and Care in Early Childhood Settings

Richard Johnson

Abstract

This chapter investigates the issues behind the development of "no touch" policies for care situations. The author refers to his personal experiences; to narratives from teachers; and to analyses of textbooks to show how moral panic about touching and sexuality has prevented the appropriate discourse from emerging and has repressed the development of a "space" where human sexuality can be confronted and explored.

> To breathe life into the imagination, a language must be found for it. For what has to be seen, there may often not be words. Or if words exist, they may be the wrong words—words which place a wedge between the being and the telling. A space needs to be found where languages can be invented, words can be applied, a voice can be found, a story can be told . . some words may become little crimped tales told in small corners whilst others become shouted expansive stories told by people aware of power dressing. Here are matters of control over space, body, face, dress, eyes and touch (Plummer, 1996, p 43).

As early childhood educators we have all witnessed a certain type of *talk* enacted in our early childhood education courses: in our respective academic settings in the following field experiences debriefing we see an example of this "talk." This is a fairly typical debriefing period whereby practicum students share with the larger class a "real life" story they encountered out in the field. This particular "talk" is a story of sexuality, a story we all face each semester, which goes something like this:

Professor: Who would like to share a story from your practicum?

Student: Today at my prac I noticed one of the 3-year-old boys standing by himself behind a tree for a very long time. After a while I began to wonder what he was doing over there by himself so I wandered over to check it out. When I looked behind the tree I discovered the front of his pants were drawn down and he was playing with his, his penis. It was erect and he told me, 'It won't go down! ' I didn't know what to say, what to do, so I went to the lead teacher and informed her about this incident."

Professor: What did you say to the boy?

Student: Well, nothing, I didn't know what to say!

Professor: Well as you all know from your reading, this kind of thing is normal for that age child, especially for boys. It is called masturbation. All children do it, even girls, and it typically happens around age 3 to 4. It is part of normal, healthy child development so don't worry about it and don't embarrass the child. If you haven't observed it yet you will some time during your practicum experiences or while you have your own classroom. OK, now let's move on and talk about anti-bias curriculum!

I remember this type of interaction, this type of "talk," all too well when I was both an undergraduate and graduate student in early childhood education. Even if we got up enough nerve to share stories of sexuality, they were readily deconstructed by our professors as typical, normative, universal truths. Issues of sexuality were never questioned *("It is part of normal, healthy child development so don't worry about it and don't embarrass the child")* and always presented as unproblematic, "fundamental, invariable truths about the nature of children". Just as Stainton Rogers and Stainton Rogers illustrated, these traditional, dominant discourses of the field "are as true for the children of today as for the children of a century ago; for the children of Newcastle as the children of New York or New Delhi" (1992).

Like those past professors, today we continue to pretend that sexuality is not an important issue, that it doesn't exist for children and for the field of early childhood education. This ignorance protects us and keeps us theoretically safe. We do this at a time when we know children of all ages understand sexual life (Johnson, 1996; Lees, 1993). We do this at a time when sexuality has shifted from the margins to the center in many disciplines that are interrelated to our own work (Adkins, & Merchant, 1996). We model our early childhood practice as we model our sexuality interactions with children by assuming, "We have a need for children to be ignorant in the face of evidence that they know a lot about sex and birth and even about AIDS and death, we continue to insist that they don't know, can't know, shouldn't know" (Tobin, 1997, p. 136). It seems this need for children to be ignorant and innocent carries well over into our practices. As the text review here illustrates, we have a similar, profound need for academics, teachers, and caregivers (i.e., our collective selves) to be ignorant in their/our understandings of sexuality.

Touch in the Care of Young Children

Some of the fondest memories I have of my early teaching experiences are intimate memories that surround the physical touch(ing) of the children I cared for. As an early childhood education teacher educator I am very much interested in how teachers today physically interact with children in their care. I recently asked several groups of preservice early childhood students the question, *"As a teacher, in what ways will you be touching your students?"* I was pleased to find that the expectations my students today have for physically interacting with children mirror my preschool teaching experiences many years ago.

These are sample expectations my students shared with me, when they thought of how they will be touching students in their care: "cuddle to comfort; pat on back-affirmation; touch them to show support; hold hands; arm around shoulder; through hugs; changing diapers; hold hands on excursion; reassuring children through holding them; patting backs to help them sleep; to assist through traumatic separation from parent(s) some children will need holding; touch to give comfort; cuddle if they are upset; administering first aid if a child hurts self; tucking clothes in and investigating an injury; arrival and departure hugs and high 5's; sitting on my lap; dressing, feeding and toileting; restraining children for their own safety; to direct them to go somewhere; touch on shoulder; hold babies if distressed; spontaneous cuddles; hygiene; rubbing and patting back and stroking hair to help child to sleep; having children on my lap during carpet time; patting their head in recognition or praise; behavior management; playing outdoors (during gross motor activities I will hold hands to help balance, jump, slide pole, etc.; push on swing or help up into a swing; during game playing, like tag); and remove a child who poses a danger to others."

The expectations these teachers share are closely aligned with my notions of how we're *supposed to* physically interact with young children in our care, my notions of touch in early education (Johnson, 1997b). For I don't remember a day of work with two-year-olds when a child and I did not exchange some kind of meaningful touch. As a preschool teacher I always remember the joy of touch as I changed diapers, rocked children to sleep, and as children sat on my lap during storytime. While I directed an inner-city school-age childcare center, touch was also an integral part of all our collective staff-child relationships. The tide has shifted dramatically between then and now, as more recent accounts of touch in early schooling are informing teachers and children that they should both incorporate and follow written and unwritten "no touch" guidelines during their daily experiences with each other (Johnson, 1997b).

Now We Can't Touch Children

Recent personal letters posted on *KIDSPHERE* (an electronic listserve for early childhood teachers) reveal how common "no touch" is becoming in American society; in this first account a young male teacher personalizes his story of touch:

> "No touch" scares me because, as you all probably know, elementary students like to hug teachers, like affection, and do not want to be treated like they have some dreadful disease. As a result of my fear I do not touch students, except maybe on the shoulder or arm, and I do not show any affect except verbally unless initiated by the student first. I'm also never alone with a student, and anytime a student has a problem which may be sensitive, I find a female teacher (regardless of the child's sex) to assist me, so that a witness is there.

Another teacher shares:

> This is scary stuff. As a male teacher I have thought about this a million times. It always seemed totally unfair that the female teachers could hug their students, some getting hugged by every student every day as they boarded the bus. However, as a male teacher, I must keep at arms' length.

Lastly, a novice teacher shares some tips he *picked up* in his teacher education program; tips which he now incorporates into his pedagogical practices with children. They include:

1. never be alone with students, male or female, without another teacher or other students around;
2. never cover up the window on the classroom door;
3. keep the classroom door open as much as possible;
4. if there are problems in clothing-sensitive areas (such as one day when I had to help a kindergartener with his belt buckle and pants zipper in the classroom) elicit the help of a fellow teacher, preferably a woman;
5. always hug from the side—avoid frontal hugs whenever possible;

6. legally, keep a critical incident file for every student.

Like the above examples from the U.S., my recent research noted similar stories becoming more popular in Australia. Several months ago, Brisbane's *Courier-Mail* newspaper included a story entitled, "Sex-charge fears put men on the outer" (O'Chee, 1997); in this story a Year 2 male teacher is said to "live in fear of being labeled a pedophile"—just because he's a man, teaching in the primary grades. This teacher reveals that, "if his students try to hug him, he instinctively raises his arms and folds them in defense. If his students come too close while they read, he must try to avoid contact. He can never be alone with a child and if he wants to talk to a student in private, he also asks another three children to stay back" (p. 3).

A month later in the national paper, *The Australian,* an article appeared entitled, "Education Chief Backs Classroom Abuse Watchdog" (Brook & Glascott, 1997). In the article, the New South Wales Department of Education's Director General said, "We have to probably resign ourselves to the fact that the proportion of pedophiles amongst teachers will be more or less the same as amongst the community as a whole, regrettably." One week later the paper included another related feature story entitled, "Suspicious Minders" (O'Neill, 1997). In that story a man talks about walking his dog past a kindergarten and listening to excited children approaching him and inquiring about his active pet. He reports, "Ten years ago I would have stopped and talked to them, let them pat him. That day I gave them a wry grin and walked straight past when he later talked to his male friends about what he had done he decided that his reactions were by no means unique" (p. 9).

As revealed in these few stories, the moral panic of "no touch" is making itself internationally known and its effects are devastating. Many teachers no longer incorporate touch as an integral part of their experiences of working with young children. Indeed, the overwhelming power with which the moral panic of "no touch" has affected our abilities to *be with children* as professional teachers has also entered more personal (home) contexts. For example, just as a male teacher questions whether he can hold a student on his lap in the classroom, a father on KIDSPHERE questioned his parenting abilities in the home *("Did I inappropriately touch her vagina when I changed her diaper?").* Most recently I've heard several anecdotal accounts of fathers who won't bathe their own young child(ren) after the recent release of the Pedophile Index (Coddington, 1997) in New South Wales.

Touch and Sexuality

I now sit in disbelief, stunned, as I listen and learn about how childcare worker exchanges of touch are changing, right in front of our collective eyes. And while the notion of *moral panic* has been helpful in my initial interrogation (see Johnson, 1995, 1997c, 1997d) of much of the hysteria surrounding "no touch," another area which I now see warrants equal energy in this project surrounds issues of sexuality.

Broad sexuality concerns have been very much in the forefront of state and national politics in Australia and America over the past several years (Altman, 1995). Exemplar issues which I recently (1997) noted include the publishing of the *Pedophilia Index* in New South Wales, the governmental push to disallow lesbian women from receiving intrauterine sperm fertilization, banning same-sex marriages, and removing federal dollars from school districts that use curriculum materials that teach about homosexuality. Similarly, Duggan (1995) feels that other issues of sexuality which recently convulsed our nation include the "content of safe-sex education, the extent of sexual abuse of children in day care centers, the sexual content of public school curricula, and the funding of allegedly *obscene* art" (1995, p. 1).

More specific sexuality issues that have entered the field of early childhood education include implementing center-based policies that disallow men from changing diapers, widespread fingerprinting and criminal checks of day care workers, incorporating "good touch" and "bad touch" practices into early schooling curricula, our zeal to "stamp out" child pornography—to protect *our* children at all costs, and our all-too-ready willingness to portray all males who (desire to) teach young children as perverts (Johnson, 1997a; Pally, 1994; Silin, 1997).

In the 1990s we can't think of such issues as "power, the family, the organization of work, identity and politics" without a clearer understanding of sexuality. Weeks and Holland (1996) note that, "Sexuality is shaped within society, and in turn helps to make and remake the variety of social relations. A sociology which ignores the sexual will fail to grasp the complexity of identities, belongings, personal relationships and social meanings in late modern societies" (p. 13). Sexuality is a vital, necessary aspect of human experience, and remains a pressing social issue throughout our society(ies) (Casper, Cuffaro, Schultz, Silin, & Wickens, 1996; Valverde, 1987).

Textual Analysis

To gain an initial understanding of the ways that sexuality is viewed in early childhood education, I decided to study popular discourses of this topic (in this case, textual evidence) in the field. To assist in this process I reviewed content on *sexuality* from a wide variety of popular early education texts, most of which would grace the early childhood library collections in teacher education programs throughout the world. I chose these particular texts because many of them were used when I was an early childhood postgraduate student. Some of them I've used before in early childhood education "foundations" courses. They were available in several university libraries. The majority of them have been reprinted multiple times. These texts have holding power as knowledge sources in early childhood education.

In order to conduct this text analysis I looked up the word *sexuality* in the index section of each text. When that word/descriptor wasn't available, I then looked up related terms, including *sex, sex-role development, gender, social development,* etc. A brief review of my preliminary findings begins with a chapter entitled "Science Activities" in the book *Introduction to Early Childhood Education* (Hildebrand, 1986). In this particular passage the author shares:

> The handling of genitals, or masturbation, is generally a harmless activity and is often observed in young children. Masturbation may have various meanings, so a child must be observed individually so that the purpose of masturbation for a given child can be discovered. Of course, masturbation can mean the child is insecure and unhappy. However, it can also mean the child is bored and needs active play, or that clothing is too tight, teachers must have an enlightened attitude around shaming the child (p. 231).

Joanne Hendrick's book, The Whole Child: Developmental Education for the Early Years (1996), informs us:

> Today, when educational emphasis tends to be placed on the value of non-sexist education, it may be necessary to remind the reader that it is also important to teach children about reproduction and gender difference and to help them value their maleness or femaleness. (p. 353)

In the book *Behaviors of Preschoolers and Their Teachers* (1991), the authors share a multitude of narrative accounts. After each anecdotal account is presented, they debrief the passage. One particular narrative flows as follows:

> By this time of day I am ready to lie down on the cots with the children. Worked with Mark today, the child is strange like his father. Oh did he put on a show for his teachers today! I do know that he humps the cot as if it were some long lost female companion. My best advice to the teachers is to ignore his behavior unless it commences to disrupt the other children or involves them. After all, what does a four year old know except a bunch of sensations guided by an erratic mental compass (Carson & Sykes, 1991, p. 162)?

After this all-too-brief deconstruction of this observation the authors then advise the reader to,

> Ignore behaviors that are only minimally disruptive and that are of no harm to others. A teacher cannot expect to respond to every behavior of each and every child, so save your energy and attention for the more significant behaviors (p. 163).

Later in the text, when discussing issues of "what do I say when they ask me about boy-girl stuff" the authors offer:

> Just listen to them when preschoolers ask about boy-girl stuff. Adults often make the mistake of proffering up, usually with a red face, more complexity or depth than the child needs, wants, or can intellectually accommodate (p. 184).

In the text, *The Whole Child: Developmental Education for the Early Years,* the author (Hendrick, 1996) states:

> The more open and matter-of-fact teachers and parents can be about differences in the anatomy of boys and girls, the more likely it is that children will not need to resort to "doctor" play or hiding in corners to investigate such differences (p. 354).

To help further frame this critique, it is important to note how sexuality is positioned within the grand early childhood narratives, so well represented in the various texts reviewed here. The topic *sexuality* was not a stand-alone chapter in any of the texts I reviewed. Depending on the text, sexuality as a topic shares textual space in chapters that discuss multiculturalism, sexual abuse, social science, special relationships, and providing cross-cultural, non-sexist education. One text included sexuality issues within the "science activities" chapter. Further, the major headings or subheadings that help frame sexuality as important early childhood education knowledge/course content included the following titles:

1. Teaching Simple Physiological facts,
2. Masturbation,
3. Meeting the Special Needs of Boys in the Preschool,
4. Sex Role Identification, and
5. Gender Role Development.

The "sexuality" content I did find in these texts was dominated by traditional notions, which treat sexuality as simple, unifying, conservative themes (Foucault, 1984; McNay, 1991). As taught in these texts, as taught in our classes, sexuality in early childhood education is all about the normative practices of reproduction (i.e., penis and vagina), social studies (a text informs us, "thinking of it as a *geography* question can make it reasonably unembarrassing to explain that a baby is growing inside the mother's uterus or that it will be born through a special hole women have between their legs.") and science (e.g., another text tells us, "some children handle their genitals more than others. This is called masturbation. It gives children a pleasurable sensation and is sometimes comforting.")

In their recent book, *Rethinking Sex: Social Theory and Sexuality*, Connell and Dowsett suggest that, "sexuality is a major theme in our culture, from the surf video to the opera stage to the papal encyclical. It is accordingly, one of the major themes of the human sciences" (1992). Yet all of the texts reviewed here and many others steer well clear of using the word "sexuality" at all. One is more likely to find "toilet training" in the index, than the term "sexuality." The popular discourse around childhood sexuality is a discourse focused not on teaching *about* sexuality, but on teaching *around* sexuality—a process of erasure.

Progressing Forward

Referring back to the title of this chapter, and the greater title and underlying theme of this book, the "landscapes" metaphor is helpful here. Collectively we must discuss the types of landscapes we should be traversing individually and as a field. Like the reconceptualist movement in early childhood education, maybe the kinds of theoretical landscapes we traverse should be less planned, less tourist-like, and less predictable. Instead, we could be seeking out more adventurous landscapes, travelling through unknown spaces, willing to take risks and venture forth and see what happens (learn along the way).

Ken Plummer recently noted that "anyone who writes about sex these days stands at the intersection of a vast literature" (1995, p. x). The literature and research in the field of early childhood education seem to be distant from the "intersection." Even while critical issues of sexuality continue to present themselves in one form or another to our field (Dollimore, 1991; Haste, 1994; Irvine, 1995), other oppositional movements intent on "renaturalizing and reinstating 'ideal' or 'necessary' forms of relations with children and families" (Johnson, 1996) gain more notice, and are placed at the forefront. At the same time that a wide variety of issues of sexuality should have dominated the political front in early education, what we've focused on instead is our typical, traditional return to safety and normalcy (Grosz, 1995; Walkerdine, 1984). And so our *talk* about sex in early education "enables certain normative discourse to emerge and be sustained" (Haywood, 1996; Madus, 1995). These views run counter to the notion that sexuality takes on "many forms, patterned in a variety of different ways—and cannot be understood outside the context in which it is enacted, conceptualized and reacted to" (Weeks & Holland, 1996, p. 1).

As I noted in the opening paragraph, as a field, we (early childhood academics) have been ignorant of intellectualizing and theorizing many of the critical, underlying issues surrounding sexuality (Tiefer, 1995). We have indeed "ignored the sexual, failed to grasp the complexity of identities" (Bristow, 1997).

Given the strong movement toward "no touch" policy in early education, I don't believe we can continue to justify our efforts to physically interact with children, to touch, or take a stance against "no touch" without traversing the many "landscapes of intimacy and sensuality" in more critical, intellectual ways. Our now common exclusionary "no touch" pedagogical practices (Sibley, 1995), and our inability to critically interrogate and stand up to "no touch" policy has influenced the field in negative ways—directors are now likely to spend more money on liability than on teacher salaries; caregivers are leaving the childcare profession en masse; potential talented male caregivers are looking elsewhere for employment opportunities; children are becoming more distrustful of adults, especially teachers. When we can honestly recognize and confront our own diverse sexual identities and those of the children in our care, then maybe we can begin to move forward. If we wish to collectively fight against "no touch" policies, then we must be willing to intellectualize our understandings of sexualities (Eisen & Hall, 1996), so to better understand ourselves and the children we care for (Johnson, 1997e). Actively "seeking space for a story to be told", I want to leave off here by sharing a story, my personal story of touch and desire—a story about me and my infant daughter Haleigh. This story describes a daily interaction(s) for me, most of which takes place well after Haleigh is fast asleep in my arms at the end of a long stay in a rocking chair, just before she is placed in her bed for what I'm hoping will be a long rest.

> The sensation of the palm of my hand gently caressing her bare back pleases me and by the contented, rhythmic sound of her breathing she seems equally encouraged with this interaction. With her arms gently placed around me we sit together, mostly silent with the exception of an occasional whisper while I continue running my hands and fingers over her skin. It is with great intent that my hand

searches out each possible spot on this bare part of her body. At times she stops me by taking my hand and removing it and at other times she redirects my touch, again taking my hand, but this time guiding it to another part of her body where she prefers to be touched. Sometimes my hands and fingers roam quickly over her body and other times they pause long enough to briefly massage a part of her skin. Typically this gratifying interaction is initiated and led by me and tends to stop only when my desires have been fulfillled, but I won't speak for her, I can't speak for her.

References

Adkins, L., & Merchant, V. (1996). Introduction. In L. Adkins and V. Merchant (Eds.). *Sexualizing the Social: Power and the Organization of Sexuality* (pp. 111). New York: St. Martin's Press.

Altman, D. (1995). Political sexualities: Meanings and identities in the time of AIDS. In R. Parker and J. Gagnon (Eds.). *Conceiving Sexuality: Approaches to Sex Research in a Postmodern World*. London: Routledge.

Bristow, J. (1997). *Sexuality*. New York: Routledge.

Brook, S., & Glascott, K. (1997) Education chief backs classroom abuse watchdog. *The Australian* (February 20, p. 6)

Carson, J.C., & Sykes, D. (1991). *Behaviors of preschoolers and their teachers: Little children draw big circles*. Springfield, IL: Charles C. Thomas.

Casper, V., Cuffaro, H.K., Schultz, S., Silin J.G., & Wickens, E. (1996) Toward a most thorough understanding of the world: Sexual orientation and early childhood education. In *Harvard Educational Review, 66* (2): 271–293.

Coddington, D. (1997). *The Australian Paedophile and sex offender index*. Sydney: PSI index.

Connell, R.W., & Dowsett G.W. (Eds.). (1992). *Rethinking sex: Social theory and sexuality research*. Melbourne, Australia: Melbourne University Press.

Dollimore, J. (1991). *Sexual dissidence: Augustine to Wilde, Freud to Foucault*. Oxford: Clarendon Press.

Duggan, L. (1995). Introduction. In L. Duggan and N.D. Hunter (Eds.). *Sex Wars: Sexual Dissent and Political Culture* (pp. 1–14). New York: Routledge.

Eisen, V., & Hall, I. (1996). Introduction to special issue on lesbian, gay, bisexual, and transgender people and education. In *Harvard Education Review 66*(2): i–ix.

Foucault, M. (1984). Nietzsche, genealogy, history. In P. Rabinow (Ed.) *The Foucault Reader.* New York: Pantheon Books.

Grosz, E. (1995). Animal sex: Libido as desire and death. In E. Grosz and E. Probyn (Eds.). *Sexy Bodies: The Strange Carnalities of Feminism* (pp. 278–299). London: Routledge.

Haste, H. (1994). *The sexual metaphor.* Cambridge, MA: Harvard University Press.

Haywood, C. (1996). Out of the curriculum: Sex talking, talking sex. In *Curriculum. Studies*, 4: 229–249.

Hendrick, J. (1996). *The whole child: Developmental education for the early years.* Columbus, OH: Merrill.

Hildebrand, V. (1986). *Introduction to early childhood education.* New York: Macmillan.

Irvine, J.M. (1995). *Sexuality education across cultures: Working with Differences.* San Francisco: Jossey-Bass.

Johnson, R. (1995). The missing discourses of pleasure and desire in early education. Paper presented at the Annual Meeting of the American Educational Research Association, San Francisco, CA.

Johnson, R. (1996). Sexual dissonances: Or the "impossibility" of sexual education. In *Curriculum Studies*, 4 (2): 163–189.

Johnson, R. (1997a). "No touch" policy in early schooling: Now we can't touch children any more. Educating Young Children: Learning and Teaching in the Early Childhood Years, 3 (1).

Johnson, R. (1997b). The "no touch" policy. In J. Tobin (Ed.). *Making a place for pleasure in early childhood education* (pp. 101–118). New Haven, CT: Yale University Press.

Johnson, R. (1997c). "No touch" policies and the erasure of physical relationships in primary schooling. In *Perspectives on Educational Leadership, 7(3).*

Johnson, R. (1997d, April) "No Touch" policies and the erasure of reality in early education. Paper presented at Children's Rights: The Next Step Australian Conference on Children's Rights, Brisbane, Qld.

Johnson, R. (1997e, April). *Touching children: A valid part of the educational process or not?* Paper presented at the Queensland institute for Educational Administration Conference on The Legal, Social and Long-term Learning Costs of the "No-Touch" Policy in Education. Brisbane, Qld.

Lees, S. (1993). *Sugar and spice: Sexuality and adolescent girls.* London: Penguin.

Madus, J. L. (1995). *Unstable bodies: Victorian representations of sexuality and maternity.* New York: St. Martin's Press.

McNay, L. (1991). The Foucauldian body and the exclusion of experience. *Hypatia* 6(3): 125–139.

O'Chee, A. (1997). Sex-charge puts men on the outer. *The Courier-Mail.* January 28.

O'Neill, H. (1997). Suspicious Minders. *The Australian.* February 27.

Pally, M. (1994). *Sex and sensibility: Reflections on forbidden mirrors and the will to censor.* Hopewell, NJ: ECCO Press.

Plummer, K. (1995). *Telling sexual stories: Power, change and social worlds.* New York: Routledge.

Plummer, K. (1996). Intimate citizenship and the culture of sexual story telling. In J. Weeks and J. Holland (Eds.). *Sexual Cultures: Communities, Values and Intimacy* (pp. 34–52). New York: St. Martin's Press.

Sibley, D. (1995). *Geographies of exclusion.* New York: Routledge.

Silin, J. (1997). The pervert in the classroom. In J. Tobin (Ed.). *Making a Place for Pleasure in Childhood Education* (pp. 214–234). New Haven, CT: Yale University Press.

Stainton Rogers, R., & Stainton Rogers, W. (1992). *Stories of childhood: Shifting concerns of child concern.* Toronto: University of Toronto Press.

Tiefer, L. (1995). *Sex is not a natural act and other essays.* Boulder, CO: Westview Press.

Tobin, J. (1997). Playing doctor in two cultures: The United States and Ireland. In J. Tobin (Ed.). *Making a Place for Pleasure in Early*

Childhood Education (pp. 119–158). New Haven, CT: Yale University Press.

Valverde, M. (1987). *Sex, power and pleasure*. Philadelphia, PA: New Society Publishers.

Walkerdine, V. (1984). Developmental psychology and the child-centered pedagogy: The insertion of Piaget into early education. In J. Henriques, W. Hollway, C. Urwin, C. Venn, and V. Walkerdine (Eds.). *Changing the Subject: Psychology, Social Regulation and Subjects* (pp. 153–201). London: Methuen.

Weeks, J., & Holland, J. (Eds.). (1996). *Sexual cultures: Communities, values and intimacy*. New York: St. Martin's Press.

Chapter 12

The Social Policy Context of Day Care in Four Canadian Provinces

Mary Lyon
Patricia Canning

Abstract

This chapter presents a discussion of the results of a study of 48 day care centers in four Canadian provinces. The study investigated the relationships between center auspice, provincial regulations, geographic location, teacher characteristics, adult working conditions, family socioeconomic status, center quality, and child development. The results are analyzed from the perspectives of the distributional and constitutional dimensions of social policy that they reflect. The authors argue that, while different distributional allotments across provinces are affecting some aspects of center quality, a fundamental shift in childcare policy is necessary for the development of high-quality early childhood programs in Canada.

This chapter presents a summary of the results of The Atlantic Day Care Study (Lyon & Canning, 1995)[1], an investigation of 48 day care centers carried out in 1993–1994 in the four Atlantic provinces of Canada (i.e., Nova Scotia, New Brunswick, Newfoundland, and Prince Edward Island). The study was designed to compile a comprehensive picture of what day care centers in the region were like as environments for children and adults. Information was obtained on the overall quality of centers, the staff who worked in them, and the families and children who used them. The relationships between center auspice, provincial regulations, geographic location, teacher and director education and experience, adult working conditions, family socioeconomic status, center quality, and children's development were examined. The major impetus for the study was the need for research relevant to the Canadian context. The findings of the study are discussed and analyzed from the perspectives of the distributional and constitutional dimensions of federal and provincial social policy with respect to childcare.

The Social and Political Context of Childcare in Canada

During the past 25 years there has been considerable discussion about day care policy in Canada. Childcare has been the subject of a number of federal and provincial task forces and special committees. Plans for national childcare programs have been included on the election platforms of the previous two federal governments. Professional organizations, academics, and advocacy groups have entered vigorously into the discussion of day care policy arguing for national standards, a national nonprofit childcare system, and universally affordable, accessible childcare (e.g., Canadian Day Care Advocacy Association, 1994; Howe & Jacobs, 1995). This professional and political debate has resulted more in the *appearance* of interest and progress than in substantial improvements brought about by increase in public and government support. The proposed childcare policies of both Liberal and Conservative governments have disappeared virtually without trace. Indeed in the most recent federal election, childcare had disappeared from the political agenda altogether.

The political and professional discussion of issues relating to day care policies in Canada has not always been grounded in relevant Canadian research nor has it taken into account the Canadian sociopolitical context. Canadian day care research has increased over the past 10–15 years (Goelmen & Pence, 1987; Jacobs, Selig, & White, 1992; Lero, Pence, Goelman, & Brockman, 1985; Pence, 1992; Hayden, 1997).

However, most of the research that has informed the discussion on day care has been carried out in other places, in the U.S. (e.g., Whitebook, Howes, & Phillips) or in Europe, e.g., Palmérus, 1991). Implications from research for policy and practice in Canada need to be based on research on the Canadian situation within the social, economic, structural, and geographic contexts of care in Canada. There are distinct differences, for example, in social programs (e.g., parental leaves, family allowances, and social assistance) and in health care between the U.S. and Canada. There are also higher standards for licensing regulations in many Canadian provinces than in many American states. On the other hand, Canadian social policies for childcare and early education are more similar to those in the U.S. than those in a number of European countries where there is much greater government support for more universal programs for families and young children (Kamerman & Kahn, 1995).

Even within the Canadian context, different provincial regulations and policies, and overall regional economic conditions and political contexts, have direct and indirect effects on childcare. Canadian provinces exercise more control and power than American states. Health, education, and social services, including day care services, are under provincial jurisdiction in Canada with the federal government providing block funding transfers to the provinces to cost share services. Each province has its own day care legislation and regulations. In spite of federal transfer payments, there are wide economic disparities within Canada to such an extent that there are well recognized "have" and "have not" provinces. The former include British Columbia, Ontario and Alberta. The latter are primarily represented by the Atlantic provinces.

In most provinces, day care falls under the jurisdiction of departments of social services and/or health. Some provinces (e.g., Ontario and Alberta and Quebec) also have preschool education programs under the aegis of departments of education but nearly all programs, full or part time, for preschool-aged children in Canada are operated under day care legislation (see Friendly, this volume). In Atlantic Canada, day care centers provide virtually the only early childhood education programs although in Nova Scotia there are a small number (four) of kindergarten programs in inner-city schools. Many day care centers offer both full-day and part-day programs. There are also a number of part-day preschools that are operated under the day care legislation for fee paying parents.

The people of Atlantic Canada for the most part live either in small towns with populations ranging from a few hundred to a few thousand or small cities with populations ranging from 25,000 to 150,000. The four provinces have a total population of two million but cover an area almost four times the size of the United Kingdom. The economy of these provinces has relied heavily on the primary resources of fisheries, mining, and agriculture, and the region has traditionally experienced relatively higher rates of unemployment and lower wages than other parts of Canada. The recent failure of the cod fishery has had a negative effect on the economy, particularly in the province of Newfoundland where dependence on the fishery was highest. At the time of the study, the high rates of unemployment meant that many centers throughout the region were operating substantially below capacity, and a number who agreed to participate were closed before data could be collected.

Until government cutbacks in the 1980s and 1990s, federal transfer payments for education, health, and social services were weighed to maintain a level of equality in services across the country. However, the high unemployment rates and overall poor economy in this region have always meant a lower level of provision of all services. For example, publicly funded kindergarten programs for five-year-olds were only begun in 1991 in New Brunswick and still do not exist in Prince Edward Island. Changes to federal-provincial transfer payments makes these differences more, rather than less, likely in the future.

As in the rest of Canada, the last three decades have seen a significant increase in the numbers of day care centers and the development of day care legislation in each of the Atlantic provinces. Each province now has at least one college level training program for ECE. Within the region there are a number of one, two, and three year college programs and two university level programs. Provincial funding for day care in the region has been relatively low compared to some traditional "have" provinces. The reason for this is not necessarily ideological but reflects economic reality. However, unlike several of these "have" provinces (e.g., Alberta and Ontario) recent government cutbacks have not decreased the level of day care funding, and in at least two Atlantic provinces there has been recent additional funding for subsidies and salary enhancement.

Government Funding and Legislation for Day Care

Government financial support to day care in Canada comes primarily in the form either of provincial subsidies for fees for parents who are economically eligible, or federal tax relief for parents who pay fees and earn sufficient taxable income to claim the benefit. Both funding mechanisms, subsidies and tax relief, are employment-related. As a social policy objective, day care is funded as a service to parents to enable them to work or study and thus maintain their careers and standard of living or, at least, to escape from poverty. It is not funded as an education program for young children in its own right.

Childcare tax relief designates day care as an allowable deduction in the same way as other employment related expenses. Use of the deduction is strongly related to income level, and level of income determines the actual tax saving—the higher the tax bracket the higher the saving. Families with incomes above $40,000 claimed the deduction three times as often as those with incomes below $15,000 (Canadian Council on Social Development, 1993).

Provincial governments set their own levels of income eligibility for subsidies. These levels are very different even within the Atlantic provinces. For example, at the time of the study a family with two children that earned $20,000 per year would cease to be eligible for subsidy in

Newfoundland while being eligible for almost full subsidy in Nova Scotia. The number of subsidies in each province is determined in the provincial budget and is not sufficient for all eligible families. The majority of subsidized spaces are allocated to single mothers and are contingent upon employment or full-time study, with the explicit aim of moving parents off welfare and into employment. The only exception to this employment-related policy is children who are placed in subsidized day care spaces by social service agencies because they are deemed "at risk" because of their family situations. Only when families and children are known to be in great difficulty is day care seen as a children's program, independent of parental employment.

All day care centers in the region operate essentially as independent small businesses, generating by far the largest percentage of their income from user fees whether these are paid by individual parents or through government subsidies. Centers are operated under two different types of auspice. Approximately 40% of centers are operated by individuals as private small businesses and are known as for-profit centers. The other 60% are operated as nonprofit centers incorporated under community boards of directors and regulated by legal bylaws. All centers must conform to the same provincial regulations.

Auspice has different financial implication in the four provinces. Nova Scotia restricts the availability of subsidized spaces to nonprofit centers. In the other three provinces, subsidies may be used in both profit and nonprofit centers. Again this does not necessarily reflect different ideological positions between provinces, although at some point Nova Scotia made the decision to support nonprofit childcare. In the other three provinces, to restrict subsidy to nonprofit centers would mean that many parents could not use the subsidy because of the lack of nonprofit centers in many rural areas. Nova Scotia also provides salary enhancement grants and small equipment grants to nonprofit centers only. Prince Edward Island provides operating grants to all center's with a percentage designated for salaries. New Brunswick provides some small equipment and other grants but overall the percentage of government funding not in the form of subsidized fees is small.

Specific regulations respecting day care centers (e.g., for adult-child ratios by age and for teacher qualifications) also differ between the four provinces. To take the example of teacher qualifications, in New Brunswick there are no specific teacher training requirements; Prince Edward Island and Newfoundland require the director and one other teacher to have at least a one-year training qualification or the equivalent (in Newfoundland this only applies to centers with enrollments of more than 25); in Nova Scotia the director and two-thirds of the staff must have at least a one-year qualification (Childcare Resource and Research Unit, 1994).

The Atlantic Day Care Study

Sample and Procedure
The Study involved detailed observations and information gathering in a sample of 48 centers in Atlantic Canada with full-time enrollments of at least 15 children. The sample was drawn at random from provincial listings of day care centers. While the minimum enrollment of 15 is low compared to centers in most day care research, it represents the population of centers in the Atlantic region where there are a large number of centers with low enrollments in small towns and rural areas. The sample of centers included equal numbers of urban and rural, profit and nonprofit centers. Within each center a sample of 10–15 children aged 28–60 months and two teachers were studied. Four teams of two researchers spent a week in each of 48 centers conducting interviews, recording observations, and administering assessments.[2]

In addition, directors filled out a comprehensive questionnaire on center policies and organization. Parents of participating children were interviewed for information on family structure, parental education, employment, income, and their views on day care.

Overall Ratings of the Children's Environment
The mean ratings of centers on the Early Childhood Environment Rating Scale (ECERS) was 4.5, indicating an overall quality in the "acceptable" to "good" range. The ECERS rates 37 aspects of the environment on a scale from 1 (inadequate) to 7 (excellent). Almost 75% of centers received ratings greater than 4.

Measured by the two factors developed for the National Childcare Staffing Study (Whitebook, Howes, & Phillips, 1990), centers were rated significantly higher on measures of the human or interpersonal aspects of the environment (Preschool Appropriate Caregiving Subscale [PAC], mean = 4.8) than on the measures of the facilities, equipment and activities provided to children (Developmentally Appropriate Activity Subscale [DAA], mean = 4.0).

The two original ECERS subscales with the lowest mean scores were Social Development and Adult Needs. The Social Development subscale includes items assessing opportunities for free play, the developmental appropriateness of group time, the overall tone of the human environment, and the cultural sensitivity of materials and activities. The lack of provision for free play was supported by consistent reports from the researchers of difficulties in scheduling the videotaping of free play. Play was often directed or constructed in some way or seen as a filler at the end or beginning of the day.

The research assistants' independent ratings of the physical environments of centers indicated that many were far from ideal. At least half were rated as "dilapidated, or dingy, or in need of repair". Only three centers were in purpose-built facilities. Half of the centers were in spaces in other buildings (e.g., schools, hospitals, church basements) or empty mall, warehouse, or industrial space.

Differences by Province, Location, Auspice and Size

There were no overall differences in the ratings of centers in different provinces or between centers in rural and urban areas. There were significant differences in ratings on ECERS between profit (mean = 4.12) and nonprofit (mean = 4.93) centers. Nonprofit centers were rated significantly higher on total ECERS ratings and on all subscales. This did not mean that for-profit centers were necessarily of poor quality. Sixty percent of for-profit centers received ratings of 4, the scale midpoint, or above.

Nonprofit centers were on average larger than for-profit centers. However, size alone was not a factor in predicting ECERS ratings. When centers with large enrollments (31 or above) and centers with small enrollments (less than 30) were analyzed separately, there was a significant size by auspice interaction. Large nonprofit centers were rated significantly higher than large for-profit centers. There was no significant difference between small nonprofit and for-profit centers.

The Teachers and Directors

Many teachers and directors in the sample were more qualified than was required by provincial regulations. Almost 68% of teachers and 92% of directors reported some kind of postsecondary education. The majority of teachers (54%) and directors (66%) had some kind of specific postsecondary qualification in early childhood education. Of the others, a further 32% of teachers and 30% of directors had some courses or in-service training specific to early childhood, many of them meeting provincial equivalency requirements for training.

There were no overall significant differences in level of teacher education in centers in different provinces, in urban and rural areas, or in for-profit and nonprofit centers. In Nova Scotia (where salary enhancement grants are paid to nonprofit centers) teachers in nonprofit centers had significantly higher levels of specific early childhood education than those in for-profit centers.

Salaries and Benefits
The overall average salary of teachers and directors was very low at $14,255 and $19,100 respectively. Average director and teacher salaries were below the poverty line for a family, and many individual teachers and day care operators received salaries significantly below the poverty cut-off for a single person (National Council of Welfare, 1997). Salaries were significantly higher in the two provinces, Nova Scotia (mean = $15,668) and Prince Edward Island ($15,097) that provide government funding to centers for staff salaries. Teachers in nonprofit centers in Nova Scotia were the highest paid group of teachers.

Teachers with higher levels of specific early childhood education earned significantly more than those with lower levels. This was accounted for largely by the higher levels of specific education and salary in nonprofit centers in Nova Scotia.

In addition to low salaries, teachers and directors reported few benefits and poor working conditions. Only 16.5% of teachers reported having a written contract. Only 18% reported that merit and only 15% that cost of living was a consideration in the determination of salary. Few provincial or urban/rural differences in working conditions emerged.

Consistent differences between for-profit and nonprofit centers in favor of nonprofit centers were reported in working conditions and benefits. For example, teachers in nonprofit centers were significantly more likely to have health, dental, and life insurance and to receive financial assistance for training, paid preparation time, and paid release time for training and professional meetings. Teachers in nonprofit centers were also more likely to have written job descriptions, formal contracts, grievance procedures, and to have salary determined by merit than teachers in profit centers.

In spite of poor salaries and working conditions, teachers and directors reported relatively high levels of satisfaction with their jobs and careers. They were most satisfied with the nature of the work with children, their coworkers, and their work environment. They were least satisfied with the level of explicit organization and policies in centers, opportunities for professional growth, and salaries and benefits. There were few differences between satisfaction levels in for-profit and nonprofit centers.

Teachers in nonprofit centers were significantly more satisfied with the "clarity of roles" in centers as defined by the presence of clear job descriptions, written contracts, and written staff and parent policy manuals. Nonprofit centers had more explicit policies.

The Children

All assessments of children's language, play, social maturity, and self-esteem indicated a normally developing group of children with mean scores and ratings within normal ranges for all measures. During free play time, children played constructively and socially with their peers 70% of the time, were unoccupied or wandering aimlessly for only 3% of the time, and behaved aggressively or appeared distressed or unhappy less than 1.5% of the time.

There were no significant differences on any of the children's measures between children in centers in different provinces or locations or between children in for-profit and nonprofit centers.

The Families

Approximately 30% of families had incomes below $20,000, while 40% earned more than $50,000. Many of those at the low end were at the very low end. There were several centers with average incomes of less than $10,000. Approximately 33% of parents were single parents, twice the national percentage (17%) for single parent families, and of these 97% fell in the lowest income group. There were also centers with average family incomes above $100,000. Families in the average income range were underrepresented in day care operations in the sample. Overall there were no significant differences between family incomes in for-profit or nonprofit centers. There were differences within provinces. In Nova Scotia, parents in nonprofit centers had significantly lower incomes than those in for-profit centers, while the reverse was true in Newfoundland, a clear reflection of provincial policy for subsidized spaces.

Parents were, on the whole, satisfied with their children's centers. A large majority (98%) felt that day care had been good for their children, particularly for their social development. However, when asked how they chose centers, the largest single category of responses related to the convenience of the location or the availability of subsidized spaces.

Parent interviews were scheduled to last 20 minutes, but many parents talked for much longer and many reported anecdotes to illustrate the support they and their child had received from centers. Most parents (98%) were satisfied with their input and involvement in their children's center and did not wish to become more involved. This is understandable given the demands of work and home on families with young children.

Relationships Between Center Quality, Teacher Education, Family Background and Child Development

There was a consistent trend for centers with staff with higher levels of teacher and director education to receive higher ECERS ratings. The link was statistically significant only between ECERS ratings and the early childhood education of the directors. There was no overall pattern of significant relationships between the ECERS ratings of centers and measures of child development, nor between teacher or director education levels and child development. There were some individual significant relationships between measures which individually need to be considered with caution but which together may indicate a significant pattern. There was a significant relationship between the early childhood education of directors and the amount of social play engaged in by children. There was also a significant relationship between children's perceptions of their acceptance by their peers and the ECERS ratings of centers. That is, centers with directors with higher levels of education specific to early childhood education were of higher quality overall, made more provision for social play, and promoted better peer relationships.

Maternal education levels were the only significant predictor of children's language development, although there was also a nonstatistically significant trend for children to have higher Peabody Picture Vocabulary scores in centers where directors and teachers had higher levels of specific early childhood education. Previous studies (e.g., Whitebook, et al., 1990) have reported stronger links between center quality and levels of teacher education and child development. These results should not be interpreted to mean that center quality and teacher education had no effect on children's development. There were consistent trends for these variables to be related and the lack of statistically significant relationships in this study is probably a function of the relative homogeneity of most of the measures. For example, there was a more restricted range of ECERS ratings than in the U.S. study. When teacher specific education levels were averaged across centers, most centers had average levels at either the college level (26 centers) or in some courses at the early childhood education level (19 centers). Even with respect to family income, although there were some centers at the polar ends of the income scale similarly, there were not the contrasts in family incomes between centers seen in studies in large U.S. cities. In many small communities there is only one center.

Summary

The standard of care provided in these 48 centers was on average between acceptable to good. Centers were rated more highly on the human dimensions of programs than on the physical facilities and activities they provide. Most teachers had some relevant education. Teachers were very poorly paid but were satisfied with, and committed to, their jobs. There were no differences between centers in provinces with different specific regulations but there were advantages to nonprofit auspice, particularly in larger centers which seemed to be linked to better organizational structures and processes. Advantages of differential funding, whether by province or auspice, directly affected staff salaries rather than center quality. Clearly, teachers and directors are providing a hidden subsidy to day care operations in the form of low salaries. User fees, which constitute the largest percentage of all centers' incomes, cannot generate sufficient revenue to pay living wages to staff.

Discussion

What conclusions or implications can be drawn from these data? What recommendations can be made for social policy and professional practice? There are two levels at which these questions can be addressed. The first is from the internal perspective of the study, of these centers, or of day care practice. At this level there are some fairly direct and logical conclusions and possible recommendations. The second is from the external perspective of the social policy context in which day care exists and at this level the conclusions and recommendations are more complex.

From an internal perspective the following conclusions could be drawn: Day care in the region is reasonably good. Centers are of acceptable quality, the children are happy, their parents are satisfied with their children's care, and teachers are satisfied with their jobs. Centers were not rated as excellent, or even as good, but given the financial constraints under which they operate they are better than anyone should expect. There are aspects that could be improved and recommendations for policy and practice that could be made.

There were significant benefits to the nonprofit auspice particularly in large centers. These benefits appear to be linked to both funding and organizational factors. It would be logical to recommend that provincial legislation either restricts the size of private centers or ensures that appropriate organizational structures and processes are in place in all centers.

Although this study did not find as many significant relationships between teacher education, center quality, and child development as have been reported in other studies, there was a consistent trend for teacher education to be related to ECERS, and for directors the relationship was significant. It would be logical to recommend that legislation respecting teacher and particularly director education should be strengthened and that training programs and legislation for programs should address the concerns raised about the lack of play.

Physical environments were poor and teacher salaries were very low. It is logical to recommend that both need improving, but understanding what needs to be done in order to do this means considering the external context in which day care operates, and from this perspective the logic of all of these recommendations becomes less clear.

Taking an external perspective involves considering the results within the social and political context of childcare and examining the intended and unintended effects of specific policies (or the lack thereof). From this perspective the results of the study clearly illustrate the contradictions, anomalies, and ambivalence that mark social policy in this area.

For whom is day care provided? Clearly, at a direct level, day care is for children. Centers are licensed and regulated as environments for children. Those directly involved (parents and teachers) consider them in these terms. The teachers in this study viewed themselves as early childhood educators, evaluated their environments, and reported their job satisfaction in terms of their work with children. They presumably rate their own work environments highly because they consider them as environments for children, as on any objective rating: for adults they are poor, often lacking even adult chairs and washrooms. Parents reported that the experience of day care was beneficial to their children. Advocacy groups, academic, professional organizations, and teachers argue the benefits of high-quality childcare for child development.

However, childcare is not funded as a service to children but as a service to parents to enable them to work, either in the form of subsidies or tax relief. The impetus for the development of government direct and indirect funding stemmed from the women's movement and the movement of women into the workforce rather than a commitment to young children. The funding of day care on the basis of individual user fees, based on what governments and parents are prepared to pay for their children to be looked after, leaves the service severely underfunded compared to other human services in education, health, or social service. Poor physical environments, with centers often in spaces no one else wants at the time and poverty-level salaries for teachers, are direct effects of the contradictions of a service funded as welfare or tax relief but providing a direct service to children.

This contradiction determines both the very low level of funding for day care and the categories of families and children who can use them. Nearly 75% of user families in this study had incomes at either end of the income scale. Families in the majority income range were underrepresented. Not all of the missing families would be looking for full-time childcare. Some were presumably one-income families where one parent has chosen to stay at home. Others were using other types of care, care by relatives or unlicensed home care or part-day programs. Other studies have reported that many families have to make do with less than acceptable childcare arrangements (Lero, et al., 1985). From the perspective of the developmental and educational needs of children current provision is clearly inadequate. Many children are de facto excluded from any kind of early childhood program.

As noted previously, the start of the study coincided with the closure of the fisheries and a significant rise in unemployment in the region. A number of centers were seeing their enrollment sink dramatically, a number were forced to close, and fewer children were attending full-time. Children's participation in centers was directly contingent upon parental employment. This may be particularly significant given the economic insecurity in the region and the consequent effects on family security. Children are likely to be removed from stable day care settings at the very time when they and their families may need them most.

Over the past 25 years there have been developments and increases in the distributional allotments to day care (e.g., in subsidized spaces, tax relief, grants for salaries, equipment, regulations, training programs, and professional organizations). These are positive developments but their effects have been limited and uneven. The development of high-quality programs for young children which meet the childcare needs of parents, and the developmental needs of children in general, will require a fundamental shift in the constitutional dimensions of social policy, in the employment-related and targeted approach to policy. These approaches, in turn, reflect the lack of priority that early childhood education and development are afforded in social policy. Programs for young children as social programs are supported directly and indirectly as a necessity for parents rather than something desirable in their own right.

It is difficult to be optimistic that there will be these fundamental shifts in social policy. Established social programs such as health and education have been cut, and there is clearly neither the political will nor public support to propose a new universally available program. Such funding as is available is more and more directed to particular groups. Canada has a high rate of child poverty compared to other affluent western nations (Canadian Council on Social Development, 1993). The increasing awareness of this fact and of the long-term social, emotional, and economic consequences of growing up poor has led to a number of policy initiatives including community health programs, parent resource centers, school lunch programs, and direct financial help in the form of child tax credits. Such initiatives are entrenching the targeted focus of funding to children consistent with trends in other aspects of family policy in Canada (e.g., once universal programs such as family allowance and old age security are now income based).

The results of the Atlantic Day Care Study indicate that, while centers offer reasonably good environments for the children who attend, they operate under severe financial constraints and serve only certain populations. The differences between provinces in distributional allotments are not sufficient to make significant differences in quality, although nonprofit auspice is a significant indicator of quality in large centers and different funding policies affect teacher salaries. The picture that emerges reflects the status of day care policy in the country and the region. Improvements in distributional allotments to day care, while desirable in themselves, have not and will not lead to the development of high-quality early childhood programs for all children. This objective will require a fundamental shift in social policy priorities.

Notes

1. The Atlantic Day Care Study was funded by the Childcare Initiatives Fund, Human Resources Development Canada. The views expressed in this chapter are solely those of the authors and do not necessarily represent the views of Human Resources Development Canada.

    This chapter presents only a summary of the results. For a copy of the complete report please contact Dr. Mary E. Lyon, Department of Child and Youth Study, Mount Saint Vincent University, Halifax, Nova Scotia, Canada B3M 2J6 E-mail: Mary.Lyon@MSVU.Ca

2. All differences reported as significant were significant at the $p < .05$ level or above. The measures for assessing day care centers included:

    1. The Early Childhood Environment Rating Scale (ECERS) (Harms & Clifford, 1980);
    2. The Early Childhood Work Environment Scale (Jorde-Bloom, 1985);
    3. The Early Childhood Job Satisfaction Scale (Jorde-Bloom, 1988);
    4. The Minnesota Job Satisfaction Scale (Vocational Psychology Research, 1963);
    5. The Peabody Picture Vocabulary Test (Dunn, 1984);
    6. The Adaptive Language Inventory (Feagans & Farran, 1979);
    7. The Pictorial Scale of Perceived Competence & Social Acceptance for Young Children (Harter & Pike, 1984);
    8. The Entwistle Personal Maturity Scale (Entwistle, Alexander, Cadigan, & Pallas, 1987);
    9. Analysis of social and cognitive levels of children's play from video recordings.

References

Canadian Council on Social Development. (1993). Center for international studies on economic and social welfare for families and children. *Focus on Childcare*, Newsletter 2. Ottawa: Canadian Council on Social Development.

Canadian Day Care Advocacy Association & Canadian Child Day Care Federation. (1994). *Caring for a living: A study on wages and working conditions in Canadian childcare.* Ottawa: Canadian Day Care Advocacy Association and the Canadian Child Day Care Federation.

Childcare Resource and Research Unit. (1994). *Childcare in Canada: Provinces and territories 1993.* Toronto, Ontario, Canada: University of Toronto, Center for Urban and Community Studies.

Dunn, L.M. (1984). *Peabody picture vocabulary test* (revised). Circle Pines, MN: American Guidance Service.

Entwistle, D.R., Alexander, K.L., Cadigan, D., & Pallas, P.M. (1987). The emergent academic self-image of first graders: Its response to social structure. *Child Development, 58*: 1190–1206.

Feagans, L., & Farran, D. (1979). *Adaptive Language Inventory.* Unpublished document, University of North Carolina at Chapel Hill.

Goelman, H., & Pence, A.R. (1987). Effects of childcare, family, and individual characteristics on children's language development: The Victoria day care research project. In D. Phillips (Ed.). *Quality in Childcare: What Does the Research Tell Us?* (pp. 89–104). Washington, DC: National Association for the Education of Young Children.

Harms, T., & Clifford, R. (1980). *Early childhood environment rating scale.* New York: Teacher's College Press, Columbia University.

Harter, S., & Pike, R. (1984). The pictorial scale of perceived competence and social acceptance for young children. *Child Development, 56*(3): 689–703.

Hayden, J. (1997). Neo conservatism and childcare services in Alberta: A case study. Occasional paper No.9. Center for Childcare Research and Resources. Toronto: University of Toronto.

Howe, N., & Jacobs, E. (1985). Childcare research. A case for Canadian national standards. *Canadian Psychology, 36*(2): 131–143.

Jacobs, E., Selig, G., & White, D.R. (1992). Classroom behavior in Grade 1: Does quality of preschool experience make a difference? *Canadian Journal of Research in Early Childhood Education, 3*(2): 89–100.

Jorde-Bloom, P. (1985). *Early childhood work environment survey.* Evanston, IL: Early Childhood Professional Development Project.

Jorde-Bloom, P. (1988). *Early childhood job satisfaction survey.* Evanston, IL: Early Childhood Professional Development Project.

Kamerman, S., & Kahn, A. (1995). Innovations in toddler day care and family support services: An international overview. *Child Welfare, 77*(6): 1281–1300.

Lero, D., Pence, A., Goelman, H., & Brockman, L. (1985). Parents' needs, preferences and concerns about childcare: Case studies of 336 Canadian families. *Background paper for the Task Force on Childcare.* Ottawa, ON, Canada: Status of Women Canada.

Lyon, M., & Canning, P. (1995). *The Atlantic day care study.* St. John's, NF, Canada: Memorial University of Newfoundland.

National Council of Welfare. (1997). *Poverty profile 1995.* Ottawa, ON: Minister of Supply & Services.

Palmérus, K. (1991). The impact of ratio of children/caregiver on social interaction and activity pattern in a day care center. *Early Child Development and Care, Vol. 71*: 97–103.

Pence, A. (Ed.). (1992). *Canadian national childcare study. Canadian childcare in context: Perspectives from the provinces and territories.* Health and Welfare Canada.

Vocational Psychology Research. (1963). *Minnesota satisfaction questionnaire.* Minneapolis: University of Minnesota.

Whitebook, M., Howes, C., & Phillips, D. (1990). *Who cares? Childcare teachers and the quality of care in America.* Final report of the National Childcare Staffing Study. Oakland, CA: Childcare Employee Project.

Chapter 13

Empowerment and Entrapment: Women Workers in Home-Based and Center-Based Settings

Andrea Petrie
Judith Burton

Abstract

This chapter focuses on women who work in the childcare industry in Australia. Specifically it focuses on women in home-based and center-based settings. Two concepts—entrapment and empowerment—are used to analyze the status and position of these workers. The benefits the women derive from such work, the burdens that the work creates, and the importance of underlying social structures in shaping their work experiences are examined. Central to this examination are assumptions that social structures largely determine the distribution of benefits and burdens among different groups in society. In the case of childcare workers, the gendered division of labor is fundamental to the construction of women as suitable and appropriate people to work with, and care for, young children. Analysis of the gendered outcomes of policy decisions demonstrates the disadvantages borne by women as childcarers.

Introduction

Equity indicators, ranging from health and education to poverty and parliamentary representation, consistently demonstrate that women have less access than men to public sources of power (Alloway, 1995). Childcare providers, who are predominantly women, occupy a position of disadvantage in the labor market not only because they are women but also because childcare generally is perceived as a low status occupation.

For the purposes of this chapter, the two concepts of entrapment and empowerment will be utilized to provide an analysis of the status and position of childcare workers. Entrapment and empowerment define the position of women in childcare in relation to the traditional stereotypical role expectations prevalent within a modern, industrialized, patriarchal society. *Entrapment* serves to perpetuate the low status of women, constraining life options and restricting opportunities for personal advancement. *Empowerment* enhances the status of women and increases life options and broadens opportunities for personal advancement (Petrie, 1995).

In order to understand the relationship of women as childcare providers to the concepts of empowerment and entrapment, it is important to take into consideration issues confronting women in terms of the public/private dichotomy: dependency; the world of work; and the development of attitudes and values. Further, it is important to examine the ways in which industrial relations policies and children's service regulation and funding policies are implicated in the entrapment or empowerment of childcare providers.

This chapter examines work and employment in childcare that is drawn from studies of women in two sectors of the childcare industry—home-based family day care providers and teachers working in center-based childcare services. The studies explored the ways in which the gendered nature of work and government policy influence care providers and the tasks they perform.

"Women's Work"

An examination of the historical context of work reveals the gendered ways that women have become socially constructed as suitable and appropriate people to work with children. Following industrialization, the redefinition of domestic and childrearing tasks as "women's work" created tensions between parenting and paid work that continue to shape women's experience of both home life and industrial citizenship. Because paid workforce participation was constructed as a secondary consideration for women, their primary focus being on family matters, they were actively discouraged, and at times excluded by law, from competing with men for work. Women's economic status became inextricably linked to their position in the social institution of the family. Thus the gendering of paid work generally confined women's employment to work that men found boring, repetitive, or saw as an extension of traditional feminine activities (Deacon, 1989; Baxter, 1990).

The structure of the public sphere is predicated upon the division of labor in the private sphere. People's labor market experiences, such as access to work, pay, and employment conditions, while influenced by the intervention of public institutions, are predominantly a function of the social reproduction of labor within the family and the policies and practices of firms (Burchell & Rubery, 1990). While women's labor market position has improved markedly since the mid-1970s, inequalities remain (Economic Planning and Advisory Commission, 1996). Three indicators of women's disadvantage in the Australian labor market are differential access to employment, workforce segmentation, and variation in returns from work.

Workers in Home-Based Childcare

The use of informal neighborhood childminding has been a traditional solution to providing "care" for young children where this "care" cannot be provided by the children's own family or extended family. The arrangements for this alternative family "care" have resulted usually from negotiations and transactions between the child's own mother and a substitute, neighborhood "mother." This interchange has been of a private and personal nature, but involving some form of reciprocity either in kind or in financial terms. This practice has been enshrined traditionally in the private sphere and, because of this, it has become taken for granted and viewed as "normalized" practice (Petrie, 1995). Private childminding remains the most common form of alternative childcare provision for young children in Australia (CPAL, 1996).

Social policy related to family day care has changed little over the last 20 years. Family day care remains a government organized system of childcare which provides childcare as a public service in the private homes of care-providers. Family day care is considered by some to be a more "normal" form of substitute "care" than that provided in institutional settings, i.e., in childcare centers. It is considered more cost effective because it is cheaper to utilize "care" provided in existing homes, rather than establish extra childcare centers. In the 1990s family day care is an integral part of childcare services in Australia yet family day care tends to be a silent, almost invisible service with a very low public profile (Petrie, 1991c).

Entrapment of Home-Based Carers

The view that children need mother substitutes to "care" for them, rather than skilled workers, is inherent in the provision of family day care as one of a range of possible types of service. The selection of "suitable" mother substitutes based on the subjective criteria of a select group of professional women within the Coordination Units of Schemes is in line with the philanthropic, protectionist, "child saving" model of social welfare policy. Women who are mothers are selected if there are no evident negative characteristics, including the absence of any perceived, or officially recorded, deviant behavior. These mothers are not selected on the basis of any qualifications for childcare (see Lane, 1986). Being a "normal" mother in a "normal" family is perceived to be the "ideal". Care-providers (generally working-class women) are required to submit themselves, their homes, and their families to detailed scrutiny and ongoing supervision by members of the Coordination Unit (generally middle-class women) and also be prepared to undertake in-service training.

It is important to understand care-providers' experience, taking into account the way it has been, and continues to be, shaped by the primacy of their family roles. Considerable numbers of home-based childcare providers experience limited mobility both as a consequence of their commitment to domestic routines and because their range of skills is limited to expertise in the domestic sphere—a consequence of social forces and of socialization processes, including schooling (Petrie,1995).

Family day care providers receive no formal training; are selected, in general, on the basis of their experience as mothers; and are classified as self-employed outside of any industrial agreement which entitles them to leave, sickness benefit, or any other industrial conditions that the average Australian worker takes for granted. Hence the pay and conditions for care-providers are low in comparison to other workers. There are a variety of reasons for this, including the devaluing or undervaluing of caring, the age of the children (infants, toddlers, three-to-five-year-olds, rather than adolescents) and the perceptions of care-providing as non-work. Part of the reason lies in the lack of access by care-providers to "internal labor markets". "Internal labor markets" facilitate the acquisition of power within the labor market through the provision of opportunities for promotion, good pay, good conditions, security of tenure, and in-service training to improve knowledge and skills. Women's domestic responsibilities often deny them access to "internal labor markets", creating the situation where they are unable to compete equally with men for internal labor market jobs.

Despite the perceived advantages, women doing paid work at home are in weak bargaining situations industrially. In the case of women working at home, it is difficult to distinguish legally between being full-time, part-time, or casual employees, or being self-employed. Despite family day care providers being considered "self-employed", i.e., independent contractors, they are not free to set their own fees and are subject to employment conditions set by the family day care Scheme to which they belong. There is resistance by both some care-providers and some coordination unit members to unionization. This resistance derives from the belief that the consequences of care-providers in losing "self-employed" status and gaining "employee" status would lead to family day care, as a childcare service, no longer being "cost effective". In addition, there is a belief that a situation would arise where care-providers would have less autonomy, less support from Coordination Unit members, and would move into informal provision of 'back yard' childcare. This would result, ultimately, in an end to family day care (National Family Day Care Council (Aust.) 1989).

Empowerment of Home-Based Centers

Alston suggests that, whereas under these circumstances women may lack recognition and status in the public domain, they may have enhanced power and status within the private domain (Alston, 1994). Care-providers are able to engage in household tasks while also caring for their own children and their day care children. It is arguable, then, that family day care not only allows for "joint products" for which the care-provider receives payment, but also allows the care-provider greater power and status within the dynamics of the family setting.

There continues to be interest from the unions, peak industry groups and care-provider organizations as to the employment status of family day care providers. Unions remain concerned to have family day care providers recognized as workers with protections, rights and entitlements that are comparable to other workers in the childcare industry. The government has concerns to balance the interests of Family day care providers with the need to provide high-quality, affordable childcare to working families. The debate continues over the employment status of family day care providers as workers.

A Paradox

Family day care represents a series of contradictions. It is both resisted (as a day care service with its use of "nonexperts") and supported if day care is unavoidable (as the better form of childcare service it replicates, albeit secondhand, the best and "natural care" of young children) by some early childhood professionals. Similarly, family day care is supported (as it offers a network of community-based day care services by "nonexperts") and resisted (as it perpetuates the domesticity of women) by some feminists. It involves public recruitment and inspection of the care-providers but there is no formal responsibility toward them as "workers". The selected care-providers are classified as self-employed, but terms and conditions are largely dictated by the Family Day Care Scheme. The Scheme's role is ambiguous. It provides a range of advisory and support services, including in-service training; home-visiting; providing advice and resources to enhance the care providing; organizing playgroups and social gatherings. The coordination unit members, the major facilitators of the service, are at the same time supervisory and inspectorial as well as supportive and befriending of care-providers. Regardless of the ways in which the coordination unit members are perceived by the care-providers, the members of the coordination units are the direct agents of state control within family day care structures.

In relation to family day care, in social policy terms, a paradox is clearly evident (Petrie, 1995). Wattenberg (1980, p. 41) describes an "interesting dilemma" in which there is a "delicate line between the urge to provide more rigorous, formalized and systematic support to a [Family] system which increasingly is one of strangers caring for children behind closed doors" (Wattenberg, 1980, p. 41). This dilemma is reflected in indecision related to formal state regulation. With the exception of a minority of states and territories in Australia, home-based childcare is largely excluded from specific public regulation. Those states/territories that remain without regulation do so, in part, in the belief that regulation through legislation represents an intrusion by the state in affairs that are the "private" concerns of families. Further, there is prevarication by governments in the establishment of a national system of accreditation for family day care. Despite the introduction in 1994 of a national system of accreditation for center-based long day care, no equivalent system for family day care has been introduced. The introduction of an accreditation system for family day care may become a double-edged sword for care-providers.

In a recent study it was shown that most women in the role of care-provider have taken on that role because they are constrained (Petrie, 1995). As workers, these women feel constrained by the need to find appropriate, adequate "quality" care for their children, directly or indirectly. The availability of care may determine whether or not the women can work at all. The recruitment of care-providers is predicated and dependent upon the context in which they live. Their decision to locate their work within the family home is based upon the experiences and values established initially within their own family contexts and reinforced, subsequently, when their own children are young and dependent. Their response to the need to find "quality" care is to provide the care themselves. This is then made available to others (Petrie & Coombes, 1994).

Workers in Center-Based Care

Most Australian long day care staff are employed on a part-time basis and nearly one in four staff members are employed on a casual basis (EPAC, 1996; Heiler, 1996). The increasing use of part-time and casual employment within the long day care sector not only denies full industrial citizenship to women workers but also has potentially damaging repercussions on continuity of care for children (EPAC, 1996).

Labor costs, the need to maintain child/staff ratios at various times of the day, and consumer demand fluctuations contribute to the employment of high proportions of part-time and casual staff. Payment in arrears for childcare assistance was introduced in January 1998. Implicit in this policy change is the potential payment for only those hours that children have actually attended services. Thus, unless all parents use all their eligible hours, centers would become liable from maintaining the standing conditions required for service provision with reduced government assistance. Such a scenario could be expected to increase the incidence of casual employment. Burgess (1996) argues that casualization appreciably enhances "the opportunities for managerial discretion at the workplace" as this employment strategy makes for a more compliant and cooperative workforce. The extent of reported award and regulation breaches within the long day care sector, which has led to increasing casualization, has the potential to not only undermine the continuity of care for children but also the ability of staff to resist employer demands.

Empowerment of Center-Based Workers

Analysis of the work of teachers in center-based services has found that these women may feel empowered within their workplace by being able to influence the policy directions of centers and finding ways to share their expertise with other staff. Also, unlike the majority of family day care providers, teachers possess qualifications which, if they are also registered with the Board of Teacher Registration, enable them to move between different educational settings.

Early childhood teachers working in childcare draw extensively on their university gained knowledge to construct positive learning environments for children. They integrate this formal knowledge with what has been, until recently, largely personal and experiential knowledge to organize and support other staff, but their knowledge-based interventions remain undervalued. In Queensland this is demonstrated by the lack of recognition that teachers fully apply their professional knowledge when working in childcare and thus have an inability to achieve parity of pay and conditions with other early teachers (see Burton & Lyons this volume). This is despite increasing expectations generated by state regulation in the area that requires a cornerstone of early childhood education's claims to professionalism—developmentally appropriate programs—and the continual improvement of service quality.

Two potential sources of professional empowerment for teachers in childcare—influencing center policy and practice and sharing expertise with other staff, are discussed below. The extent to which teachers feel empowered by these potential expressions of their additional knowledge and skill is problematized by considering the tensions between these two elements and the extent of overwork required to achieve this level of professional practice.

Influencing Center Policy and Practice

The Childcare (Childcare Centers) Regulations 1991 (Qld) set out the responsibilities of center directors. These managerial and human resource functions not only place a significant degree of responsibility on directors but also provide them with a potentially powerful resource because such discretion may enable directors to define "employee work roles and shape structures of coordination" (Gardner & Palmer, 1992, p. 278).

Teachers' ability to influence policy and practices in center-based care operates in a number of ways. Principally the authority of teachers who are directors rests in being able to determine core aspects of center philosophy, such as the curriculum framework adopted, and to influence the selection, employment, and fostering of staff. Furthermore, as they are in more direct contact with sponsors, they feel satisfaction if able to achieve improvements in conditions for staff. Teacher group leaders were predominantly responsible for the intellectual work of giving shape to children's learning, in particular analyzing patterns in children's behavior, planning worthwhile experiences, and documenting observations and programs. In addition, teacher group leaders had more input into the processes of formalizing center policies and procedures for accreditation purposes. Thus, teachers at centers hold responsibility for key educational and human resource management decisions.

Sharing Expertise

The directors' responsibility for human resource functions generates tensions for them, with staffing being the most challenging and difficult aspect of their role (Hayden, 1996; McCrea, Mobbs, & Nailon, 1995). Teacher-directors resisted making unilateral decisions. An important factor contributing to decision making strategies was the need to trust staff who, through their interpretative work of implementing such decisions, also influenced service provision. Directors generally needed to negotiate with other staff members when policies were changed or formalized. Reaching consensus was a time-consuming and stressful process littered with unacknowledged conditions and fraught with unintended consequences.

While teamwork is characterized as central to the provision of adequate services in centers, by both design and default teachers assume more responsibility and thus have greater say in decision making processes. Teamwork is central to the interactive phase of working with children and families. Yet teachers' personal/professional sense of responsibility, the difficulties of setting up, resourcing and evaluating the program while children are present, and the labor cost pressures of human service work generate imperatives that lead individuals to assuming more responsibility for center-wide decisions. Work performed when children are not present is almost exclusively unpaid. To experience a sense of professional satisfaction and undertake the work expected of them by regulatory bodies, teachers tend to work longer hours in the independent documentation and evaluation of curriculum.

Criteria for successful or effective teamwork in early childhood settings typically include valuing staff members' contributions irrespective of their status (O'Connor, 1990; Fleet & Clyde, 1993; Simpson, 1994) and being willing to self-disclose and empathize with others (Fleet & Clyde, 1993). The interpersonal delicacy required to find ways to both value others' skills and share expertise is reflected in Sebastian-Nickell and Milne's (1992) assessment that staff members need to negotiate and compromise as they work toward a common vision. However, teachers' supervisory responsibilities could be seen as providing numerous opportunities to share their expertise.

Staff supervision is seen in terms of professional development and establishing center-wide program coherence. Some formal professional development and appraisal is carried out at centers, with staff meetings seen as essential forums for whole staff discussion. Directors believed it important to move around centers in order to observe the quality of interactions, model teaching, and care strategies, and be available for consultation.

Teacher group leaders also have some responsibility for supervising the work of the assistants and some responsibility for center-wide supervision. As staff work in shifts, teachers believe it essential to gather observations of children. Teachers are also responsible for orienting new staff into the center's programs and providing in-services for new staff. Directors draw on the expertise of these teachers in formulating center-wide policies and procedures and in articulating, most notably during staff meetings, the underlying principles and illustrating how these can be practically implemented.

Entrapment of Center-Based Workers

Teachers' influence over centers' policies and practices by organizing and supervising work and sharing their expertise with other staff is established and maintained not just by drawing on the authority delegated by employers or possession of additional qualifications but mostly by performing significant amounts of unpaid work. The lack of recognition of core aspects of the work of care-providers contributes to the insufficient resourcing and thus "a pattern of overwork", particularly in family day care and long day care (Heiler, 1996, p. 21). Not only do teachers have to work longer hours in long day care, they also perceive a need to put more effort into their work.

Professional ethics directly contribute to the overwork of teachers of young children. In addition, workplace and industry structures also interact to shape teachers' willingness to work, and organize others' work, to meet professional rather than industrial obligations. Teachers feel responsible for the quality of children's experiences and view many provisions of industrial awards as incompatible with educational and organizational beliefs. Within the center-based setting, individual responsibility is important for four sets of reasons: professional and personal satisfaction; the immediacy and intensity of the labor process; legislative and job description reasons; and reasons to do with the delegation of accountability.

Individual responsibility is important because of the nature of the physical, mental, and emotional labor process involved in caring for and educating children. In comparison with early childhood teachers in other settings, teachers in childcare work much longer hours in contact with children. As children's hours of attendance increase, early childhood beliefs about the continuousness of teaching and the utility, in terms of individualizing programs, of knowing about the entirety of children's curriculum experiences, lead teachers to increase their effort. Teachers experience feelings of incompleteness because they cannot see what happens over the *whole* of a child's day at a center. Their training has alerted them to the value of studying children's reactions to the program they provide.

Additional unpaid work is also necessary as teachers cannot accomplish responsibilities central to their work, such as preparing the learning-environment and documenting and reflecting on programs, within rostered hours.

The nature of work with young children can lead to emotional attachments between staff and children. The emotional bonds contribute to teachers' increased work effort. Teacher-directors believe that childcare staff members develop a compelling moral obligation to meet children's needs due to the "strong relationship" they build with children over the extended period that children attend. They speak of feelings of role overload, emotional effort, and lack of extrinsic rewards for long day staff.

The work of teachers in center-based services also involves intensive interaction with other adults. The interactive nature of curriculum decision making is more apparent when staff are working in shifts. The discretionary power of assistants is enhanced, as is that of other staff who may be responsible for children when groups are joined or play spaces shared. Para-professional staff also have many insights and much knowledge to contribute. Teachers strive to establish collegial work relations with other staff members. Interpersonal continuity is seen as a key element of building knowledge of particular children. As individual teachers are not able to assume full responsibility for such continuity, the relationships developed between adults over time become an important determinant of curriculum coherence. Sharing knowledge and agreeing on practice is important for the coherence and continuity of children's experiences not only on a daily basis but also over their possible five years of attendance. This professional responsibility draws on traditional early childhood beliefs that teachers should share physical tasks with assistants and value their contributions and is reinforced and shaped by the requirements of regulations and the accreditation process.

Conclusion

Since the 1970s in Australia, childcare has been the subject of considerable political and community debate. But the debates are riddled with contradictions. There are many differences between center-based and home-based care providers. Most notably the location of their work, the nature of their relationship with sponsors, educational levels, and regulatory structures indicate a gulf between these women. Nonetheless, both work in a feminized occupation where lack of social recognition of the nature and extent of their abilities and responsibilities contribute to similar undervaluing of the contributions they make to the well-being of children and families. We have argued that the social construction of gender is central to the construction of women as care-providers, with concomitant disadvantages. Despite the provision and regulation of the services in which childcare personnel work, there is only a tokenistic and superficial recognition of the services they provide. The gendered nature of the policy landscape is evident in the calculation of care-providers' worth, which is underpinned by the assumption that these services compete with the "free" provision of care by children's families. Recognition of the value of these women's work in material terms—greater remuneration and improved conditions—would constitute a "fundamental challenge to existing assumptions and frameworks, as well as to the 'masculine' economy" (Pringle, 1988, p. 267). The challenge is long overdue.

References

Alloway, N. (1995). *Foundation stones: the construction of gender in early childhood.* Carlton: Curriculum Corporation.

Alston, M. (1994). Women and the rural crisis. In *Country Women at the Crossroads: Perspectives on Rural Australian Women in the 1990s.* (Eds.). M. Franklin et al. (pp. 17-24) NSW: University of New England Press.

Baxter, J. (1990). Domestic labor: Issues and studies. *Labor and Industry,* 3, (1): 112-145.

Burchell, B., & Rubery, J. (1990). An empirical investigation into the segmentation of the labor supply. *Work, Employment, and Society,* 4, (4): 551-575.

Burgess, J. (1996). Workforce casualization in Australia. *International Employment Relations Review,* 2(l): 33-53.

Deacon, D. (1989). *Managing gender: The state, the new middle class and women workers 1830-1930.* Melbourne: Oxford University Press.

Economic Planning and Advisory Commission. (1996). *Future labor market issues for Australia.* Commissioned paper No. 12. Canberra: AGPS.

Fleet, A., & Clyde, M. (1993). *What's in a day? Working in early childhood.* Sydney: Social Science Press.

Gardner, M., & Palmer, G. (1992). Employment relations: Industrial and human resource Management in Australia. Melbourne: Macmillan Education.

Hayden, J. (1996). *Management in early childhood services: An Australian perspective.* Sydney: Social Science Press.

Heiler, K. (1996). *Childcare in a changing industrial relations environment.* ACIRRT Working Paper No. 42, Sydney: Australian Center For Industrial Relations Research and Training.

Lane, S. (1986). Women and childcare: Factors influencing social work dealings in women's lives. *British Journal of Social Work, vol. 16,* 1980 (Supplement).

McCrea, N., Mobbs, J., & Nailon, D. (1995). *Identifying and understanding the "easy" and challenging everyday tasks of directors managing childcare centers.* Paper prepared for the 1995 Australian Council for Educational Administration International Conference, Sydney.

National Family Day Care Council. (Aust.) (1989). *Newsletter,* NFDCC, Avoca Beach, NSW, September.

O'Connor, B. (1990). *The complexities of teamwork in childcare.* Paper submitted to the QIRC Re Case R54 / 90.

Petrie, A. (1991c). Keynote Address, An Australian fairytale: Does the Cinderella of early childhood services get to go to the ball? Proceedings of the Third International Family Day Care Organization Conference, September, Sydney.

Petrie, A., & Coombes, K. (1994). Parents' and Providers' Ideologies of Childcare. In K. Coombes and E. Mellor. *Issues in Early Childhood: Australian Perspectives* (pp. 65–81) New York: W.C. Brown.

Petrie, A. (1995). *Determined to care: Women as care-providers.* Unpublished Doctoral Thesis, Griffith University.

Pringle, R. (1988). Secretaries talk: Sexuality, power and work. Sydney: Allen and Unwin.

Sebastian-Nickel, P., & Milne, R. (1992). *Care and education for young children.* Melbourne: Longman Cheshire.

Simpson, L. (1994). Staff/staff interaction. *Rattler,* 30, Winter: 5–8.

Wattenberg, E. (1980). Family day care: Out of the shadows and into the spotlight. *Marriage and Family Review, vol.3, no.3/4:* 35–62.

Chapter 14

Exploring Parental Involvement in Canada: An Ideological Maze[1]

Evelyn B. Ferguson
Susan L. Prentice

Abstract

This article explores the political and philosophical meaning of parental involvement in childcare centers. Through an analysis of legislation and regulations in Canada's ten provinces and two territories, we find that there are four policy approaches to parental participation, ranging from "silence" to full "parent control". We argue that these constitutional options are drawn from either a market-based model of parents as consumers/purchasers or a citizenship model of parents as collaborators, entitled to involvement and control. These findings reveal that jurisdictions can and do use constitutional arrangements to favor or enhance their preferred philosophical approach to childcare service, with implications for the professions of early childhood education and policy advocates.

Introduction

Whether labeled "parental involvement", "consumer participation", "parent education" or "family/program relationships", the role of parents in early childhood education has long been perceived as an important, if at times difficult, feature of care. Approaches to the parent/caregiver relationship have varied widely, reflecting different and often opposing ideological views of family values, the role of the state in the lives of families, and the helpfulness or intrusiveness of professionalism. These differing approaches have surfaced differentially over time and place, and are mirrored in professional, popular, and legislative discourses and practices.

How the state perceives, facilitates, or ignores the parents' role in childcare is established within legislation, regulations, and practice. Public policy and services are affected by a range of players beyond elected decision makers. Early childhood educators, parents, policy analysts, administrators, professional organizations, and advocacy groups also influence how statutory arrangements influence service delivery.

Parental participation is thus a complex feature of childcare policy and delivery. Importantly, parental involvement is one of the few aspects of childcare that is influenced more by constitutional arrangements than by distributional allotments. In other words, instituting ways and means to ensure parental decision making is affected far more by legislative and regulatory practice than by resource allocation. It does not directly cost a jurisdiction more money to empower parental control, but it does require an ideological commitment that parents have such a right. How various jurisdictions mandate (or fail to mandate) parent involvement, then, reflects their philosophical orientation to childcare—and, by extension, also reflects their views of the family, the role of the state, and the role of professionals.

In this chapter, we explore parent involvement as it has been encoded in policy and legislation in Canada. Through an analysis of recent legislation and attendant regulations of Canada's ten provinces and two territories, we demonstrate how different models of parent involvement rest on varying approaches to the delivery of childcare service. We find that there are four policy approaches to parental participation, ranging from "silence" to full "parent control", and argue that these constitutional options are drawn from either a market-based model of parents as consumers/purchasers or a citizenship model of parents as collaborators, entitled to involvement and control. We suspect that these varying approaches find echoes in the policies and practices of other Western countries reviewed in this book.

Canadian policy is affected by national as well as international political and professional trends. These include pressures to privatize and commercialize service provision, concomitant government cutbacks to childcare funding in many jurisdictions, and the trend to further professionalize service to enhance the status and incomes of childcare providers. In light of this, we conclude our chapter with a discussion of the political implications of parent involvement in childcare programs; what constitutional arrangements and outcomes benefit early childhood educators and parents and why? In a time of social policy upheaval, which models of childcare do we want to support for our children, parents, and caregivers?

Meanings of Parental Involvement

What do we mean by parent involvement? In the early childhood education, the term is used to refer to a broad cluster of approaches. This definitional imprecision reflects unresolved tensions in the field about how and to what extent programs should accommodate parental interests (Powell, 1989). Consequently, terms range from "parent education" (which denotes a compensatory approach toward parental capabilities) to "parent control" (which rests on the view that parents should actually control the policy and direction of a childcare center.)

Several different ways of categorizing parent involvement have been described in the research literature. These different definitions speak to the varied meanings and forms of parental involvement found in policy, legislative, and professional discussions. Shimoni (1992) delineates three primary *goals* behind programs and activities for parents: parent education, parent influence or control, and ensuring continuity of the child's experience. Mayfield (1990) describes six different *types of parental activity*—namely, parents as audience, as adult learners, as teachers of their own child at home, as volunteers, as para-professionals or paid workers, and finally, as decision makers. Powell (1989) describes *the nature of the relationship* between parents and childcare providers. Powell's notion of "parent-teacher collaboration" evokes an image of parents and teachers representing major influences on the child that needs coordination. He identifies the parental role as consumers or customers, a role which emerges in relation to childcare as a service industry.

Like Powell, we are most interested in parent influence and control. For the purposes of this article, we define parental involvement as activities relating to decision making by customers/consumers. Our primary focus is licensed programs for full or part-time daytime care for children under 12 years of age in group centers or family-based homes. In Canada, the licensed childcare system does not include residential programs or programs delivered within the public education system except for school-age care in some jurisdictions.

The Canadian Childcare Landscape

Licensed childcare, with public subsidy and regulation, has been a reality in Canada since 1946, although the major development of services occurred post-1966 (Friendly, 1994). Provinces and territories have the primary responsibility for childcare service, and the federal government's role has been limited to providing cost-sharing expenses, primarily fee subsidies for low-income parents. Major developments in legislation, standards, and regulation took place over the mid-to-late-1980s, as jurisdictions established conditions for funding and regulating childcare in their respective provinces or territories. Much of this legislation still stands, although some jurisdictions revised their legislation or regulations during the 1990s. Manitoba (a small western province) and Ontario (a large central province) have recently completed extensive reviews of their regulations, although changes have not yet been encoded in law.

The political landscape across Canada reflects trends found in a variety of Western countries. Concern about the public debt and deficit has dominated public discussion at both the federal and provincial levels, and there have been extensive layoffs of civil servants, scaling-back of publicly provided services, liberalization of trade laws (particularly with the U.S.), and an enhanced focus on the privatization of services (Friendly & Oloman, 1996). Federal governments during this period have been dominated by the two major political parties (the Progressive Conservatives and the Liberals), each taking an increasingly fiscally conservative position, while a new right-wing coalition based in western Canada (the Reform Party) has gained increasing power, and became Her Majesty's Loyal Opposition in 1997. The labor/socialist party (the New Democratic Party [NDP] has diminished in power, and temporarily official party status in the early 1990s. Possible separation of Quebec from the rest of Canada has become a serious possibility with a federal separatist party (The Bloc Québecois) based in Quebec, which held the position of Official Opposition from 1993—1997.

Provincial governmental politics range across a wide spectrum: the NDP (Saskatchewan and British Columbia), Progressive Conservative (Manitoba, Alberta, and Ontario), Liberal (New Brunswick and Newfoundland), and Parti Québecois (the provincial separatist party of Quebec). Different governments have vastly differing approaches to childcare. For example, the 1995 election of a Conservative government in Ontario (on the heels of a short NDP term) saw the introduction of sweeping social policy reform, including a review of daycare regulations. In Alberta, two successive Progressive Conservative governments in the 1990s have also endorsed a right-wing platform that has included the closing of hospitals and cutbacks to public kindergarten programs. In other provinces, changes have not been so dramatic but the pressure of public debt, reduced federal transfer payments from the federal government for health and postsecondary education, and changes in the funding mechanism for social programs have all contributed to increased financial pressure for governments of all political orientations.

Parental Involvement in the Informal Sector

Canadian parents use a variety of childcare arrangements for their preschool and school-age children. These include licensed childcare centers and family homes, unlicensed care within a child's home or in a provider's home, and unpaid care by parents, relatives, and siblings (Goelman, Pence, Lero, Brockman, Glick, & Berkowitz, 1993; Ferguson, 1991 & in press). The vast majority of Canadian children use unlicensed care; spaces in the licensed sector meet less than 20% of the need (Goelman, et al., 1993; Friendly, 1994). In the informal and unlicensed sector, state regulation is minimal and is restricted to investigations by child welfare authorities for complaints of child abuse or neglect, or in some jurisdictions, investigation if a provider is caring for too many children who are not her own.

In unlicensed care settings, parent involvement is of necessity informal and personally negotiated. Research suggests that unlicensed caregivers view parents in a range of ways. Parents are seen as consumers or customers in settings where the provider perceives herself running a small business; as employers when parents are employing a nanny or a provider in their home; as neighbors; or as friends in a neighborhood-based informal setting (Nelson, 1989; Arat-Koc, & Villasin, 1990).

In all these settings, parental involvement is a function of the specific privatized arrangement between provider and parent. Many factors influence such arrangements, including the supply and demand of the specific service in a particular location, the citizenship status of the provider (particularly in an in-home arrangement), the hours of care needed, and the personalities of the individuals involved, as well as demographic variables such as the socioeconomic levels of parents and providers and their respective education and knowledge about childcare (Nelson, 1989; Ferguson, 1991 & in press). In settings where parents are employers, they may be very powerful: complaints of abuse in in-home settings, particularly by immigrant care-givers, are not uncommon (Arat-Koc, & Villasin, 1990). In other settings, parents may feel they have very limited power or control. For example, parents may experience themselves as relatively powerless under conditions where they have limited financial resources and/or limited access to a supply of providers (because of location, nonstandard work hours, or a special needs child). Class differences, level of experience, and professional expertise may also influence parents' or providers' perception of their own authority (Prentice, & Ferguson, 1997).

In the final instance, parental control in unlicensed settings rests on the power to select a care provider and to quit that care provider if dissatisfied. This form of consumer power corresponds to a market model of service, and in that sense is no different from any other service a family may purchase—such as insurance, groceries, or housecleaning help. In unlicensed care, the state plays virtually no role, and rarely ensures even minimal consumer protection. Enhanced protection and parent control are restricted to the licensed regulated sector.

Parent Involvement in the Regulated Sector

Across Canada, licensed childcare differs in its approach to parental involvement. We identify four statutory models of parent involvement across the country. The first model is characterized by silence on parent involvement. This approach is practiced by four provinces and territories. In what we term "silent" provinces, a role for parents is not specified by the state, even though individual centers are free to practice parent participation. The second approach we label "informed choice" and is practiced exclusively in Alberta, which goes one small step further than the silent provinces to specify a process that must be taken at the point of initial choice by parents. "Parent input" makes up the third model, and in these jurisdictions a continuing process of parent input must be in place in each childcare center. This third model can vary by auspice: In some "parent input" provinces, the requirement for parent involvement may be restricted to nonprofit centers. Finally, in "parent control" provinces and territories, all nonprofit centers must have a parent-majority board of directors, effectively ensuring that policy control rests with parents.

These four different policy orientations are discussed in more detail below. Each, we argue, reflects different values toward childcare delivery and the roles of parents and professionals, as well as reveals policy stances toward sponsorship of delivery. Out of this analysis, we gain a picture of the dominant ideological models that influence childhood delivery in our country at a critical time in our social policy history.

Model One: Silent Provinces (Newfoundland, Prince Edward Island, Ontario, British Columbia)

Legislation regarding parent involvement in silent provinces is minimal.[2] It is important to note that statutory silence does not mean that parents are necessarily powerless or absent from boards of directors, advisory committees, meetings, or other forms of input. On an individual basis, centers may implement any or all of these processes. These provinces are "silent" because the province does not *require* that centers ensure vehicles for parent input. Additionally, these provinces—like every jurisdiction except Quebec—are also silent on the issue of parent involvement in licensed family homes. In this sense, virtually all jurisdictions are equivalent on the issue of parent involvement, and Quebec's changes in this regard are very new and untested.

The "silent" provinces supply over half of the licensed spaces in Canada. Ontario provides just under 37% of Canada's spaces, British Columbia serves another 13%, and PEI and Newfoundland between them account for an additional 2%. This means that 52% of the group center spaces in Canada have no specified requirement for any mandated involvement (Childcare Resource and Research Unit, 1997). When these "silent spaces" are added to the near-universal silence of licensed family homes across the country, we conclude that the vast majority of licensed childcare has no statutory expectation for parental participation.

Given the importance of auspice, it is worth noting that each of the silent provinces has a significant commercial sector. Childcare Resource and Research Unit data (1997) shows that 66% of the spaces in Newfoundland, 32% in Prince Edward Island, 20% in Ontario, and 39% in British Columbia are all delivered in the commercial sector. Since nonprofit centers are more likely than commercial centers to have boards of directors with parent and community representation, the proportion of commercial centers is an important variable (Prentice, 1999).

Model Two: "Informed" Choice (Alberta)

Since 1994, Alberta has moved from being a "silent province" to a province that attempts to ensure front-end informed parental choice. Alberta's Family and Social Services Day Care programs notes that "parent involvement continues to be a focus for day care in Alberta" (personal correspondence, 1997). Alberta's focus on parent involvement assumes a unique form, with a philosophical base that distinguishes it from the other provinces that ensure parent involvement.

Unique to Alberta is a focus on informing and educating parents at the time they choose their day care center. Alberta, in fact, demands written records that parents have been educated. While other jurisdictions may have handbooks, brochures, and checklists, no other province or territory requires that parents sign documents guaranteeing that they have read provincially supplied information about parent involvement, vowing that they have reviewed their day care center in relation to it.

Curiously, at the same time, Alberta is silent regarding any provision for parent participation beyond standard notification and authorization for various activities (related to medication, transportation, and disciplinary methods). At point of licensing, centers are required to state what their process of parental involvement might be, but there is no actual requirement that there be a board of directors, advisory committee, or any other structure established.

Alberta's statutory requirements are consistent with the philosophy articulated by the Deputy Minister in his preamble to the licensing manual, that parents' "primary responsibility is choosing the day care center and monitoring it" (Alberta Family and Social Services, 1993). There is no discussion of parent influence on curriculum, programming, policy development, or administration. Albertan philosophy is that once parents choose a center, their role is to monitor it and withdraw their child if they are dissatisfied. In this sense, the role for parents specified in this province corresponds to Powell's (1989) notion of parents as consumers or customers (see Hayden, 1997).

Of Alberta's 12% share of licensed spaces in the country, 62% are delivered in the profit sector (Childcare Resource and Research Unit, 1997). Its pro-business Progressive Conservative government has reduced the public debt through cutting educational, social, and health services. It is not surprising that Alberta's approach to parent involvement is consistent with a market model of parents as consumers/customers. Alberta stands as an example of how a province with a strong commitment to a market model of delivery can design a parent involvement process consistent with that philosophy. Other governments that might share the ideological approach reigning in Alberta have not yet emulated its policy.

Model Three: Parent Input (Manitoba, New Brunswick, Nova Scotia, Yukon Territories)

These provinces and territories reflect a statutory orientation toward parent participation that is consistent with parent influence or control as decision makers (Shimoni, 1992; Mayfield, 1990). Despite their differences, each of these four provinces mandates some form of parent input within legislation and/or regulations. In three of the four jurisdictions, parental influence is oriented toward democratic decision making within the center and/or limiting professional control by early childhood educators. In total these provinces represent 8% of the total number of regulated spaces and 69% of those spaces are delivered in nonprofit sectors.

As with other jurisdictions, provinces that mandate ongoing parental input differentiate between commercial and nonprofit centers. For example, certain grants and subsidies may be available for nonprofit centers but not commercial centers. In part, this differential treatment reflects a commitment to limiting the development of the for-profit sector (Prentice, 1997 & 1999; Friendly, 1994). Additionally, this difference is a relic of the federal cost-sharing provisions established by the 1966 Canada Assistance Plan (CAP). Under CAP legislation, provinces and territories could choose from two funding streams to obtain federal funding of childcare spaces; but one stream, the welfare provision route for families "in need," was limited to regulated nonprofit services (Prentice, in press; Friendly, 1994). It is noteworthy that this federal incentive for nonprofit service was eliminated by the 1996 Canada Health and Social Transfer (CHST), which replaced CAP. The CHST is a block funding program that permits provinces to disburse funds for health and social services any way they wish. Provinces do not have to fund childcare at all, and if they do they are free to support whichever programs (licensed, unlicensed, profit, or nonprofit) they prefer (Friendly & Oloman, 1996).

Among these jurisdictions, the Yukon is the most lukewarm on parent involvement. Like Alberta, the Yukon articulates that parent involvement is important, but does not mandate any form of parent influence or control beyond ensuring information relating to the parents' own children is available to them. On paper, the Yukon goes a step beyond the silent provinces by articulating a position on parental involvement within its legislation and regulations, but in practice, it goes no further than the silent provinces.

Manitoba, New Brunswick, and Nova Scotia each have an articulated policy mandating parent involvement on boards of directors in nonprofit centers. Each jurisdiction enhances parental decision making authority while limiting early childhood professional decision making authority. Manitoba is most explicit, restricting employee membership on boards of directors to a maximum of 20%, while setting a parent minimum of 20% or more. Likewise, Nova Scotia also limits professional membership, but at the same time also limits parents and community members as well, so that no single constituency controls the board. New Brunswick only requires that parents make up a minimum of 25% of the board, and sets out no minimums or maximums for center employees or community members. In Manitoba and New Brunswick, parents could make up the majority of a board of directors; in Nova Scotia, this possibility is expressly prevented. Overall, the legislation and regulations in these three jurisdictions favors a mixed community board model, leaving the actual make-up to the discretion of each center.

Mandatory ongoing parent input only applies to nonprofit centers—in Manitoba 88% of the spaces, in Nova Scotia 60%, and in New Brunswick 60%. What about regulations for other centers, primarily profit centers? Each jurisdiction has a set of expectations for all day care centers, but none involve boards of directors. Nova Scotia requires a meeting of parents every three months, New Brunswick an annual information meeting, and Manitoba a parent advisory committee with unspecified structures and responsibilities. None of these processes attempt to mandate parental influence and instead emphasize informing consumers.

A certain policy contradiction characterizes these "mandatory ongoing parent input" provinces. In nonprofit centers, statutory provisions call for mixed community boards with considerable parental influence and limited professional control. In contrast, control in commercial centers rests with professional and ownership interests. While commercial centers are the minority, they comprise a significant number of spaces in each jurisdiction. Additionally, in a political climate where privatization and pressures to commercialize services are being felt across the country and at a moment when early childhood educators are advocating for more professional control, these legally permissible differences in parental involvement are critical.

Model Four: Parent Control (Northwest Territories, Saskatchewan, Quebec)

The fourth model is exemplified by parent-controlled childcare centers, which establish parents as decision makers. In addition to enhancing the decision making power of parents, this model also effectively limits the policymaking control of the professional childcare staff. Of the three jurisdictions in this model, Quebec is unsurpassed, since it has recently introduced parent boards of directors and parent committees into home day care agencies as well as centers.

With approximately 93,581 licensed spaces, 82% nonprofit or public, Quebec is a large and influential province. Uniquely, nearly 44% of licensed spaces in Quebec are delivered by the public sector. The North West Territories, a physically large but numerically small legal entity in the Arctic, has just over 1,000 licensed spaces, of which 92% were nonprofit. Saskatchewan, a smaller prairie province, has about 4,600 licensed spaces, 98% in the nonprofit sector (including a very small number of publicly operated centers).

As is common in other jurisdictions, the Northwest Territories are also characterized by a policy gap between commercial and nonprofit care.

The Northwest Territories mandates two different parent involvement models, depending on auspice. Operators of nonprofit centers must establish boards of directors in which parents hold the majority of seats, thus effectively giving parents policy control of the center. In contrast, operators of commercial centers or family day care homes must only confirm in writing some unspecified means of involving parents or guardians (Child Day Care Standards Regulations of the Child Day Care Act, 1988, section 47[1] and [2]).

A similar situation exists in Saskatchewan, although it lays out stronger pressure to establish centers with parent-controlled boards of directors. Groups establishing day care centers must be nonprofit centers, unless specifically exempted from this requirement by the provincial minister. While the requirements for centers with boards are different from those without, the norm is parent-controlled centers. Even in the situations where the minister grants an exception, there must still be a parent-controlled advisory committee, with clearly articulated membership and responsibilities. Saskatchewan thus goes further than all jurisdictions except Quebec in guaranteeing significant parental input for all parents, not just those using nonprofit centers.

Significant parental input is demanded by Quebec's childcare legislation, which establishes parent cooperatives, parent-controlled nonprofit centers with parent majority boards, as well as parent committees for all other centers, including those run by municipalities, school boards, and commercial enterprises. Recent 1996 amendments to the Quebec Act further specify that home day care permits can only be issued to organizations that include either boards of directors with parents or nonstaff members as majority directors, or to organizations that establish parent committees of five persons elected by and from the parent users of the agency (Quebec National Assembly 35 Legislature 2 session Bill 11, 1996, chapter 16). Quebec thus becomes the first and so far only province to establish parent input into home day care settings.

Quebec now gives priority to nonprofit care in both centers and family homes, through the revised Act, whose purpose is to foster the harmonious development of day care services, giving priority to the development of nonprofit day care centers and home day care agencies (Quebec National Assembly 35 Legislature 2 session Bill 11, section 2, p. 2). In the future, only home day care agencies and day care centers eligible for public funds will be cooperatives, nonprofits (with parent-user majority boards) and services operated by public institutions, school boards, or municipalities.

Quebec is phasing in a flat parent fee of $5.00 per day, as the state assumes an increasing percentage of the cost. Concurrently, Quebec's education system will deliver more services, including full-time kindergarten services. While these exciting changes have yet to be implemented, most observers are supportive of the policy direction. Yet questions remain, including some crucial concerns about staff/child regulations and the overall impact of swift change. One observer wonders whether "in the longer term the existing community network may be transformed into a para-public network, with all of the disadvantages that this may represent in terms of costs, efficiency, flexibility, and parental involvement" (Berthiaume, 1997, p. 5).

Implications and Conclusions

We have two major findings that converge to raise troubling questions for the future of childcare and the childcare profession in Canada. Our first finding is that "silence" is the dominant model in both licensed centers and family daycare homes; our second is that the degree of statutory silence is linked to the issue of commercial/nonprofit delivery model. When situated in light of current political trends, these findings suggest a future where the quality of care and the quality of the parent-child caregiver relationship may be threatened.

We have pointed out that Canadian jurisdictions can be grouped by how they address parent involvement. From a policy framework, the least parent involvement is found in the "silent" provinces and the most parent involvement is found in those jurisdictions that mandate parent control. Low statutory requirements for parent involvement generally correspond to jurisdictions with a high percentage of commercial care; high statutory requirements for parent involvement correspond to jurisdictions with a low percentage of commercial care.

In every province and territory of Canada, there is both a commercial and a nonprofit childcare sector. All jurisdictions must accommodate the tension between a profit model that perceives parents as customers or consumers (e.g., Alberta) and the nonprofit community-based model that perceives parents as decision makers and collaborators with early childhood education professionals (e.g., Quebec & Saskatchewan). Some provinces resolve the tension by staying silent on parent involvement (Newfoundland, PEI, Ontario, and British Columbia), or by articulating systems of parent involvement that fall short of parent control (Manitoba, New Brunswick, Nova Scotia, & Yukon Territories).

This relationship between parent participation models and auspice suggests that jurisdictions can and do use legislative and regulatory practices about parent involvement as benchmarks to establish their policy preferences in relation to these dominant models. For those jurisdictions wishing to create largely nonprofit childcare systems, parent control of nonprofit centers is both a helpful tool and a *raison d'être*. In provinces favoring nonprofit care, parents are conceptualized as "collaborators" with caregivers, entitled to control and input. By staying silent in legislation and regulations, "silent" provinces enable market forces to dominate. By preferring some parent involvement, but stopping short of parent control, "parent input" provinces subtly favor nonprofit care, but much less explicitly than jurisdictions that mandate parent control. By contrast, in jurisdictions that favor a profit model, parents are conceptualized simply as consumers with the power to "choose" and "exit".

Power to "choose" is often illusory in the childcare field, particularly for parents with the fewest resources. Social factors (such as class, race, disability) and limited service (accessibility, availability, affordability, and proximity) mean that parents are rarely able to "choose" the care they want. For many parents, finding and keeping childcare is an exercise in constraint and compromise, not choice. Likewise, power to "exit" is rarely parents' first preference when there are emotional costs to children and practical costs to parents for leaving. The "consumer" model corresponds to a preference for the commercial sector and is consistent with conservative fiscal and social values: it prioritizes parents as decision makers because they are purchasers, not because they are citizens or partners in care.

Early childhood educators dominate the organizational structure and management of centers, and shape the programming, curriculum, and practices of staff. One can conclude therefore, that in the absence of other sources of power and influence, professional power will predominate. It is no accident that, in both "parent input" and "parent control" provinces, the power of professionals and staff are directly challenged and limited. It is also worth noting that, although early childhood professionals may dominate the organization and practices of centers, they do so, in Canada, for remarkably low wages compared to other professionals such as public school teachers, social workers, and those working in medical settings. So we must not overestimate the power of early childhood professionals. If the silent jurisdictions leave them power, it is a very constrained power.

Like the state, the early childhood education profession is also characterized by varying approaches toward parents. Currently, the professional consensus establishes an important role for parents as collaborators with caregivers (Shimoni, 1992; Friendly, 1994). While working with parents within a collaborator model may be difficult and conflictive at times, it is nonetheless one that the profession has historically accepted, although with some ambivalence (Powell, 1989; Shimoni & Ferguson, 1992). Many professionals argue that parent-staff collaboration is in the best interests of children, since it ensures continuity of care for children while at the same time treating parents with respect (Shimoni, 1992; Mayfield, 1990). Some studies conclude that parent involvement enhances the quality of care (Doherty-Derkowski, 1995). In the current social policy environment, the collaboration model (and its implicit preference for non-market service) is at risk. Political trends toward privatization may have negative impacts on the profession of early childhood education. From the perspective of workers, the commercial sector has consistently provided the worst wages and working conditions (Canadian Day Care Advocacy Association and Canadian Childcare Federation, 1993). As importantly, the philosophy of the profit model is at odds with many of the ideals and goals of the profession. For example, serving parents who see themselves as "consumers" may be no less intrusive than working with parents as collaborators. Moreover, it could have the added disadvantage of reinforcing a "service" mentality, which is not necessarily respectful, especially when it is accompanied with poor working conditions. For our children and our childcare system as a whole, the consumer model commodifies the care of human beings, a trend that analysts have noted particularly puts our vulnerable populations at risk (Kagan, 1991).

Our analysis of parent involvement, one part of the early childhood policy landscape, reveals the importance of underlying policy alternatives. These findings reveal that jurisdictions can and do use constitutional arrangements to favor or enhance their preferred philosophical approach to childcare service with implications for the profession of early childhood education, parents, policy advocates, and children. These constitutional practices in different jurisdictions within Canada are likely mirrored in other western countries. Political trends suggest an increasing reliance on the market model of purchaser-rights. With the ascendance of market models, governments pay decreasing attention to the role of citizen involvement as a matter of social entitlement. It is important for those of us in the childcare field to consider the implications of such trends for caregivers, parents, children, and our childcare system as a whole.

Notes

1. The authors wish to thank the Universities of Manitoba and Toronto and the Social Sciences and Humanities Research Council for the support of this project. We gratefully acknowledge the work of our research assistant, Jodi Lee.

2. These silent provinces all have regulations requiring that parents be informed about important aspects of the center, such as discipline methods and notification of inspections, as well as requiring parent authorization for medications, transportation, and other safety issues. Such requirements are found in all provinces and territories, regardless of their approach to parent involvement.

References

Arat-Koc, S., & Villasin, F. (1990). *Report and recommendations on the Foreign Domestic Worker Program.* Toronto: Intercede (Organization for Domestic Workers' Rights).

Berthiaume, D. (1997). The development of early childhood services in Quebec. *Interaction* 11(2): 4–5.

Canadian Day Care Advocacy Association and Canadian Childcare Federation. (1993). *Caring for a living: A study on wages and working conditions in Canadian childcare.* Ottawa: Canadian Day Care Advocacy Association and Canadian Childcare Federation.

Childcare Research and Resource Unit. (1997). *Childcare in Canada: Provinces and territories: 1995.* Toronto: Childcare Research and Resource Unit, Center for Urban and Community Studies, University of Toronto.

Doherty-Derkowski, G. (1995). *Quality matters: Excellence in early childhood programs.* Don Mills, Ontario: Addison Wesley.

Ferguson, E. (1991). The childcare crisis: The realities of women's caring. In C. Baines, P. Evans & S. Neysmith (Eds.). *Women's Caring: Feminist Perspectives on Social Welfare.* (pp. 26–38). Toronto: McClelland and Stewart.

Ferguson, E. (in press). Shifting sands and changing boundaries: Changes in childcare policies in the late 1990s. In C. Baines, P. Evans & S. Neysmith (Eds.,). *Women's Caring: Feminist Perspectives on Social Welfare* (2 ed.). Toronto: McClelland and Stewart.

Friendly, M. (1994). Childcare policy in Canada: Putting the pieces together. Don Mills, Ontario: Addison-Wesley.

Friendly, M., & Oloman, M. (1996). Childcare at the center: Childcare on the social, economic and political agenda in the 1990s. In J. Pulkingham and G. Ternowetsky (Eds.). *Remaking Canadian Social Policy.* (pp. 16–24). Halifax: Fernwood Publishing.

Goelman, H., Pence, A. R., Lero, D. S., Brockman, L. M., Glick, N., & Berkowitz, J. (1993). Canadian National Childcare Study: Where are the children? An overview of childcare arrangements in Canada. Ottawa.

Hayden, J. (1997). *Neo-conservatism and childcare services in Alberta: A case study.* Occasional Paper No.9. Childcare Resource and Research Unit. Toronto: University of Toronto.

Kagan, S. (1991). Examining profit and nonprofit childcare: An odyssey of quality and auspice. *Journal of Social Issues* 47(2): 87–104.

Mayfield, M. (1990). Parent involvement in early childhood programs. In I.M. Dovey *Childcare and Education: Canadian Dimensions.* Toronto: Nelson Canada.

Nelson, M. K. (1989). Negotiating care: Relationships between family daycare providers and mothers. *Feminist Studies,* 15(1): 586–605.

Powell, D.R. (1989). *Families and early childhood programs* Washington, D.C.: National Association for the Education of Young Children.

Prentice, S. (1997). The deficiencies of commercial day care. *Policy Options* 18(1): 42–45.

Prentice, S. (1999). Who should be in the business of childcare? The history and politics of childcare auspice in Canada. In L. Prochner & N. Howe (Eds.). *Early Childhood Care and Education in Canada: Past, Present, and Future.* Vancouver: UBC Press.

Shimoni, R. (1992). Parental involvement in early childhood education and day care. *Sociological Studies of Child Development* 5: 73–95.

Shimoni, R. & Ferguson, B. (1992). Rethinking parent involvement in childcare programs. *Child and Youth Care Forum,* 21: 105–118.

Legislation Consulted

Alberta Family and Social Services. (1993). *Day care licensing policy manual.* Government of Alberta.

Alberta Family and Social Services Daycare Programs. (1995). *Choosing a day care center: A guide for parents.* Calgary: Alberta Family and Social Services.

Gouvernement du Québec. (1992). An act respecting child day care. *Gazette Officielle du Québec*, 125(l): 4–11.

Gouvernement du Québec. (1993). Regulations. *Gazette Officielle du Québec*, 125(6): 744–751.

Government of British Columbia. (1996). *Community care facility act: Childcare regulation.* Vancouver: Queen's Printer for British Columbia.

Government of British Columbia. (1996). Order of the Lieutenant Governor in council: *Amendments to community care facility act, 0884.* Vancouver: Queen's Printer for British Columbia.

Government of British Columbia. (1996). *Order of the Lieutenant Governor in council: Excerpt from B.C. Reg. 264-96 amends B.C. Reg. 319-89, 1109.* Vancouver: Queen's Printer for British Columbia.

Government of New Brunswick. (1985). *Child and family services and family relations Act.* New Brunswick: Queen's Printer for New Brunswick.

Government of New Brunswick. (1993). *Day care facilities standards.* New Brunswick: Department of Health and Community Services.

Government of Newfoundland. (1990). *An act respecting day care and homemaker services* St John: Government of Newfoundland.

Government of Nova Scotia (1990). *Day care act and regulations: revised statutes, 1989.* Halifax: Queen's Printer for Nova Scotia.

Government of Ontario. (1995). *Day nurseries act — Revised statutes of Ontario. 1990.* Ottawa: Queen's Printer for Ontario.

Government of Prince Edward Island. (1988). *Childcare facilities act.* Charlottetown: Queen's Printer for Prince Edward Island.

Government of Prince Edward Island. (1993). *Amendment to health and community services act,* Charlottetown: Queen's Printer for Prince Edward Island.

Government of Quebec. (1991). *Regulation respecting day care centers.* Quebec: Quebec Official Printer.

Government of Saskatchewan. (1990). *An act to promote the growth and development of children and to support the provision of childcare services to Saskatchewan families.* Saskatoon: Queen's Printer for Saskatchewan.

Government of the Yukon. (1995). *Childcare center program regulation.* Whitehorse: Yukon Regulations.

Government of the Yukon. (1995). *Childcare subsidy regulation: Childcare act.* Whitehorse: Yukon Regulations.

Government of the Yukon. (1995). *Family day home program regulation: Childcare act.* Yukon Regulations.

Manitoba Childcare Office. (1992). *The community child day care standards act.* Winnipeg: Queen's Printer for the province of Manitoba.

Manitoba Childcare Office. (1994). *The community child day care standards act: Child day care regulation.* Winnipeg: Queen's Printer for the province of Manitoba.

Northwest Territories Daycare. (n.d.). *Interpretation of child day care act.* Yellowknife: Government of Northwest Territories.

Northwest Territories Education, Culture and Employment. (1994). *Child day care manual: Child day care act and child day care standards regulations.* Territorial Printer: Yellowknife.

Nova Scotia Round Table on Daycare (1994). *Report of the Nova Scotia Round Table on Daycare.* Halifax: Minister of Community Services. *Struggles, strategies and options.* Halifax: Fernwood.

Quebec National Assembly 35 Legislature 2 session. (1996). *An act to amend the act respecting child day care and the other legislative provisions.* Quebec: Quebec Official Printer.

Saskatchewan Childcare Association (1991). The childcare story: The struggle, the reality, the vision.

Saskatchewan Social Services. (1995). *The Saskatchewan childcare regulations.* Court of Saskatchewan.

Statutes of the Yukon. (1989-90). *Childcare act.* Whitehorse: Yukon. Yukon Health and Social Services. (n.d.). *Regulatory guidelines for family day homes and childcare centers*, Statistics Canada.

Chapter 15

Immigrant Families in Early Childhood Centers: Diverse Expectations

Marjory Ebbeck
Anne Glover

Abstract

This chapter presents the findings of a South Australian study which investigated the views of 101 immigrant families in relation to their expectations of early childhood centers. These views were compared with 100 early childhood teachers working in the centers. Areas of congruence and dissonance are identified and implications of the research are discussed.

Introduction

Australia is a multicultural society with some 100 ethnic groups, each of which differs in their history, language of origin, religious beliefs, family mores, customs, political experience, and expectations of their new country. Of the current 18.2 million people, 4.2 million have immigrated to Australia since the Second World War (Shu, Goldlust, McKenzie, Struik, & Khoo, 1996).

The endorsement by the federal government of a policy of multiculturalism in 1976 was, perhaps, the most significant response to Australia's diversity since European colonization. The policy's three foci—cultural identity, social justice, and economic efficiency—were to provide a way of ensuring that, within a framework of shared fundamental values, all groups could retain core cultural values such as language, traditions, and religion. In practice this policy has been difficult to implement. The shared values are not clear for many Australians; cultural and ethnic differences often exist on a competitive, rather than a complementary basis; and opportunities for all Australians to share their cultural heritage have been denied in some social arenas (Taylor & MacDonald, 1994; Fotiades, 1995; Hartley, 1995). Despite this, Australia is regarded internationally as being at the forefront of success in managing its cultural diversity (Smolicz, 1997; Creaser & Dau, 1996).

At the state level, there is variance in responses to cultural and ethnic diversity. In South Australia (the focus for this chapter) the government has recently reaffirmed its commitment to diversity with *The Declaration of Principles for a Multicultural South Australia* (Olsen, 1997). This policy affirms the right of all individuals to maintain, develop, express, and share their cultural heritages within the social framework of the state.

The challenge for any human service organization is to ensure that all individuals or groups, regardless of culture or ethnicity, can participate in and benefit from the service; and that families are assisted in ways to share their cultural heritages as appropriate (Aina, 1994; Kiriakon, 1996).

Views about Immigrant Families

Immigrant families are faced with a number of problems and issues as they make Australia their new home. The social adaptation and integration of immigrant families is contingent on a number of factors, one being the degree to which family expectations are met in the early childhood and schooling sectors (Baker, 1994; Bowman & Stott, 1994). There has been a tendency on the part of some early childhood professionals to assume that early childhood services in Australia are similar to those offered in other countries. Likewise, there is a tendency by a number of professionals to assume that immigrant families have similar views about what they want for their children's early education (Taylor, 1994; Neuman & Roskos, 1994).

Although there is a dearth of information on the childrearing practices of immigrant families in Australia, research in other countries suggests that there is a wide variation in practices amongst different cultural groups (Swick, Boutte, & Van Scoy, 1995). There are differences also between professionals and their immigrant client groups as to what they expect early childhood centers to provide in their educational programs and overall service delivery (Ebbeck & Glover, 1996).

In the Australian context, Rodd has written that professionals who work with children and families need to be aware that immigrant parents often do not have the same access to traditional normative guidance and support on childrearing when compared with families who reside in their country of origin. Rodd (1995) also proposed that professionals working with children and families need to be aware of the potential dissonance in respect of cultural expectations between professionals' views of immigrant families of their childrearing practices. Ranford describes aspects of Vietnamese childrearing and notes that because of family dispersal once in Australia, young Vietnamese families have no senior family members to turn to for advice and support (Ranford, 1992).

Another consideration is that some professionals are poorly informed about the wide variation in childrearing practices and expectations amongst different cultural groups (Ebbeck, 1995). Unfortunately, some professionals have stereotypic views about the behaviors and beliefs of ethnic groups. Immigrant groups are far from homogenous in the values, beliefs, and expectations they have for their children. Most families are very concerned for the future success of their children even before they attend school.

In support of this statement, research by Gonzales-Mena (1991) has shown that there are differences in educational and cultural expectations between parents and early childhood staff working in centers. These differences are particularly evident in the cultural values that families have for children. If educational programs are to support the child and the immigrant family, then there must be some basic understanding and acceptance by professionals of childrearing practices and the expectations of parents (NAEYC, 1996).

It would seem then that the early childhood professional has to make a determined effort to understand the role and place of the family, especially for recent immigrant children to Australia, if they are to provide those kinds of services that will benefit both child and family.

Many families have views that are not congruent with those of mainstream Australia however much they value and celebrate their children. Petrick (1992: p. 21) wrote of Cambodian families in Adelaide, that children are highly valued. The interesting additional observation she made highlights why the professionals have to rethink their values and practices. She reported that some Cambodian families find it difficult to make provision for "play" in the home as it creates disorder in the crowded accommodation in which they live. How, then, would this action fit in with the traditional early childhood professionals' belief that play is the process through which children grow and develop?

The Study

Sample and Method
This chapter presents an extract of the findings of a wide-scale study that examined the views of 101 South Australian immigrant families as to

their educational expectations for their children who are in the age range of birth to eight years. The views of 100 early childhood teachers working in early childhood centers were examined in relation to their educational expectations. A comparison was then presented noting the commonalities and differences between parents and teachers.

Through structured interviews with immigrant families living in South Australia, the study aimed to gather reliable data about aspects of their social integration in relation to their expectations about early childhood education. A sample of five ethnic groups was obtained using the following criteria:

1. emigrating to Australia within the last six years;
2. having a child in the age group of birth to eight years; and
3. country of origin being in the Pan-Pacific Region.

Ethnic groups available in sufficient numbers for the sample were from the following countries—Vietnam, Cambodia, People's Republic of China (PRC), Indonesia, and the Philippines—totaling 101 families in all. Mothers were sought from early childcare centers and the purposes of the study were explained to them. Where needed, the interviews were conducted in the native language of the family using bilingual early childhood workers. The interviews occurred either in the early childhood center or in the home. The mean age of the mothers was 30.6 years.

The study also gathered information from 100 early childhood teachers working in early childhood centers in South Australia. The mean age of the teachers was 34.7 years.

Questions about their expectations of early childhood education were presented to both parents and teachers. The questions included the items listed below:

How important is it for the early childhood center to:

1. involve parents in decision making about what happens in the center?
2. help parents understand their children better?
3. help parents enjoy being a parent?
4. provide help to families in times of emergency?
5. give parents some time to themselves?
6. give parents an opportunity to work with their child in an early childhood center?

Respondents were asked to rank order their response from *unimportant* to *very important*. Statistical analyses were conducted with the pooled parent responses compared against the teacher responses. It was necessary to pool all of the parent groups for the statistical significance tests because of the small numbers of cells. However, in the discussion of responses, significant differences appeared between parents and teachers on all of the items.

Findings[1]

1. Parent involvement in decision making
The study showed predictable responses from the teachers with some 86% ranking parent involvement either very important or important. The response rate from the parents was also strong in support of involving parents in decision making in the early childhood center, with 95% of the Indonesian group ranking it as either very important or important, 90% of the Vietnamese group ranking it as either very important or important, followed by families from Peoples Republic of China (PRC) with 75% ranking it as very important or important.

*2. Center's role in enhancing parents'
understanding of their children*
All the five ethnic groups reported that the center should help parents to better understand their children. The average number of families amongst the five groups ranking this as important or very important was 96%. Similarly, 94% of teachers ranked this as important or very important.

3. Center's role in helping parents enjoy their role
Cambodian and PRC parents especially, but also many of the other groups, named this as an important part of the role of the center. Most teachers also saw this as a very important part of their work (94%).

4. Center should provide emergency help to families
Differences between parents and teachers were marked. Almost all teachers (97%) saw this as an important or very important role for the center. Most immigrant parents rated this lower. Ratings of important or very important were recorded as follows: Cambodians 55%, Philippine families 89%, Vietnamese 95%, PRC families 60%, and Indonesians 80%. This supports earlier comments in this chapter about how different the services in Australia are when compared with those in the Pan-Pacific countries. In fact, many immigrant families may not be aware of the total range of services, including emergency care, that centers offer. Results here indicate that early childhood teachers view emergency care as an important way of supporting their family/clients. Finding ways of com-

municating the availability of such services to immigrant families needs to be a priority.

5. Centers should allow parents to have time for themselves

Results show that parents ranked this a lower priority than did teachers. In the sample from Vietnam, some 23% ranked this as unimportant. This may highlight the need for continuous communication between parents and centers and also the need to provide information in a variety of languages. Teachers' responses indicate that they see value in parents having some time to themselves and that this is a quite legitimate use of the early childhood center. A strong majority of teachers (80%) rated this as an important role for the center. Again, communication with families is vital to allow families to make maximum use of the services being provided.

6. Centers should provide opportunities for parents to work with their child in the early childhood setting

Differences were marked between parents and teachers. While 94% of teachers noted this as important or very important, parents were less supportive of this statement. Less than half of the Cambodians and only two thirds of the Philippino and Vietnamese families rated this as important. Conversely, the majority of Indonesian and PRC families rated this as important (85%). However, only 45% of Cambodians and 63% of Philippino families saw this as an important role for the center. 85% of PRC and Indonesian families, and 63% of Vietnamese families rated this as important. The discrepancy in value placed on parents working in the center could be linked to cultural views which project authority and reverence onto the teacher (Lee, 1995). In some cultures the teacher is seen to be a conveyor of knowledge, not as a peer or friend. Parents who subscribe to this viewpoint may believe that it is detrimental to be in the center for it might remove some authority from the teacher. Other views which prevent parents from wanting to work in the centers are related to perceptions of prolonged dependence by the child. Some parents believe that children will learn independence more readily when not exposed to parents in centers.

Implications of the Findings

Migrants from the Philippines, Vietnam, Cambodia, PRC, and Indonesia are likely to have had little experience of social services comparable to those in Australia, and could hold different views to those of Australian-trained early childhood professionals, especially in terms of a commitment toward involving parents in program delivery.

These cultures prefer to use the extended family as their welfare "net". Thus, Asian parents may be more wary of intervention by early childhood service providers than are families who are familiar with the Australian welfare system.

Policies in early childhood need to be developed with a full understanding of the possible range of family cultures. This study has shown the dangers of stereotyping immigrant families.

Policies that emphasize the decision making role of parents are needed at both the micro and macro levels of government. Clearly, immigrant families need opportunities for empowerment and their potential as decision makers within services needs to be considered by professionals. The early childhood professional has a strong advocacy role in this regard and needs a sound understanding of the complexity surrounding being an immigrant family in today's ethnically diverse Australia.

Conclusion: Parental Involvement in Context

The Australian National Childcare Accreditation Council (1993) defines parental involvement in terms of participation in program development and evaluation as well as the more traditional activities such as fundraising, maintenance, cooking experience, and assistance on excursions. The involvement of parents in planning and evaluating the program is controversial. This wider involvement requires that parents have, or seek to acquire, an informed understanding of children and their development in a social setting.

This study has revealed a number of factors that must be considered regarding parental involvement in early childhood services. Primarily, it reveals that we cannot take for granted that all parents *want* to be involved to the same extent. Parent involvement has been identified as a challenge for early childhood staff in Australia and elsewhere (Advisory Council on Multicultural Affairs, 1998). The National Childcare Accreditation Council of Australia gives highest rating to parent involvement when interactions between staff and parents are characterized by exchange of information and mutual respect for similarities and differences in childrearing practices (NCAC 1993, p. 31). In addition, childcare accreditation requirements expect parents to be involved in setting all center policies, in formulating long- and short-term goals, in consulting on and evaluating the center's program, and participating in center management.

These requirements are the same for private (commercial) centers as they are for community-based ones. The philosophy behind such requirements is that *"children develop security and trust when there is continuity in the care they receive at home and in the center"* (NCAC 1993, p. 31).

While it is expected that the kind and degree of involvement will differ from parent to parent, from center to center, and from community to community, the establishment of a relationship between parent and professional based on mutual respect remains fundamental to the notion of quality in childcare. Developing mutual understanding must become the goal of parent and professional cooperation. This is especially important for immigrant families who are struggling to maintain their own cultural identity while becoming part of multicultural Australia.

Notes

1. For more detailed analyses of the findings, contact Professor Marjory Ebbeck at deLissa Institute, University of South Australia, Magill, SA, Australia 5074.

References

Advisory Council On Multicultural Affairs. (1988). *Toward a national agenda for a multicultural Australia*. A Discussion Paper. Canberra: Australian Government Publishing Service.

Aina, E. (1994). Teaching children from culturally different backgrounds. *Early Childhood Education* Vol. 27, No.1: 18–20.

Creaser, B., & Dau, E. (Eds.). (1996). *The anti-bias approach in early childhood*. Melbourne: Harper Educational.

Baker, G. (1994). Teaching children to respect diversity, *Childhood Education*, Vol. 71, No. 1: 33–36.

Bowman, B., & Stott, F. (1994). Understanding development in a cultural context: The challenge for teachers. In *Diversity and Developmentally Appropriate Practices*. (Eds.). B. Mallory & R. New. Columbia: Teachers College Press.

Ebbeck, M. (1995). Purposes of early childhood education: Expressed views of teachers and parents in Hong Kong, *International Journal of Early Years Education*, Vol. 3, No. 2: 3–18.

Ebbeck, M., & Glover, A. (1996). *Immigrant Families: Childrearing and Education Expectations*. A Report to the Bureau of Immigration, Multicultural and Population Research, Melbourne, Australia.

Fotiadas, K. (1995). Multiculturalism in education: An Australian perspective *Multicultural Teaching*, Vol. 13, No. 2: 35–37.

Gonzalez-Mena, J. (1991). *Multicultural issues in childcare*. Toronto: Mayfield Publishing.

Hartley, R. (Ed.) (1995). *Families and cultural diversity in Australia*. Sydney: Allen & Unwin, Australia.

Lee, F.Y. (1995–March). Asian parents as partners, *Young Children*, Vol. 50, No. 4: 4–8.

NAEYC. (1996). National Association for the Education of Young Children position statement. Responding to linguistic and cultural diversity–recommendations for effective early childhood education, *Young Children*, January: 4–12.

National Childcare Accreditation Council. (1993). *Quality improvement and accreditation handbook*. Canberra: Commonwealth of Australia.

Neuman, S., & Roskos, K. (1994). Bridging home and school with a culturally responsive approach. *Childhood Education*, Vol. 70, No. 4: 210–214.

Olsen, J. (1997). Declaration of Principles for a Multicultural South Australia. Adelaide: Government of South Australia.

Petrick, S. (1992). Babies in hammocks: Cambodian childrearing practices. *Professional Digest*, vol. 3, No. 2: 21–30.

Ramsey, P., & Derman-Sparkes, L. (1992). Multicultural education reaffirmed. *Young Children*, Vol. 47, No. 2: 10–11.

Ranford, R. (1992). Families in the Vietnamese culture. *Professional Digest*, Vol. 3, No. 2: 31–33.

Rodd, J. (1995). Early socialization attitudes and practices of recently arrived immigrant mothers in Australia. A pilot study. *Australian Research in Early Childhood Education*, Vol. 1: 121–130.

Shu, J., Goldlust, J., McKenzie, F., Struick, A., & Khoo, S. (1996). *Australia's Population: Trends & Prospects*. Bureau of Immigration, Multicultural and Population Research. Canberra: Australian Government Printing Service.

Smolicz, G. (1997). Extract from Opening Address, MECCS Conference, Adelaide.

Swick, K., Boutte, G., & Van Scoy, I. (1995). Families & schools: Building multicultural values together. *Childhood Education*, Winter: 75–80.

Taylor, J., & MacDonald, H. (1994). *Disadvantage and children of iImmigrants: A longitudinal study*. Canberra: Australian Government Publishing Service.

Taylor, J. (1994). *Issues of childrearing and poverty among Asian immigrants*. Victoria: Brotherhood of St. Laurence.

The Professional Landscape

Chapter 16

Preparing the Early Childhood Profession: An Australian Analysis

Collette Tayler

Abstract

This chapter addresses change in early childhood teacher education programs in a postmodern world and explores opportunities to review traditional approaches and uncontested pedagogical assumptions about early childhood education. In a period of fiscal constraint on human service provision and an ideological climate of conservatism, the challenge of preparing professionals who work in diverse social and cultural environments with families espousing different and competing values is substantial.

The Challenge of Changing Landscapes

The social world in which early childhood teachers operate reflects marked generational changes in the composition, culture, and diversity of families. Needs for, and expectations of, early childhood services have changed considerably in the previous decade and continue to change. Correspondingly, the roles of early childhood teachers are diversifying as they link the personal, social, and educational worlds of children and families and try to produce the services needed. All of this work is done in an economic climate of fiscal constraint.

Universities preparing teachers, and technical and further education colleges preparing childcare professionals, have also changed markedly. Government fiscal constraint and an ideological climate of conservatism influences preservice programs as well as early childhood services in the community. Responsiveness by university staff to the changing profession is complicated by the lead-time necessary to shift focus in courses of four years duration. The competency-based approach prevalent in the technical and further education sector prompts other challenges for staff preparing professionals for rapidly changing work contexts.

Preparing the Australian early childhood profession of a new millennium calls for models that integrate change theory within and across preservice programs and enable socially critical frameworks to be applied. Maintenance of traditional programs risks detaching preservice education from the world of early childhood work. Preservice teacher education programs are addressing the context and culture of the students and expanding social and cultural understandings in order to produce responsive teachers.

This chapter addresses the work of the early childhood profession by analyzing relationships between the changing directions of Australian early childhood teacher education programs, the wave of reforms in universities and TAFE Colleges, and demographic data on the health and well-being of children and families who are the users of early childhood services.

Images of the Australian Early Childhood Profession

Most children and parents construct positive images of the early childhood professionals with whom they have daily contact. Yet images of the profession as a whole are imbued with dissonance about the place of children in Australian society, the role of women, and the need for services provided by a well-qualified, professional workforce. On one hand, rhetoric about the importance of the early childhood years flows through government agendas and programs aimed to facilitate a "good start" for children, while at the same time ambivalence prevails about the content of programs and the specialist expertise necessary to work effectively with very young children. Traditional images of kindergarten as a social play experience for children exist alongside images of early childhood classes preparing children to read and write early so their chances of success in school are enhanced. To some adults early childhood services are of little value unless they escalate the onset of literacy in children. To others, early childhood services provide social development for a child while also providing respite for parents. To many, early childhood services are provided by "well meaning women who have pleasant dispositions, patience and warmth" (Ashton & Elliott, 1995) but who neither engage in nor need to pursue rigorous, scholarly study of young children's development and learning in the dynamic social, cultural, educational, and political context of Australian care and education.

The kaleidoscope of images of the early childhood profession include those of a group different and separate from other areas of the teaching profession, expressed by a call for early childhood professionals to "entertain perspectives other than their own" (Stonehouse, 1992, p. 161); a group misunderstood, "a cinderella area seriously neglected" (Cross, cited in Senate Employment, Education and Training Reference Committee, 1996, p. 94); a group fractured and divided across childcare, preschool, and school sectors of the field (Senate Employment, Education and Training Reference Committee, 1996; Tayler, 1994); a group having expertise primarily for work in childcare or preschool rather than the early primary school (Senate Employment, Education and Training Reference Committee, 1996); and a group traversing a span of services that make the profession "problematic" (Mellor & Gifford, 1992, p. 208). All of these images reflect in some way the challenge of developing a cross-sectoral, cogent view of the profession to which all sectors can relate.

These images also underscore the challenge of early childhood teacher education courses to prepare professionals for early childhood work. The work of the early childhood profession is distributed widely across education and care settings, but is also closely connected to tacit values about family, schooling, and childhood espoused by different cultural and social communities across Australia. Building in rigor and depth of study, flexibility, and professional practice in courses where the field is broader than "the school as model" challenges staff resourcefulness as well as the capacity of institutions to ensure that funding is sufficient to deliver effective programs.

As in all professions, mixed views prevail on the relevance and significance of early childhood professional work in the lives of Australian children and families. The nexus between family and school, between private and public spheres of children's lives, is core early childhood work and yet this nexus is problematic in society as a whole. Different ideologies and political agendas exist in regard to the relative responsibilities of family and the community or state in the care and education of young children. Early childhood work is carried out in a wide variety of settings, including schools, and through provision of a diversity of services ranging across health, welfare, community development, and education. The degree to which early childhood professionals succeed in inducting children and families into formal education services makes the work of primary teacher colleagues more or less complex (see Hayden, this volume chapter 8). Because of this, some schools give special attention to preschool and early years provision as security that children will commence formal school education with success. Others pay scant attention to the area, believing whatever is done in early childhood classes will be acceptable (Stamopoulos, 1995).

Recent literature also questions traditional directions in early childhood curriculum (Fleer, 1995; Mallory & New, 1994; Kessler, 1992). Matters of knowledge and its social construction; the relative value of different knowledges in education and in the community at large; the relationships of culture, language and learning; and constructions of family and society in a postmodern world challenge the primary focus in preservice early childhood education courses given to traditional child development content. Although the particular culture and characteristics of a country must be central to any analysis of curriculum and early childhood services, David Wu reports, in discussing early childhood education across nine Asia Pacific countries and the United States, that early education is "ninety percent politics and ten percent pedagogy" (Wu, 1992, p. 21). Ideological, class, gender, economic, and political struggles are resident within most early childhood curriculum. Early childhood in China, for example, is a "sensitive thermometer for measuring the correct or incorrect thoughts on human nature, intelligence, psychology and pedagogy, women's liberation, family planning and, most crucially, the future of China and its spoiled children" (Wu, 1992, p. 21). Social, cultural, and educational dimensions of Australian early childhood programs need challenge and reform in the light of current child and family contexts. Garbarino's report of this issue in the United States context construes the challenge there as "educating children in a socially toxic environment" (Garbarino, 1997, p. 12). Early childhood curriculum and the type of courses provided for professionals entering this field is under scrutiny in many countries.

Preservice Education and Qualification

Australian early childhood professionals are prepared in university programs, technical and further education (TAFE) colleges, and in private colleges and institutes that offer courses registered through government industry training boards. In Australia, the level and type of preservice education experienced by an early childhood professional varies according to the type of institution enrolled, the state in which the professional is prepared and, in some cases, the target-setting in which the professional plans to work. State governments have varying (although similar) requirements for qualifications of childcare, preschool, and school personnel in early childhood services. For example, most teachers working in government preschools and kindergartens have three- or four-year degrees in early childhood education. All Australian teachers working in early years primary school classes (K–3) have three- or four-year degrees, some in primary education, some in early childhood education. In childcare settings, some states have mainly degree level teachers and others have two- or three-year diploma professionals along with staff who have completed courses of several weeks to a year. There are also staff in some childcare centers who have no specialist preservice early childhood preparation. Unqualified staff in some parts of Australia continue to receive exemptions from state qualification requirements because qualified staff are not available in the locality, or owners of the centers fund positions at minimum salary levels that do not attract professionals with above the minimum qualifications.

Notwithstanding the irony of separating the "care" and "education" functions of any service for young children, a setting construed as providing predominantly "care" or "education" prompts reference to different requirements in legislation pertaining to qualifications and conditions of staff. Professionals who work in education-focused settings such as schools and preschools are teachers who completed courses in education faculties at universities (or colleges and institutes of education subsequently amalgamated with universities). Professionals who work in "care" settings may come from university, TAFE, or private courses. Some staff may, by dint of their qualifications, be able to move across the early childhood sectors of school, preschool, and childcare whereas others may be unable to move into schools or preschools without further study. Because university, TAFE, and private providers have different accreditation processes and practices, and because state governments have different regulatory frameworks affecting courses, students, or graduates who wish to move across institutional groups or across state borders can encounter problems in articulating coherent study or career pathways. Much has been done in Australia since the 1980s to coordinate preservice education and workplace regulation, removing many disparities, and yet federal and state government legislation pertaining to working conditions and requirements remain varied. Bureaucratic ambivalence about coordination and regulation in the face of national workplace deregulation accounts for some of the sustaining differences affecting early childhood workplaces across Australia.

Structural and Government Change

The style, content, sequence, and manner of delivery of any nation's teacher education courses cannot be viewed in isolation from the nature of teaching, schooling, education, and the society in which a course functions (Judge, 1989). Although the review of Australian early childhood courses by Tayler (1991, 1994), outline of issues (1992b), and preferred models of early childhood teacher education programs (1992a) detailed many of these characteristics, the Australian political landscape has changed since that time. The social and educational climate remains volatile and all courses have been reconsidered, revised or redeveloped in correspondence with federal government fiscal constraint. Some university programs integrated the early childhood and primary courses in response to severe staff reductions. Others made closer links with TAFE programs, forging new distributions of content and course focus. Yet others have held to original structures but operated with reduced resources. All programs are affected by recent political changes and structural reform at all levels of government. The bureaucratic and management language of government is now well established in university faculties.

University-based early childhood programs in faculties of education also encounter pressure to include teaching staff who have neither specialist early childhood qualifications nor experience of working with young children. In addition, all programs have difficulty finding sufficient, suitable field placements for students across the range of early childhood service settings, particularly as the total student population in early childhood courses (university, TAFE, and private) increased substantially throughout the nineties.

Fundamental Change

Little has been reported on the degree to which early childhood courses have changed in underlying philosophies and direction as a consequence of the changes in university structure and resources and the merging of early childhood and primary specialist staff in university settings (see Hayden, this volume, chapter 8). Whether early childhood preservice education courses have altered philosophical or pedagogical bases in response to recent and increasing data on the cultural diversity of Australia and the general well-being of its children and families is open to question. Ashton and Elliott (1995) described stereotypic views of childcare as prevalent in teacher education programs. Hayden reported on a street survey in which the majority of respondents did not perceive work in childcare as needing professional or extensive tertiary preparation (Hayden, 1996a). Similarly in Britain, this circumstance contributed to remarks such as those of a recent British Minister of Education that "an army of intelligent mums" would do for teaching children under eight (see Gammage, 1995, p. 97).

Fleer (1997, p. 13) asserts the need for guidelines for the preparation of early childhood professionals to "guarantee the quality of our early childhood programs in Australia" and goes on to argue that documents such as the guidelines on preparing early childhood professionals set by the National Association for the Education of Young Children (1996) and the position paper of the Association for Childhood Education International (1997) give explicit direction about the content of preservice education courses. Although these documents, and equivalent Australian discussion papers and documents such as the national competency framework for beginning teachers (Australian Teaching Council, 1996) and the Board of Teacher Registration Queensland discussion paper on early childhood teacher education (1997), provide useful information for those designing and delivering preservice education programs, all of these documents fail to address explicitly ways to integrate changing social, cultural, and political dynamics while also negotiating "shared understanding of the key features of high-quality courses of study that prepare early childhood teachers to work in a range of settings" (Board of Teacher Registration, 1997, p. 3). It is a myth to believe that a set of guidelines can assure the quality of programs relevant to a postmodern world.

Sources of Information

One clear trend in early childhood teacher education in the past five years has been the replacement of American textbooks with those written by Australian authors (see, for example, Arthur, Beecher, Dockett, Farmer, & Death, 1996; Briggs & Potter, 1995; Fleer, 1995; Hayden, 1996; Wright, 1991). This trend acknowledges the importance of context and culture in any analysis of professional issues and provides support for the notion that knowledge is socially constructed and integrally related to the time and place in which it develops. Bereday (1964) sets out clearly the importance of context when comparing settings or promoting certain types of programs. Moreover, the knowledge, beliefs, and understandings held by students on entry to a program are important to the way in which they accommodate new knowledge and confront new ideas. A survey of literature indicates little published information on whether preservice courses routinely collect data on the types of students entering programs, the views and attitudes of students on issues such as childcare, child rearing practices, conceptions of childhood, conceptions of what it is to be educated, beliefs about early childhood practice, and beliefs about family life, diversity, and culture. The limited data available describe stereotypic attitudes held by entry early childhood students on issues of childcare, parenting, and family life. The need for courses to increase tolerance and broaden understandings of multiculturalism and ways of Australia's diverse families is apparent from these data (see, for example Kelly, 1986; Ashton & Elliott, 1995; Elliott, 1996).

If one accepts the argument that preservice education is to prepare teachers for work in a diverse and vibrant Australian community, then assessment of entry and exit understandings related to child and family matters is as important as assessing understanding of teaching strategies and techniques, or espousing recorded theory. If practical teaching is assessed specifically around technical components, and academic units are assessed in ways that do not capture the outcomes of student learning regarding social policy, equity, values, and culture and their impact on early childhood pedagogy and practice, then the chances of preparing a responsive early childhood profession for a new millennium diminish.

Candidates Entering the Profession

In the context of the United States, the Carnegie Report (1986) highlighted the lack of recruitment into teaching of people from minority groups. Although teacher education reports in Australia have not specifically focused on the need to recruit candidates representative of the cultural diversity of the population, this area deserves attention if the profession is to be responsive to context and culture in teaching and learning. Arguments for ensuring access of minority groups to teacher education courses are based on moral imperatives and a sense of justice rather than on any expression of need for an ethnic or cultural minority group to be taught by people from the same group (Raths, 1989). A challenge to ensure that the diversity of a nation's population is represented in the candidates who seek to become early childhood professionals exists when public responsibility for education is supplanted by private responsibility, a trend emerging in Australia. In such circumstances, candidates from poor communities have diminished opportunity to take part in tertiary education as costs increasingly transfer from the state to the individual.

In the case of early childhood teaching, men are also poorly represented across Australia. Data are not readily available on the current cultural and socioeconomic composition of candidates entering early childhood teaching, but anecdotal evidence indicates little growth in the representation of men or of groups such as Aboriginals and people from diverse non-Anglo backgrounds in courses across the country. Perhaps because of the traditions that are the foundation of early childhood services in Australia (see Piscitelli, McLean & Halliwell, 1992; Kerr, 1994) the field has been dominated by monolingual women from the middle classes. A notable progression is the postgraduate programs for training early childhood teachers that have recently been introduced in New South Wales and elsewhere (see Hayden, 1997) for the express purpose of diversifying the field (see also Greive & Maloney, this volume). Whether the style and form of delivery of early childhood programs in the field and in the university have a part to play in regard to the kinds of people who enter the field is an important consideration. Most Australian universities are expanding their flexibility of delivery to address this issue.

The Impact of Postgraduate Programs

The nineties have brought rapid growth in postgraduate studies in early childhood where progress in research across a wide variety of areas is occurring. This development is indeed positive and also has an impact on undergraduate programs. How closely preservice course developers have analyzed the postgraduate work with a view to preparing undergraduates better for research remains to be seen. However, recent changes in federal government support to postgraduate studies may impede the advances made in early childhood research at a time when the Senate Inquiry highlighted a vital need for more research in Australian early childhood development, education, and care (1996). Rigorous study of inquiry methods are perhaps not what undergraduates enter early childhood courses to do (see Ashton & Elliott, 1995), but attention to this area would strengthen the capacity of students to analyze their work beyond that of doing child observations.

Demographic Data on Australian Children and Families

Children bring to early childhood services (day care, preschool, and early primary) a variety of experiences, beliefs, expectations, and challenges that arise from home. The general health and family conditions of children clearly influence educational achievement. For some children the prevailing conditions of their lives ensure the likelihood of success whereas for others this assurance is absent. Success may come with extraordinary effort and persistence.

Study of family and general health data provide critical contextual information in early childhood teacher education programs. These data beg questions of how well Australian social policy supports families and enables a "fair go" to all children. In a field that prides itself on catering to the needs of the child, early childhood teachers must become conversant with demographic data on Australian families and debate the philosophy and direction of current early childhood programs in view of such data. Family groups have changed substantially in recent decades. For example, the median age of mothers is higher now than a decade ago, and there are more multiple births now than a decade ago (McLennon & Goward, 1997). These, and many other demographic data, affect the work of early childhood educators (see also Gammage, this volume). Preservice programs in early childhood that include cursory address to family studies and social policy and which provide insufficient rigor in the assessment, management, design, and development of child, family, and community data do little to build student knowledge and sensitivity to the field in which they are to work. It is one thing to say the field has changed. It is another to understand how it has changed and to match professional work more specifically with the changes.

The UNICEF "Progress of Nations" report (1996) locates the nutrition, health, and education of Australian children in relation to children for all other countries. These data confirm that young Australians are relatively well-off but that one in five Australian children (before taxes and transfers) lives below the poverty line. Over 50% of children in sole-mother families are living in poverty. The study acknowledges that many children are happier and better cared for in sole parent families than in miserable marriages. However, the Report notes that "separation and divorce are associated with poorer school performance, greater risk of teen pregnancy, higher rates of delinquency, and a worsening of the mental health of both mothers and children". Further, data in the Commonwealth health monitoring study of Australian children (Mathers, 1995), the Western Australian child health studies (see Zubrick et al., 1995, 1997; Silburn et al., 1996) and the analysis of poverty in Australia (Healey, 1997) also starkly point out poverty as the major inhibitor of child well-being and future success. Teachers and teacher educators have a role to play in realizing the importance of these data, profiling the demographics of their own classes and debating and designing responsive programs that link with initiatives in allied fields.

The general condition of the population, particularly in regard to mental, social, and emotional health, indicates some sense of the load placed on teachers in the 1990s. This load is probably characterized differently from that carried by teachers in past eras because of the changes that have taken place in the Australian family and society. There is a growing body of knowledge from other places that shows changing family patterns and community life pose particular risks and opportunities in child socialization and education (see, for example, Amato, 1987; Bronfenbrenner, 1991; Leach, 1994; Rutter & Rutter, 1993; Webster, 1990). Each child is embedded in a family, a community, a culture, and a society.

Teacher education programs clearly need to address the broad context of supporting children's learning, and research data is central to this work. The need for early childhood teacher education programs to develop in students a set of research, mediation, and advocacy skills alongside pedagogy is clear if teachers are to know and respond to the contexts in which they work. Doing so with a code of ethics in place would give considerable facility to early childhood professionals as they question and help regulate policy (Gammage, 1995; see also Newman, this volume).

Uncertain Progress

Australian early childhood teacher education is at a critical juncture. The rapid growth and changes in early childhood services call for vigilance on the part of teacher educators who must predict and plan for differing demands placed on graduates in childcare centers, preschools, and in the early years of school. On the other hand, teacher educators need to lead developments in the field, and be critical of changing trends that lack accompanying scrutiny and evaluation.

Courses that integrate change into all aspects of their programs and which provide critical analysis of changes are more likely to prepare early childhood professionals for work in a postmodern world. Initiatives across Australia to develop models more sensitive and responsive to change and diversity are positive and are being supported as Australian teacher education programs expand into neighboring countries, particularly in the Asian region.

Gammage (1995, p. 98) points out that most countries of the developed world build initial teacher education around certain core principles and areas of knowledge distilled "from consensus, from research and from practical experience". Areas of content common to early childhood courses (Gammage, 1995, pp. 100–101) include knowledge of human development and human learning; high level conceptual knowledge, usually in a discipline; knowledge of curriculum content areas; ability to communicate effectively; ability to manage and organize; knowledge of sociology; values clarification, ideology, and beliefs; and regular, well-integrated field experience. Although general directions seem similar in many parts of the world, what counts as valid knowledge for both children and their teachers is a task much wider than interpreting subject curricula. The task brings politics, culture, society, and context into focus.

As Australia goes through a reinvention of social and educational policy with the federal, conservative government, the discernible community ambivalence about childhood and the rights and needs of children have an impact on early childhood work. Gammage points out that effective schooling should take place "in a culture and atmosphere where children are valued and held dear; in short, in a culture which actually *likes* children" (1995, p. 96). Cross reports some harrowing examples of an embedded negativity toward children in Australia (Cross, 1992).

Decades of attention to economic imperatives at the expense of social and community values have taken a toll on children, their needs, and their rights. Australian early childhood teaching is poised in a time where the community and country expects program achievements to be considerable in regard to socializing children, modifying difficult behavior, advancing cognitive skills, diagnosing special needs, motivating children, and providing imaginative experiences through which children emerge as flexible, independent, problem-solvers who have resilience and can succeed in the world.

The reforms of higher education, along with a government disposition to construe education programs as commodities that can be "delivered" and "measured" like products, fundamentally misunderstands the subtle and dynamic nature of early learning and the development of self-esteem which furthers the joy of learning. On the one hand, government is clear in its recognition of the value of early education (see, for example, federal government early literacy initiatives, and state government effective early learning projects). On the other, early childhood teacher education, like all areas of teacher education, gets little positive "fair-play" or support. As preservice early childhood programs advance in their scrutiny of change and take more socially critical perspectives, their impact in the community at large will increase.

Conclusion

The changing social world of Australia in the late 1990s is an ecological barometer for early childhood professionals and for teacher education course developers. The social dynamism of Australian families should be prompting early childhood professionals to review traditional approaches and uncontested pedagogical assumptions, and to establish itself as a profession at the forefront of educational reform, attuned to the needs of children.

The price of lack of attention to the dynamic nature of the social world of children and families would be early childhood services and teacher education courses that are irrelevant. Early childhood cannot afford to live in a cultural vacuum built at a time when "nice ladies looked after children". The world has clearly moved on. Many Australian early childhood professionals have recognized the need for change and for growing scholarship across the profession. Early childhood educators need to be bold and confident in their collective power.

References

Amato, P. (1987). *Children in Australian families: The growth of competence.* Melbourne: Prentice Hall.

Arthur, L., Beecher, B., Dockett, S., Farmer, S., & Death, E. (1996). *Programming in early childhood settings.* (2nd ed.). Sydney: Harcourt Brace.

Ashton, J., & Elliott, A. (1995). *Student teacher perceptions of early childhood care and education issues.* Paper presented at the Australian Association of Research in Education Annual Conference. Hobart, Tasmania, 27-30 November 1995.

Association for Childhood Education International. (1997). *Preparation of early childhood teachers.* Position paper. Childhood Education. Spring: 164-165.

Australian Teaching Council. (1996). *National competency framework for beginning teaching.* National project on the quality of teaching and learning. Leichhardt, NSW: Author.

Bereday, G. (1964). *Comparative method in education.* New York: Holt, Rinehart and Winston.

Board of Teacher Registration Queensland. (1997). *Early childhood teacher education. Discussion paper.* Brisbane, Queensland: Author.

Briggs, F., & Potter, G. (1995). *Teaching in the first three years of school.* (2nd ed.). Melbourne: Longman.

Bronfenbrenner, U. (1991). What do families do? *Family Affairs* 4(1): 1-6.

Cross, T. (1992). Early childhood: A national priority or an uneconomic agenda. In *Educational Imperatives: Never mind the width, feel the quality.* Papers of the 32 National Conference of the Australian College of Education. (pp. 60-74). Darwin.

Elliott, A. (1996). *Student attrition in early childhood teacher education.* Paper presented at the Australian Association of Research in Education Annual Conference, Singapore, (pp. 24-29). November.

Carnegie Forum of Education and the Economy. (1986). *A nation prepared: Teachers for the twenty-first century.* Washington DC: Author.

Fleer, M. (1997). Guidelines for early childhood professionals. *Education Review.* December: p. 13.

Fleer, M. (Ed.). (1995). *Dapcentrism. Challenging developmentally appropriate practice.* Canberra: Australian Early Childhood Association Publications.

Gammage, P. (1995). Initial teacher education. In *Early childhood education: The way forward.* P. Gammage & J. Meighan (Eds.). (pp. 95–111). Nottingham, England: Education Now Publishing Cooperative.

Garbarino, J. (1997). Educating children in a socially toxic environment. *Educational Leadership,* 54 (7): 12–16.

Hayden, J. (1996). *Management of early childhood services. An Australian perspective.* Sydney: Social Science Press.

Hayden, J. (1996a). Beyond Mr. Bubbles: An analysis of the public image of early childhood care and education in Western Sydney. *Journal of Australian Research in Early Childhood Education,* Vol.1: 65–77.

Hayden, J. (1997). Facing the future together: New programs in early childhood education at UWS, Nepean. *Rattler:* 44:19.

Healey, K. (Ed.). (1997). *Poverty in Australia.* Issues for the Nineties Volume 77. Sydney: The Spinney Press.

Judge, H. (1989). Forward to special issue on teacher education. *Childhood Education.* 65(5): 259–260.

Kerr, R. (1994). *The history of the kindergarten union in Western Australia 1911–1973.* Perth, Western Australia: Meerilinga Young Children's Foundation.

Kelly, J. (1986). Day care—an unfortunate necessity or a desirable community resource? *Australian Journal of Early Childhood.* 11(1): 3–9.

Kessler, S.A. (1992). The social context of early childhood curriculum. In S.A. Kessler & B.B. Swaddener (Eds.). *Reconceptualising early childhood curriculum.* (pp. 21–42.) New York: Teachers College Press.

Leach, P. (1994). *Children first. What we must do and are not doing for our children today.* London: Michael Joseph.

Mallory, B.L., & New, R.S. (Eds.). (1994). *Diversity and developmentally appropriate practices.* New York: Teachers College Press.

Mathers, C. (1995). *Health differentials among Australian children.* Australian Institute of Health and Welfare Health Monitoring Series. No. 3. Canberra: AGPS.

McLennon, W., & Goward, P. (1997). *Australian women's yearbook 1997.* ABS Catalogue No. 4124.0. Canberra: Australian Bureau of Statistics.

Mellor, E., & Gifford, J. (1992). Early childhood education: What does the future hold? In E.J. Mellor & K.M. Coombe (Eds.). *Issues in Early Childhood Services. Australian Perspectives.* (pp. 203–210). Melbourne, Australia: WCB Publishing Inc.

National Association for the Education of Young Children. (1996). *Guidelines for the preparation of early childhood professionals.* Guidelines developed by NAEYC, the Division for Early Childhood of the Council for Exceptional Children and the National Board for Professional Teaching Standards. Washington DC: Author.

Piscitelli, B., McLean, V., Halliwell, G. (1992). Early childhood education in Australia, In S. Feeney (Ed.). *Early Childhood Education in Asia and the Pacific.* (pp. 197–236). New York: Garland Publishing Inc.

Raths, J. (1989). Reformers' visions of tomorrows teachers, a U.S.A. perspective. *Childhood Education,* 65 (5): 263–267.

Rutter, M., & Rutter M. (1993). *Developing minds.* Middlesex, England: Penguin Books.

Senate Employment, Education and Training References Committee. (1996). *Childhood Matters.* The report on the inquiry into early childhood education. Parliament House, Canberra: Author.

Silburn, S.R., Zubrick, S.R., Garton, A., Gurrin, L., Burton, P., Dally, R., Carlton, J., Shepherd, C., & Lawrence, D. (1996). *Western Australian child health survey: Family and community health.* Perth, Western Australia: Australian Bureau of Statistics.

Stamopoulos, E. (1995). *The professional background and perceptions of principals on their leadership role in preprimary.* Unpublished med. thesis. Perth: Edith Cowan University.

Stonehouse, A. (1992). Early childhood grows up. In B. Lambert (Ed.). *Changing Faces. The Early Childhood Profession in Australia.* (pp. 150–163). Canberra: Australian Early Childhood Association.

Tayler, C. (1994). Perspectives on early childhood course development in universities and TAFE colleges. *Australian Journal of Early Childhood,* 19(3): 14–19.

Tayler, C. (1992a). Preferred models of early childhood teacher education: A Western Australian perspective. *Australian Journal of Teacher Education,* 16(1): 11–21.

Tayler, C. (1992b). Issues in pre-service early childhood teacher education in Australia. *Australian Journal of Early Childhood,* 17(2): 35–41.

Tayler, C. (1991). Early childhood teacher education in Australia. *Early Child Development and Care,* 76: 3–25.

United Nations Children's Fund. (1996). *The progress of nations.* Sydney: UNICEF.

Webster, S.C. (1990). Long-term follow-up of families with young conduct problem children from preschool to grade school. *Journal of Clinical Child Psychology,* 19: 144–149.

Wright, S. (Ed.) (1991) *The arts in early childhood.* Sydney: Prentice Hall.

Wu, D.Y.H. (1992). Early childhood education in China. In S. Feeney (Ed.). *Early Childhood Education in Asia and the Pacific. A Source Book.* (pp. 1–26). New York: Garland Publishing Inc.

Zubrick, S.R., Silburn, S.R. Garton, A., Burton, P., Dally, R., Carlton, J., Shepherd, C., & Lawrence, D. (1995). *Western Australian child health survey: Developing health and wellbeing in the nineties.* Perth, Western Australia: Australian Bureau of Statistics.

Zubrick, S.R., Silburn, S.R., Guru, L., Tech, H., Shepherd, C., Carlton, J., Lawrence, D. (1997). *Western Australian child health survey: Education health and competence.* Perth, Western Australia: Australian Bureau of Statistics.

Chapter 17

When Does a Teacher Teach? The Queensland Early Childhood Profession on Trial

Judith Burton
Michael Lyons

Abstract

This chapter examines the professional status and industrial relations of early childhood teachers in day care centers in the Australian state of Queensland. Two features of professional status, abstract knowledge and state sponsorship, are discussed with reference to a core element of early childhood theory and practice—developmentally appropriate practice. It is suggested that the blurring of the distinction between "education" and "development" permitted employers to highlight development over education, implying that education is not "necessary" in Queensland day care centers and, thus, denying teachers in day care a status comparable to teachers in other settings. This outcome was made possible by reference to the instruments of state sponsorship and the teamwork norms of equality found in centers. While the abstract knowledge-base of early childhood was not questioned in this "trial", the early childhood field's predilection for the term "development" over education in both day care center practices and when designing the instruments of state sponsorship only furthered the employers' arguments. The case study illustrates that professional status is a complex web of an occupation's knowledge-base, state sponsorship, workplace, and industrial issues.

Introduction

The case study presented in this chapter examines the issue of professionalization in Australian day care by analyzing a recent matter before the industrial relations tribunal of the state of Queensland. The tribunal hearings dealt with claims that early childhood teachers working in day care should receive parity of pay with teachers in other settings. During these hearings it was suggested that the matter could be reduced to one simple issue: whether teachers employed in day care centers in Queensland were *teaching*. It was decided that most were not. Rather, these practitioners were portrayed as "only" providing "developmental" programs, which required less skill and thus deserved less pay. This view of early childhood programs and the work of early childhood teachers underlines the urgency of more rigorously examining relationships amongst professional recognition, children's service policies, and industrial relations. In contributing to the debate regarding the professional status of early childhood, its practitioners, and the community standing of the children's services "industry" (see Fleer & Waniganayake, 1994; Hill, 1976; Smith, 1990; Stonehouse, 1990; Tayler, 1994), this case study questions whether early childhood professionals are shaping their own destiny or whether other elements, such as the state and employers, are determining key features of children's service provision.

This examination of professional recognition focuses on two characteristics generally required for occupational groups to be seen as professions. One, that a profession is an occupation with the capacity to generate and develop, interpret, then apply the abstract knowledge-base of the occupation (Hall, 1975, p. 71). Two, that there is a degree of state sponsorship to regulate practitioners (Bradley, 1993, p. 38).[1] State sponsorship, that is the intervention of various government and regulatory bodies to regulate the practice of an occupation by determining that practitioners require formal qualifications, is significant to the success of professionalization strategies (Witz, 1992, pp. 202–203). In this case, state sponsorship involves legislation and regulations, the day care center accreditation process, and employment regulation through industrial awards.

In assessing the level of state sponsorship of early childhood professionals in day care we critically examine the ability of the instruments of state sponsorship to support a core element of early childhood theory and practice: developmentally appropriate practice. While acknowledging that practitioners with a range of qualifications can be found in day care, we focus on staff with teaching degrees.[2] The Australian Bureau of Statistics defines early childhood teachers as professionals.[3] This, together with the fact that their formal training is conducted in education faculties at a university with cohorts who go on to teach in school settings, suggests that elements of professionalization are already present. Therefore, if recognition of teachers' professionalism is not evident here then it is unlikely to be recognized in other day care staff or in other services for children that lie outside the "education" system.

This case highlights the contradictory features of state sponsorship of early childhood and the ability of employers to exploit the notion that there is a clear division between development and education to serve their commercial interests. We argue that merely asserting that degree-trained early childhood practitioners are necessary to achieve quality outcomes in day care is not sufficient. This has to be expressly stated in the forms of state sponsorship. This chapter suggests that industrial relations considerations, the design and development of formal instruments of state sponsorship and issues of professional practice, are all conducted in isolation from each other. Together with the norms of equality found in day care, this permits employers and the formal industrial relations system to deny professional recognition for staff in children's services in general, and early childhood teachers in day care in particular.

Disregarding the Nexus between Development and Education

The terms "development" and "education" are core concepts within the early childhood professional knowledge-base. Psychological theories of child development were used to provide a "scientific knowledge-base" when substantiating early childhood teachers' claims to professional status (Silin, 1988, p. 124). The continuing importance of developmentally appropriate practice to Australian early childhood educators is illustrated by the use of such principles and practices as found in the influential Bredekamp (1987) statement as the foundation for the Quality Improvement and Accreditation System (QIAS) for day care services (Cross, 1995). However, vigorous debate in America (Kessler & Swadener, 1992) and Australia (Fleer, 1995) has renewed the argument that the field over-emphasizes the theory and language of developmentally appropriate practice. Of interest here are concerns that this emphasis contributes to difficulties in terms of communicating early childhood educators' knowledge. In particular, little attention has been directed to articulating teachers' role in children's learning and development (Cross, 1995) or the ways teachers' relationships with those who collaborate with, provide resources and organize their work have an impact on educational practice and the development of teacher knowledge (Halliwell, 1992). As this case study demonstrates, the fields' strong emphasis on the language of development in preference to education has unintended consequences in terms of professional recognition.

While early childhood professionals have been debating these complex issues, those charged with decisions affecting the regulation and resourcing of early childhood services have tended to construct definitions of development and education that suit their own practical purposes. As women's traditional work of caring for young children has increasingly shifted into the public arena, the costs of recognizing the value of such work to society become evident. Nonetheless, recent community acceptance of the necessity of providing children in day care with an accredited standard of service requires abandoning portrayals of work in these services as merely "caring" and not requiring skill. For the state and for employers, reliance on the dichotomization of care and education will no longer suffice. Assuring voters and consumers of the quality of day care services while continuing to suppress staff wages and conditions requires a new rhetoric. Disavowing the nexus between processes of education/teaching and "outcomes" of development/learning not only sits comfortably with community perceptions that education implied formal programs of study but also provides an argument for the denial of professional recognition.

Professional Recognition, Industrial Relations, and State Sponsorship

Professional recognition of female-dominated occupations shapes and is shaped by outcomes of the Australian industrial relations system (Rafferty, 1989, 1991). Unlike other industrial jurisdictions in Australia, both degree-trained staff and vocationally trained and untrained staff in day care in Queensland are represented by one trade union. In 1991 this union, the Australian Liquor Hospitality and Miscellaneous Workers Union (LHMU), applied to the Queensland Industrial Relations Commission (hereafter the "Commission") to rescind the *Kindergarten Teachers Award* (KTA) and create a new award entitled the Early Childhood Education Teachers in Childcare Award—(State Matter R27-3 of 1991). The LHMU's application sought parity of pay with teachers employed under other teaching awards (QIRC Transcript: 3).

State sponsorship of day care in Australia generally, and in Queensland in particular, may imply that there is a widespread community demand for the skills, knowledge, and practice of degree qualified staff. The level of expenditure by the state clearly suggests that more than minimal standards are expected (EPAC, 1996, pp. 29-36). Moreover, the involvement of the state in regulating quality of service provision through the QIAS would again suggest increasing expectations of professional practice by both governments and the community. Indeed, the policy of linking payment of federal funds to quality standards suggests this (NCAC, 199, pp. ii-ix). In addition, Queensland regulations have, since 1991, specifically stated that directors of centers licensed for over 30 children must hold at least three-year tertiary qualifications with an early childhood specialization (s.26[1]). Further, an object of the *Childcare Act 1991* (Qld) is "to ensure that childcare services provide care that is a safe, positive, nurturing and *educational* experience for children" (s.[4][1])—emphasis added. Clearly, both implicitly and explicitly, state sponsorship of day care brings with it an expectation from both practitioners and the community that education is a vital part of center-based children's services.

Notwithstanding the expectations of state sponsorship for educational programs in day care centers in Queensland, the 1996 decision of the Commission regarding the role of early childhood teachers in day care suggests state sponsorship has only limited capacity to advance the professionalization of employees in this area (see also Hayden, 1992). The Commission was persuaded by employers' arguments that teachers do not fully apply their professional skills and abstract knowledge and that education does not form a vital ingredient of quality outcomes in day care.

The Trial

At the outset of this case, the Commission made it clear that the teachers and their union would have to demonstrate "that teachers teach in childcare centers" (QIRC Transcript, p. 31). In contrast to teachers' efforts to argue their case by reference to theoretical and practical elements of their work and comparisons with the work of early childhood teachers in other settings, employers' arguments centered around the proposition that teachers were not needed in childcare:

> If Teachers [sic] are to have a specific place in childcare it needs to be on the basis that they are doing something conceptually and identifiably different to other childcare workers. If this is not the case and the view is maintained that they do the same thing as other workers only a whole lot better, then the simple reality is that the childcare industry does not in most cases want or need what they have to offer. (Local Government Association final submission. p. 11)

Employer applications basically called for payment of teachers salaries only if a teacher was "employed as such". Further, it was argued that only if a center was "offering and advertising an 'educational program' conducted by 'fully qualified teaching staff' should employers be obliged to employ a teacher and pay them teacher rates" (The Queensland Professional Childcare Centers Association [QPCCCA] and Childcare Centers Association of Queensland [CCCAQ] final submission, p. 7). A number of employers testified that although they employed teachers, they did not require teachers to provide educational programs. For example, one employer testified that "three-year trained employees" were not allowed to run educational programs and while teachers might be "using their knowledge and skills. We're only paying them for what we're requiring them to use which is the same skills that we're paying and requiring a [two-year trained] group leader to use" (QIRC Transcript, pp. 791–793). The proposition that a range of factors contribute to the quality of children's experiences was used to argue that "it's not very easy to see the difference between, say a teacher and a [two-year trained] associate diploma in terms of relative value" (QIRC Transcript, p. 444).

The Ephemeral Nature of State Sponsorship

Teacher unionists expected that reference to the national day care center accreditation system would support their claims for parity with other teachers (teacher interview, 12 August, 1994). Indeed, the QIAS states that salaries, working conditions, training, and job satisfaction are all contributing factors to "good quality care and education" (NCAC, 1993, p. iv; see also Brennan, 1994, pp. 201–204; Wangmann, 1994, p. 150). However, employers argued that all but a few of the 52 principles of the QIAS were covered by the Queensland regulations. This is contrary to accreditation literature, which notes that "regulations are minimum standards and, although essential for good quality care, they are not on their own sufficient to guarantee it" (NCAC, 1993, p. iii). Further, employers submitted that the founding principles of the system were "based on the assumption that qualifications do not necessarily guarantee good quality outcomes for children" (Exhibit 20, point 18). Their arguments appear to have been persuasive. The only reference to the QIAS in the Commission's decision was with respect to the additional cost to *employers* of implementing the system (QIRC Decision, p. 23).

Central to employer arguments that teachers employed as "group leaders' should not be paid teacher rates were two requirements of the regulations issued pursuant to the *Childcare Act 1991* (Qld): the provision of developmental programs (s.8) and two-year qualifications for "group leaders" (s.28[1][a]). Legislation governing the education system, most notably the *Education (General Provisions) Act 1989* (Qld) and the *Education (Teacher Registration) Act 1988* (Qld), were also drawn on. In short, these require establishments claiming to provide "education", employ teachers who are registered with the Board of Teacher Education. It was further submitted that "the statutes don't require teachers unless in the delivery of an educational program for children in the year immediately prior to year one" (QIRC Transcript, p. 453). The union contented that teachers working as group leaders not only taught but also provided curriculum leadership (Exhibit 16). The employers' counterargument was simplistic in the extreme: as there were "no classrooms and the regulations don't require curriculum leadership, employers should not be required to pay for such services even if they could be shown to be performed" (QIRC Transcript, p. 284). When a teacher argued that parents enrolled children at a center where she worked because there were teachers employed in group leader positions, employers characterized this as a "marketing strategy" that should not be allowed to influence the entire industry (QIRC Transcript, p. 308).

When Does an Early Childhood Teacher "Teach"?

Key elements of developmentally appropriate practice were not regarded as "teaching" and presented as not requiring skillful application of abstract knowledge. The central role of play within the early childhood curriculum challenged the Commission's understanding of educational practice. When outlining programs for children, a teacher witness was twice questioned on assertions that "large blocks of play time were regarded as teaching time" (QIRC Transcript, p. 848). A similar lack of recognition of the knowledge used by early childhood teachers was demonstrated when a commissioner asked whether the ability to maintain and plan from developmental records could be gained by "on the job training" (QIRC Transcript, p. 196). An employer characterized the more visible extent of learning and development in children's early years as meaning that "at that time in a child's life everything's educational" (QIRC Transcript, p. 450). Nonetheless, attempts were made to denigrate the relevance of teachers' knowledge of child development by noting its absence from primary and secondary teacher preparation programs (QIRC Transcript, p. 269). Arguably, such comments reflect old-fashioned or "commonsense" understandings of education. They also reflect the general lack of recognition of the skills required to work with young children (see Petrie & Burton, this volume).

Employers also challenged the relevance of teaching qualifications to the work of center directors. The Regulations' schedule of approved qualifications for directors of centers licensed for over 30 children at that time listed only teaching/education degrees with majors in early childhood. However, the Regulations do not mention that teacher registration and explanatory documents, such as schedules, are not the law. The law is what the Act and the Regulations say (QIRC Transcript, p. 403). Furthermore, employers argued that although teacher-qualified directors possessed the knowledge and skills to "oversee the workings of group leaders programming", such qualifications should not entitle them to teachers' pay because they were "not actually teaching, they're more supervising and controlling" (QIRC Transcript, p. 751). Paradoxically, employers also argued that teacher group leaders should not be entitled to teachers' pay because, regardless of their qualifications, they still had "to present their program weekly to the director for her approval and working through" (QIRC Transcript, p. 51).

The Decision

The Commission's long awaited decision in March 1996 bitterly disappointed teachers and their union. They were denied access to the full salary scale available to early childhood teachers outside of day care centers on the grounds that:

> ... the vast bulk of persons engaged in long day childcare activities, although they might be 3 or 4 year qualified professionals, are not engaged in the delivery of an educational program but rather the delivery of a developmental program appropriate to the needs and age of the children. Whilst there might be particular abilities which a higher qualified person can bring to such activities, *such extra qualifications are not required by the Childcare Act 1991, nor the Childcare (Childcare Centers) Regulation 1991* [sic], nor, based on the evidence, by various licensees [employers] who operate long day care centers. In many instances *the attainment of higher qualifications is a personal choice of the individual* designed to assist them in their own promotional or career objectives and, presumably, *to give them some advantages over other applicants for positions they might seek which do not require the use of the full range of qualifications* possessed by them. (QIRC Decision, p. 34, emphasis added)

Day care centers were described as generally providing "only" a developmental program that called on a narrower range of skills than teaching in recognized educational settings (QIRC Decision, p. 32). Even if a teacher was "delivering" an "educational program" the Commission doubted that the program would be of "the same depth and intensity" as programs provided by teachers in other settings (QIRC Decision, p. 35). The Commission was not convinced that the additional skills 4-year-trained teachers brought to their "profession" were "anywhere near as evident in the delivery of programs in this sector" (QIRC Decision, p. 35). The Commission decided that to be eligible to be employed under the Kindergarten Teachers' Award a person would have to hold a three- or four-year qualification in early childhood studies and be registered with the Board of Teacher Education and be *required* by their employer to deliver an educational program (QIRC Decision, p. 33). Therefore, only registered teachers who worked in centers advertising an educational program need be employed as "teachers".

The Limits of State Sponsorship

One of the most notable features of this case was the parallax view of state sponsorship accepted by the Commission at the urging of the employers. This restricted interpretation of Queensland legislation and the QIAS denied the vital role teachers play in day care. In that arena the limitations of relying almost solely on state sponsorship to assert the professionalism of early childhood practitioners was evident. Employers were able to draw on commonsense understandings about educational practice and contrast this with developmentally appropriate practice. They capitalized on the perception that working with young children does not require skill or abstract knowledge: it's "just" catering for individual needs and supervising "play" at a stage in life when "everything's educational". It would appear that just such notions about education and its role in day care can be supported by the formal documents associated with state sponsorship of day care. The legislation governing "educational" services mentions only the year immediately prior to compulsory schooling. The approval of teaching qualifications was not held to be law; hence regulations stipulating "developmental" programs can unproblematically be divorced from the early childhood educator's knowledge-base.

Even if the formal documentation of the QIAS could be analyzed to claim that "education" is not implicit in the process, the Commission's reliance on the legislation to come to a similar view defies some logic. For example, the argument that teacher-directors do not "teach" when fulfillling center director duties contradicts the submission that teacher group leaders do not teach because their program has to be approved by the director. University qualified practitioners have to defer responsibility to a superior prior to discharging duties in most organizations; yet this does not dilute the skill and knowledge that the practitioners apply to their work (Brewer, 1996). Even if teacher group leaders did not fully utilize their expertise because of the subordinate relationship to the director it would then be the director's role to apply this expertise. The fact that attachments to the regulations at the time approved only registrable teaching qualifications for larger centers is an explicit acknowledgment that directors perform teaching tasks. In short, the employers cannot have their cake and eat it—either teaching knowledge and skills are accessed by teacher qualified group leaders or teacher directors (or both). At best, the employers and the Commission were extremely selective in evaluating what forms of state sponsorship were to be the basis of the decision. A less kind analysis could claim that this process was disingenuous, manipulative, and patriarchal.

Is Early Childhood Education Necessary for Day Care?

The arguments put by the day care employers and the decision of the Commission should not be seen as an atypical understanding of the division between "education" and "development" in day care. The tribunal hearings also reflect the ongoing debate over the role of university trained staff with "educational' degrees in contrast to TAFE trained staff with qualifications in "care" or "development" (EPAC, 1996, p. 145). Indeed, the early childhood field has, since the early 1930s, debated the purposes and benefits of services deemed to provide care or education and the training needs of staff working in them (Petrie, 1988; Hayden, 1992; Kelly, 1994). In the midst of the debates some consensus exists: education programs contain elements of care and care programs contain elements of education (Senate References Committee, 1996, pp. 1–28). Indeed, the inability of the Commission to identify the educational aspects of day care reflects a feature common to traditional professions. Professional or abstract knowledge can be called upon in either a "technical" or "indeterminate" manner with the unique outcomes of the latter being almost solely dependent on the capacity of the professional to apply the knowledge-base to each particular circumstance (Brewer, 1996, p. 34).

The belief that two-year-trained staff perform the same duties as university qualified early childhood practitioners in day care is not unique to either the Queensland employers or the Commission. The proposed national *Standards for Center Based Long Day Care* (Commonwealth Government, 1993, p. 40) make no distinction between the two- and three-year qualifications recognized for "staff working in qualified positions". Similar notions are held by non-degree qualified staff. This, in addition to the work organization and work practices of day care discussed below, made the employers' arguments all that more credible.

Teacher section meetings of the LHMU held while the case was being arbitrated made this point evident. Teachers noted that two-year-trained staff also considered themselves professionals (union meeting, 12 May, 1993). Early childhood beliefs about valuing the contributions of those they work with are reflected in teachers' assertions that the same employment conditions should apply to any group leader with programming responsibilities irrespective of qualifications.

It would be a mistake to assume that the lack of recognition of teacher qualifications, additional skills, and specialized knowledge-base is a feature common to day care staff only in Queensland, or a result of having both early childhood teachers and other staff represented by the same union. This is also noticeable in other states of Australia. The notions emanating from the Queensland data are confirmed by interviews conducted in early 1997 with day care staff employed in Melbourne and Sydney. Of the 14 staff interviewed with a two-year qualification only one could identify a clear difference in the approach of teacher qualified staff with that of two-year trained staff. The general perception detected was that much of the abstract knowledge-base obtained from a university qualification appeared irrelevant to day care. The only major differences evident in the two-year-trained staff was that a teaching qualification earned greater extrinsic rewards (e.g., higher pay and faster promotional prospects) and greater "status". Not unexpectedly, all but one of the ten qualified teachers interviewed were able without hesitation to articulate the additional skills and knowledge that university education brings to day care even when staff basically undertake the same duties. The major difference between the two types of training was generally seen to be that two-year trained staff were more "practical" in their approach whereas the teacher trained staff were more "theoretical". However, university qualified staff freely admitted that a degree in itself does not automatically make a staff member more proficient; rather the abstract knowledge has to be applied to the tasks associated with the work found in day care (see Lyons, 1997).

Working Knowledge in Day Care:
Teamwork Relations and Consistency of Approach

It is, perhaps, not surprising that the employers were able to dominate the Commission proceedings and have the decision largely reflect their arguments given the work organization of day care, which is, in many respects, different from other teaching settings. Conceivably then, restricted definitions of teaching as delivering programs to children fail to capture the "working knowledge" of teachers (Yinger & Hendricks-Lee, 1993, p. 112). Arguably, the ability of teachers and their union to clearly demonstrate the ways teachers apply their knowledge is not enhanced by the teamwork nature of day care.

Understanding how teachers in day care create conditions within which children can learn and develop requires rethinking assumptions about teaching. Viewing knowledge as interacting with setting and jointly constructed by all participants (Yinger & Hendricks-Lee, 1993, p. 104) allows us to consider that many early childhood practices have been constructed over decades of theorizing on practice in quite different social and physical settings, typically sessional programs. The teachers in a study by the first author found it was often counterproductive to try to reproduce traditional sessional practices in long day care (see, for example, Burton, 1997). Teachers' responsiveness to setting variables leads them to reflect on ways to create curriculum with the resources they perceive to be available. That is, they draw on underlying principles of the early childhood knowledge-base to search for ways of achieving core purposes in different ways. Most notably, directors can use their delegated discretion as service managers. As argued in the Commission, teacher-directors are "supervising and controlling" the work of other staff, but the ways they set about these tasks demonstrate "the dynamic processes involved in reaching agreement about the nature of appropriate practice" (Halliwell, 1992, p. 358).

Teachers' curriculum decisions in day care reflect their knowledge about the powerful influence the social environment has on the curriculum dynamic. In day care, productive work relations amongst members of the center team are "a critical factor in the operation of a quality program" (Fleet & Clyde, 1993, p. 103). While early childhood teachers have traditionally worked closely with other adults—most notably assistants, parents, and management committees—teamwork situations confront early childhood teachers' knowledge about the need for consistency and continuity in children's experiences. Unlike most educational settings, individual teachers are not able to assume full personal responsibility for continuity in learning due to long operating hours. Thus, adopting a consistent center-wide approach to children's learning and development is vital (Fleet & Clyde, 1993, p. 83). While a director will have a degree of control over the curriculum framework adopted for a center, the immediacy and intensity of work in day care highlights the role of all staff in the curriculum process. The interactive nature of curriculum is more apparent when staff work in shifts and the discretion of other team members is further enhanced if groups are joined or facilities are shared. Nonteacher-trained staff, most notably two-year-trained practitioners, possess a range of knowledge and skills essential to the services that centers provide. Therefore, the relationships developed among adults are an important determinant of curriculum coherence and the quality of care. As Grundy and Bonser (1997, p. 11) observe: "the development of a collaborative, interdependent profession has profound implications for teachers' work".

An organizational principle that helps build effective teamwork relations is organizing work and allocating physical tasks on the basis of a "norm of equality" (Pettygrove & Greenman, 1984, p. 95; see also O'Connor, 1990). These norms are reinforced by small workforce size and similarity in accountability expectations of variously qualified group leaders. However, norms of equality render teachers uncomfortable about claiming the legal rights they are entitled to under industrial awards for to do so may be seen as "unprofessional". Expecting different employment conditions may also be seen as "lacking sensitivity toward the conditions and pay rates" of other staff and contributing to staff resentment and reduced commitment (see also Brennan, 1994, p. 128). Another way norms of equality counteract teachers' claims to professional recognition is that, as very little child-free time is provided, teachers (and probably other group leaders) work beyond rostered hours, documenting observations and programs. That they perform this work may not be evident to other staff. For example, a teacher reported working unpaid overtime to justify her additional teachers' rights in a work climate where other staff saw themselves working just as hard. Indeed, one director in this study explicitly rostered all staff on the basis of equality. This resulted in the majority of staff benefiting. However, early childhood teachers' conditions, including her own, were diminished.

Despite the benefits of norms of equality in enhancing continuity of and consistency of children's experiences, such work practices do not enhance the recognition of teacher expertise, partly because their expertise is dispersed around the systems designed to achieve their educational purposes such as curriculum frameworks and the relationships they foster amongst staff. Such knowledge-based influences on service quality are, as demonstrated by the Commission proceedings, difficult to articulate in ways that converse with either general perceptions or legalistic definitions of teachers' work (see also Fleet, Duffy, & Patterson, 1995). Furthermore, such work practices lead to increasing dissociation from the conditions available to teachers in other settings and involve even greater effort for the already relative substandard pay, thus further reducing teachers' organizational commitment. These informally negotiated norms mirror the Commission's decision to combine the two awards covering most day care staff and move toward common conditions of employment (QIRC Decision, p. 32). This illustrates the "intimate and continuing reciprocity between workplace and company-level bargaining and the conciliation-arbitration process" in shaping professional recognition (Kennoy & Kelly, 1996, p. 247).

Conclusion: Implications for Professional Recognition

The decision in the Queensland teachers' tribunal hearings and the workplace evidence, together with the other research cited, points to a number of critical factors that could advance the community's understanding of the professionalism of early childhood practitioners. Although the Commission case illustrates the continuing devaluation of day care services, it is fortunate, and encouraging, that the case did not question to any great extent the abstract knowledge of early childhood education. In fact, this was the basis for delineating the distinction between "education" and "development" programs. Indeed, the early childhood field has emphasized developmental appropriateness to distinguish its approach from both rigidly structured, academically oriented programs and custodial programs. While a clearer articulation of the ways teacher knowledge is used within day care programs appears necessary, the first criterion selected for examination here—the possession of a knowledge-base that is largely abstract yet capable of practical implementation—does not appear to be a problem.

The central issue of the case involved questions as to whether early childhood education, and therefore teachers, is an inherent component of day care. So when elements of state sponsorship were relied upon by the union and teachers to argue that education does form a necessary ingredient in day care, this was unsuccessful. While clearly the comments of the Commission indicate an ignorance of early childhood principles and contemporary notions of educating young children, these beliefs were supported by the formal documents associated with state sponsorship. Overcoming the understanding of nonuniversity-qualified staff that there is little difference between the skills and knowledge-base of early childhood teachers and other qualified staff is more difficult. This outcome probably has more to do with the small workplace aspects of day care and employment conditions such as the lack of time for staff to discuss and reflect on their work than any notions that early childhood education theories and practice are of limited utility in day care (Fleer & Waniganayake, 1994, p. 4).

Therefore, the key lesson to be learned from this case study is that relying solely on state sponsorship for professional recognition has its limits. For instance, the failure of the QIAS to explicitly state that child-centered outcomes in day care are predicated on "education" was significant in the Commission's decision, as was the weight given to the Queensland legislation and regulations to assert that education is not "necessary" in day care, the selectivity of the Commission and employers in this regard notwithstanding. In this context, then, the short-term strategy would seem to be axiomatic. When early childhood educators participate in the process of designing and developing the formal instruments of state sponsorship, it must be explicitly stated that "education" is a vital component of day care. Such a move may challenge the field's traditional preference for the term "development". Furthermore, such strategies could be perceived by nonteacher-trained practitioners as exclusionary rather than being aimed at enhancing the status of all day care staff.

Witz (1992, p. 208) argues that the professionalization of female-dominated occupations has been "more successful in the pursuit of legalistic tactics seeking state sponsorship". For example, Queensland teachers in day care could make more use of legislation covering the registration of teachers and the provision of educational programs in the preschool year. Registration would be one way to demonstrate professionalism and help substantiate claims for rates of pay similar to other teachers. However, the limited evidence available suggests that effective use of this instrument of state sponsorship, teacher registration, would be highly problematic. Moreover, legalistic tactics will not enhance recognition if pursued in isolation—a point illustrated by Bradley's (1993) analysis of the professionalization of nursing; issues of state sponsorship, competency standards, and industrial conditions were viewed as interconnected and addressed in a coherent manner. Consequently, it needs to be recognized that the knowledge-base of early childhood teachers, the role of state sponsorship, and workplace and industrial relations issues all influence the way professionalism is conceived and made visible to the community. Therefore, we conclude by suggesting that the obstacles to professional recognition of early childhood practitioners in day care can be overcome but that this process rests mostly in the hands of early childhood practitioners themselves, for nobody else will do it for them.

Notes

1. A more extended discussion of professionalization strategies is beyond the scope of this chapter. Most notably there is insufficient space to scrutinize important questions surrounding the collective organization and identity of early childhood practitioners.

2. Children's services in Australia are regulated by the six State and two Territory governments. Regulations refer to the postschool qualifications required by early childhood practitioners in center-based day care—the most common being the two-year diploma or "associate" diploma obtained from colleges of technical and further education (TAFE) and university degrees in early childhood education of either three or four years duration. Each educational institution usually applies differing titles to the respective qualification (see Fleer & Waniganayake, 1994 and Rosier & Lloyd-Smith 1996: p. 99). For reasons of consistency TAFE qualifications will be referred to as "two-year" qualification and a university degree as either a "three-year" or "four-year" qualification.

3. The decision states that "if a person met the first two (2) [requirements] and their employer was advertising an educational program that should, in *normal* circumstances, result in the employee(s) involved in the delivery of such programs being classified as a 'teacher'" (QIRC Decision: 33—emphasis added). Perhaps evidence of employers' expectations of this outcome can be found in the 1996 Brisbane *Yellow Pages* business telephone directory. Here, of the over 12 pages of day care centers listed, only 39 advertised an "educational program". However, many offered parents—perhaps unaware of the nuances of the Commission's decision—"progressive developmental programs," "educare," and "learning and development".

References

Bradley, D. (1993). Competency standards for female dominated professions: A dual closure strategy. *Labor and Industry*. 5,3: 33–56.

Bredekamp, S. (Ed.). (1987). *Developmentally appropriate practice in early childhood programs serving children from birth through age 8*. Washington, DC: National Association for the Education of Young Children.

Brennan, D. (1994). *The politics of Australian childcare: From philanthropy to feminism*. Melbourne: Cambridge University Press.

Brewer, L. (1996). Bureaucratic organization of professional labor. *Australian and New Zealand Journal of Sociology*, 32, 3: 21–38.

Burton, J. (1997). Teaching dilemmas and employment relations in childcare centers. *Journal of Australian Research in Early Childhood Education*, 1: 123–31.

Childcare (Childcare Centers). Regulations 1991 (Qld).

Cross, T. (1995). The early childhood curriculum debate. In M. Fleer (Ed.), *DAP Centrism: Challenging Developmentally Appropriate Practice*. Canberra: AECA: 87–109.

EPAC (Economic Planning Advisory Commission). (1996). *Future childcare provision in Australia: Childcare task force interim report, June 1996*. Canberra: AGPS.

Fleer, M. (Ed.). (1995). *DAP centrism: Challenging developmentally appropriate practice*. Watson: Australian Early Childhood Association.

Fleer, M., & Waniganayake, M. (1994). The education and development of early childhood professionals in Australia. *Australian Journal of Early Childhood*, 19,3: 3–13.

Fleet, A., & Clyde, M. (1993). *What's in a day? Working in early childhood*. Wentworth Falls, Australia: Social Science Press.

Fleet, A., Duffie, J., & Patterson, C. (1995). Capturing the essence of early childhood teaching (K–3) through work-based vignettes. *Journal for Australian Research in Early Childhood Education 1: 82–90.

Grundy, S., & Bonser, S. (1997). Choosing to change: Teachers working with student outcome statements. *Curriculum perspectives*, 17, 1: 1–12.

Hall, R. H. (1975). *Occupations and the social structure*. Englewood Cliffs, N.J.: Prentice-Hall, Inc.

Halliwell, G. (1992). *Dilemmas and images: Gaining acceptance for child-responsive classroom practices*. Unpublished doctoral thesis. University of Queensland.

Hayden, J. (1992). Early childhood care and education: Social justice versus economic rationalism—Will the real purpose please stand up. In R. Hunter & A. Hickling-Hudson (Eds.). *Education and the real world. Education and economic rationalism*. Selected proceedings of the 20 Annual Conference of the Australian and New Zealand Comparative and International Education Society. Brisbane, December.

Hill, B.V. (1976). Professional parity for the early childhood educator. *Australian Journal of Early Childhood*, 1,2: 15–17.

Kelly, J. (1994). *Making a new professional: The childcare worker*. Paper presented at the National Association of TAFE Child Studies Teachers. Sydney, June.

Kessler, S., & Swadener, B. (Eds.). (1992). *Reconceptualizing the early childhood curriculum: Beginning the dialogue*. New York: Teachers College Press.

Lyons, M. (1997). Will you respect me in the morning? The "professional" status of early childhood. Paper presented to the Australian Early Childhood Association National Triennial Conference. Children in the balance. Melbourne, 20–23 September 1997.

NCAC (National Childhood Accreditation Council). (1993). *Putting children first: Quality improvement and accreditation system handbook*. Sydney: National Childcare Accreditation Council Inc.

O'Connor, B. (1990). The complexities of teamwork in childcare. Paper submitted to the QIRC Re Case R54/90. Childcare Industry Award—State (Exhibit 30).

Petrie, A. (1988). Education and care: The false dichotomy. *Australian Journal of Early Childhood*, 13, 3: 26-30.

Pettygrove, W.B., & Greenman, J.T. (1984). The adult world of day care. In J.T. Greenman & R.W. Fuqua (Eds.). *Making Day Care Better: Training, Evaluation and the Process of Change*. New York: Teachers College Press.

QIRC (Queensland Industrial Relations Commission). *Decision: Matter Nos. R27-3 of 1991 and B561 of 1994 Kindergarten Teachers Award—State; Childcare Industry Award—State*. 22. March 1996.

QIRC (Queensland Industrial Relations Commission). *Transcripts of proceedings: Matter Nos. R27-3 of 1991 and B561 of 1994. Australian Liquor, Hospitality and Miscellaneous Workers Union, Queensland Branch, Union of Employees*.

Rafferty, F. (1989). Equal pay—past experience, future directions: A practitioner's perspective. *Journal of Industrial Relations*, 31,4: 526-537.

Rafferty, F. (1991). Equal Pay: An industrial relations anomaly? *Journal of Industrial Relations*, 33,1: 3-19.

Rosier, M., & Lloyd-Smith, J. (1996). *I love my job, but . . . childcare workforce attrition study*. Melbourne: Community Services and Health Industry Training Board.

Senate Employment, Education and Training References Committee. (1996). *Childhood matters: The report on the inquiry into early childhood education*. Parliament House, Canberra.

Silin, J. (1988). On becoming knowledgeable professionals. In B. Spodek, O.N. Saracho & D.L. Peters (Eds.). *Professionalism and the Early Childhood Practitioner*. New York: Teachers College Press.

Smith, A.B. (1990). Early childhood on the margins. *Australian Journal of Early Childhood*, 15, 4: 12-15.

Standards for center based long day care. (1993). Canberra: Commonwealth Government.

Stonehouse, A. (1990). An open letter to Australian early childhood professionals. *Australian Journal of Early Childhood*, 15, 4: 6-11.

Tayler, C. (1994). Perspectives on early childhood course development in universities and TAFE colleges. *Australian Journal of Early Childhood*, 19, 3: 15–19.

Wangmann, J. (1994). Accreditation in Australia. In E. Mellor & K. Coombe (Eds.). *Issues in Early Childhood Services: Australian Perspectives*. Melbourne: WBC Publishers International. Inc.

Witz, A. (1992). *Professions and Patriarchy*. London: Routledge.

Yinger, R., & Hendricks-Lee, M. (1993). Working knowledge in teaching. In C. Day, J. Calderhead, & P. Denicolo (Eds.). *Research on Teacher Thinking: Understanding Professional Development*. London: Falmer.

Chapter 18

The Politics of Restructuring and Professional Accountability: A Case Study of Curriculum Choice for Early Childhood Programs

Loraine Corrie

Abstract

This chapter considers the effects of educational reform on the early years' curriculum. Specifically, links are made between new restructuring policies and the inclusion of a controversial program in the curriculum for three- to eight-year-old children, namely a perceptual-motor program (PMP).[1] The chapter is divided into three sections. First, some conceptual issues inherent in the restructuring reforms are discussed. Second, the PMP and the research evidence are described. Third, the decision to include the PMP in the curriculum is analyzed and conclusions are drawn.

Restructuring Policies and Early Childhood Education

Changes in education embody complex issues. Many changes are driven by political processes rather than research findings (Hopkins, 1994). Currently, the political process is reflected in the constitutional dimensions of policy that construct schools as sites of self-managing enterprise that enact the "three Es"—economy, efficiency, and effectiveness (Reynolds, 1994). The three Es shape notions about teacher accountability, which is judged by the measurement of students' learning outcomes.

The framework of current educational reform rests on restructuring policies that devolve power from a centralized bureaucracy to individual schools. Restructuring policies are consistent with the constitutional agenda promoting individualism and competition. Current restructuring policies mean that individual schools are held responsible for children's educational outcomes, although the bureaucracy maintains control over key policies and levels of funding.

Restructuring the System

Restructuring policies have been debated worldwide, with the argument focused on the top-down versus bottom-up dichotomy. Proponents of restructuring point to the deleterious effects of centralized bureaucratic organizations. They insist that restructuring improves school productivity and accountability because individual schools are free to make decisions that enhance the quality of education for their students.

Critics of decentralization argue that restrictions under a centralized system were more imagined than real. Critics say that before restructuring reforms, few policies were mandated; most were written as guidelines that helped educators to make their own professional judgments based on their knowledge of a specific context.

Fullan (1993) points out that decentralization lacks credibility because centralization is protected in most education systems. Decentralization is seen through policies that prescribe systemwide curriculum, assessment, and accountability practices. These policies reflect an entrenched centralizing imperative that ensures top-down control of schools. Decentralization ensures that bureaucrats remain in control over the purposes, aims, priorities, and outcomes of education. Decentralization means that the individual schools are responsible for achieving the objectives of the policies.

Restructuring Reforms and Early Childhood Education

Policymakers speak about reform being directed at improvements to the quality of education, but critics say that distributional outcomes drive the reform agenda (Hartley, 1994). However, there tends to be less public scrutiny of budget reductions when policies are presented as educational reform.

Before decentralization, early childhood education attracted special conditions that set it apart from other sectors of education. Many programs for four- and five-year-old children were provided by local communities in spacious, purpose-built centers with large, well-equipped outside playing spaces. There were ample supplies of equipment and materials; a generous allowance for teachers of one day a week for planning and preparing programs; and a full-time teacher assistant. Teachers had a great deal of autonomy concerning the day-to-day running of the center, the program, the content of the curriculum, and levels of parent involvement. Specialist early childhood personnel from the "head office" visited centers regularly to advise teachers and provide professional development.

As a result of reforms, four- and five-year old children were relocated to the primary school site, where the school principal took control of the administration of the program. Early childhood teachers lost autonomy and were required to report to the principal. After the reforms, many of the early childhood specialist support staff disappeared, and less specialized early childhood professional development was provided. In addition, provision of physical amenities was reduced, with some teachers being moved to small transportable buildings situated in sparse outside playing areas.

The move to the school site created difficulties for some early childhood teachers. Often there were only one or two early childhood trained teachers on the school staff. Anecdotal evidence suggested that some early childhood teachers felt isolated because they held values and beliefs about education that reflected early childhood pedagogy, rather than the traditional primary school pedagogy of other staff members. Teachers reported that they were the butt of jibes about being "baby-sitters" and not being "real" teachers (see Hayden, this volume, chapter 8).

Restructuring Reforms and School Principals
School principals were expected to take leadership roles in administering the early years' programs and evaluating teachers. However, principals reported that they lacked knowledge and expertise in early childhood education and that professional development was not provided by the system (Stamopoulos, 1995).

Principals needed to understand the philosophical underpinning of early childhood pedagogy in order to support early childhood teachers. However, anecdotal evidence suggested that some principals found it hard to understand the noise, movement, and activity levels generated by child-centered programs and did not understand the teacher's role. Some principals were comfortable with teacher-directed whole class activities, which were similar to traditional primary school pedagogy, and some teachers were instructed to incorporate more of these activities in the daily timetable.

The system's failure to provide induction for principals into early childhood education can be interpreted as a lack of commitment to early childhood at the constitutional level. Before reforms, distributional outcomes had enabled early childhood programs to attract special conditions, but these did not fit the reform agenda of economic rationalism. It is inferred that changes at the constitutional level meant that the expensive differences between the early childhood and primary sectors were not acceptable.

Before the reforms, the special conditions that early childhood education received were rationalized by the differences in pedagogy between early childhood and primary school education. Incorporating a teacher-directed, whole class, lock-step program (such as the PMP) into the curriculum may have been viewed to make early childhood look like primary school education, and thus justify more equal funding arrangements.

In addition, the need for the government to provide for children with educational difficulties had been highlighted in a government inquiry (Shean Report, 1993), which had received media exposure throughout the state. The PMP claimed this seemed especially timely. PMP was said to provide intervention for children with educational and behavioral difficulties, and to cost each school only $6,000, which made it a cheaper option than providing extra specialist staff.

The Perceptual Motor Program (PMP)

The use of the PMP in the curriculum became apparent in a survey that asked school staff about children who were of concern to teachers, and the types of programs being provided to meet the needs of these children. The survey included 200 school principals and 230 teachers of five to seven-year-old children. The survey showed that schools used the PMP more frequently than any other intervention (Corrie & Barratt-Pugh, 1997). As a result of these findings, a thorough search was made of the research literature about PMPs, and anecdotal evidence was collected from practitioners in the field.

Teachers who used the PMP believed that it prevented educational difficulties by enhancing skills in normally developing children. In addition, teachers believed that the PMP served as appropriate intervention for children at-risk of educational difficulties in the physical, cognitive, language, and/or psycho-social domains.

The PMP is a commercial program that was sold to schools (see Bulluss & Coles, 1994). Teachers learned how to implement it by attending inservice sessions that were conducted by the promoters of the program. The program consisted of a manual, workcards, and special equipment. Some state government schools received funding of up to $6,000 to implement the program. The money came from a fund allocated for children with educational difficulties as a result of the Shean Report (1993).

Use of the PMP
Typically the program was administered to the whole class. The teacher followed a sequence of activities in the program manual. Workcards gave precise steps for adults to follow when instructing and supervising the children. Usually three other people were needed to help implement the program, and often parents acted as assistants.

Children were taught the same skill at the same time by the teacher during whole group "floor" sessions. They practiced the skills later three times a week in small supervised groups. Each skill was taught and practiced according to specific instructions, and children were not allowed to deviate from these instructions. The program did not allow children to create their own movements; to select, improvise, or experiment; or to plan and collaborate. There were a variety of activities, but a strong emphasis was placed on eye-tracking and patterning exercises, as it was claimed that these exercises helped children achieve academically and behave appropriately.

The promoters of the PMP ran inservice courses for teachers that included presentations by "developmental optometrists", who reinforced the need for eye exercises to remediate and prevent difficulties in reading and learning. Anecdotal evidence suggested that some parents heard about PMPs from other parents and exerted pressure on their school to buy the program.

PMPs and the Research Evidence
The rationale for the perceptual-motor programs was established by Ayres (1972), who published research evidence purporting to show positive results for children with learning disabilities. Ayres stressed the importance of eye training and neurological organization, including laterality and patterning training. Ayres' work was used as the basis for many different diagnostic and remedial perceptual-motor programs. Many studies assessed the effects of the programs, but researchers failed to replicate Ayres' original positive results.

A meta-analysis of 180 studies showed that the approach was not an effective intervention technique for academic, cognitive, or perceptual-motor variables (Kavale & Mattson, 1983). Other later studies supported Kavale and Mattson's findings (Kaplan, Polatajko, Wilson, & Faris, 1993).

In 1991, Cummins examined some of Ayres' original research and found that the analyses were flawed and did not accord with rigorous research methods (Cummins, 1991). In summary, Ayres' research has been criticized for lack of validity and reliability. Later research studies showed that PMPs did not benefit children, and many researchers have concluded that perceptual-motor programs neither prevented difficulties nor cured them.

However, the promises of the programs have proved to be seductive, and new programs based on Ayres' flawed theory emerge at regular intervals. Analysis of the program sold to schools in Western Australia (Bulluss & Coles, 1994) showed that there were many links to Ayres' work, although the promoters claimed it was a new and different program. Many of the exercises were similar to Ayres' exercises, and there was the same emphasis on eye exercises.

The effects of eye exercises is disputed by the Royal Australian College of Ophthalmologists (RACO), who have expressed serious doubts about optometrists' work in the area of learning difficulties. A joint policy statement by RACO and the Australian College of Paediatrics (1990) stated that there is "no known scientific evidence" to support the use of visual training or neurological organizational training to improve academic abilities.

Similarly, the National Health and Medical Research Council (1997) reported on interventions for children with behavior problems and learning difficulties, and found that there was no evidence to support the use of patterning exercises, optometric training, or perceptual motor programs.

In summary, research has failed to find support for the use of PMPs. In addition, an examination of the pedagogic principles of the program used in Western Australian schools shows that they did not align well with worldwide standards of appropriate pedagogy in early childhood.

The PMP and Early Childhood Pedagogy
An analysis of the pedagogical principles encapsulated in the PMP showed that some principles do not fit with principles articulated by the National Association for the Education of Young Children or the Australian Early Childhood Code of Ethics (Corrie & Barratt-Pugh, 1997). The PMP reflected the aspects of education classified as "regulated" rather than "flexible" in the Schools' Council (1992) paper. Furthermore the PMP did not match the Education Department of Western Australia's (1996) draft "Guidelines for Best Practice in the Early Years", which reflected the Schools' Council document. An analysis comparing some aspects of the PMP and the guidelines is given in Figure 1.

As shown in Figure 1, there were differences between the principles underpinning the PMP and Education Department's own guidelines for early years programs, which makes its decision to fund the PMP seem contradictory. It seems even more surprising that early childhood

Perceptual Motor Program	**Guidelines for Best Practice**
The program is based on didactic principles of teaching	**The program is based on constructivist principles of learning**
Children learn when a predetermined task is given to them, regardless of their strengths or needs.	Children learn when the teacher plans learning experiences that match individuals' interests, strengths, and needs, identified by objective observation.
Specific skills can be taught to every child in a group in a lock-step way.	Children in one group will be at different developmental levels, and therefore a range of learning experiences is required.
Children will learn the same skill in the same way.	Different children have different learning styles, and require a variety of types of learning experiences.
Children benefit from following adults' instructions in order to complete the tasks in the one "right" way.	Open-ended learning experiences facilitate skills of problem solving, planning, discussion, and result in different solutions.
Children benefit from being taught fragmented skills that are practiced in an isolated context.	Children learn specific skills that they use to explore, experiment, discover, improvise, and innovate in a range of meaningful contexts.
All children have the same cultural and linguistic understandings.	Cultural and linguistic diversity is recognized through a range of learning experiences.
The teacher enacts the role of instructor.	The teacher enacts a variety of roles that include facilitator, instructor, player, observer, and planner.

Figure 1   Principles Underpinning PMPS and Best Practice Guidelines

teachers would include the PMP in their curriculum willingly. However, several factors conspired to influence teachers' decisions, and these factors are discussed in the following section.

Factors Influencing the Decision to Include the PMP in the Curriculum

Teachers' use of the PMP was at odds with the knowledge and beliefs that underpin their pedagogy. However, it is suggested that a set of factors combined to influence teachers' judgements. The factors that shaped teachers' decisions resulted from the state government's decentering and recentering policies.

Move to the School Site

The state government's election promise resulted in the rapid inclusion of four and five-year-olds on the primary school site, which led to a shortage of appropriate buildings. Many children were housed in temporary "transportable" rooms which were inadequate in size. Other groups were housed in converted primary school classrooms that were situated next door to the older children.

The lack of appropriate physical amenities and need to control noise and movement influenced teachers' decision making processes. In some cases, the type of learning experiences teachers could make available to children was restricted by the cramped spaces. Some teachers responded to the difficulties by providing more "seat work" activities, which involved photocopied worksheets and other whole-group teacher directed tasks that are part of traditional primary school classrooms, rather than early childhood programs. The drift to primary school pedagogy set the scene for the inclusion of the didactic PMP.

Sessional to Full School-Day Programs

The inclusion of the PMP in the curriculum came at a time when children's attendance was changed by a government dictate, from "sessional" (attending four half-days a week) to "full-time" (attending four full school days a week). However, specialist professional development had been reduced and teachers received little guidance about changes to programming and timetabling. Many teachers expressed anxiety about how to use the extra time with the children, and implementing the PMP was a time-consuming exercise that filled a substantial part of the day.

The Power Hierarchy of the School
Early childhood teachers had to act on the principal's instructions when they became part of the primary school. Some principals required particular information from teachers for the "School Management Plan", which was based on traditional primary school curriculum areas. Some principals made decisions about the content of the early childhood curriculum and timetable, which lead to a reduction in child-initiated learning and play. Many principals supported the use of the PMP, and some instructed teachers to include it in the curriculum. However, some principals lacked knowledge about early childhood and did not have access to resources in the system to guide them in their decision making processes.

Many temporary teachers experienced professional conflicts but wanted to keep the principals happy in order to keep their job, particularly as teaching positions were in short supply. Job prospects of early childhood teachers hinged on good assessment reports and high grades from the principals.

Teacher Accountability
The push for teacher accountability had gathered momentum and was aligned with evidence of students' learning outcomes. Some principals insisted that early childhood teachers used the same format for reporting to parents as the primary school teachers, which meant assessing children in the curriculum learning areas. However, traditionally early childhood teachers assessed children's progress in developmental domains, and changing assessment procedures to the curriculum learning areas diverted some teachers away from early childhood pedagogy.

There was a great deal of confusion about the assessment of the five-year-old children, because the student outcome statements did not include this younger age group. Many teachers were not sure about appropriate assessment methods. Teachers received little guidance from the system and were pressured by principals to assess children formally.

The PMP came with tests that claimed to assess children's progress, and these were used by some teachers. In some schools, the results of the PMP assessments were used to decide whether children should proceed to the first year of compulsory school, which meant important decisions about children's education were made on the basis of an invalid test. However, teachers could claim to have met their principal's requirements by assessing children's progress.

Multi-Age Grouping

There was a system-level initiative for some schools to restructure classes of five-, six-, and seven-year-olds into "multi-age group" classes. Many teachers appointed to teach in these classes were primary trained, rather than early childhood trained.

The multi-age group classes were provided with less (a) classroom and playground space, (b) teacher assistant time, and (c) materials and equipment because it was argued that each class now had only one-third the number of five-year-olds.

Many teachers found it difficult to manage the multi-age group classes in small classrooms with reduced materials and equipment. In addition, primary teachers experienced difficulties in programming across the age range, and they lacked knowledge of early childhood. Consequently, they welcomed the structured teacher-directed PMP that claimed to benefit children of all ages.

Children with Special Needs

Policy changes meant that increasing numbers of children with high levels of additional needs in the cognitive, physical, or psycho-social domains were integrated into the classroom. In some cases, a special assistant was provided for part of the day.

However, many teachers were expected to integrate children with special needs into their classes with little guidance from early childhood specialists. In addition, staff reductions at the system level meant there were fewer school psychologists to help teachers plan appropriate programs. The PMP claimed to help children with a wide range of physical and cognitive needs, and teachers believed it provided the intervention required by some children.

System Level Funding for the PMP

Schools received funding from the state government's education department to implement the PMP. The bureaucrats' decision to fund the PMP had three results:

1. some children experiencing difficulties at school participated in an ineffectual program, and they did not receive help at school for their academic or behavioral difficulties;
2. normally developing children participated in a costly and invalid program; and
3. funding spent on the PMP meant that money was not available to fund high-quality educational interventions needed by some children.

Most importantly, schools assumed that the program must be credible because it was being funded, and, therefore, the use of the program spread throughout the state.

The Marketing Campaign
Vigorous marketing ensured that the PMP was the name on every teacher's lips. Anecdotal evidence shows that some teachers who did not like the program were worried that they were being "left behind" or getting "out of date" by not using the PMP. Gradually more teachers or principals asked for the PMP. The word spread, and consequently, parents began to complain to schools if their children did not participate in the program.

The PMP gathered a groundswell of support among teachers and parents based on a marketing campaign that relied on anecdotal stories, testimonials, and esoteric jargon to sell its message. Few people understood the theory underpinning the program, and it assumed considerable mystique. The PMP was promoted with zeal by its supporters, who greeted its critics (such as Blackmore & Corrie, 1995) with hostility and anger.

Funding was withdrawn after a change in leadership of the state education department, and a slow movement away from the program was apparent. Although some teachers continued to use the program as prescribed, many others changed the format by using the equipment as part of the free-play activities, and some stopped using it. Two years after funding ended, some teachers reported that the specialized equipment sat abandoned in storerooms of schools as a daily reminder of a costly error.

Discussion

The inclusion of the PMP into the early childhood curriculum is linked inextricably to the restructuring policy. The policy was based on the constitutional imperative to make schools economically viable, efficient, and effective in producing results. However, it is speculated that achieving the policymakers' aims meant reducing the level of constitutionalized commitment to early childhood education, which was enacted by a reduction in distributional outcomes.

Decisions were shaped by policies that constructed schools as sites of commercial enterprise. Schools focused their goals on the need to be cost-effective and competitive, which inevitably resulted in changes in the special conditions awarded to early childhood. Funding policies shaped the type of interventions that schools provided for children struggling to learn. Many schools felt that $6,000 was a bargain price compared to the specialized educational interventions that were needed by some young children.

The rhetoric of decentralization is posited on the notion that schools should be autonomous, self-managing units, which matches the values of a democratic consumer society. However, decentralization meant that there was no central information system to advise schools of research findings related to innovations being marketed by the promoters of PMP. In the case of the PMP, schools had no central body to check the validity of the claims made about the program.

Devolving power to schools resulted in fewer support structures for early childhood teachers. In addition to dealing with school staff and principals who had little understanding of their pedagogy, early childhood teachers no longer had the systemic supports to affirm the pedagogical knowledge that underpinned their practice (Corrie, 1997). In turn, it became harder for early childhood teachers to enact their role of advocates for young children, and their voices were silenced.

Decentralization is reflected in systemwide curriculum, assessment, and accountability policies. By using the assessment protocols of the PMP, teachers based their professional judgments about children's progress on an invalid behaviorist set of competencies. However, the assessments produced by teachers enabled them to fulfilll the accountability demands imposed on them by their principals.

The policies about student assessment and teacher accountability resulted in a drift away from early childhood pedagogy. Other policies changed early childhood teachers' working conditions substantially. Teachers' attempts to manage the changes with little support led to an erosion of the principles of early childhood pedagogy.

The inclusion of the PMP in the early childhood curriculum leads to many questions about professional accountability. The PMP appeared to be a quick fix solution to some important educational issues, but it proved costly in terms of wasted resources and lost opportunities for children to learn. Who will accept responsibility when decisions are shown to be imprudent? Are the teachers, the principals, the bureaucrats, or governments responsible for erroneous decisions? The view taken here is that accountability is governed by the extent to which early childhood issues are constitutionalized within the education system.

The case of the PMP highlights the need for constitutional support for early childhood education, which could have been shown by policies that:

1. provided appropriate physical amenities for four- and five-year-old children;

2. provided principals with professional development in early childhood education; and
3. ensured professional support for early childhood teachers.

Accountability for the quality of programs cannot be separated from constitutional commitment to early childhood education. School principals and early childhood teachers are responsible for the content of the curriculum. However, to a large extent, distributional outcomes of policies govern the provision of high-quality programs.

Restructuring the system to promote economy, efficiency, and effectiveness in schools may be a worthy idea within an economic rationalist's framework. However, there is a need to address the hidden costs of restructuring policies in order to avoid the repetition of wasteful ventures.

Notes

1. Perceptual-motor programs were promoted in the United States of America in the late 1960s by Ayres. Many different types of programs have been devised based on Ayres' work, and all emphasize neurological patterning and eye exercises. The program promoted in Australia is known as "Smart Start with PMP" (see Bulluss & Coles, 1994). It is worth noting that the Brain Gym program was being used in some schools in Western Australia at the same time as the PMP. Brain Gym is an off-shoot of PMPs and includes similar patterning exercises. While PMPs and related programs offer quick fixes that have great appeal, the promoters provide no reputable research evidence to support their claims of success.

References

Ayres, J. (1972). Improving academic scores through sensory integration. In *Journal of Learning disabilities*, 5(6): 23–28.

Blackmore, A.M., & Corrie, L. (1995). When is a job worth doing? Perceptual-motor programs examined. In M. Wild & L. Corrie (Eds.). *Wild Beasts and Other Curiosities.* (pp. 11–21). West Australian research, issues, and innovations in early childhood education. Perth, W.A.: Edith Cowan University.

Bulluss, J., & Coles, P. (1994). *Perceptual motor programs. A manual for teachers.* Mordialloc, Victoria: P.J. Developments.

Corrie, L. (1997). The interaction between teachers' knowledge and skills when managing a troublesome classroom behavior. *Cambridge Journal of Education* 27(1): 93–105.

Corrie, L., & Barratt-Pugh, C. (1997). Perceptual-motor programs do not facilitate development. Why not play? *Australian Journal of Early Childhood*, 22(1): 30–36.

Cummins, R.A. (1991). Sensory integration and learning disabilities: Ayres' factor analyzes reappraised. *Journal of Learning Disabilities*, 24(3): 160–168.

Fullan, M. (1993). *Change Forces. Probing the depths of educational reform.* London: Falmer.

Hartley, D. (1994). Devolved school management: The "new deal" in Scottish education. In *Journal of Education Policy*, 9(2): 129–140.

Hopkins, D. (1994). School improvement in an ERA of change. In P. Ribbins & E. Burridge (Eds.). *Improving Education. Promoting Quality in Schools.* (pp. 183–193). London: Cassell.

Kaplan, B.J., Polatajko, H.J., Wilson, B.N., & Faris, P.D. (1993). Re-examination of sensory integration treatment: A combination of two efficacy studies. *Journal of Learning Disabilities*, 26(5): 342–347.

Kavale, K., & Mattson, P.D. (1983). One jumped off the balance beam: Meta-analysis of perceptual-motor training. *Journal of Learning Disabilities*, 16(3): 165–173.

National Health and Medical Research Council. (1997). *Attention Deficit Hyperactivity Disorder*. Canberra: Commonwealth of Australia.

Reynolds, D. (1994). School effectiveness and quality in education. In P. Ribbins & E. Burridge (Eds.). *Improving Education. Promoting Quality in Schools*. (pp. 165–173). London: Cassell.

Royal Australian College of Ophthalmologists and Australian College of Paediatrics. (1990). *Learning disabilities, dyslexia and vision*. Joint Policy Statement. Canberra: RACO.

Schools Council. (1992). *Developing flexible strategies in the early years of schooling: Purposes and possibilities*. Project Paper No. 5. Canberra: Australian Government.

Shean, R. (1993). *The education of students with disabilities and specific learning difficulties*. Perth, W.A: Ministry of Education.

Stamopoulos, E. (1995). *The professional background and perceptions of principals on their leadership role in preprimary*. Unpublished master's thesis. Edith Cowan University.

Chapter 19

The Emergent Professional: Training and Credentialing Early Childhood Teachers—an Australian Case Study

Ann Veale

Abstract

This paper traces the development of early childhood professional education in South Australia from 1907 to the present day. Beginning as a two-year course of training apart from mainstream teacher education, early childhood courses were separated until the 1970s when the commonwealth government funded colleges of advanced education for teacher training institutions. The two pathways have merged in the 1990s in a four-year degree course called a Bachelor of Early Childhood Education. The pathway includes specialized higher degrees with honors, masters degrees by coursework or research, up to Ph.D. This South Australian case study is a reflection of the rites of passage of early childhood professional training in Australia, which evolved from philanthropic concerns about the welfare of children to fully credentialized choices from a spectrum of specialized training, professional organizations, and a developing research base.

Introduction

In 1994 a four-year teaching award was conceived in South Australia, with the object of providing a "key step in the development of a single coherent academic/training career path for early childhood service personnel" (University of South Australia, 1994, p. 4). At one stroke, three existing degree awards were blended together: the Bachelor of Social

Science (Human Services-Childcare), the Bachelor of Teaching (Early Childhood Education), and the Bachelor of Early Childhood Education. The new award had articulation agreements with the Associate Diploma in Social Science (Childcare) offered by the Department of Technical and Further Education, and offered credit for two subjects available through Open Learning Australia (OLAA). Thus a seamless professional path opened for men and women for study and employment in early childhood services for children from birth to eight years.

Early childhood education had come a long way from its simple beginnings. The growth of early childhood education began in philanthropic concerns of volunteer groups of women for the welfare of children in cities. By the 1970s childcare and education became a central political focus where the goals were linked to the needs of women to take their place in the workforce and their consequent need for childcare for their children. The organization of children's services and the training programs are now housed in large bureaucracies. Teacher credentials need to be nationally recognized as the professional staff wish to be free to move and have their qualifications and experience recognized across state and national boundaries. But the central issues of care and education remain the same. The debate about quality of services is an ongoing concern with two critical issues. These are: *who pays for quality in care*; and *is care a public or private concern*?

Case Study of South Australia

Early childhood teacher education began in South Australia in 1907. The initiative for the provision of early childhood services came from a Church of England clergyman who had witnessed the work being done in Woolloomooloo in Sydney and arranged for two of the Sydney pioneers to come to Adelaide to promote the kindergarten method. From this philanthropic start in 1905, the Kindergarten Union movement was born. Thereafter it led to the creation of a training system for staff for the kindergartens and the generation of children's services as we know them today. The pioneers were Lillian deLissa and her colleagues, graduates of the Sydney Kindergarten Training College. The principles upon which the programs were based were those of the European Kindergarten movement and were influenced by educators such as Froebel and Montessori. They were also influenced by progressive educators such as Dewey and other educational reformers (Dowd, 1983, p. 13).

The issue about whether training was necessary for their teachers was a matter of some debate. It was a moot point as to whether it should be the province of the employing body or whether kindergarten teachers should undertake their training in University alongside other teachers. Mellor believes that "the decision to retain control of kindergarten teacher training effectively placed kindergartens outside the mainstream of education in those states. It also limited the opportunities for students teacher training to those who could afford to pay the necessary fees" (1990, p. 122). In Mellor's view this shaped the outcomes for many years. It created a self-perpetuating group that dominated both senior kindergarten administration and teacher training into the 1970s (op cit., p. 123). Brennan comments, "setting up independent training colleges outside the state education system was a bold decision for these voluntary groups. It was also a statement of their desire to retain their status as independent organizations, offering a service that was not governed by politicians or bureaucrats" (Brennan, p. 28). Lillian deLissa argued that "the Government Training College was purely intellectual" and that if teachers trained there, "kindergartens would become merely places of instruction like the infant schools, instead of places for the development of character". (Brennan, p. 29).

The programs provided care and education for children over a short day extending from 9.00 a.m. to mid-afternoon. A "meal and sleep" was included. The children were provided with a balance of care and stimulation and indoor and outdoor play.

Courses for Early Childhood Teachers

The newly created kindergartens were in need of a supply of trained personnel to staff them. The state could not continue to rely on Sydney trained graduates, and the South Australian University training college did not make provision for teachers who wished to work with children below the age of seven years (Dowd, p. 23). While Lillian deLissa wanted a two-year undergraduate program as in Sydney, there were others who had reservations about this idea. Dowd reports "many people in Adelaide and elsewhere were of the opinion—often strongly held—that the only attributes needed by someone who worked with young children were common sense and sympathy. To put her [sic] through two years of intensive specialized training was a pretentious waste of time. After all, *anybody* could mind a baby" (op cit., p. 22).

Back in 1906 it may have seemed pretentious to set up a training college when there was only a single kindergarten, but Lillian deLissa foresaw the need for future expansion. The new kindergarten training program was begun in February 1907 at the Franklin Street kindergarten. The "Franklin Street properties fulfillled the three-fold functions of free kindergarten, experimental training college, and residence" (op. cit.). The teacher education program consisted of practical teaching experience, and lectures on educational theory, academic and general studies, and crafts with "practical experience in the mornings with the children, under supervision and with help, and theory in the afternoons" (Sixty-first Annual Report Kindergarten Union of South Australia, 1966, p. 12).

In the early years, concern was felt for the health of the children in centers. This was shown by provision of a midday meal, followed by a sleep. "The plan of having a midday meal and sleep at the kindergartens has quite justified itself in the improved health of the children . . . The Directors all report on the satisfactory state of children's health owing to the regular routine and carefully selected diet" (p. 18).

This policy of having the same person responsible for the training program for teachers, and the educational program in the kindergartens, continued until 1945 while the numbers of students remained low (Dowd, p. 35). In the 1943–1944 Annual Kindergarten Union Report, the Principal reported the "important development—the forming of a new College syllabus". One main feature of the new syllabus is that it is identical in general outline to the courses offered in the other states and commonwealth, so that in future all Australian preschool teachers will receive the same type of training (p. 8). The content of the course was to "stress a wider training in both cultural and academic subjects" and "opportunity to develop their individual interests and abilities" (op. cit.). This report also announced new opportunities for courses of postgraduate training to be held in Adelaide, Melbourne, and Sydney for one term. Graduates of these courses were later to return as lecturers who were able to further enhance the professional training.

In 1968, the principal, Betty Davis, reported that the government had allocated $670,000 to the College "for rebuilding in order to double the present enrollment to two hundred students" (1968, p. 12).

The year 1972 was a landmark in early childhood education. The Liberal-National Party passed the Childcare Act, which effectively took on an increased Commonwealth Government role in early childhood services. When the Labor Government came into office in 1972 it shifted the responsibility for the Childcare Act from the Department of Labor and National Service to the Department of Education. The effect of this, comments Brennan, was "that the distinctions between childcare and preschool became blurred and that educationalists with very little knowledge about childcare now had responsibility for implementing the Government's policy in this area" (Brennan, 1994, p. 78).

The Dual System of Education and Care

June 2, 1976, was another landmark date when "the Government established an Office of Childcare within the Department of Social Security to plan, coordinate and provide policy advice, to identify needs and allocate funds to community groups and State governments for a range of childcare services" (Evatt, 1977, vol. 4, p. 49). The philosophy behind this policy states "we see the role of government as recognizing that families of young children need community support. Childcare should be available to all parents, means tested in accordance with present policy and with preference for those in greatest need" (op. cit., p. 49). The government involvement was rationalized thus, "the facts are that thousands of parents are using inadequate forms of childcare with possible consequences to the whole of society. Not to provide and subsidize childcare is to penalize the poor, particularly as commercially operated services are beyond the reach of lower income families" (op. cit., p. 50).

The Evatt Report also recognized the needs of other groups in Australian society. They said "we believe that as a general policy, childcare services catering for groups with special needs (e.g., migrants, Aboriginals, handicapped children, isolated children) should be integrated with other childcare services in terms of planning and provision of funds . . . Aboriginal people should be encouraged and assisted to train in childcare work and special short term training programs should be devised for this purpose" (op. cit., p. 50). Such initiatives were not long in coming in South Australia.

Teacher Education Merges with Tertiary Education

There were two reports by Karmel into "Education and Change in South Australia" (Final Report, 1982). Karmel recommended that the isolation of teacher education in single purpose colleges be replaced by converting teachers colleges into multipurpose colleges of advanced education (op. cit., p. 213). Early childhood education became part of a large multicampus institution. The early childhood school thus formed retained its identity and was named in honor of Lillian deLissa. The deLissa Institute of Early Childhood and Family Studies was born in this period of rapid change.

The pace of change induced by the government was so rapid that students who began their three-year course in one institution would graduate with the award of another.

The 1970s not only brought changes to the tertiary training organizations, but also saw the emergence of childcare as the priority in children's services. Many new training programs were introduced, the most significant one being the two-year childcare certificate courses in colleges of technical and further education. This offered choices for entrants to the profession of a two-year qualification from TAFE or a three-year teaching qualification from a college of advanced education. Brennan points out that the choice of courses attracted different students. "The Care Certificate tended to attract students from working class as well as middle class homes" (1994, p. 125). The childcare industry has been a growth area of employment. Women in the workforce has resulted in reduced demand for sessional preschool services and directed need to long day care programs.

In the Final Report of the Committee of Enquiry into Education in South Australia, Karmel commented that "formal distinctions between preschool and childcare were rapidly disappearing, and that the major sponsors of early childhood services were engaged in or associated with the provision of both preschool and childcare programs" (1982, p. 6).

The Current Landscape
By 1993 there was government recognition that the number of children in Australia in childcare outside their homes had escalated and that the amount of time spent in childcare before a child starts school may be only 500 hours less than time spent in their entire years of schooling *(Putting Children First, 1993)*. To address this significant development a quality improvement and accreditation system was developed and administered by the National Childcare Accreditation Council (NCAC). The system is intended to "assist childcare providers and parents with the advice, support and training they need to help ensure that all children receive high-quality care" (op. cit., 1993, Foreword). At the heart of this process is a collaborative endeavor between the management and staff of centers with the parents of the children. It is a self-study process in which staff engage in reflection and accountability measures that enhance their self-perceptions of their own professionalism. This process and its effects upon the staff has benefits to the children, and has professional development impact on staff, which raises the standard of the quality of care.

Governments have gone a long way toward setting quality standards for children's services, although there are gaps in newer areas such as out-of-school hours care. Rising costs have seen students in training employed to provide out-of-school hours care on very limited budgets catering for children from 5 to 12 years. Whereas regulations have been successful in addressing such issues as ratios of staff to children in care services, there are still some newer areas that need to be scrutinized and provided with guidelines. Wangmann points out that, in contrast to the purpose of legislation, "Accreditation focuses on the *determining* components of quality which are likewise essential, but intrinsically not susceptible, to regulation". The fact is that the "development of a national accreditation system for childcare services in Australia has evolved from professional and political initiatives" (Wangmann, 1995, p. 92). That this has emerged from *within the early childhood profession* seems to indicate a growing awareness of the need "for establishing its own standards of quality" (op. cit.). The evaluation process involves staff in the self-assessment of their programs according to guidelines, which is assessed by an expert panel. A detailed evaluation of the benefits of the accreditation process may hold the key to staff development aspects which unite the care and education aspects of the profession working together. In the report "Childhood Matters" (1996, p. 24), there is a subheading "Integration: an emerging reality for childcare and preschools". The report says "while shifts in thinking regarding the relationship between, and the importance of, care and education have been taking place in research, the same shifts were becoming evident in childcare and preschool centers. More childcare centers began employing preschool teachers and more preschool centers began employing various kinds of care: out-of-school hours care, occasional care and vacation care. Preschools and childcare services established links with schools. Schools began offering out-of-school hours care" (op. cit.)—thus improving arrangements for continuity of care across a child's early schooling.

Conclusion

This South Australian case study represents one approach to the blending of the professional credentializing of early childhood teachers in ways that merge care and education of young children. The economics of childcare provisions and differential salary structures for staff in childcare still exist, but the profession itself is taking on the challenge of setting the standards in the process of accreditation. Both national government policy initiatives are necessary to ensure that provision of services is spread equitably across the country and the ability of the profession to determine standards of quality over which they have some control and responsibility. Early childhood education has always been a blend of government and nongovernment initiatives. Contemporary influences flow from changes in the reduction of government funding to community childcare centers, with subsequent fee increases, and the withdrawal of children from center-based care. Up to now the political landscape has driven changes in the professional context. The challenge is to reverse this sequence.

References

Brennan, D. (1994). *The politics of Australian childcare from philanthropy to feminism*. Melbourne: Cambridge University Press.

Clyde, M. (1994). A comparative study of Australian and American center based caregiver perceptions of their role. *Journal for Australian Research in Early Childhood Education*: 124–131.

Clyde, M., & Rodd, J. (1995). Survey of the perceptions of the definitions of caregiving. *Journal for Australian Research in Early Childhood Education*, 1: 23–30.

Dowd, C. (1983). *The Kindergarten Teachers College. A history 1907–1974*. Adelaide: South Australian College of Advanced Education.

Evatt, E. (1977). *Royal Commission on Human Relationships Final Report*. Volume 4, Canberra, Australia Government Publishing Service.

Hill, S., & Veale, A. (1997). Love, care and politics in low income early childhood settings: The process of constructing a professional identity. *Australian Research in Early Childhood Education*, Vol. 1: 40–48.

Keeves, J. (1981). *Education and change in South Australia*. First Report. Committee of Enquiry into Education in South Australia, Feb.

Keeves, J. (1982). *Education and change in South Australia*. Final Report. Committee of Enquiry into Education in South Australia, Jan.

Kindergarten Union of South Australia (1938–1974) *Annual Reports*.

Mellor, E.J. (1990). *Stepping stones. The development of early childhood services in Australia*. Marrickville: Harcourt Brace Jovanovich.

National Childcare Accreditation Council. (1993). *Putting children first, quality improvement and accreditation system handbook*. First Edition. Commonwealth of Australia.

Palmer, G., & Ebbeck, M. (1990). *On home ground: The Magill Aboriginal early childhood program*. Adelaide: Meranda Media.

Ross, J. (1994). *Leadership*. Sydney: Allen & Unwin.

Saracho, O.N. (1993). Preparing teachers for early childhood programs in the United States. In B. Spodek (Ed.). *Handbook of Research on the Education of Young Children* (pp. 412-426). New York: Macmillan Pub. Co.

Saracho, O., & Spodek, B. (1993). Professionalism and the preparation of early childhood practitioners. *Early Childhood Development and Care, 89*: 1-117.

Senate Employment, Education and Training References Committee. (1996). *Childhood matters: The report on the inquiry into early childhood education*. Canberra-Commonwealth of Australia, July.

Social Welfare Commission. (1975). *Report on project care: Children, parents and community*. M. Coleman (Chairman). Canberra: The Parliament of the Commonwealth of Australia.

South Australian College of Advanced Education. (1988). *A submission for the accreditation of the Bachelor of Social Science (Human Services)*. Adelaide, August.

University of South Australia. (1994). Stage 2 Submission. *Bachelor of Early Childhood Education and Bachelor of Early Childhood Education (with Honors)*. deLissa Institute of Early Childhood and Family Studies, Faculty of Education, July.

Veale, A. (1991). *The emergent profession*. ERIC Clearinghouse on Elementary and Early Childhood Education, ED343 666, Urbana-Champaign, University of Illinois.

Wangmann, J. (1995). *Toward integration and quality assurance in children's services*. Australian Institute of Family Studies, Early Childhood Study Paper No. 6. Melbourne: Australian Institute of Family Studies.

Willer, B., & Bredekamp, S. (1993). A "new" paradigm of early childhood professional development. *Young Children*, Vol. 48, No. 4: 63-66.

Chapter 20

Early Childhood Services in Rural and Remote Areas: Four Case Studies

Tracey Simpson
Jan White

Abstract

This chapter explores the distributional and constitutional dimensions of early childhood service provision in rural and regional areas of New South Wales, Australia. Developments of the past 25 years as well as some generally unrecognized struggles, which continue through the 1990s, are described in terms of a landscape of contrasts—marginalization versus community strength and ownership; rural cultures versus service standardization. The authors conclude that the need to recognize and value the individuality of each rural situation is critical.

Location: Geographical and Political

Much has been documented about the effects of geographic isolation. Sinclair and Squires (1997, p. 10) emphasize the psychological dimensions of isolation and refer to factors distinguishing rural communities and contributing to rural disadvantage, as reported in *Toward a National Education and Training Strategy for Rural Australians*:

1. sparse distribution of government agencies,
2. high service costs,
3. high costs of living,
4. the sensitivity of non-metropolitan areas to fluctuations in international prices of agricultural and mining conditions,

5. less comfortable or convenient travel due to infrequent or absent transport services or poor road conditions,
6. poor knowledge of and access to information on services and facilities,
7. floods, fires, drought, and extremes of temperature sometimes destroying both life and the means of essential services and facilities,
8. infrequent or unreliable supply services,
9. lack of stimulus and social opportunities from a varied cultural environment and limited employment bases in any one locality.

These factors are also identified in research done in the early childhood field and specifically in New South Wales (McGowan, 1994; Simpson, 1993, 1996). However, there is somewhat of a paradox. A recent study carried out by Sarantakos (1997) presents a positive perspective of rural family life and part of the *Australian Living Standards Study*, reported by Kilmartin (1996), highlights the discrepancies between parents' and providers' perceptions of factors of isolation and the identification of problems in their rural settings.

Farm families—City families (Sarantakos, 1997) compared 124 farm families with 124 city families based on nine aspects of family life: overall happiness, marital satisfaction, family togetherness, family tensions, appreciation, community support, family functioning, community involvement, and religiosity. The author concludes that:

> farm families are functional and effective and, despite the distance and isolation as well as reduced services in areas such as health, education, and social services, they demonstrate standards of performance which are more than satisfactory. (p. 4)

Further it was revealed that, compared to city families, farm families perform either at the same or at a higher level in all measures employed in the analysis. Sarantakos concludes that these results lead to questions about how and at what costs these families manage to succeed in their task as primary units and socialists of children. There are two aspects of these questions that are pertinent to rural early childhood services: First, are there early childhood services which aid families in this task? And, second, where there are services, what relationship is there between the family and the service?

Social justice and equity have been discussed in the general education sector, but the outcomes related to the early childhood field are being challenged as the field develops. Understanding the social context and the values held within each rural and regional community is something that cannot be done from a distance or even by visiting service providers (Stevens, 1994; Kilmartin, 1996). While some providers situated in particular communities may be aware of underlying values and social stratification, their ability, as "blow-ins", to interpret the effects for specific families is restricted by their own understanding of, and more importantly, their acceptance in, the community.

Local, state, and federal governments all play a part in rural early childhood services, but the specific relationship to service provision often has as much to do with models of funding for service types as it does with characteristics and needs of the communities. Depending on the location and social attitudes of those in power at the local government level and the values of the community, there may also be a conflict between the timing of what appears to be constitutional change at a federal level and social change at a local level.

Advocates of the early childhood field and researchers acknowledge the differences and perceived difficulties of rural settings and support moves for what is seen as innovative practice to fill the gaps between metropolitan and nonmetropolitan service provision. Unfortunately, little has been addressed regarding the development of quality services which reflect their communities.

Distributions: Reports, Inquiries, and Recommendations

Problems associated with rural and remote early childhood service provision have been identified and recommendations have been made in a number of recent reports and inquiries.

In 1994, the National Council for the International Year of the Family[1] emphasized the importance of consultation with local communities as a base for family policy development. Access to affordable childcare was identified as a basic right and the Council recommended an increase in the availability of all types of services in rural and remote areas based on local needs. Partnerships between community-based organizations Commonwealth, state, and local governments, were suggested as a means to achieve appropriate service provision in the long-term.

The 1995 report from the Council of Australian Governments (COAG) Childcare Working Group[2] highlighted the possible benefits of flexible service provision at local level, especially in relation to the provision of more integrated services tailored to meet a range of local needs.

The concept of flexibility in approaches to service provision was repeated again in the 1996 recommendation from the Senate Employment, Education, and Training References Committee:[3] "that the State and Territory Ministers review their guidelines for licensing childcare centers to allow for greater flexibility to address the needs of small and remote communities" (1996, p. xv).

The Economic Planning Advisory Commission's Report[4] (1996, p. xv) revisited aspects of previous inquiries when it recommended that "a system which makes available affordable, high-quality care to all children and families, irrespective of their backgrounds, location or special needs" and "a system which can respond to the changing needs of working parents and community expectations for childcare" should be national objectives of childcare policy.

The absence of policy and action based on the recommendations, however, points to a lack of embedded commitment that indicates not only an absence of distributional allotment but also clearly shows there is no constitutional change. The call for strong family and child policy continues to be echoed by advocates for the whole early childhood field suggesting that constitutional change must occur before effective distributional allotments will flow to the rural sector of the early childhood field.

Case Studies: What is Really Happening?

It is the very specific nature of each setting that makes case studies of rural services difficult to generalize. The "quaintness" or the remoteness of particular services can also detract from the description of the factors of quality and true innovative practices. For the purpose of this discussion, reference to a range of situations in a wide area of rural New South Wales will provide a more realistic picture of how some of the issues identified in the aforementioned reports influence different communities. The overall problem to be addressed is finding ways to provide appropriate early childhood services in rural settings in New South Wales.

Case Study 1: No Cuts in Professionalism
The community preschool in a rural village was walking the tightrope of survival to maintain a two-day operation so that parents would not need to travel the extra 60 kilometers (at least) round trip to the nearest preschool service. Staff employed at the service were aware that funds in the preschool account may not cover their paychecks. In addition, the old church hall building used by the preschool was barely adequate in providing an appropriate physical environment for children and staff.

In 1991 preschools statewide felt the impact of the freeze of state government funding to their services. Many had some breathing space but for this little village service the pressure was enormous. Not only was the funding frozen but running costs were increasing and the downturn in the rural economy was having dramatic effects on parents' ability to pay fees. Parents, management committee, and staff felt they were fund raising to a point of overdependence on the community. The staff and management committee were also becoming more concerned about the physical environment of the service and the effect it was having on their ability to continue to provide a quality program.

In 1992, a crisis meeting was held involving management committee, staff, families, interested members of the local community, members of the wider early childhood, and education sectors. A suggestion was put forward that the staff should accept a cut in their wages until the crisis was over. Remembering that the community as a whole was suffering economically, this was seen as a reasonable solution and an extension of the community philosophy of "sticking together". It was the influence of the members of the early childhood community that changed the direction of the discussion, having argued that this was an inappropriate strategy and that staff were already doing more than their job required. After much long and often heated discussion, it was the realization that the preschool might be lost altogether that motivated members of the village community to become more active. Despite the fact that the service did not meet all their needs, this community had already, over time, made a huge commitment to their preschool.

The community supported the management committee and staff in successfully seeking funds from the Department of Community Services to get them over the crisis. The parents and interested community members joined the management committee and staff in developing a proactive approach to fund raising in order to keep their preschool open and to make improvements to the physical environment. They were successful in securing one-off funding to make more substantial improvements to the building in 1997. Despite these achievements, the fight to be financially viable and meet the needs of all the community continues. The long-term future of the preschool is no clearer than it was throughout the most difficult times.

In this case the lack of distributional allotments led to the empowerment of the preschool and wider community. The expectation that the staff should forgo rights as employees presents the complexity of combining professional and community roles and a double-edged sword in terms of support for the preschool on one side and devaluing the position of employees on the other. Nonetheless, the power of the early childhood community to influence the local community must be acknowledged as a constitutional allotment despite poor "distributions" (resources).

Reclaiming ownership of a service allowed for a move toward constitutional change at the local level, which in turn was responded to with distributional allotment from the state. Yet the problem still remains as the recognition from state level was of a "one off" response to the calls from a minority group who "made noises" when they were desperate. Future commitment to all small rural preschools was not considered nor was the real problem of inappropriate funding models for services which must respond to the needs of small communities.

The actual cost to the state was minimal while the cost to the community was great. The pressure to fund-raise was greater than ever and the local area was already supporting this service and others (education, health, aged care, and emergency and support services). Parents, staff, and other community members had to spend precious time away from their families and workplaces in fund-raising efforts that often required travelling to larger communities in the area to tap into other sources of support. The emotional and financial strain that was felt in the early days of the crisis had been projected onto the individual level.

Case Study 2: A Director's Dilemma

A remote rural community has the services of a preschool and a childcare center. The preschool runs an enrichment program for children selected from the community through a testing process. Many in the local community still see preschool as providing an educational program and the childcare center as a form of babysitting. This perception is encouraged by the fact that a bus collects and returns children from the childcare center so that they are able to attend preschool sessions. Furthermore, at times the childcare center has been run without qualified early childhood staff as it is difficult to attract appropriate staff to the isolated community.

A new qualified teacher/director was employed by the childcare management committee after some considerable time in advertising for the position. The director was enthusiastic in efforts to work with all staff, families, and committee to develop positive attitudes about the service provided and at the same time improve the quality of the overall program. Health and hygiene practices and staff-child interactions were of great concern. However, after many hours of consultation and hard work, the center was able to achieve one year's accreditation through the Quality Improvement and Accreditation System (QIAS).[5] This achievement was not without its casualties.

While the staff knew that the accreditation process was compulsory and they needed to work through the steps, they did not all agree with the standards identified as quality nor did they see the importance of quality staff-child interaction. Some staff wanted a more structured program "like preschool" rather than one that catered for individual needs and required all staff to observe and plan for children. Some families were frustrated by the policies that did not allow sick children to attend the center, and discussion of fee increases as a result of federal government funding changes were a problem. The center began to lose children as there were backyard babysitters who were more than willing to take children, even when they were ill, at a small fee per child. The director suffered stress from the difficult work environment as well as harsh treatment from some in the community and as a result decided to resign despite the support received from some families. Once again the director's role was taken over by an untrained staff member and the cycle recommenced.

In this scenario the distributional allotment of two early childhood services, funded in two very different ways, did not reflect an understanding of the cultures of this community nor the local attitudes.

The delight of finding an enthusiastic teacher/director willing to take a position in a remote location cannot shape the attitudes of staff and the community. This takes constitutional change. The problem in this community goes much deeper than simple provision of services (distributions). Education, information, consultation, and respect for the whole community are issues that occur at a different level. Meeting the criteria for national accreditation is not a reward for a childcare service when the attitude of many is "who cares?"

In this situation there are numerous factors which are out of the direct control of the early childhood field. However, the involvement of early childhood professionals could have an impact on future change in this and other remote rural communities. When considered in the light of the local community and its culture, there is room for considering greater flexibility in establishment of standards and the provision of services.

Case Study 3: "Small Populations Need Not Apply"

A large rural council area with a relatively small population of 11,757 identified the need for childcare services, other than preschools, which ran sessions varying from one half-day to five days a week. This unmet need resulted from a depressed economic climate; both partners wanting to or needing to work; and a changing population, some of whom did not have the support of family networks.

A group of early childhood professionals and interested parents working alongside the local council sought funding for a mobile or family day care service. As the model for mobile services did not allow for a long day care service, it was decided to explore the funding opportunities for a family day care scheme. Despite the enthusiasm of this group, they continually met opposition because council resources were determined by population, not geographical size. After many hours of frustrating telephone conversations with government funding bodies and advisers in capital cities, the group was sent away to consider other alternatives. The suggestion of combining with a neighboring council area, which also had a small population, had to be explored. The size of the two council areas presented one problem while the initial reluctance from some members of this council to have anything to do with "childcare" presented another. A barrier of conservative views about mothers caring for their own children had not been expected in this bid for what the group had seen as a move toward developing appropriate quality children's services.

Nonetheless, the development of a joint submission for funding for a family day care scheme appeared to be the only hope for acquiring a service in the area. The advisers for the appropriate funding body did not mind how the partnership was achieved but were more impressed by the figure for total population. Before the ink was dry on the agreement to fund the scheme, there was already discussion about how extra funding for the amount of travel, which was going to be necessary, might be obtained.

The family day care scheme continues to go from strength to strength although facing problems of finding a range of appropriate caregivers in very small villages and on properties. The tasks of educating the population about this quality early childhood service, changing attitudes in small communities, and coordinating a service in such a large area are faced with professionalism and enthusiasm. The quality of this and other rural services that are "different" and continuing to find ways of being flexible, should be recognized for their strengths in achieving service delivery that reflects the community.

Case Study 4: Farm-Based Multipurpose Care

The *Farm Based Childcare Project* (McGowan, 1994), centered around rural communities in south-east New South Wales and north-east Victoria, was a pilot program funded to trial a model of integrated rural childcare. The steering committee had representatives from women in agriculture, the local early childhood community, the local adult and community education organization, the tertiary sector, and government departments. The project aimed to find an effective model of childcare that took into consideration factors overlooked in mainstream services. These factors included the relatively small numbers of children, workplaces which combine home and work, seasonal labor requirements, irregular work hours, and patterns and provision for care on specific occasions such as for attendance at agricultural field days or before and after school when parents need to go to town.

Factors of distance, cost, time, lack of services, conservative attitudes, and misinformation were identified as barriers in accessing childcare services. These factors were interpreted as resulting from lack of flexibility of service provision rather than the service type. As the project's outcomes were bound by the children's services regulations from both New South Wales and Victoria, another barrier identified was that some regulations worked *against* the viability and relevance of any proposed model!

The model decided upon consisted of traditional services: multipurpose childcare with long day care, family day care, occasional care (including extended hours of care), out of school hours care, mobile service, and emergency care in the home. However, the organization of these services is flexible to meet local needs.

While there are signs of decision makers displaying a commitment to meeting the needs of rural families, the depth of this commitment will only be seen in the future if the support for such projects continues and each situation is viewed as being unique. Using this case as an example of the type of flexibility that works will suggest a move toward constitutional change. The ability to transcend barriers such as state regulations will be an indicator of such progression.

Conclusion

Is it only outsiders who see rural communities as disadvantaged? Rural families manage their lives with greater satisfaction than urban onlookers would expect. The power of families and communities to respond to the situations that are often out of their control, whether it be in the realm of early childhood services or other areas, suggests that they may have more innovative ways of approaching the provision of unique, quality childcare than the current situation allows.

Flexibility in regulations, funding, models of childcare services, and attitudes to the culture of rural communities would allow for the development of services which reflect local values. Valuing the strengths of the local community assists in the creation of an environment in which the values of the wider community can be introduced. Harnessing the professionalism of early childhood staff in responding to the uniqueness of their situation should be an extension of valuing the rural community. Advice and training from those who do not respect the culture of the setting must be seen as a shallow distributional allotment.

The development of Multifunctional Aboriginal Children's Services (MACS) is a federally funded initiative that provides for the specific needs of Aboriginal communities. The MACS' model reflects some of the aspects lacking in the provision of other children's services in rural communities: flexibility and consideration of community values and culture in the provision of the most appropriate types of childcare. A model such as this has the potential to be developed and successfully applied in many communities.

Decision makers must be confident in providing services which in meeting the local needs might not conform to the norm. Much is said about greater tolerance, antibias, and flexibility, but translating these into action at this level is quite a task. Through strong, well-informed advocates for the early childhood field, players at government level need to be encouraged to see the uniqueness of each rural situation before the process of constitutional change can even begin. Who is strong enough to bite the bullet and recognize the tenacity in the early childhood sector of rural Australia? They dare to be different and somehow survive by the rules of the "norm". How well might they function if advocates and decision makers gave them the respect and autonomy they deserve?

Notes

1. The National Council for the Year of the Family was established as an independent advisory body by the Commonwealth Minister for Family Services. The Council consulted widely with the community, encouraged public debate, advised the Minister on issues and challenges posed by existing social and economic change which impacts on Australian families, and recommended measures for improved standards of service which meet the needs of Australian families.

2. The Council of Australian Governments' (COAG) review of children's services was undertaken by a Commonwealth-State Working Group comprised of officials from all Commonwealth and State/Territory governments. The Working Group developed a draft national framework for children's services in 1995 with the aim of identifying possible areas of reform producing more efficient and effective arrangements for the delivery of services.

3. The Senate Employment, Education and Training References Committee carried out an inquiry into the experience of Australian children up to age seven. The inquiry included examination of recent research related to early childhood factors that have an impact on various aspects of future cognitive abilities, analysis of the cost of remedial and intervention strategies, assessment of the relationship between the early childhood services sector and the schools sector, and examination of recent early childhood education initiatives in Australia and the implications for Commonwealth policies in education and child support.

4. The Economic Planning Advisory Commission (EPAC) established a Task Force to investigate and report on the prospective demand for childcare, best practice in the provision of childcare, and the links between the provision of childcare and other children's and family services (Terms of Reference, EPAC, 1996, p. 175).

5. The Australian Quality Improvement and Accreditation System applies to all long day care centers. The process for improvement based on 52 principles involves ongoing evaluation by staff, families, community, and management and review by an experienced outsider. In order to be accredited, a center must achieve a specified standard for each principle. Those centers which exceed the required standards are given longer periods between reviews (see Glossary of Terms, this volume).

References

COAG Childcare Working Group. (1995). *Discussion paper on a proposed national framework for children's services.* Canberra: Australian Government Publishing Service.

Economic Planning Advisory Commission. (1996). *Future childcare provision in Australia: Task force final report.* Canberra: Australian Government Publishing Service.

Kilmartin, C. (1996). Local differences in problems for families: Views of providers and parents. In *Family Matters* (43): 38–42.

McGowan, C. (1994). *Country kids— who cares? Childcare, a work-related issue for farm families.* Report of the Farm Based Childcare Project sponsored by "The Hub." Adult and Community Education Provider, Tallangatta, Victoria.

National Council for the International Year of the Family. (1994). *Creating the links: Families and social responsibility.* Canberra: Australian Government Publishing Service.

Sarantakos, S. (1997). *Farm families—City families.* Preliminary report. (Wagga Wagga: Faculty of Arts, Charles Sturt University).

Senate Employment, Education and Training References Committee. (1996). *Childhood matters: The report on the inquiry into early childhood education* Canberra: Australian Government Publishing Service.

Simpson, T. (1993). *The effectiveness of the current system in providing early childhood services in rural New South Wales: A case study of Cabonne Shire.* Report from Cabonne Council, Molong, New South Wales.

Simpson, T. (1996). *Parents' perceptions of planning for and provision of early childhood services in rural and regional NSW.* Unpublished Masters research project report, Macquarie University.

Sinclair, R., & Squires, D. (1997). *Country areas program: Outcomes.* The Full Report Bathurst: Charles Sturt University.

Stevens, K. (1994). Rural education, policy and teaching. In E. Hatton (Ed.). *Understanding Teaching: Curriculum and the Social Context of Schooling.* (pp. 363–382). Sydney: Harcourt Brace.

Chapter 21

Implementing the Australian Early Childhood Association Code of Ethics: A Constitutional Strategy

Linda Newman

Abstract

Early childhood teachers report anxiety over ethical dilemmas during their preservice field experiences. While codes of ethics and codes of conduct are available for early childhood education, these need to be more than token distributions that are displayed as wall posters and forgotten about. Codes can be moved toward a more embedded *constitutional* feature of the profession by incorporating improved preparation for ethical judgment into preservice courses for early childhood teachers.

In this chapter, research and resources that are being developed in Australia to assist early childhood student teachers to develop ethical judgment abilities are described and a framework for the development of ethical judgment is suggested.

Introduction

Preston explains that the ethical responsibilities of professionals stem from the role they are performing or the institution they are serving, leading to the idea of *role morality* or an *ethic of agency*. Indeed, clarification of a coherent set of ethical responsibilities is an important defining characteristic of a profession. The test of professional ethics is acting in ways that are consistent with the duties entrusted to one in a professional capacity. Professional ethics tend to place a strong emphasis on community service, including a willingness to provide service gratuitously beyond the call of duty (Preston, 1996).

According to Hostetler, the ethical dimensions of teaching have not received a great deal of attention in the literature (Hostetler, 1997). Yet nearly all aspects of teaching reflect the need for awareness of ethical practice. Teaching is a moral exercise in which power is used, ends and means are chosen, and decisions constantly reflect values. Teachers, from their first day on the job, must be able to exercise sound judgment about ethical issues. Ethical issues involve the *critical* incidents such as physical, sexual, and emotional abuse, as well as the subtle *or open to interpretation* issues involving application of policy, developmentally appropriate practice, and the use of power and control (Coombe & Newman, 1997a; Prilleltensky, Rossiter, & Walsh-Powers, 1996).

In 1991 the Australian Early Childhood Association (AECA) introduced their Code of Ethics and supporting materials (Fasoli & Woodrow, 1991). Two years later, in a representative survey, less than half of a group of 225 early childhood practitioners reported being aware of the AECA Code (Pollnitz, 1994). Of those who were, it was the more highly qualified and experienced practitioners who reported that they found the code useful (Pollnitz, 1994).

This is understandable. New teachers tend to be concerned with everyday issues of survival (Katz, 1977). "Graduands are unlikely to focus upon esoteric notions of ethics, values, or professional morality" until later in their careers (Clyde, 1989, p. 15). However, the complex issue of accelerated movement toward higher order skills such as ethical judgment and advanced advocacy, if addressed appropriately within tertiary preparation courses, will reduce, not add to, new teacher anxiety.

Student Teachers and Professional Ethics

It is increasingly common for students to return to their tertiary institutions following professional experience to describe problematic situations in which they were involved (Coombe & Newman, 1997b; Edwards, 1993; Skaff, 1997). These most frequently include dilemmas that involve conflicts of interest between parties involved in fieldwork (students, cooperating center/school staff, tertiary supervisors, institution administrators). The result is feelings of powerlessness in students. While student teachers are being taught to implement best practice, they do not always see best practice in action. Thus the student teachers come to question their role as players in the field. At what point should they be beginning to influence practice rather than observing and replicating it?

Student teachers appear to move developmentally, from beginner to practitioner, but the acquisition of ethical judgment does not necessarily develop in predictable stages for all students. This acquisition often depends upon the chance of being confronted and having to deal with, reflect upon, and resolve an ethical issue. Preservice tertiary educators can assist in developing pedagogic practices that provide opportunities to move their student teachers toward higher levels of ethical judgment.

In 1995 and 1996, members of The Early Childhood Practicum Council of New South Wales developed *Guidelines for Ethical Practice in Early Childhood Field Experience*.[1] These guidelines grew out of the AECA Code of Ethics and were targeted at all stakeholders involved in fieldwork programs.

The Pilot Project

A pilot project aimed at empowering early childhood student teachers to effectively make appropriate and ethical judgment using the AECA Code of Ethics and the *Guidelines for Ethical Practice in Early Childhood Field Experience* was undertaken. The project involved the preparation of student teachers for their fieldwork placements.

In order to identify what student teachers saw as ethical issues, and what their experiences during field experience had been, pilot research was conducted to investigate student teacher experiences of dilemmas during field experience (Coombe & Newman 1997a, 1997b; Newman & Coombe, 1999). It was found that students encountered a number of situations of dilemma. Many dilemmas arose because students were in a situation of powerlessness, did not know how to refuse to comply with a request, and did not like what they were seeing. Many students were concerned that if they took action, their final grade would suffer (Newman & Coombe, 1999). These findings led to the production of a video to be used as a teaching tool (Newman, 1996). The video showed student teachers facing dilemmas and was accompanied by discussion starters for the tertiary classroom, for use before or after fieldwork sessions. Students reported that role playing the resolution to the scenarios with follow-up discussion was a useful method for the introduction of issues that may arise during fieldwork.

Further research involved evaluation of the video. Data were sought about the fieldwork priorities and experiences of students, cooperating fieldwork staff, employers and tertiary supervisors. The research provided previously undocumented information about the resolution of dilemmas, both ethical and practical, in early childhood field experience programs. Issues most often identified by respondents revolved around power and control, communication, and dilemmas involving gender (Newman & Pollnitz, 1997).

Following the pilot project, extended resources to facilitate a deeper level of preparation for students were developed. As Baumgart (1996) argues, "ethical behavior is likely to be more effective and more pervasive when developed through education, reflection and deliberate modeling". The resources aim to help tertiary educators to guide students through the maze of ethical judgment and dilemma. A second video was developed. This video addresses all stakeholder interests; reviews ethical dilemmas; is accompanied by a manual that outlines the difference between types of dilemmas; proposes models for ethical decision making; and includes teaching resources.

Findings: A Taxonomy of Ethical Judgment

Based on findings from the pilot project and follow-up research, as well as other reported student experiences, it became evident that preparation for ethical judgment can follow on set pathways. A taxonomy was developed as a framework for tertiary teaching. The taxonomy (Figure 1) outlines the conceptual elements of ethical judgment. Levels within the taxonomy are not intended to be strictly hierarchical but to be used as a guideline to give a sense of progression in the development of ethical judgment.

A complex process is involved as students make the shift from being members of the general public to becoming fully practicing early childhood professionals. Codes of ethics cannot ensure that practitioners act ethically because "ethical thinking and decision making are not just following the rules" (Baumgart, 1996; Strike & Soltis, 1985, p. 3). Teachers, as well as knowing legal rights and duties, need to assume an ethical perspective that requires "critical understanding of the moral basis of teaching and working knowledge of the value principles and processes of inquiry involved in ethical thinking, feeling, and acting" (Strom, 1989, p. 268).

While it is agreed that ethical judgment cannot be taught or imposed (Baumgart, 1996; Hostetler, 1997; Prilleltensky, Rossiter, & Walsh-Powers, 1996), students can address issues of morals and ethics and benefit from assistance in applying their knowledge to professional situations (Strom, 1989). The taxonomy shown below describes the stages toward embedding ethical judgment as student teachers move through stages from graduands to professional.

The taxonomy begins at the point of entry to tertiary study, where it should be noted that students come with a vast range of experiences and backgrounds. It culminates at the point where students are ready to graduate and are beginning to gain confidence in their judgment.

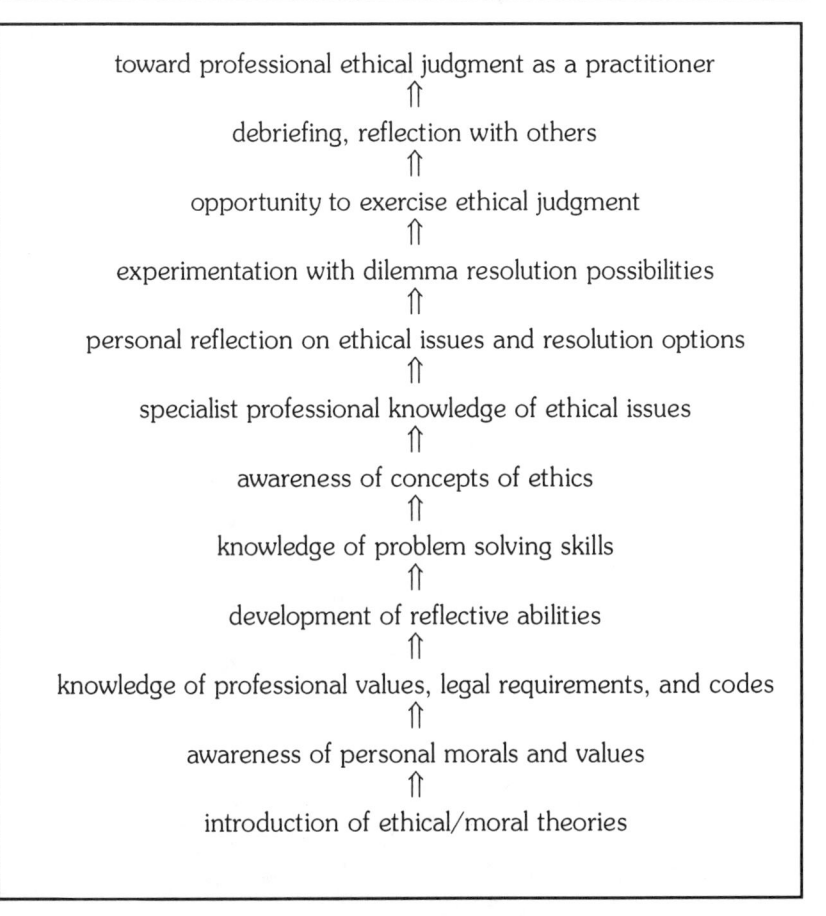

```
toward professional ethical judgment as a practitioner
⇑
debriefing, reflection with others
⇑
opportunity to exercise ethical judgment
⇑
experimentation with dilemma resolution possibilities
⇑
personal reflection on ethical issues and resolution options
⇑
specialist professional knowledge of ethical issues
⇑
awareness of concepts of ethics
⇑
knowledge of problem solving skills
⇑
development of reflective abilities
⇑
knowledge of professional values, legal requirements, and codes
⇑
awareness of personal morals and values
⇑
introduction of ethical/moral theories
```

Figure 1   A Taxonomy of Movement Toward Ethical Judgment and Professionalism

Conclusion

Graduands of early childhood courses will be entering a rapidly changing professional world. They need to have the knowledge, skills, and confidence to assume a strong ethical stance. In the present climate of change, some, or much, of the content of their preparation courses could be outdated within a few years. Student teachers have reported a need for greater scope and depth in their preparation for movement toward ethical judgment and professionalism. The ability to reflect upon the ethical dimension of teaching may be the most important tool that tertiary educators can supply.

In this case study, a process has been described that is aimed at supporting and extending use of the AECA Code of Ethics. The study and resources developed will move early childhood teachers toward a better understanding of the need for professional ethics with some guidelines for acting appropriately in situations of dilemma.

Notes

1. For further information or copies of *the Guidelines for Ethical Practice in Early Childhood Field Experience* contact the author at the University of Western Sydney, Nepean, PO Box 10, Kingswood, NSW, Australia 2747; l.newman@uws.edu.au

References

Australian Early Childhood Association. (1991). *Code of Ethics.* Australian Capital Territory: Australian Early Childhood Association.

Baumgart, N. (1996). Codes of ethics on assessment practice: Confronting a quandary or inculcating ethical character?—Overview of two sample documents. *Assessment in Education,* 3 (3): 393–396.

Clyde, M. (1989). *Ethical concerns of early childhood workers: Planning for the future.* In Research and Future Development of Education in Australia. Unpublished papers presented at the annual conference of the Australian Association for Research in Education, held at the University of Adelaide, 1989. AD No. 46016.

Coombe, K., & Newman, L. (1997a). Ethics and the practicum: A pilot study. *Journal for Australian Research in Early Childhood.* Vol. 1: 1–9.

Coombe, K., & Newman, L. (1997b). Ethical quandaries for early childhood practitioners. *Early Childhood Folio 3: A Collection of Recent Research. SET.* Wellington: New Zealand Council for Educational Research.

Early Childhood Practicum Council of New South Wales. (1996). *Guidelines for Ethical Practice in Early Childhood Field Experience.* Sydney: Early Childhood Practicum Council.

Edwards, M. (1993). What is wrong with practicum? Some reflections. *South Pacific Journal of Teacher Education,* 21 (1): 33–43.

Fasoli, L., & Woodrow, C. (1991). *Getting ethical: A resource book for workshop leaders.* Canberra: Australian Early Childhood Association.

Hostetler, K. (1997). *Ethical judgement in teaching.* Boston: Allyn & Bacon.

Katz, L. (1977). *Talks with teachers: Reflections on early childhood education.* Washington, DC: National Association for the Education of Young Children.

Newman, L. (Project Manager). (1996). What *should I do? Issues in early childhood field experience.* Sydney: Summer Hill Films.

Newman, L., & Coombe, K. (1999). Facing the hard questions: Ethics for early childhood fieldwork programs. *Australian Journal of Early Childhood*: 46–59.

Newman, L., & Pollnitz, L. (1997). *Partnerships in professional experience: toward resolution of dilemmas.* Paper presented at "Children in the Balance". Australian Early Childhood Association National Conference. Melbourne, September, 1997.

Pollnitz, L. (1994). *The AECA Code of Ethics: A good beginning?* Conference on Disk. Proceedings of "Good Beginnings Never End". 20 Triennial Conference. Perth: Australian Early Childhood Association.

Preston, N. (1996). *Understanding ethics.* Sydney: The Federation Press.

Prilleltensky, I., Rossiter, A., & Walsh-Powers, R. (1996). Preventing harm and promoting ethical discourse in the helping professions: Conceptual, research, analytical and action frameworks. *Ethics & behavior,* 6 (4): 287–306.

Skaff, K. (1997). *Exploring student views on the ethical impact of their clinical experience.* Paper presented at the Annual Conference of the Australian Association for Professional and Applied Ethics, Melbourne, October.

Strike, K., & Soltis, J. (1985). *The ethics of teaching.* New York: Teachers College Press.

Strom, S. (1989). The Ethical dimension of teaching. In M. Reynolds (Ed.). *Knowledge Base for the Beginning Teacher.* Oxford: Pergamon Press.

Chapter 22

Empowering the Migrant Worker: The Childcare Assessment and Bridging Project

Vicki Greive
Carmel Maloney

Abstract

This chapter describes the development and delivery of a program designed to provide bridging training for 50 migrant women with overseas qualifications relevant to the childcare field. It analyzes the factors that influenced and shaped the program and explores current changes in the political landscape that may influence the development of such projects in the future.

The Historical Context

In 1995, an innovative Childcare Assessment and Bridging Project was launched in Perth, Western Australia. The program was developed to meet an extreme shortage of qualified staff in childcare centers. In addition, the program was perceived as supporting the training and employment of migrant women and responding to the demand from the childcare field for more flexible approaches to assessment and training.

The National Training Reform Agenda and Industry Training Councils

The political and economic climate of the early nineties was ripe for encouraging the development of alternative initiatives in training. The Heads of Government Agreement of July 1992 resulted in the establishment of the Australian National Training Authority (ANTA). This development was significantly driven by economics and the requirement to make better use of the training dollar. Thus, the initiative resulted in a shift of emphasis from identifying a fixed period of study to obtain a credential, to a more flexible approach to training that focused on outcomes.

The importance of vocational and tertiary education and its importance in improving the nation's economic performance has become a major issue in Australia today. This is commonly referred to as the "training reform agenda". The main goals of the training reform agenda are:

1. a more highly skilled workforce;
2. diversifying the range of training providers;
3. increasing industry's commitment to train its workforce;
4. greater recognition of the skills people have achieved;
5. equity and access to training and employment opportunities; and
6. a system that is more responsible and relevant to the needs of industry.

These goals are seen to support an increase in the skill and competency base for Australia's economic development needed to achieve and maintain greater international competitiveness.

Equity and access to training affects all sections of the community. At present many workers possess skills that are not recognized because of the way credentials are awarded and accredited. Among those identified as particularly disadvantaged are migrants. For example, in Western Australia a pool of some 150 overseas trained and experienced childcare workers were identified as unable to utilize their skills when their qualifications were not recognized (Dimovich, 1996). According to the Minister for Employment, Education and Training "it is estimated that the non-use of existing migrant skills and the failure to address only skills gaps, costs Australia $100–350 million dollars per annum" (Consultants' Final Report, 1996).

In Western Australia, Industry Training Councils (ITCs) have been established to actively promote the availability of more flexible and accessible education and training options. One of the key responsibilities of the ITCs is to identify areas where there is a shortage of trained workers and to encourage the development of industry-driven strategies to address this shortage. One key area identified in Western Australia was the childcare field.

Childcare Need

Due to the increasing participation of women in the workforce, there has been a growing demand for the provision of childcare services. Consistent with the national trend over the past ten years, the number of childcare centers operating in Western Australia (W.A.) has risen significantly. Since 1991 the number of licensed services in Western Australia increased from approximately 120 to more than 320 (Dimovich, 1996). The childcare field has experienced unprecedented growth and development in many areas including policy, funding, program management, and service delivery. As a result of this sudden and rapid growth, it has been difficult for childcare centers to meet demand and recruit qualified staff. There has been a critical shortage of trained childcare workers in Western Australia for some years. In recent years the shortage became so critical that for the first time ever, the recruitment of qualified staff from the United Kingdom into Western Australia occurred. A recent survey, funded by the Department of Training through the Industry Analysis Branch and the Overseas Qualifications Unit investigated the need for trained workers in the country and metropolitan regions of Western Australia against projected graduate rates and confirmed that shortages would be ongoing. The Department of Employment, Education, Training, and Youth Affairs identified the childcare sector as a priority area for the provision of training programs (Consultants' Final Report, 1996). In addition, the Department of Immigration and Ethnic Affairs was asked to place childcare workers on their priority list for migrants (Consultants' Final Report, 1996).

Clearly, existing childcare training has been unable to meet the need for qualified childcare workers. This has been partly due to the fact that the major childcare training providers in Western Australia are the Technical and Further Education colleges (TAFE) which, prior to the training reform initiatives, were restricted in their student quotas.

Given the number of overseas trained personnel submitting applications to the Childcare Qualifications Committee (a state committee responsible for the validation of acceptable childcare qualifications), key stakeholders in the childcare industry recognized the wealth of untapped talent in the migrant community. Although many of the applicants' qualifications did not strictly meet Australian standards, they nevertheless were seen to have only minimal gaps in their training. The National Women's Vocational Educational and Training Strategy (March, 1996) states "Research shows that labor force participation of people from non-English speaking backgrounds had declined during the 1990s and these women received less vocational training on or off the job than any other group." The lack of recognition of migrants' skills and qualifications and the shortage of qualified childcare workers were, therefore, key factors influencing the development of the Childcare Assessment and Bridging Project for migrants.

The Need for Diversity

At the time when childcare centers in Western Australia were having difficulty in recruiting appropriately qualified staff, there was also an increased demand for the field to conform to quality standards through the introduction of a national childcare Quality Improvement and Accreditation System (QIAS) in 1995 (see Glossary of Terms, this volume).

The QIAS was implemented as a means of establishing and monitoring provision of high-quality childcare. It contains 52 principles or benchmarks for maintaining quality standards. One of the core principles of the QIAS states "staff treat all children equally and try to accommodate their individual needs: They respect diversity of background" (National Childcare Accreditation Council, 1993, p. 5.). This principle addresses the need in the childcare field, to move beyond tokenism toward a serious attempt at developing understanding and empathy of diverse cultural groups. The employment of staff from a variety of cultural backgrounds is considered an important way to promote antibias approaches to multiculturalism as it exposes young children to people from diverse cultural backgrounds at a time in their lives when the formulation of values and attitudes are critical (Wallis Consulting Group, 1994). It also provides excellent opportunities to model acceptance and tolerance as staff members from different cultures develop into effective teams and work side by side. The employment of staff from a variety of cultures provides an opportunity for diversity to infuse all aspects of the childcare curriculum in ways that can be made meaningful and relevant to the children and to families, many of whom may be from diverse cultural backgrounds themselves.

The Childcare Assessment and Bridging Project

Because the training institutions in Western Australia were unable to meet the demand for early childhood graduates, many childcare centers were applying for exemptions from staffing regulations in order to maintain basic staffing requirements.

Rapid developments in the delivery and accessibility of childcare services throughout the state resulted in a differential between supply and demand for trained personnel. In response to this situation, many childcare personnel began to advocate for reform of the training system and the provision of more flexible approaches to training delivery. In this time of shortage the Childcare Qualifications Committee had been receiving an increasing number of applications from migrant women. This situation led to a submission for funding of the Childcare Assessment and Bridging Project. The project aimed to provide:

1. a more detailed and comprehensive assessment of currently held qualifications with an emphasis on Recognition of Prior Learning (RPL);
2. the development of a more accurate system of identifying training needs of individual applicants; and
3. the development of flexible training delivery to bridge identified gaps between existing qualifications and skills and those skills needed to meet the requirements for employment as a qualified childcare worker.

The submission had widespread support from a number of key stakeholders from both within and outside the field of early childhood care and education, including the Department of Family and Children's Services, the Overseas Qualifications Unit of the Department of Training, the Department of Employment, Education, Training and Youth Affairs and the Community Services, Health and Education Industry Training Council. From the point of view of these stakeholders, the Childcare Assessment and Bridging Project was perceived as addressing both the shortage of qualified childcare staff and the issue of migrant unemployment through the provision of support and training for a minority community group.

The 44 participants selected to take part in the project came from 30 different countries including Burma, Hong Kong, Singapore, South Africa, Vietnam, El Salvador, and Thailand. The majority of the participants had an education qualification from their country of origin. The selection criteria was developed to identify those applicants with a combination of a formal educational qualification closely aligned to the knowledge required of a qualified childcare worker, together with experience working in the childcare field.

The project was implemented in two phases. Stage one comprised an extensive Recognition of Prior Learning (RPL) assessment phase, conducted over a period of four months. Stage two included the training phase of the program.

The Assessment Process

During stage one, a range of procedures was used for assessing RPL including portfolio submission, informal interviews and discussion, fieldwork assessments, practical demonstrations, oral questions, and minimal use of written responses.

Assessment was conducted by a selected group of childcare directors experienced in RPL assessment and the delivery of training programs. A key factor in the assessment was the face-to-face contact between assessors and participants. During this personal contact, assessors were able to establish rapport and lines of communication with the participants, and to explore, through discussion and interview, each participant's knowledge, skills, and experience. The learning outcome statements of an accredited Diploma level course in childcare were used as the benchmarks for the assessment process. Based on the assessment, a comprehensive profile of each participant was compiled and an individualized training program developed.

The Training Phase

Stage two, the training phase, was implemented over a period of nine months. The training program was developed to meet specific individual needs of the participants based on the outcomes of recognition of prior learning assessments. The average amount of training required was 462 hours. Most of the participants were identified as requiring training in the area of programming and planning. A nine-month timetable was devised aimed at meeting the majority needs first, thus enabling those requiring the least amount of training to qualify most expediently.

A combination of workshop sessions and childcare fieldwork experience was used. Supervision training was offered to childcare center staff prior to the student placement so they were informed about the course and better able to meet the needs of this particular group of students. The workshop sessions were presented by two trainers from an accredited training institution in W.A. Participants were encouraged to mentor and support one another and to work in small group situations.

According to the Consultants' Final Report (1996), every attempt was made to ensure that the course was accessible and recognized the needs of the target group. For example, the training venue was chosen for its central location and access to public transport. There was flexibility in both the training delivery and the practicum component of the course to accommodate the individual's background, work, and family responsibilities. The training program was structured and delivered taking into account the level of experience and diverse cultural backgrounds of the individuals in the group. There was an emphasis on celebrating cultural diversity by encouraging individuals to contribute and share ideas from their cultural background, including their cultural perspectives on aspects of the curriculum. Individual support and counseling was also made available. Formative evaluation of the course was conducted to ensure the needs of the group were being met.

Evaluation of the Project

Upon completion, the project was independently evaluated by an external consultant (Greive, 1996). The participants' written evaluations and verbal feedback in two focus group discussions confirmed the success of the range of strategies adopted and offered comments for future consideration. Participants acknowledged and supported strategies that recognized and allowed for constraints due to their cultural and linguistic background. They felt that the project had opened many doors and provided new opportunities for them. Many commented on their improved self-confidence and self-esteem as a consequence of their involvement with the project. Participants felt it had enhanced not only their knowledge, but also their language and communication skills. It had provided a useful opportunity to meet others and expand their networks and professional contacts.

The participants supported the project as a model of more flexible training options for the field and a means of creating alternative pathways for others to obtain a qualification. Participants reported the view that the assessment and bridging training not be restricted to a "one off" initiative. This was related in particular to their perception that they had been a test (pilot) group, and that their credibility might be threatened should there be no more graduates. Further, they felt that the project would be seen as inequitable if access was restricted to those with overseas qualifications (Greive, 1996).

The Outcomes of the Project

The Childcare Assessment and Bridging Project met the objectives for the project. The feedback from the field indicated that the work performance of the graduates was perceived as being comparable to that of graduates from conventional, full-term training programs (Greive, 1996). The employment outcomes for the graduates of this program have been encouraging. Many were offered employment during the training phase of the project with 35 graduates being employed as childcare workers, level

"B." According to the W.A. Community Services (Childcare) Regulations (1988), Level "B" refers to a holder of a two-year certificate in childcare studies and includes a specialist course on the principles and practices of the care and education of children from birth to two years. An indication of support from the field was also apparent in the large number of childcare centers prepared to offer fieldwork placement to the participants.

What was notable from the project was that a smaller training provider was in a position to be responsive and flexible in meeting the needs of this group, while the more complex bureaucratic systems of universities and larger training providers were perceived as being more inflexible in their admissions criteria and, therefore, limited in accessibility.

The feedback on this project indicated that it has been positively received by many of the key agencies and interest groups associated with childcare and the provision of training. The project has done much to promote and advance the concept of RPL as a way of customizing and individualizing training delivery in the childcare field in W.A. It has incorporated many elements of best practice as outlined in the Department of Training Guidelines (1997) such as:

1. community involvement in the design and development of the course;
2. meeting the needs of individual learners;
3. providing service and advise to students; and
4. promoting input from participants in setting personal goals.

In addition, the program responded to many of the initiatives outlined in the Training Reform Agenda. The Childcare Assessment and Bridging Project has been successful in both meeting an urgent need for qualified staff and advancing the range of fast track, flexible training options that had been in demand for some time.

Discussion

The Australian Political Context
There are ominous signs that, at least in the immediate future, the childcare field is facing some very difficult and demanding times. The constitutional context of present policy developments in this area is suddenly somewhat out of harmony with the development of innovative training programs designed to provide more qualified personnel to the field. In the broader national political context there have been a number of economic and political decisions that will have a severe restraining effect upon the childcare

sector, dismantling many of the policy advancements made under the previous Federal Labor Government.

Recent changes instigated by a Liberal Federal Government has seen a dramatic turnaround in childcare policy. The most pessimistic are predicting the end of the community-based sector in childcare. In Australia this is the sector of childcare which has until recently received much support, including an operational subsidy from the federal government. Receipt of baseline funding from government provided this sector with the support needed to implement many of the practices widely associated with the provision of quality childcare. Most relevant to this discussion was the tendency to be more generous in meeting quotas of qualified staff and the option to employ older and frequently more experienced staff. In the current climate of cutbacks, centers are expected to close and more carers will lose their jobs. In addition, it is likely that directors will be forced to employ less experienced (less costly) childcare workers.

Another development on the current Australian political landscape is the increasing support for extreme right wing policies, which has seen the growth of the One Nation Party. Ms Pauline Hanson, leader of One Nation Party, advocates an anti-Asian, anti-Immigration stance as central tenets of her political platform and calls for abolition of the multicultural policy and the halting of immigration as being in the best interest of the nation (1996). The recent federal government announcement of future cuts to immigration has also been disturbing for many members of ethnic minority groups. While this may have only a minimal impact on the overall number of migrants seeking employment in childcare settings, at a deeper level it may create an ideological shift and have a more indirect and negative impact on attitudes and tolerance toward diversity in the wider community.

Distributional Outcomes

The allocation of funding to this project was a clear indication of government recognition and commitment to addressing the shortage of qualified childcare staff through the provision of more flexible and innovative training options for the childcare field. It also provided a training and employment opportunity for a group traditionally found to be disadvantaged in the workforce. Strong industry support for this project was evident through the involvement of the Industry Training Council, which allocated managerial and administrative expertise and support to the development and implementation of the project. The commitment demonstrated by the Industry Reference Group meant that the project was always well guided by key people from the field. Many childcare centers participated in the project through the provision of fieldwork placements to the students. All of the graduates from the Bridging Project seeking employment quickly found positions in childcare centers, indicating the field's willingness to accept graduates from this type of training program.

Constitutional Outcomes

At the conclusion of the first Childcare Assessment and Bridging Project in 1996, there was evidence to suggest growing support in the Western Australian childcare field for a wider range of flexible training strategies, including the RPL process and bridging training programs. The Childcare Assessment and Bridging Project is one useful, tangible strategy to promote new and innovative training courses. However, graduates from these training courses will be subjected to close scrutiny and it is essential that standards and expectations required by the childcare field are met. Those working in the field will begin to lose confidence if there is no ongoing support and commitment which allows these projects to be viewed as a legitimate, long-term training option. An *ad hoc* approach to the delivery of these types of programs may restrict opportunities to develop recognition and credibility for the graduates.

Conclusion

The history of childcare in this country has been patchy, with many ambivalent emotions and reactions expressed toward the widespread provision of childcare services, particularly for younger children (Hayden, 1994). While the mid-1990s gave hope for consolidation and increased respectability of the early childhood field, current policies and fiscal constraints have created a swing back to survival mode for many childcare services.

Recent media reports on the changing fortunes of childcare have tended to highlight the importance of the Quality Improvement and Accreditation System in ensuring Australia maintains high-quality childcare services, despite the cutbacks of government funding to this area. However, one program cannot address the complexities of providing quality and accessible services. While QIAS is certainly an important component in ensuring quality, there is a need for systematic evaluation of the process and outcomes, an examination of the factors influencing accreditation, and research into how standards can be sustained when resources are reduced. Such evaluations will no doubt reveal that plentiful supply of well-qualified and experienced staff from diverse training and cultural backgrounds are essential to the provision of quality programs.

Initiatives such as the Childcare Assessment and Bridging Project developed as a result of demand from the field for more highly skilled and credentialed workers. It is particularly gratifying that a bridging course specifically designed to assist non-English-speaking migrants was able to attract funding and generate such a high level of support from those in the childcare field. Equally gratifying is the recognition given to the program through the 1996 Adult Learners Award for an Outstanding Group of Learners, presented by the W.A. Department of Training. The project also received two training excellence awards for access and equity.

Current economic, political, and social trends at the macro level of policy development appear to be responsible for a constraining effect on the childcare sector, at least in the short term. Much of the energy and effort of the field is being channeled into ensuring the mere survival of many services. In the prevailing political climate it is not easy to imagine that projects such as the Childcare Assessment and Bridging Course will be high on the list of the priorities, or that even small distributional allotments will be as readily available as previously.

The integration of the bridging course with programs related to employment and immigration provided a unique opportunity to broaden the experience for early childhood professionals. From a program created out of necessity, the bridging course was able to propel early childhood into a more mainstream constitutional place in the social, cultural, and political arena.

References

Consultants' Final Report. (1996). *Childcare assessment and bridging project.* Western Australia: Department of Training.

Dimovich, C. (1996). *A study into the shortage of qualified childcare workers in Western Australia and the feasibility of providing alternative modes of training delivery.* Western Australian Department of Training: Overseas Qualifications Unit, Perth.

Greive, V. (1996). *Evaluation of the childcare assessment and bridging project.* Western Australia: Department of Training.

Hanson, P. (1996). Maiden speech Australian House of Representatives. *Hansard* for 10 September, 1996. Available at: http: Hwww.geocities.coni/capitolHill/9637/Speech.html.

Hayden, J. (1994). Half full or half empty? Children's services policy and the missing bits. In Mellor, E. & Coombe, K. (Eds.). *Issues in Early Childhood Services. Australian Perspectives.* New York: WCB: 11–25.

National Childcare Accreditation Council. (1993). *Quality improvement and accreditation handbook.* Sydney: NCAC.

State Training Board. (1996). *Quality standards for vocational education and training in Western Australia.* Western Australia: Department of Training.

Wallis Consulting Group. (1994). *Supplementary services (SUPS) program evaluation.* Melbourne.

The Classroom/Curricular Landscape

Chapter 23

Family Literacy: Challenges for Early Education

Trevor H. Cairney

Abstract

This chapter argues that literacy has many forms and that family literacy has a vital relationship to the literacy of preschool and school. It suggests that not only is the family a key site for the development of early literacy, it is a rich source of language, knowledge, and ongoing support of children's learning. As such, close and effective relationships are important between families and educational institutions. Further, it suggests that genuine partnerships are necessary between parents and teachers, which will ultimately lead to greater understanding of the shared responsibility for children's learning. Using a case study of one successful family literacy program, the chapter demonstrates how such partnerships can be established and challenges readers to seek other vehicles for achieving changes in education that respond more fully to the diverse needs of learners.

An Emerging Interest in Families and Parent Involvement

The importance of family support to children's educational success has long been recognized. However, often this has been little more than the portrayal of families and the home as different (but related) sites for learning and development. Families have been seen as having specific roles to play, while educational institutions have been seen to have quite different and at times almost unrelated functions. While it is clear that the homes are different sites for learning when compared with early childhood or school institutions, there is a clear and important relationship between them. In recent years much attention has been given to the different social and cultural practices of home, school, and community, and the importance of understanding such differences in order to build educational opportunities that provide equal access and opportunity for all students.

It is within this broad context that family literacy has emerged as an area of considerable interest. Family Literacy is one of the "new" literacies that have been the focus of discussion, writing, and research in the past decade. The labeling of specific literacy practices in this way reflects an underlying concern to understand the complexities of literacy demands outside the school context, and a long overdue acceptance that a great deal of literacy learning starts before a child commences formal schooling or participation in early childhood education. As a descriptive label, it has emerged from a number of related, and at times overlapping terms. These terms have included "parent literacy", "parent involvement", "intergenerational literacy", and "community literacy". This has created some degree of confusion. As Nickse (p. 35, 1993) points out, there has been a "strange mix of titles and names". A second order confusion has been the addition of the words "involvement", "participation", and "partnership" to the major term.

There is little doubt that parent involvement in children's education is an important element in effective schooling (Epstein, 1983; Delgado-Gaitan, 1991). This is reflected in findings of high positive correlations between parent knowledge, beliefs, and interactive styles, with children's school achievement (see Schaefer, 1991, for a detailed review). Differences in family backgrounds appear to account for a large share of variance in student achievement. School factors (e.g., resources, class sizes, classroom organization, and methods) simply cannot account for the variability that occurs in student achievement (Hanushek, 1981; Jencks, et al., 1972; Thompson, 1985). Some have gone as far as to suggest that the cumulative effect of a range of home related factors probably accounts for the greatest proportion of variability in student achievement (Rutter, Tizard, & Whitmore, 1970; Thompson, 1985; Cairney, 1995a).

Attempts to explain this relationship have varied, as have the programs devised in recognition of the relationship. It appears that just as programs are often based on notions of deficit, so too are some attempts to explain this relationship. Some children are seen as having received "good" or "appropriate" preparation for schooling while others are seen as having received "poor" or "inappropriate" preparation. This view has been criticized because of its failure to recognize that schooling is a cultural practice (Auerbach, 1989). What it ignores is the fact that much of the variability of student achievement in school reflects discrepancies that exist between school resources and instructional methods, and the cultural practices of the home, not deficiencies (Scribner & Cole, 1981; Heath, 1983; Au & Kawakami, 1984; Cazden, 1988, Moll, 1988).

One of the difficulties with this emerging field of educational interest is the fact that frequently there has been a failure to problematize the issues surrounding family literacy, parent involvement in schooling, and related issues. For example, one needs to ask, why are we seeking to identify differences between home and school literacy? Why are we involving parents at school? Is someone always "involved" as a participant? But, more importantly, what is a participant, a family, or even a community? Does participation lead to partnership? These are just some of the questions raised by the use of these terms. Implicit within the questions raised in this chapter is a belief that literacy is a social practice that has many specific manifestations (Gee, 1990, Luke, 1993; Welch & Freebody, 1993; Cairney, 1994) and which is learned in rich sociocultural contexts as humans relate to one another. Literacy is not simply a unitary cognitive skill to be imposed or passed on to people.

Not surprisingly, there has been a great deal of debate about initiatives in this area in recent times because of the vastly different philosophies that seem to be driving the work. Broadly, there appear to be two extreme positions. At one end of a continuum we have what can be called deficit-driven initiatives. These are based on a faulty assumption that there are families which lack the specific skills to enable them to create an environment of support that will enable their children to succeed at school. At the other end of the continuum are those I call collaborative partnership initiatives, which seek to develop partnerships between families and other institutions (typically schools or preschools) that offer educational support and aim to increase awareness by each party of the other's literacy practices and needs. The latter initiatives often aim to enable specific students to cope more effectively with school, but are based on the assumption that this requires changes, adjustments, and learning on the part of families, teachers, and school administrators. As well, the content and nature of the initiatives devised are developed collaboratively, and reflect the needs of all parties. In contrast, deficit driven initiatives are often tightly structured programs devised for other people and involving little choice in what is done within the program.

In a Australian federal government funded review of family and community literacy initiatives in Australia, (Cairney, Ruge, Buchanan, Lowe, & Munsie, 1995) it was found that:

1. there has been little evaluation of the effectiveness of family and community literacy initiatives;

2. the majority of programs are initiated by schools;
3. initiatives vary greatly in terms of content, process, participant control, and purposes, but offer little recognition of the richness of literacy practices within the wider community;
4. many initiatives are "tokenistic" (see Cairney & Munsie, 1995a) and pay little attention to the needs of communities, focusing instead on the needs of the school;
5. in spite of some of the limitations noted, there is evidence that some programs have the potential to lead to the development of significant partnerships between the home and school, which in turn may lead to increased understanding on the part of parents and teachers of each other's needs, attitudes, and roles in children's learning.

The Cairney, et al. (1995) study confirmed that few programs offered the potential to either empower previously marginalized groups, or to bring about significant changes in educational programs to make them more responsive to the diversity of needs of students.

Schools engage in specific discourses and hence inconsistently tap the social and cultural resources of society, privileging specific groups by emphasizing particular linguistic styles, curricula, and authority patterns (Bourdieu, 1977). To be a teacher or student in any setting demands specific ways of using language, behaving, interacting; as well as adherence to sets of values and attitudes (Gee, 1990). There is obvious potential for mismatches between these discourses and those that have been characteristic of some children's homes and communities. Scribner and Cole's (1981) work showed that what matters is not literacy as an isolated skill, but the social practices into which people are enculturated (or apprenticed) as a member of a specific social group. Not surprisingly, one gets better at specific social practices as one practices them. It would seem that those children who enter school, already having been partially apprenticed into the social practices of schooling (of which literacy is a part), invariably perform better at the practices of schooling right from the start.

Views on literacy are inevitably reflective of a specific ideology and, as a consequence, arbitrarily advantage some while disadvantaging others (Street, 1984; Lankshear & Lawler, 1987). To understand literacy fully we need to understand the groups and institutions through which we are socialized into specific literacy practices (Bruner, 1986; Gee, 1990).

As a consequence of this recognition of literacy as cultural practice, rather than simply a cognitive skill, some schools and community groups have sought to develop a greater sense of partnership and collaboration between the school and its community. These schools have generally recognized and valued the language and culture of communities and sought to acknowledge and respond to their richness and diversity by modifying school curricula and classroom practices.

But there is obviously a fine line between acknowledging a community's diversity and seeking to conform it to school expectations of what it is to be literate. The initiators of any family literacy initiative immediately put themselves in a position of unequal power and hence begin to shape the agenda (no doubt unwittingly) to reflect their personal agendas. Since schools have typically been responsible for initiating many family and intergenerational initiatives, it is not surprising that many such initiatives have typically been dominated by concerns with school literacy. As Delgado-Gaitan (1992) argues, we need to find ways to help schools recognize the cultural practices of the home and community and build effective communication between these parties.

Evaluating Current Parent Education and Family Literacy Initiatives

One of the keys seems to be a need for educators at early childhood and school levels to closely consider the underlying assumptions of what they are doing in the name of family literacy, parent education, parent involvement etc. At one level, there have been many attempts to describe in a categorical way the diversity of parent and family literacy initiatives (see Petit; 1980; Rasinski & Fredericks, 1989; Epstein & Dauber, 1991). Nickse (1993), for example, has developed a classification system that is defined in terms of the target group (adults or children) and the relationship between the adults and children (adults and children working together, or only indirect contact). While this is helpful, like all such attempts to classify anything, it can mask diversity, something Nickse acknowledges herself. As well, the classification systems developed have often been influenced strongly by analyses of content, target group, and purpose, without a detailed examination of some of the underlying principles and assumptions driving the initiative.

In response to the need for more detailed analyzes of family literacy initiatives, Cairney, et al. (1995) developed a framework for evaluating such initiatives in a far more comprehensive way. This framework was developed in response to the need to describe the complexity of some 261 programs that were identified in a national evaluation of family literacy. The framework attempted to assess any family literacy initiative on a number of key variables, and consists of four broad areas of assessment within which a continuum of variability exists. The four broad areas are defined through a series of questions:

> *Content*—What information is shared? What is the focus of group discussions, demonstrations, home tasks, and so on? What is the stated purpose of the content?
> *Process*—How is information shared? Who acts as the facilitator or leader for any program and how does this person structure opportunities for discussion, observation etc.?
> *Source*—Who has initiated the involvement? Was it a parent, school, community, or government initiative?
> *Control*—Who is in control of the program? Where is the program located (home, school, community building)? How do parents become involved in programs (nominated self selected)?

Using frameworks like the above it is possible for us to critically examine the family literacy programs and initiatives that are being used or that we are planning to implement. It is only when we begin to do this that we will be in a better position to create genuine partnerships between preschools and schools and the communities that they serve.

While many programs claim to "involve" parents, or attempt to develop "partnerships", one needs to test the voracity of such claims. Can a program lead to partnership if the initiator of the program is a school that does not involve parents in its planning and conduct. While there may be a rich array of initiatives, some educators have begun to question the programs that have been implemented. Auerbach (1989) has argued that some programs are based on a model designed simply to transmit school practices to the home. Considerable criticism has been leveled at those programs that are designed to exert a central influence on parents' caregiving roles. These issues are not only important for individual teachers but for policymakers as well. Many of the well-known national initiatives in the U.S., UK, and Australia have done little to chip away at educational inequity experienced by marginalized groups.

It would appear that some schools and government agencies frequently adopt very narrow definitions of parent involvement, which seek primarily to determine what parents can do for teachers, or how schools can make parents "better" at their role in the home, rather than how schools and parents can develop close relationships of mutual support and trust (Cairney & Munsie, 1995a). As argued elsewhere, we need to go beyond token involvement and recognize the vital role that parents play in education (Cairney, 1995b; Cairney & Munsie, 1995a). As Kruger and Mahon (1990, p. 4) point out, "parental involvement in literacy learning has much greater value than as an add-on to what teachers do". Harry (1992) also argues that such parent initiatives must forge collaborative relationships that create mutual understanding between parents and teachers—a "posture of reciprocity"—and which are associated with a shift from the school to parents and the community.

In essence, what some of these educators are arguing for is not the transmission of knowledge from schools to parents and their children but rather a process of reaching mutual consensus between the partners. This process of reaching shared understanding is what Vygotsky called "intersubjectivity" (1978). It involves a shared focus of attention and mutual understanding of any joint activity. Fitzgerald and Goncu (1995) suggest that this requires reaching agreement on the selection of activities, their goals, and plans for reaching the goals. Programs that are imposed by teachers on communities "for their own good" obviously fail to meet the conditions necessary for intersubjectivity to occur. Such programs frequently end with no appreciable impact on teachers and the school, and little long-term benefit for parents and their children.

While accepting the difficulties that surround some (if not all) of the programs in family literacy, these initiatives have flourished because parents, teachers, and educators recognize that they offer access to specific literacy practices that help students and parents to cope with school literacy and learning. This presents us with a conundrum that I have already addressed earlier in this chapter, how does one respond to the cultural mismatches of home and school? As Lareau (1991) asks, should one focus on developing initiatives that provide parents with the cultural practices that enable them to cope with the limited practices of the school, or do as Delgado-Gaitan (1992) suggests, find ways to help schools recognize the cultural practices of the home and community and build effective communication between these parties? The answer is probably both, but the starting point should be first to develop genuine partnerships with parents.

If the mismatch between home and school literacy practices does in fact make it more difficult for some students to succeed at school, then any strategy that counteracts such mismatches is difficult to reject (see Cairney & Ruge, 1998). Studies of low income families have shown that these parents, who often have limited needs for literacy, may not encourage the literacy practices of their children, thus setting up an intergenerational pattern of literacy difficulties (Goldenberg, 1987).

There is still much to be learned about this topic. What we do know is that classrooms are not simple places; they are dynamic interactional spaces where individuals come together for the purpose of schooling to construct situated definitions of teacher, student, knowledge, values, and so on (Green, Kantor, & Rogers, 1991). They are places for negotiating and refining culture. But whose culture, and on what (and whose) terms is this culture negotiated? Furthermore, what impact do such practices have on the achievement of all students? We already know that talk associated with literacy within the home is related to differences in culture and language (e.g., Heath, 1983; Cairney, Ruge, Buchanan, Lowe, & Munsie, 1995; Freebody & Ludwig, 1995) and that this is related to school success.

We also have some preliminary evidence suggesting that the way teachers shape classroom discourse is at times limited in scope and not reflective of the diversity of student language and culture (Gutierrez, 1994; Cairney, Lowe, & Sproats, 1995; Freebody & Ludwig, 1995; Cairney & Ruge, 1998). We have further evidence to suggest that there are variations in literacy practices in rural and urban schools and communities (Breen, et al. 1994). As well, there is evidence to indicate that changes in classroom programs and environments can be made to make them more reflective of the cultural and linguistic diversity of students (e.g., Neumann & Roskos, 1995). Finally, we have evidence concerning the nature of family and community literacy practices (e.g., Heath, 1983; Teale, 1986; Wells, 1985; Breen, et al. 1994; Cairney, Ruge, Buchanan, Lowe, & Munsie, 1995; Freebody & Ludwig, 1995; Cairney & Ruge, 1998).

However, there are still a number of issues for which the evidence is inconclusive and which are of critical importance for ongoing research (Cairney & Ruge, 1998). These are:

- There is a need for a richer description of home and community literacy practices in English literacy as well as in the literacy of other common community languages.
- We need more comprehensive descriptions of literacy practices within schools including sanctioned "school literacy" and "unofficial" literacy used at school. For example, we know that much literacy goes on at school that teachers have not "approved", including note writing, graffiti, reading magazines, reading and writing popular music, playing computer games etc. (see Cairney, 1987, and Barton, 1994 for a discussion of this important issue).
- We need a better understanding of the consequences of matches and mismatches in the language, literacy, and culture of school and the home and community.

- Research is necessary that explores the mechanisms for creating a climate of analysis and reflection within the teaching profession that will lead to self-analysis of classroom discourse and its impact on children.
- We need more systematic research that examines the way parents, educators, and communities support people to develop shared understandings about literacy, the role of adults in supporting children's literacy development, and the importance of the development of partnerships between schools and their communities.

Moving Toward Partnership in Family Literacy Initiatives

Many of the earliest attempts to recognize the relationship between home factors and school success were little more than parent education programs. Some of the most significant early initiatives in this area occurred in the United Kingdom. The Plowden report (Department of Education and Science, 1967) was one of a number of factors that probably facilitated the significant number of initiatives. This report argued strongly for the concept of partnership between home and school.

Many of the early programs focused on the need to offer parents a limited range of reading strategies to use with their children. One of the most commonly used was the paired reading technique. This simple technique was first designed by Morgan (1976) and was later refined by Topping and McKnight (1984) and Topping & Wolfendale (1985). Some more recent programs in Australia have also utilized this strategy.

A number of the most successful British programs were designed for parents whose children have reading problems. While some of the programs showed encouraging outcomes, there was a degree of inconsistency (see Hannon, 1995). For example, the Haringey Reading Project found that some of the children whose parents were involved in their program made significant gains in reading achievement (irrespective of reading ability), while others made little (Tizard, Schofield, & Hewison; 1982).

In the United States there have been numerous attempts to design programs that aim to involve parents more fully in their children's literary learning. The major source of funding for these programs has been from a variety of state and federal government programs including Head Start, Even Start, and the Family School Partnership Program (PACE). However, while considerable effort and money has been put into these programs, Nickse (1993) points out that evidence concerning their effectiveness is modest. As well, most of these programs have been school-centered and have done little to acknowledge the language, literacy, and cultural diversity of communities.

Notable recent programs that have attempted to move toward partnerships with communities include Project FLAME (Shanahan & Rodriguez-Brown, 1993), the initiatives of the *Illinois Literacy Resource Development Center* (ILRDC, 1990), and *Schools Reaching Out* (SRO) (Jackson, Krasnow, & Seeley, 1994). In contrast with many of the early parent literacy programs, these programs have attempted to develop a sense of partnership with parents and communities. In each case, an attempt has been made to recognize the significant cultural differences between communities and to adapt programs accordingly. For example, project FLAME has been designed for Mexican American and Puerto Rican families, and involves components in "parents as teachers", adult learning, summer institutes and community experiences. An interesting feature of the program is its ability to adapt to the specific cultural and educational characteristics of the families. Programs like this have increasingly begun to recognize that relationships between home and school achievement are complex, and hence require initiatives that do more than simply offer parents information.

Similarly, in Australia there have been a number of more recent attempts to involve parents more fully in their children's literacy and learning through integrated programs that seek to involve parents, children, and teachers. One example is *Making a Difference* (Furniss, 1991). This is an intensive program that requires teachers to work with Year 7 students who are experiencing difficulties with literacy. Parents and community volunteers are trained by a Making a Difference teacher to work with the students. Contained within the program is a volunteer tutor manual that trains parents and community volunteers to work with students.

Talk to a Literacy Learner (TTALL) Program

Talk to a Literacy Learner (TTALL) was developed in response to the growing understanding of the literacy diversity and needs of families (Cairney & Munsie, 1995a).[1] One of the aims in developing TTALL was to go beyond simply offering information to parents. The aim was to open up dialogue between teachers and parents in order to develop reciprocal relationships. TTALL has the dual aim of offering parents insights into school literacy and learning (and strategies to support this) and at the same time developing a relationship between teachers and families that enables more responsive literacy programs to be planned. The major goal of TTALL is to empower children and their families to take greater control of their literacy learning.

The TTALL program was first developed for parents with children from birth to age 12 years (Cairney & Munsie, 1992) within a preschool and associated primary school in Sydney. The development of the program was guided by a planning committee consisting of staff from the preschool and primary school, the research team, and parent representatives. As the title suggests, its focus is on the way parents and children interact with each other in and through literacy. It is a program centered both on the adult and the child. TTALL aims to offer parents practical guidance on how they support their children's literacy and learning. It also aims to act as a starting point for the development of more effective partnerships between home and school.

The content of the program covers basic child development, the nature of the reading and writing processes, strategies for assisting children with reading and writing (e.g., directed reading and thinking, conducting writing conferences, etc.), the use of the library for research, and the development of self-esteem. The program is presented to parents using a mixture of short talks, workshops, and the demonstration of a number of literacy support strategies. It requires attendance at 16 two-hour workshops, and between-session work with their children. All parents completing the program receive a certificate of completion presented at a celebratory function attended by parents and their families, and also school, center, and community representatives.

Since the sessions are very much learner-centered, they are responsive to the needs and questions of the participants. Group members are given (and take) frequent opportunities to talk with each other, to share personal insights, to ask questions of each other, to provide opinions, and to reflect on their own learning. One of the earliest observations of TTALL in action was that it helped to create a community of parents who were able to support each other and also to challenge schools to consider the needs of the children.

The program is run by a facilitator with strong knowledge of literacy who has experience in working with adults. This person's role is to engage participants in discussion and to encourage them to reflect on their experiences of learning as well as those of their children.

The program has been evaluated using a variety of qualitative and quantitative measures. This has shown that the program leads to positive changes in parent/child relationships, the relationship between parents and teachers, and the literacy learning of students whose parents complete it (Cairney & Munsie, 1992, 1995a). The evaluation showed the following benefits of the program.

1. It offers parents strategies they did not have previously.
2. It helps parents to choose resource material, help children with book selection, and use libraries more effectively.
3. Parents gain new knowledge about literacy, learning and schooling.
4. Families are affected as members' use of time and involvement in literacy activities changes.
5. Parents begin to share their insights outside the family.
6. Parents gain a greater understanding of schools.
7. Parents grow in confidence and self-esteem.
8. Children whose parents complete the programs make greater gains (relative to children of non-participating parents), in literacy performance, as well as attitudes to and interest in literacy.
9. Teachers develop more positive attitudes to parent involvement in schooling.
10. Teachers gain new knowledge about parents and children.
11. Parents become more involved in school activities.

The response of thousands of parents who have now completed TTALL in a variety of forms is enthusiastic. Over 450 schools and early childhood centers are now implementing the program in Australia, and systemwide support has been given in New South Wales and Tasmania. The program is also in use in the UK, U.S.A., Canada, Papua New Guinea, and New Zealand. As well, additional programs have been devised in response to the parents' needs. For example, parents who had completed the TTALL program requested (and participated in the planning of) an additional program designed to allow them to share their experiences with other parents. This program, called the *Parent Partnership Program* (Cairney & Munsie, 1995c), equips graduates of TTALL to run four one-hour informal discussion sessions in other parents' homes using a series of 10 resource sheets on topics of relevance to parents of preschool and school-aged children. Similarly, parents requested help with their secondary-aged children and helped to secure funding to develop the Effective Partners in Secondary Literacy Learning program (Cairney & Munsie, 1993). The TTALL program materials have also been translated into a variety of community languages, and it has been modified by many groups to cater for the specific needs of their parents.

It is clear that programs like TTALL can have an impact on the lives of the parents and children associated with such programs. As well, they can act as a bridge between families and institutions like schools and preschools. This, in turn, can enable teachers to respond more effectively to the needs of all children, enabling responsive curricula to be developed, and increasing every child's chances of success at school.

The description of TTALL in this chapter is not provided because it is seen as the ideal program to solve all problems. This is simply one attempt to consider how home and school might be bridged in ways that offer significant increased educational opportunities for students who have traditionally struggled with schooling.

There is a challenge in such work to consider broader definitions of literacy and different relationships with families and our communities. It is only by developing closer relationships with our communities that parents gain real insights into what it is that we as teachers do to support learning. As well, it is through such relationships that we learn enough about the diversity of family language, literacy, and culture to design the type of responsive curricula that children need if they are to be given equal opportunities to learn and succeed.

Where Do We Go from Here?

Family literacy initiatives provide considerable promise, and yet at the same time they have the potential to contribute inadvertently to the mismatches between the literacy practices of home and school, by emphasizing a limited range of literacy practices. The latter will be the case if teachers continue to view parent involvement as simply an opportunity to have parents "help" in the classroom, or a means to improve their parenting skills. There are many challenges for teachers, one of the most obvious is the need to build more effective partnerships with families and communities. Those interested in partnerships between parents and schools need to consider whether the programs and curricula they construct in early childhood centers and schools meet the diverse needs of all learners, or whether they continue to privilege some at the expense of others. There is also a need to consider if the literacy practices that we privilege as teachers are reflective of the diversity of the multiple literacies that they will encounter outside formal education.

Gee (1990, p. 671) has suggested that "short of radical social change" there is "no access to power in society without control over the social practices in thought, speech and writing essay-text literacy and its attendant world view". We need to ask constantly, what does this mean for the way literacy is defined and used in early childhood and school settings, the programs we initiate with and for families, and the relationships that exist between educational institutions and communities?

At the level of program initiatives we need to continue to explore the use of the many programs that are in existence and to develop other initiatives that open up greater possibilities for the development of effective partnerships between schools and communities; partnerships characterized by:

1. Genuine involvement of parents in dialogue with teachers concerning what literacy is, how it is used, the match and mismatches of literacy practices at home and at school, the needs of children and their literacy behavior;
2. More equal sharing of responsibility for initiating dialogue such as the above;
3. Attempts by schools to acknowledge the enormous diversity present in community literacy practices;
4. The use of community-based sites for programs;
5. The involvement of parents in the setting of agendas for family literacy initiatives so that programs reflect their needs.

The main challenge that early childhood and school educators face is how to transform centers and schools into sites for learning that are responsive to the social and cultural diversity of the communities that they serve. Educational institutions are amongst the most stable in society, and short of a total transformation in the society within which they are embedded, they will not be moved quickly. However, given the continuing inequities in student opportunities to learn and to develop the literacy practices they need in a complex world, change must occur. We need to engage in social evolutionary development by providing opportunities and alternative programs and curricula which challenge existing educational practices (Cairney, 1994). The work in family literacy, if based on deficit views of learning, will do little to break down educational inequities present within our society. What is needed is a commitment to build genuine partnerships between communities and educational institutions that meet the diverse needs of children. If such partnerships enable shared understanding to develop between teachers and parents, then there is some hope for the changes that are necessary to ensure greater equity in the access that all children have to the literacy practices of schooling and the "outside" world.

Notes

1. The TTALL program and additional information are available from the author, University of Western Sydney (Nepean), PO Box 10, Kingswood, NSW, Australia 2747 or from the Australian Council for Educational Research, Camberwell, Victoria, Australia 3124.

References

Au, K., & Kawakami, A. (1984). Vygotskian perspectives on discussion processes in small group reading lessons. In P. Peterson & L.C. Wilkinson (Eds.). *The Social Context of Instruction* (pp. 209–225). Portsmouth (NH): Heinemann.

Auerbach, E. (1989). Toward a social-contextual approach to family literacy. *Harvard Educational Review,* 59:165–181.

Barton, D. (1994). *Literacy: An introduction to the ecology of written language.* Oxford: Blackwell.

Bourdieu, P. (1977). Cultural reproduction and social reproduction. In J. Karabel & A.H. Halsey (Eds.). *Power and Ideology in Education.* New York: Oxford University Press.

Breen, M.P., Louden, W., Barratt-Pugh, C., Rivalland, J., Rohl, M., Rhydwen, M., Lloyd, S., & Carr, T. (1994). *Literacy in its place: Literacy Practices in Urban and Rural Communities,* Vols I & 2. Perth: DEET.

Bruner, J. (1986). *Actual minds. Possible worlds.* Cambridge, MA: Harvard University Press. Cairney, T.H. (1987). Supporting the independent learner: Negotiating change in the classroom. In J. Hancock, & B. Comber (Eds.). *Independent Learners at School.* Sydney: Methuen.

Cairney, T.H. (1994). Family literacy: Moving toward new partnerships in education. *Australian Journal of Language and Literacy,* Vol. 17, No.4: 262–275.

Cairney, T.H. (1995a). *Pathways to literacy.* London: Cassell.

Cairney, T.H. (1995b). Developing Parent Partnerships in Secondary Literacy Learning. *Journal of Reading.* Vol. 38, No. 7: 520–526.

Cairney, T.H., Lowe, K., & Sproats. E. (1995). *Literacy in transition: An investigation of the literacy practices of upper primary and junior secondary schools* (Vols. 1–3). Canberra: DEET.

Cairney, T.H., & Munsie, L. (1992). *Talk to a literacy learner* Sydney: UWS Press.

Cairney, T.H., & Munsie, L. (1993). *Effective partners in secondary literacy learning (EPISLL).* Sydney: University of Western Sydney.

Cairney, T.H., & Munsie, L. (1995a). *Beyond tokenism: Parents as partners in literacy.* Portsmouth, NH: Heinemann.

Cairney, T.H., & Munsie, L. (1995c). *Parent partnership program.* Sydney: University of Western Sydney.

Cairney, T.H., Ruge, J., Buchanan, J., Lowe, K., & Munsie, L. (1995). *Developing partnerships: The home, school and community interface* (Vols. 1–3). Canberra: DEET.

Cairney, T.H., & Ruge, J. (1998). *Community literacy practices and schooling: Toward effective support for students.* Canberra: Department of Employment Education and Youth Affairs.

Cazden, C. (1988). *Classroom discourse.* Portsmouth, NH: Heinemann.

Delgado-Gaitan, C. (1991). Involving parents in schools: A process of empowerment. *American Journal of Education,* 100: 20–45.

Delgado-Gaitan, C. (1992). School matters in the Mexican-American home: Socializing children to education. *American Educational Research Journal,* 29: 495–516.

Department of Education and Science. (1967). *Children and their primary schools: A report of the Central Advisory Council for Education (England) Vol.1: Report & Vol. 2: Research and Surveys (Plowden Report).* London: HMSO.

Epstein, J. (1983). *Effects on parents of teacher practices of parent involvement.* Baltimore: The John Hopkins University, Report No. 346 (pp. 277–294).

Epstein, J., & Dauber, S.L. (1991). School programs and teacher practices of parent involvement in inner-city elementary and middle schools. *The Elementary School Journal,* 9: 289–305.

Fernie, D., Kantor, R., & Klein, E. (1988). Becoming students and becoming ethnographers in a preschool. *Journal of Childhood Research in Education.* Vol. 3, No. 2:

Fitzgerald, L.M., & Goncu, A. (1995). Parent involvement in urban early childhood education: A Vygotskian approach. In S. Reifel (Ed.). *Advances in Early Childhood Education and Day Care: A Research Annual,* Greenwich, CT: JAI Press.

Freebody, P., & Ludwig, C. (1995). Everyday literacy practices in and out of schools in low socioeconomic status urban communities: A descriptive and interpretive research program, Vols. 1 & 2. Canberra: Department of Employment, Education and Training.

Furniss, E. (1991). *Making a difference.* Melbourne: Ministry of Education and Training.

Gee, J. (1990). *Social linguistics and literacies: Ideology in discourses.* London: The Falmer Press.

Goldenberg, C.N. (1987). Low-income Hispanic parents' contributions to their first-grade children's word-recognition skills. *Anthropology and Education Quarterly,* 18: 149–179.

Green, J., Kantor, R., & Rogers, T. (1991). Exploring the complexity of language and learning in the classroom. In B. Jones & L. Idol (Eds.). *Educational values and cognitive instruction: Implications for reform,* Vol. 2 (pp. 333–364) Hillsdale. (NJ): Erlbaun.

Gutierrez, K.D. (1994). How talk, context, and script shape contexts for learning: A cross-case comparison of journal sharing. *Linguistics and Education,* Vol. 5 (3 & 4): 335–365.

Hannon, P. (1995). *Literacy, Home and School: Research and practice in teaching literacy with parents.* London: The Falmer Press.

Hanusheck, E.A. (1981). Throwing money at schools. *Journal of Policy Analysis and Management,* 1: 19–41.

Harry, B. (1992) An ethnographic study of cross-cultural communication with Puerto Rican-American families in the special education system. *American Educational Research Journal,* 29: 471–494.

Heath, S.B. (1983). *Ways with words: Language, life and work in community and classrooms.* Cambridge, UK: Cambridge University Press.

Illinois Literary Resource Development Center. (1990). *The mechanics of success for families.* Rantoul (111): Illinois Literacy Resource Development Center.

Jackson, B.L., Krasnow, J., & Seeley, D. (1994). *The League of Schools Reaching Out: A New York City Cluster Building Family-School-Community Partnership.* Paper presented to the American Educational Research Association Conference, New Orleans, 4–8 April.

Jencks, C., Smith, M., Acland, H., Bane, M.J., Cohen, D., Gentis, H., Heynes, B., & Michelson, S. (1972). *Inequality: A reassessment of the effect of family and schooling in America.* New York: Basic Books.

Kruger, T., & Mahon, L. (1990). *Reading Together: Magical or Mystifying.* Paper presented to Australian Reading Association Conference, Canberra. 7-10 July.

Lankshear, C., & Lawler, M. (1987). *Literacy, schooling and revolution.* London: Falmer Press.

Lareau, A. (1991). *Home advantage.* New York: Falmer Press.

Luke, A. (1993). Stories of social regulation: The micropolitics of classroom narrative, In B. Green (Ed.), *The Insistence of the Letter: Literacy Studies and Curriculum Theorising.* London: The Falmer Press.

Moll, L. (1988). Some key issues in teaching Latino students. *Language Arts,* 65: 465-472.

Morgan, R.T.T (1976). "Paired Reading" Tuition: A preliminary report on a technique for cases of reading deficit. *Childcare, Health and Development,* 2: 13-28.

Neuman, S.B. & Roskos, K. (1995). *Access to Print for Children of Poverty: Differential Effects of Adult Mediation and Literacy Enriched Place Settings on Environmental and Functional Print Tasks.* Paper presented to American Educational Research Conference. San Francisco, 18-22 April.

Nickse. R. (1993). A typology of family and intergenerational literacy programs; implications for evaluation. *Viewpoints,* 15: 34-40.

Petit, D. (1980). *Opening up schools.* Harmondsworth: Penguin.

Rasinski, T.V., & Fredericks, A.D. (1989). Dimensions of parent involvement. *The Reading Teacher,* Nov: 180-182.

Rutter, M., Tizard, J., Whitmore, K, (1970). *Education Health and Behavior.* London: Longmans.

Schaefer, E. (1991). Goals for parent and future parent education: Research on parental beliefs and behavior. *Elementary School Journal,* 91: 239-247.

Scribner, S., & Cole, M. (1981). *The psychology of literacy.* Cambridge, MA: Harvard University Press.

Shanahan, T., & Rodriguez-Brown, F. (1993). *The Theory and Structure of a Family Literacy Program for the Latino Community.* Paper presented at the American Educational Research Association Conference, Atlanta (U.S.A.), 12–16 April.

Street, B. (1984). *Literacy in theory and practice.* Cambridge, UK: Cambridge University Press.

Teale, W.H. (1986). Home background and young children's literacy development. In W. Teale & E. Sulzby (Eds.). *Emergent Literacy* (pp. 173–206). Norwood, NJ: Ablex.

Thompson, W.W. (1985). Environmental effects on educational performance. *The Alberta Journal of Educational Psychology,* 31: 11–25.

Tizard, J., Schofield, W., & Hewison, J. (1982). Collaboration between teachers and parents in assisting children's reading. *British Journal of Educational Psychology,* 52: 1–15.

Topping, K. & McKnight, G. (1984). Paired reading—and parent power. *Special Education—Forward Trends,* 11 (pp. 12–15).

Topping, K., & Wolfendale, S. (Eds.). (1985). *Parental Involvement in Children's Reading.* Beckenham, UK: Croom Helm.

Vygotsky, L. (1978). *Mind and society: The development of higher mental processes.* Cambridge, MA: Harvard University Press.

Welch, A.R., & Freebody, P. (1993). Introduction: Explanations of the current international "Literacy Crises." In P. Freebody & A. Welch (Eds.). *Knowledge, Culture & Power: International Perspectives on Literacy as Policy and Practice.* London: Falmer Press.

Wells, G. (1985). Preschool literacy-related activities and success in school. In D.R. Olson, N. Torrance & A. Hildyard (Eds.). *Literacy, Language and Learning: The Nature and Consequences of Reading and Writing.* Cambridge: Cambridge University Press.

Chapter 24

Literacy in the Preschool: An Australian Case Study

Bridie Raban
Christine Ure

Abstract

This chapter describes preschool teachers' beliefs and knowledge base with regards to young children's literacy development. Data were gathered from preschool teachers across the State of Victoria (Australia). The teachers' beliefs, attitudes, and curriculum practices for early literacy development are explored against a context of contemporary research evidence concerning children's acquisition knowledge about print and its function. This chapter argues for a reconceptualization of young children's development which takes account of the role of the adult in structuring opportunities and experiences that support both the progress and process of development.

The Study

The government of the State of Victoria, like governments across the developed world, is concerned about the educational standards of its school students. A particular focus of this attention is the perceived low levels of literacy among primary school-age students and the ways in which lack of literacy militates against further school achievement. Indeed, as Hill (1995) and others have pointed out, failure in learning to read and write during the early years of schooling has a profound impact on later school success. Because of this understanding, a variety of initiatives have been taken by educational systems in different countries, for instance, Reading Recovery (Clay 1993a), Success for All in the U.S. (Slavin, et al., 1996),

The U.K. National Literacy Project (Stannard 1997), and the Early Literacy Research Project—ELRP (Crevola & Hill, 1997) in Victoria, Australia (see also Cairney, this volume).

These projects have been designed to influence children during the early years of schooling so that each child has the maximum opportunity to succeed in learning to read and write. However, because of the ways in which funding and schooling are organized in Victoria, this initiative by the Department of Education excludes preschools (which are not funded by the Department of Education). The implication here is that children learn to read and write when they begin school, which is true; and that they do not learn to read and write during their preschool years, which is not the case. While this point of view may not be explicit in the Victorian Early Literacy Research Project, there could be a powerful implicit message for preschool professionals and for parents.

In order to counteract this possible misperception, a further project was linked to the ELRP, the Preschool Literacy Project (PLP), and considerable work has been conducted in preschools in the state.[1] The ELRP at school-level invited schools to make a commitment to their students' literacy development and through this commitment fifty two primary schools serving populations of low socioeconomic status were chosen to take part in the study. Twenty-seven schools acted as trial schools and 25 acted as reference (control group) schools. These schools were asked to gain information on preschool centers which their prep grade students (aged five yrs) had attended during the previous year. A typical response from these school teachers was that these children had not attended preschool provision of any form. However, when pressed for this information, it was discovered that 75% of this total cohort, which was in excess of 4,500 children, had attended kindergarten.

Some preschools fed all their children to a single primary school, especially those in country areas. Other preschools had children who left them for more than a dozen different primary schools and this was found to be the case in many metropolitan preschool contexts. Therefore, out of a possible 236 preschool centers which sent children to the ELRP project schools, only those who sent five or more children to a PLP project school were contacted. One hundred and fifty-two preschools were formally contacted and asked if they would be interested in exploring their children's early literacy development as part of the project. This would involve them in answering a survey, being interviewed, and taking part in a program of professional development across a period of 18 months. Few replies were received to this initial contact and follow-up phone calls were required to take the invitation further. After extensive discussions and explanations, 40 preschool centers agreed to take part in the Preschool Literacy Project. During these phone calls there was a large number of early childhood professionals who rejected the idea of the project completely. They stressed that literacy was not an issue for them or their center and they did not wish to be involved in this project.

This first experience of refusal was unexpected and provided us with much to consider. We were operating with an understanding that literacy is a social construct and available to all children born into a literate culture. Our understanding was based on our reading of current literature, which indicates the power of individuals to make sense of their surroundings, through both spoken and written language, and the role of adults in that successful endeavor. We were not prepared for the negation of this stance at whatever levels of development children may be achieving.

Early Literacy Development

With respect to this apparent reluctance on the part of many Victorian preschool teachers to become involved in the Preschool Literacy Project, it is interesting to note that literacy development has seen a continuing change of focus throughout the twentieth century (Raban, 1997). We have achieved an awareness, if not an understanding, that developing literacy is a profoundly social process (McLane & McNamee, 1990). Literacy is embedded in social relationships, especially in children's relationships with people in their immediate family; grandparents, friends, caregivers, and teachers. These are the ones who act as models, provide experiences and materials, offer support, establish expectations, instruct, and encourage. Children who start school with little experience of literacy in their lives can soon experience failure as they are increasingly confronted by texts that are too difficult for them to read. Allington reports on a sample of six-year-old children (1984) that their experience of literacy at school extended from 16 words read in one week by one child with little experience of literacy, to a high of 1,933 words read by another who lived with a rich literacy background.

In this sense, literacy feeds itself. Children with the experience of literacy as an immediacy in their lives understand and benefit from formal schooling in a way that other children do not. Grasping the significance and nature of print and the many ways it can function in the lives of people has been called having the *big picture* (Purcell-Gates & Dahl, 1991). This understanding of the contexts for written language and the ways in which it supports everyday lives of adults is basic to any future knowledge, forms, and conventions of print that children might develop (Purcell-Gates, 1996). In Purcell-Gates' study (1996), this knowledge appeared to be learned more by children in preschool environments in which print was used to a greater degree and who experienced more interaction with significant adults around print, regardless of experience with formal literacy instruction, when they attend school.

Children begin to learn about the nature and forms of written English language, as well as its alphabetic code as they experience their parents and other significant literate people reading and writing more complex text, both for their own purposes and for the purpose of their children. The results of Purcell-Gates' study (1996) suggest that the development of the *big picture* was predictive of early literacy success in school for low SES children, and this *big picture* knowledge and understanding is affected by the frequency of experiences of print in use around them. By living and participating in an environment in which others use print for various purposes, children come to infer and understand the semiotic and functional nature of written language. It is claimed in this study that children who experience many uses of written language to which they attend and personally experience have more opportunities to build the important conceptual basis of literacy development—that print is symbolic and serves communicative purposes.

Purcell-Gates claims (1996) that preschoolers who have already begun to construct knowledge about the forms and concepts of print of written English and its alphabetic nature will begin formal literacy instruction in school with schema for literacy, which puts them at an advantage over their peers who have yet to begin this learning. The issue is not, thus, getting preschool children ready to learn, but rather creating literacy environments within which the learning that they already do on an ongoing basis includes the different emergent literacy understandings needed for school success. Children's early attachment of meaning to print in their environment is seen as a result of the combination of repeated exposures to print and of many interactions around them with more competent others, usually their parents.

Vukelich (1994) reports her study in which she invited young children to engage in self-sponsored play with their peers and adults during the children's free-play period. Literacy was built into the children's environment in ways that encouraged literacy events to occur as a part of the usual flow of the everyday experience, and they did so in ways that increased children's contact with literacy materials without disturbing the ecology of the children's preschool experience. They discovered that this enhancement of play environments increased children's engagement in literate behaviors. In addition, they discovered that these enhancements positively affected children's literacy learning as determined by their performance on such measures as a function of print test and *Concepts About Print* test (Clay 1993b). In this study, the adult interactional style was like that which children experience in the world outside the preschool, a world they shared with their parents and with significant others, a style where the environmental print-meaning associations were woven naturally into the adult-child interactions.

Neuman and Rosko (1997) set out in their research to capture the multifaceted knowledge and behaviors that may constitute early literacy practices for three- and four-year-old preschool children, viewing literacy in its development not as a series of skills acquisition, but as a series of transformations and adaptations across events and settings. Environmental design factors were examined that might best provide opportunities for literacy within the contexts of children's play. This was done in the belief that young children reveal what they know and can do to the extent that an environment is supportive of their efforts (Bjorklund, Muirs-Broaddus, et al., 1990) Contexts that incorporate everyday literacy practices of families and their community suggest settings with identifiable frameworks that encourage children to use what they know to generate new knowledge. (see Cairney, this volume).

A combination of exposure to environmental print and many functional experiences with others with this print are now known to result in young children making important meaning-making connections (Taylor 1983; Harste, et al., 1984; Reynolds 1997)—associations believed to be important precursors to conventional reading (Goodman 1990; Clay 1991).

Literacy and Developmental Practice

What we experienced at the beginning of the Preschool Literacy Project in Victoria was an apparent denial of the value of preschool experience by primary school teachers and a lack of association with children's early literacy development by preschool teachers. Indeed, there has been a noticeable reluctance by early childhood educators to embrace literacy in their preschool programs. Campbell (1996) suggests that one of the grounds for this reluctance may stem from the notion of developmental "readiness" in preschool education. This stance is further elaborated by those who believe that reading readiness is linked to the idea that certain abilities, skills, and understandings are essential before a child learns to read (Raban, 1997). Hannon and James (1990), in their study of preschool teachers and parents of preschool children, indicate that preschool teachers are aware, for instance, of the parents' interest in the literacy development of their children, but they worried about parents using inappropriate methods, parents putting too much pressure on children and they, as teachers, didn't see literacy as a central concern of the preschool curriculum. These views were further supported in this study.

Espousing a child-centered philosophy and having this embedded in play-based practice is one of the axioms of current early childhood educators in the Australian state of Victoria, although this concept has been interpreted in a number of different ways. Bredekamp (1987) indicates that what this philosophy means is a commitment to the planning and implementation, in preschool programs, of appropriate experiences. The National Association for the Education of Young Children (NAEYC) also states that:

> . . . developmentally appropriate practices for teaching strategies are based on knowledge of how young children learn. Curriculum derives from many sources such as the knowledge base of various disciplines, society, culture, and parents' desires. (Bredekamp 1987: 53)

This influential position statement goes on to suggest that children should be exposed to literate opportunities and that literacy development should be promoted within meaningful contexts.

David (1990) purports that, depending on the overriding philosophy, some ambivalence is evident amongst early childhood educators in the U.K., for instance, concerning the role of adults in providing for children's learning needs. If, for example, early childhood educators interpret "child-centered" to mean providing an environment in which children engage in their own interests with the exclusion of adult intervention, other than by invitation, then there will be little or no obvious determined structure in the program. Alternatively, in an adult-dominated and directed setting, a rigid and highly noticeable structure would be evident. The emphasis in this latter case would be directed toward pushing children forward with little regard to their interests and understandings.

On the one hand, we have adults hanging back and waiting for children to prompt their own development and, on the other hand, we have them taking over from the children. Both points of view provide us with a paradox. We are aware of the considerable power of children to act on their environment and make sense of their experiences (Piaget, 1955), we understand that success is cooperatively achieved (Vygotsky, 1978) and we are reminded by Bruner (1986) that inquiry and resolution are learned through interacting with more knowledgeable others. How can these three perspectives be reconciled within a framework of emergent literacy development and the dominant preschool educational philosophy found among this group of teachers?

Paradoxes for Preschool Teachers

The postal survey we sent to 40 preschools across the state of Victoria, as the first step of the Preschool Literacy Project, asked preschool teachers to let us know any questions they might have regarding children's early literacy development. Their overwhelming response was to be better informed. They wanted information concerning their own role, how to address parents' questions, and what children would encounter when they entered school. They identified that children in their programs were reading and writing because they were being asked for words and spellings by the children. They found this challenging and wanted to know how to foster literacy development.

Views of the Teachers' Role

One teacher expressed her concern by saying "Should I be doing more?" In questioning their role, they asked how to further extend children's literacy development, how to provide for readiness, and how to incorporate literacy informally into their programs. They wanted to know how to promote children's interest in literacy, what do about three-year-olds who expressed an interest in literacy, should they model, provide for, even facilitate literacy learning? "Will it come, or should I point it out?" "Should I make it happen or should I wait for it to happen?" These teachers wanted to know the best books to buy for preschool children, what to suggest to parents about, for instance, writing capital letters and mirror writing. They asked how to appropriately share information with other early childhood professionals like speech therapists and other support services so that parents would not be confused.

An overriding concern was their feeling that their expectations of children might be too low and that they should be expecting more of children. They felt ignorant of what would be expected of children when they started school, both by parents and by primary school teachers. They believed that they must not encroach on what children would experience when they went to school, so they wondered how far they could go with children's literacy learning in their preschool program. They were concerned for children who had difficulty learning to read and write and wanted to know how reading and writing were taught in the primary school.

Clearly these teachers were curious and keen to learn more about young children's literacy development. Children in their four-year-old programs spanned a wide range of age and experience as there is only one date for school entry in Victoria at this time. Children enter Victorian primary schools at the beginning of the school year that they turn five on 30 April. This means that a child with a birthday on May 1 might not enter school until the following February. These teachers, therefore, had experience of children whose literacy development was expressed through their wanting to know what words said and how to spell words for their own writing.

Preschool Teachers' Knowledge about Literacy

With their interest and enthusiasm for more information, we planned a professional development package that would be tailored to the teachers' expressed needs. On the last page of the postal survey we asked teachers to indicate their willingness to be further interviewed. These interviews focused directly upon their understandings concerning young children's literacy development.

The interviews confirmed that this group of teachers were highly motivated to learn more about early literacy development and that their current practices were limited in focus. Descriptions of the daily events of their preschool program illustrated little provision for experiences and did not address an understanding of the role and uses of literacy. However, there was an example of a teacher who planned to incorporate reading and writing into children's dramatic play and another example where a teacher had designed a reading room for the purpose of allowing children enriched experiences with books and print. Many of these teachers described how their program provided a wide range of experiences that established important prereading and prewriting skills such as eye control and visual tracking skills, left to right movement activities, hand-eye coordination, an appropriate pencil grasp, and perceptual skills associated with sequencing and visual discrimination. One teacher said "my job is to give children experiences which will lead to reading and writing".

The goals of the preschool programs we observed and discussed with the teachers were found to be marginally linked to the development of knowledge about literacy. Some of these teachers indicated that they expected most children to be able to recognize their own name by the end of the preschool year. Many also noted that some children were able to write their own name, although they did not expect this of all their children.

Some teachers commented that there were a few children who commenced the preschool year with the ability to recognize and write their own name. When questioned further, no strategies were identified for this skill to be used or further extended, beyond allowing the child to write his/her name on his/her work, if they chose to do so. Some teachers noted that some children became less inclined to write their name as the year progressed!

Most of these teachers included more literacy-based experiences for the four-year-old group in the latter part of the year as part of their school transition program. During this time they were inclined to encourage children to have a go at writing their own name and to positively appreciate their efforts. Some teachers used a range of prepared worksheets to foster pencil and paper skills through circling correct responses to simple visual discrimination tasks, for instance. However, the view that literacy and its development is a curriculum issue that should be left until schooling has appeared to cause many of these preschool teachers to be concerned that they might "get it wrong" if they encourage reading and writing within the preschool. The teaching of literacy was also believed to interfere with other areas of development within the child and that this could mean that children would be "pushed" inappropriately. One teacher stated that "when children start writing, they lose their creativity".

Preschool Teachers' Views of Parents

These teachers also held paradoxical views about the role that parents played in young children's literacy development. There was recognition, on the one hand, that "those preschool children who can read have a lot of parental support" and that children who exhibited interest in literacy in the preschool did so because it had been fostered by their parents. On the other hand, there were concerns that parents were too competitive, their expectations were too high, and that children's interest in literacy was stifled by too much parental pressure. Parents were also perceived to "get it wrong" and to use inappropriate methods for teaching their children to read and write. For example, many teachers were of the view that parents taught their children to write using capital letters. They were concerned that this was incorrect and would cause these children difficulty at school. Most teachers distributed copies of the Victorian cursive script to parents to avoid this problem. However, copies of this script for children to use in the preschool program were rarely evident.

Children Entering School

This group of preschool teachers believed that school teachers didn't listen to their concerns and that records of preschool development weren't consulted, and this was in order to avoid the stimulation of preconceived notions, with school teachers wanting to give their students a fresh start. These preschool teachers also feared that their reports might be misinterpreted and, because of this, they were less inclined to share documents. They expressed anxiety concerning their children's progress in school. Some believed that children would be threatened by being asked things they didn't know and that children might be perceived to fail if not found "ready" for school. They felt that they were in the front line, battling for children's freedom from pressure and protecting their opportunities for learning through play before their life was changed forever by the didactic experience of school.

There was a strong suggestion that children would be bored at school if they were reading and writing before they got there and that if the children encountered resources and activities they had already experienced in the preschool, then they would also be bored. In addition, some believed that young children found school boring because there was no play, it was adult-directed, and too intensive ("too full on"). Importantly, some of these teachers expressed the view that as long as adults didn't direct or intervene, children wouldn't be judged to have failed. Two opposing views were expressed concerning children's experience with their early days at school; first, that school teachers would expect children to be "ready" to learn to read and write, and second, that school teachers do preschool-like activities during the children's first year in school. Indeed, there is a growing movement in Victoria at this time to include prepreparatory grades into Victorian primary schools that would in effect prolong young children's preschool experience and give them more time to become "ready" for school.

Conclusion

Many dilemmas are expressed through these data. Clearly, there is a lack of appreciation concerning the different roles of professional educators in both school and preschool settings. Differences are found in the focus of the curriculum and in the orientation toward children's learning. There can be very different expectations for children of the same age—dependent on which service they are in at age five years, i.e., preschool or school. This may well be a result of the training provision in Victoria, which is separate in many cases. Primary student teachers (of 5–11 year-olds) take a different training program from their preschool student colleagues (of 0–5 years), and these preschool teachers are not now licensed to teach in primary schools. These two groups also have separate funding sources, professional organizations, professional development provision, and locations. Clearly, their sense of each other's purpose and function is difficult to achieve. However, many voluntary early years networks are beginning to bring these two groups together across the state. In an important way, these two groups are trying to listen to and understand each other's discourse, which presently appears to militate against any simple reconciliation of views. These networks are attempting to reflect the international definition of early childhood that spans the age range 0–8 years.

This group of preschool teachers, while signaling their concerns about their lack of knowledge about children's literacy, are caught between notions of developmental "readiness" and any proactive notion of their own role in children's learning. They are expressing a model of development that is one of developmental *progress,* with skills and abilities unfolding in sequence, culminating in a state of developmental readiness or maturity. Their major concern is to ensure children are not pressured and have time to achieve this in a natural way before starting school. An alternative and more proactive view of developmental *process* has not been found in their intellectual repertoire. Such a view would acknowledge that children's learning is guided by what is socially significant in their experience and that adults have to acknowledge their role in supporting children's quest for meaning by being proactive in curriculum design and implementation. Importantly, children learn all the time and form hypotheses from whatever information is available, requiring more experience and opportunities to refine their conjectures, making approximations toward full achievement. Coupled with this, these teachers appeared to lack a sure knowledge that children, through targeted interaction with them and capable others, would benefit most in the depth and breadth of their development.

This view of development leaves us with a fresh interpretation of practice. The skill of leaving the initiative with the child (child-centered) and yet offering opportunities and experiences that extend children's understanding and ability (developmentally appropriate) is indeed a matter of fine judgment and intellectual sophistication on the part of preschool teachers. Nevertheless, it is at the heart of early childhood educational philosophy and this developmental *process* and, therefore, best practice needs much sharper and successful articulation. The central purpose and function of early childhood education, which is to deliberately encourage, sustain, and support the full development of young children, needs to be clearly articulated by the early childhood community.

Within a political and social landscape, which is in danger of rejecting preschool education because it is too costly or too difficult for other reasons, it will be necessary to reinstate professional obligations and purposes that give early childhood education a more definite place in the critical development of a nation's human resource. It would appear from these data that there has been neglect, intentional or otherwise, of a reinterpretation of the role of the adult in the earliest and most important years of a child's development. To gain maximum effect from educational initiatives at the levels of theory, policy, and practice, then these three need to be in careful alignment (Monk, 1992). We have reported here from data collected in early childhood settings in Victoria, Australia. There is some nonalignment of policy and practice with now well-established theoretical perspectives. These theoretical perspectives are gaining credibility through research evidence reviewed earlier in this chapter and should not be ignored by those generating policy and practice for early childhood educators. While many may claim that early childhood education is too costly, we would maintain that it repays all the attention and resourcing that a community devotes to its support. If attention and resourcing for early childhood are impoverished, either financially or intellectually, then so will be the returns in both the short term and in the future.

Notes

1. The PLP focused on four main questions concerning the provision for literacy in preschool programs:
   1. What are the typical experiences that are planned, or occur incidentally, that involve young children in written language experiences?
   2. What attitudes and beliefs do preschool staff hold in relation to the literacy development of young children?
   3. What information do preschool staff need in order to plan and evaluate the literacy experiences they provide for young children?
   4. What is the relationship between a preschool literacy program and young children's early reading development in school?

   Data sources included answers to a postal survey, follow-up interviews, inventories of preschool centers, policy documents, and diaries of practice.

References

Allington, R.L. (1984). Content coverage and contextual reading in reading groups. *Journal of Reading Behavior* 16: 85–96.

Bjorklund, D.F., Muirs-Broaddus, J., et al., (1990). The role of knowledge in the development of strategies. In D.F. Bjorklund (Ed.), *Children's Strategies*. Hillsdale, NJ: Erlbaum.

Bredekamp, S. (1987). *Developmentally appropriate practice in early childhood programs serving children from birth through age 8.* Washington DC: National Association for the Education of Young Children.

Bruner, J. (1986). *Actual minds, possible worlds.* Cambridge MA: Harvard University Press.

Campbell, R. (1996). *Literacy in nursery education.* Stoke-on-Trent, UK: Trentham Books.

Clay, M.M. (1991). *Becoming literate: The construction of inner control.* Auckland, NZ: Heinemann.

Clay, M.M. (1993a). *Reading recovery: A guide book for teachers in training.* Auckland, NZ: Heinemann

Clay, M.M. (1993b). *An observation survey: of early literacy achievement.* Auckland, NZ: Heinemann.

Crevola, C., & Hill, P. (1997). Initial evaluation of a whole school approach to early literacy prevention and intervention. *International Adaptations of Success for All.* Annual Conference, American Educational Research Association Conference, Chicago.

David, T. (1990). *Under five—under educated?* Buckingham: The Open University Press.

Goodman, Y. (1990). *How children construct literacy.* Newark, DE: International Reading Association.

Hannon, P., & James, S. (1990). Parents' and teachers' perspectives on preschool literacy development. *British Educational Research Journal* 16,3: 259–272.

Harste, J., Woodward, V., & Burke, C. (1984). *Language stories and literacy lessons.* Portsmouth, NH: Heinemann.

Hill, P. (1995). School effectiveness and improvement. *Deans Lecture Series.* Faculty of Education, Parkville VIC: The University of Melbourne.

Hill, P., & Crevola, C. (1997). The Early Literacy Research Project: *Success for All in Victoria, Australia.* Paper presented at the American Educational Research Association Conference, Chicago.

McLane, J., & McNamee, G. (1990). *Early Literacy.* Cambridge, MA: Harvard University Press.

Monk, D. (1992). Education productivity research: an update and assessment of its role in education finance reform. *Education Evaluation and Policy Analysis,* 14: 307–332.

Neuman, S.B., & Rosko, K. (1997). Literacy knowledge in practice: contexts of participation for young writers and readers. *Reading Research Quarterly* 32,1: 10–32.

Piaget, J. (1955). *The child's construction of reality.* London: Routledge & Kegan Paul.

Purcell-Gates, V. (1996). Stories, coupons and the TV guide: Relationships between home literacy experiences and emergent literacy knowledge. *Reading Research Quarterly* 31,4: 406–428.

Purcell-Gates, V., & Dahl, K. (1991). Low SS children's success and failure at early literacy learning in skills-based classrooms. *Journal of Reading Behavior,* 23: 1–34.

Raban, B. (1997). Reading skills: Emergent literacy. In V.K. Edwards (Ed.)., *Literacy* Vol. 2 *Encyclopedia of Language and Education.* D. Corson (Ed.). Dordrecht, Boston: Kluwer Academic Publishers.

Raban, B. & Ure, C. (1997). Systemic issues and preschool teachers' practice. *Melbourne Studies in Education,* 38,2: 85–99.

Reynolds, B. (1997). *Literacy in the preschool: The roles of teachers and parents.* Stoke-on-Trent: Trentham Books.

Slavin, R.E., Madden, N.A., Dolan, L.J., Wasik, B.A., Ross, S.M., Smith, L.J., & Dianda, M. (1996). Success for all: A summary of research. *Journal of Education for Students Placed at Risk 1*: 153–170.

Stannard, J. (1997). *Frameworks for teaching: The national literacy project.* London, UK: Crown Copyright.

Taylor, D. (1983). *Family literacy: Young children learning to read and write.* Portsmouth, NH: Heinemann.

Vukelich, C. (1994). Effects of play interventions on young children's reading of environmental print. *Early Childhood Research Quarterly* 9: 153–170.

Vygotsky, L.S. (1978). *Mind and society: The development of higher psychological processes.* Cambridge, MA: Harvard University Press.

Acknowledgments

Funding for this project has been obtained through the University of Melbourne, the Faculty of Education, and the Center for Applied Educational Research. The Center staff—Professor Peter Hill, Carmel Crevola, and Ken Rowe have been generous in their advice and support through enabling us to link our study with the Early Literacy Research Project (Hill & Crevola, 1997).

Chapter 25

Effects of Sociocultural Contexts and Discourses on Science and Technology Teaching in Early Childhood Education

Alison Elliott

Abstract

The strong constitutional dimension that shapes the production, transmission, and valuation of knowledge about science and information technology in early childhood contexts is considered in this chapter. Implicated in this constitutional dimension are the wider social and political landscapes that determine science, math, and information technology curricula, early childhood teacher training, and teaching in early childhood classrooms. Of particular interest are images of science and information technology in the community, particularly their "masculine" orientations, and perceptions of the social uses and responsibilities of science-related domains. It is argued that a further moderating effect comes from deeply embedded beliefs about what constitutes appropriate practice in the care and education of young children, especially preschoolers. Illustrations are drawn from a recent study of 90 preservice and 34 inservice early childhood teachers' beliefs about and experiences with science and information technology.

Introduction

In this chapter, I explore some of the sociocultural and pedagogic processes that appear to contribute to the gap between policy and practice in relation to science and technology teaching in early childhood education. The main foci are on the production, transmission, and evaluation of knowledge about science and information technology in the community and in early childhood contexts and how these processes affect decisions about classroom practice. It is argued that in both domains there is a strong constitutional dimension that affects sociocultural discourses and pedagogic practices, which in turn structure and shape what's considered legitimate and valued knowledge about science and information technology.

Implicated in this constitutional dimension are the wider social and political landscapes that have shaped the attitudes and policies that frame science, math, and information technology curricula, early childhood teacher training, and teaching in early childhood classrooms. The constitutional dimension encompasses very powerful images of science and information technology in the community, perceptions of its social uses and responsibilities, and specifically, the masculinity of perceptions and images. Of particular interest are the links between teacher attitudes to science and information technology and relationships between policy and practice in curriculum decision making, especially choice and definition of classroom learning experiences. Equally powerful are the deeply embedded beliefs about what constitutes appropriate practice in the care and education of young children, especially preschoolers.

Understanding the gulf between rhetoric and practice involves more than a superficial look at resourcing and teacher attitudes to science and technology. It requires analyses of the sociocultural context of policymaking and implementation and deconstruction of the pedagogical discourses that shape teaching and learning practices in early childhood classrooms. Of significance, too, is the predominance of female teachers and support staff in early childhood education. Examples illustrating aspects of the discussion are drawn from recent investigations of preservice (n = 90) and inservice (n= 34) early childhood teachers' beliefs about, and experiences with, science and information technology in early childhood classrooms.

Science and Information Technology in Early Education

The limited focus on science and use of information technologies in the preschool and early school sector has been well documented (Elliott, 1995a; Haplern, 1992a; Perry & Rivkin, 1992). Science is often considered to be the weakest component of an early childhood program and early childhood teachers, and indeed most teachers at the primary school level, are generally considered to have limited personal knowledge of science and ability to teach it effectively. Compounding the negative effects of this situation is the fact that many science concepts that must be introduced to young children are actually difficult for adults to understand, let alone explain to children (Hawkins, 1985).

Acceptance of the role of computers as legitimate learning tools, especially in the preschool sector, is low. Rarely are the scope and potential of computers exploited in early childhood contexts, despite the fact that computers are common everyday tools, and the results of a plethora of studies highlighting the cognitive benefits of various types of computer-based learning activities (Clements & Nastasi, 1992; Elliott, 1988, 1995a; Elliott & Hall, 1997). The reasons for this low acceptance are complicated. While a partial explanation lies in teachers' early beliefs about negative effects of children's computer use on social skills, concerns about poor software, and a view that young children were unable to interact meaningfully with symbolic and two dimensional screen-based images (Elliott, 1984, 1995a), the continuing resistance to implementation of computer technologies in purposeful ways suggests more complex factors are influencing teacher beliefs and practices.

In a paper to the *First Years of School Conference* in 1986, I spoke of the ways in which early years' teachers viewed computers as "novelty items" for when the "real business of teaching" was over (Elliott & Hall, 1986). The computer was located in the "computer corner" and children had a "turn" on the computer. Some fifteen years later, while children's involvement with computers has increased substantially, the novelty model of implementation still dominates, as was shown in the study of early childhood teachers referred to here.

Equally well documented is at least a decade of community discussion about the value and importance of computers in education—and a range of policy initiatives to encourage meaningful use of computers in education, including early childhood settings. These initiatives have had varying effects in primary and secondary schools with some schools embracing information technology as a means of enhancing learning across the curriculum and others virtually ignoring its potential. As late as 1996, few students left secondary school with anything but the most superficial experience of learning with technology in the classroom despite the expenditure of millions of dollars on computers and computing infrastructure (Elliott, 1996).

In recent focus group sessions with 34 early childhood teachers, a Year 1 teacher reported: "Most money for computers is spent in the primary school classes. We get what they don't want—if we're lucky. This year we got another hand-me-down (computer). It's so out-of-date it really belongs in the home corner with the dress-ups, old phones, typewriters, and the ironing board."

While this teacher's efforts to incorporate computer-based experiences were clearly hampered by lack of appropriate technology, other early childhood classrooms, while rarely as well resourced as their counterparts elsewhere in schools, are nevertheless, better served. Results of a recent investigation of preservice teacher education students' experiences of computer use in 90 Kindergarten to Year 2 classrooms across Sydney suggested that most classrooms now had one or more computers, many with multimedia capabilities. Yet children's use, at least over the four-week period while the students were with the class, averaged about 10 minutes each per week. Computers were used mainly for games and story typing, on a rotational basis, and often as a reward or "filler". As one student commented, "computers are for Friday afternoon when everyone has run out of other things to do." No students saw children using the Internet and only five students had the opportunity to use a computer in their teaching. This all too common situation of the computer-in-the-corner, so children can have a "turn" playing games, albeit "educational", makes a mockery of policy initiatives, parents' fund raising efforts, and of course, the technology itself. Teachers may just as well have bought Nintendos.

Understandably, given these experiences, most students believed computers had limited impact in the classroom and on children's learning. But they reported the very strong view that computer-based learning experiences were important in enhancing children's learning. Most (80%) mentioned the importance of technology as a tool for the Twenty First Century. Fewer (55%), however, felt confident integrating computers in meaningful ways in a classroom. On the whole though, they felt positive about their knowledge of the technology. Their self-ratings were in stark contrast to their ratings of the qualified teachers to whom they were assigned during their professional experience. Generally students perceived that their classroom teachers had limited skill and confidence in using computers to enhance children's learning. Students rated only 30% of the 90 teachers as being able, in their opinion, to effectively implement computer-based learning experiences for children.

In the case of science teaching, in the same 90 classrooms, experiences were similarly limited in nature and scope. Only 35% of students saw what they described as an activity designed explicitly to focus on scientific ideas. This is not to say, though, that children did not experience any science activities. In fact, the preservice teachers reported that scientific ideas were often incidental to other activities, such as art. Rarely was there any observable effort to articulate or highlight key scientific ideas through the use of scientific language or references. There were few concerted efforts to involve children in the scientific discourses that Greeno (1992) argues are so important for facilitating children's scientific thinking.

Interestingly, where students described science as being well and explicitly taught, it was often taught by a teacher who specialized in "science teaching", not by the classroom teacher. It was taught while the classroom teacher had her rostered time off (known as *relief from face-to-face teaching*). Only 22% of the preservice teachers taught one or more science lessons over the four weeks of their professional experience in schools.

An interesting finding from my ongoing research into preservice early childhood teachers' experiences of, and attitudes to, science, math, and technology is that only about 20% of each cohort entering our undergraduate teacher education programs has completed higher level science or math subjects in their senior secondary school years. Further, most students claim not to have enjoyed science and math at school.

A major aim of conversations with the 35 practicing early childhood teachers was to explore their beliefs about and the actual teaching of science and information technology. Most teachers reported that children in their classes had rostered turns at the computers and mainly for games involving math, language, and occasionally, scientific ideas. Children sometimes typed a final version of a story, but rarely did they compose at the computer. Generally, teachers emphasized "distributional" considerations such as lack of money and availability of resources, especially software, coupled with lack of time and expertise, as the major reasons computers were not used more effectively to support their teaching and children's learning. In the case of science teaching, most claimed that it was incorporated as part of other activities, for example, themed units on "the sea" or "our community". They agreed that they did not usually focus on scientific problem solving in a systematic or explicit manner, confirming claims of Haplern (1992) and Rivkin's (1992) claims of scant attention to science, and consistent with the views of the undergraduate teacher education students about their observations in classrooms.

Analyses of teachers' conversation, however, together with more in-depth discussions with individuals from the preservice group and educational policymakers, suggest a much more complex web of distributional and constitutional attributions that seemed to underpin the limited emphasis on science and technology shown in these and other early childhood classrooms.

These analyses suggest that the limited inclusion of science and information technology experiences in early childhood classrooms were likely to be affected by a complex interactic.. of constitutional factors at both a macro and micro level. At the macro level are community and teacher beliefs and perceptions about science and information technology, including the gendering of experience. At the micro level are the sociocultural discourses and structural characteristics of early education settings, including decision making about infrastructure support for implementation of relevant curriculum policy.

Community and Teacher Beliefs and Perceptions

There is generally a very strong and positive community image and acceptance of computer technology, both in the workplace and the home. The dramatic rise in home computing over the last year or two means that many students, especially those from more economically advantaged backgrounds, are likely to have access to a computer at home (Elliott, 1996). Some 40% of Australian homes have computers, with the percentage rising to 60% in homes with incomes over $50,000 (Australian Bureau of Statistics, 1997).

Despite overt community support for and involvement with computers in the home, there is substantial anecdotal evidence to suggest that activity is largely male-driven and sustained (Spender, 1995). Evidence from the focus group sessions with practicing teachers and follow-up interviews with selected preservice teachers, suggested that it was the males in their families—brothers, fathers, husbands, boyfriends, and sons—who were the most active users of the home computers. Generally, women used the home computer for a narrow range of instrumental tasks, such as completing a university assignment or writing a business-oriented letter. Rarely did they use computers for the same range of recreational and instrumental tasks or for the same lengthy periods of time as did the males in the family.

As one teacher said: "Of course we have a computer at home, but it's different from having one at school. At home it's the boys' toy. My sons and husband play boys' games and I get to use it late at night if I have to type something for work. It's quite different from having a computer in the classroom." She went on, as did several other teachers, to emphasize that using a computer at home bore little resemblance to incorporating computer experiences in meaningful and purposeful ways to enhance learning in a classroom.

The apparent dominance of men and boys in home computing is both shaped by, and reflected in, the strong masculine images, especially in the media, of science and technology. In a key discussion paper *Women in Science, Engineering and Technology* (Office of the Chief Scientist, 1995), it was claimed that the predominance of males and male images has "a consistently negative impact upon girls and women wishing to enter, contribute and progress through higher levels of science, engineering and technology education, training and employment" (p. 3). Further, the report emphasized that this situation is "apparently accepted as normal and unremarkable by the dominant culture" and that "it is rare to find references which directly attribute the exclusionary behavior which women and girls experience to their male colleagues and from boys" (p. 3). The reality is that far fewer girls than boys study science and technology at high school: Fewer women study science, engineering, and technology at university and fewer are employed in science, engineering, and technology fields. For example, women make up only 12.5% of all engineering students (p. 12).

Clearly, masculine images of science and technology have a powerful influence on women's perceptions of science and beliefs about its value in the community. Related images of physics and engineering are seen as not socially responsible or people-oriented, inflexible and arbitrary, and unrelated to the human condition (Byrne, 1994), which suggests that the almost exclusively female dominated early childhood teaching profession is likely to hold a negative image of science and technology, which translates to the classroom context.

Enculturation and Social Construction of Beliefs

Beliefs about science and technology develop through processes of enculturation and social construction (Stigler & Baranes, 1988). According to Nisbett and Ross (1980), beliefs are so personal and deeply held that they are unaffected by persuasion. As early beliefs are the most enduring it is important to consider that teachers' negative attitudes to science and technology may be unconsciously communicated to children in their care (Mandler, 1975; Nisbett & Ross, 1980). Indeed, Pajares (1992) argues that teachers' beliefs have stronger, affective, and evaluative effects than knowledge and that these are good predictors of classroom decision making. While referring particularly to beliefs about mathematics, the same is likely to be true for the related areas of science and technology.

While secondary teachers with relevant professional and academic background are likely to be confident about their understandings and knowledge in mathematics and science (Stodosky, 1988), early childhood and primary teachers usually have more limited and often poor academic backgrounds in science, math, and technology. This means they may have limited declarative and procedural knowledge (Quilter & Harper, 1988; Pajares, 1992; Chi, et al., 1982) report that novices' declarative knowledge is relatively devoid of the procedural specifications routinely incorporated by experts. Indeed, there are now studies indicating differences between expert and novice teachers' understandings of subject areas and subsequent abilities to teach effectively (Tweney & Walker, 1990). Claims that elementary teachers may have limited backgrounds in science, mathematics, and technology are confirmed by my own tracking of entry level early childhood teacher education students' academic backgrounds in, and attitudes toward, math, science, and technology (Elliott, 1996).

Negative cultural experiences and related beliefs and attitudes constitute substantial problems for early childhood science and technology and for mathematics education. They result in an unwillingness to implement day-to-day science and technology activities that are knowledge-building in nature, let alone embrace the newer information technology developments. Not only are masculinist societal images of science and information technology reinforced in the preschool and early school contexts, undoubtedly influencing the well-documented marginalization of girls in science and technology, but appear to have a long-term impact on girls' post secondary school involvement in science and information technology (Burkham, Lee, & Smerdon, 1997).

There has long been evidence claims that school texts, especially in science and mathematics, were designed to appeal to boys rather than to girls. And, while images in children's books have generally changed in the last decade with the appearance of similar numbers of males and females in illustrations and examples, and the use of "gender neutral" images (usually a cute child, with longish curly hair, dressed in overalls, that could possibly be interpreted as being either a girl or boy, but is usually interpreted as being a boy), a new generation of highly sex-typed materials has emerged—computer software.

A glance at any computer or toy catalogue reveals a host of children's software with space, pirate, dinosaur, disaster, and monster themes, and packaged in dark colors, designed to appeal mainly to boys' interests. And, as is the case for books, while it is claimed that masculine environments are neutralized through the portrayal of players who might be interpreted as male or female, they are frequently construed as "male" by both boys and girls. The maleness of the themes is further masked by claims that their fantasy, technical, or scientific natures are neutral. Having explored these male-oriented themes and found them unappealing, girls' lack of interest is frequently interpreted as technological immaturity or lack of imagination or creativity.

Pedagogical Discourses In Early Childhood Education

A second micro constitutional dimension sets science and information technology within a more specific educational framework and highlights educational discourses that impact on early childhood teachers' attitudes to, and classroom practice with, science and technology. Especially powerful here are the deeply embedded beliefs about what constitutes appropriate practice in the care and education of young children, particularly those under five years of age. Close links between mothering and nurturing roles and the related, largely Frobelian and Piagetian inspired notions of fostering development through unstructured play experiences, are often at odds with more recent Vygotskian inspired conceptions of enhancing learning and development more explicitly through guiding and scaffolding (Elliott, 1995b; Fleer, 1995; Vygotsky, 1978).

Traditionally, most ideological positions within early childhood preservice education have emphasized the caring and social dimensions of early childhood education and focus on the notion of the Piagetian-grounded developmentally appropriate practice (Fleer, 1995). There is far less emphasis on fostering cognition in an explicit manner or on thinking and problem solving as a foundation for early academic learning. Indeed, there is some resistance from educators in the childcare sector to see their key function as "education." The common practice in many circles of using the term "childcare workers" instead of early childhood educators, while ostensibly to ensure that all staff—even those without degree level or professional qualifications—are valued equally, reflects a prevailing non-educational orientation of elements within the childcare sector.

Given entrenched ideological and structural perspectives about the relative value and status of care and education in preschool and childcare settings, and the predominant emphases on children's social and emotional development, it is not surprising that science and technology, with their overtly "intellectual" and "impersonal" connotations (Office of the Chief Scientist, 1995), are not highly valued as legitimate and desirable curriculum endeavors in many early childhood contexts.

Conversations with the early childhood teachers from the preschool and kindergarten sector elicited consistently the view that early childhood classrooms are settings for play and social experiences that should not be "contaminated" with the technological tools of society, except as playthings. There seemed to be a view that there is enough time in the primary school years to focus on pursuits that are "academic" in nature. In general it was believed that computer-based activities and "science" were far too closely aligned with the formality of "schooling".

Focus group discussions with the early childhood teachers about who participates in the process of policymaking, the nature of that participation, the extent of participants' involvement, and the degree to which stakeholders are involved in policy formulation, suggest that few early childhood classroom practitioners actually contribute to science and technology policy, unless they are in very small or single unit operations. In the noncompulsory preschool sector there are very few systemwide policies to govern curriculum implementation. And in the early years (K–2) of school, where policy development occurs at a systems level, the prevailing view was that the early childhood teachers had almost no impact on policy despite some systematic efforts to consult practitioners. There was a very strong belief that the early childhood classrooms got the technological crumbs and that real business of learning with computers was something for the primary and secondary school years.

Also important in shaping early childhood teachers' attitudes and skills are policies and practices in teacher education and development that affect students' engagement with math, science, and technology. Science and math, and now information technology, rarely have a strong base in early childhood teacher education, and women's frequently negative entry-level attitudes and often limited science, math, and information technology experiences are not usually addressed explicitly. It can be expected that this situation might have a negative impact on early childhood teacher education graduates' confidence and competence to create rich, positive, and relevant science experiences or their employment of information technologies (Elliott, 1996).

Relatedly, the major foci in most early childhood teacher education courses are on learning through play, the concept of "developmentally appropriate practice", and children's physical and social and emotional development. There seems to be less explicit emphasis on cognition and scaffolding learning, and particularly the facilitation of problem solving, thinking skills, and knowledge-building in areas such as math, science, and technology. While many teachers argue that scientific ideas are embedded in everyday play experiences, the focus groups revealed that few teachers were able to articulate exactly what scientific ideas they highlighted in day-to-day activities or the long- and short-term importance of science to children. They were much clearer about the importance of information technology in children's occupational futures, but far less confident about how computers could be used to support learning in a classroom context. One important task for teacher education must be to reconcile the apparent tensions between the notion of "play" and the more cognitive and scientific conceptions of "technology", problem-solving, and knowledge-building.

Pedagogical Futures for Science and Technology

In recent years there have been a plethora of reports, initiatives, and projects to promote the use of information technology in education. At the formal level, the role of various government initiatives, committees of inquiry, and professional training and literature affect curriculum implementation in the systemic school sector. The filtering process, though, means that recommendations from such reports have varying impacts between and within organizations. Recommendations from such documents have little, if any, impact at the level of an individual preschool or childcare center. At the same time, the sociocultural context in this landscape works to mediate policy by influencing the production, transmission, and evaluation of knowledge to structure and shape what is valued by teachers as legitimate knowledge. The result is the current mismatch between policy, both overt and implied, and practice.

If policymakers, educators, and parents are serious about enhancing young children's participation in science and technology, the *status quo* must be challenged. Statements about the encouragement of thinking and problem solving in authentic scientific and technological contexts are strong in the research literature (Burkam, Lee, & Smerdon, 1997) and are generally well represented in educational policy and curriculum documents. Yet, evidence on children's experiences in mathematics and science, and now with technology, together with information on young people's (especially women's) pursuit of careers in math, science, and engineering fields, suggest that interest and skill in scientific problem solving is at an all time low (Burkam, Lee, & Smerdon, 1997; Haplern, 1992b).

Recently, the immediacy of global access to unimagined volumes of interconnected knowledge and information via the Internet has challenged traditional conceptions of teachers, teaching, and learning. Early childhood teachers, like other teachers, must be skilled in facilitating children's abilities to access, process, and construct knowledge. They must embrace the pedagogical possibilities of computers and related technologies to change the models of knowledge construction that prevail in early childhood classrooms. In science they must deal explicitly and thoughtfully with problem solving in scientific and technological domains. Ideally, education is about leading and guiding people to be the thinkers and doers in their world. Early childhood educators must prepare children for a world that is even more information rich than today's. Children must be empowered to be critical thinkers, problem-solvers, and writers. And this empowering must commence from their very first experiences in group educational settings.

Clearly, in decision making about the provision of science and information technology experiences, both distributional and constitutional attributions have affected current policy and practice in early childhood settings. But, as has been argued here, it seems that the barriers blocking initiatives to integrate meaningful science and computer-based experiences across the curriculum are not necessarily the infrastructure and resource problems that are most readily and frequently identified as inhibiting implementation of appropriate learning experiences. Also implicated are the more complex constitutional dimensions at both the micro and macro levels. And, as suggested by Hayden in chapter 1, it is the informal dimensions—the nonpolicies—that are perhaps the most powerful mediators of policy and practice.

Creating environments to facilitate authentic experiences does not require complete overhauls of existing practices and structures. Rather, it involves processes of adapting existing strategies and, at least for some, reconceptualizing views of science and technology, and the processes of learning and teaching about it in early childhood education. Importantly, it means recognizing that each teacher's actions are stimulated by needs that are subordinated to personally constructed goals. While these personal needs and goals are at odds with those of organizational policies, there will be little interest and effort to focus on science and technology in meaningful ways.

What is clear is that teacher knowledge, support, skill, and commitment are central to planning environments that incorporate effective, hands-on, scientific, and computer-supported learning and facilitate thinking and problem solving through explicit as well as implicit means. It is the teacher who must plan learning experiences that engage children in thinking that is conceptually rich, coherently organized, and persistently knowledge-building (Lipman, 1991) and enriched, rather than constrained, by the vastness and interconnectedness of scientific and related knowledge. Rarely though, according to Haplern (1992a), are children taught how to discover and solve novel problems, evaluate the strength and nature of evidence, use reasons to support conclusions, recognize propaganda and other persuasive techniques, consider likely outcomes of actions, and question claims, especially in science.

Conclusion

In this chapter I have explored some of the influences that have an impact on decisions about science and information technology practice in early childhood settings.

Perhaps the most important pedagogical challenge currently facing early education is how best to enhance children's thinking and problem solving skills in areas such as science and technology. Growing largely from concerns that many students function poorly when it comes to applying complex thinking in these areas, enhancing science and technology teaching should be high on the policy agenda.

It was suggested that explanations for the limited focus on science and adoption of computers in early childhood settings are more complex than first thought. While teachers may report that they have not used technology because they can't afford the equipment, examination of constitutional processes—the sociocultural context of early education, the structural characteristics of the teaching-learning processes, and the role of classroom mediational devices, particularly teacher beliefs—confirms that much more influences decision making than money and policy documents. As I have argued, while science and technology are commonly considered of limited interest and value to women, the task of encouraging the largely female early childhood teacher population to plan and implement appropriate scientific and technological learning experiences for children will continue to present a major challenge for education.

The limited confidence and expertise in science and technology of many early childhood teachers and support staff acts to both shape and mirror girls' limited experiences in science and information technology at school. But if our communities are serious about enhancing young children's participation in science, information technology, and related problem solving activities, there needs to be a concerted effort to challenge the social construction of science and information technology discourses and practices. Specifically, one might conclude that early childhood teachers must be actively supported to gain personal confidence with science and technology as a means of better understanding the world and become more knowledgeable about enhancing young learners' conceptions of science and technology. All children, and especially girls, must have regular, hands-on experimentation, which they are required to report on and from which they should draw conclusion; but as Burkam, Lee, and Smerdon (1997) admit, moving teachers to provide more appropriate science teaching is not an easy task.

References

Burkam, D., Lee, V.E., & Smerdon, B.A. (1997). Gender and science learning in high school: Subject matter and laboratory experiences. *American Educational Research Journal,* 34(2): 297–331.

Byrne, E. (1994). *Critical Filters: Hidden Helix. Policies for Advancing Women in Science and Technology.* A discussion paper prepared for the Women in Science, Engineering and Technology Working Party. University of Queensland.

Chi, M., Glaser, R., & Rees, E. (1982). Expertise in problem solving. In R. Sternberg (Ed.). *Advances in the Psychology of Human Intelligence.* Vol. I (pp. 7–75). Hillsdale, NJ: LEA.

Clements, D., & Nastasi, B. (1992). Computers and early education. In M. Gettinger, S.N. Elliott, & T.R. Kratochwill (Eds.). *Advances in school psychology: Preschool and early childhood treatment directions* (pp. 187–246). Hillsdale, NJ: LEA.

Elliott, A. (1984). Computers in the preschool: Thinking it through. In J. Hughes (Ed.). *Computers and education: Dreams and realities* (pp. 43–46). Sydney: CEGNSW.

Elliott, A. (1988). Preschoolers' communicative behaviors while participating in computer based learning activities: Some preliminary findings. In F. Lovis & E.D. Tagg (Eds.). *Computers in Education* (pp. 132–144). Amsterdam: Elsevier Science Publications B.V.

Elliott, A. (1995a, July). *Pedagogical Issues and Computer-Supported Learning in Early Childhood.* Paper presented at the World Computers in Education Conference, Birmingham, UK.

Elliott, A. (1995b). Scaffolding young children's learning in early childhood settings. In M. Fleer (Ed.). *DAP Centrism. Challenging Developmentally Appropriate Practice* (pp. 23–34). Canberra: AECA.

Elliott, A. (1996, March). Are schools making a difference? Changes in students' computer experiences and attitudes 1987–1994. In *Proceedings of the Thirteenth International Conference on Technology and Education,* Vol. 2 (pp. 679–691). New Orleans.

Elliott, A., & Hall, N. (1986, May). *Across Curriculum Computer Based Activities in the First Years of School.* Paper presented at the First Years of School Conference, Sydney.

Elliott, A., & Hall, N. (1997). The impact of self-regulatory teaching strategies on "at-risk" preschoolers' mathematical learning in a computer mediated environment. *Journal of Computing in Childhood Education,* 8(2/3): 187–198.

Fleer, M. (1995). Challenging developmentally appropriate practice. In M. Fleer (Ed.). *DAP centrism. Challenging Developmentally Appropriate Practice* (pp. 1–10). Canberra: AECA.

Greeno, J. (1992). Mathematical and scientific thinking in classrooms and other situations). In D. Haplern (Ed.). *Enhancing thinking skills in the sciences and mathematics* (pp. 39–61). Hillsdale, NJ: LEA.

Haplern, D. (1992a). A cognitive approach to improving thinking skills in the sciences and mathematics. In D. Haplern (Ed.). *Enhancing thinking skills in the sciences and mathematics* (pp. 1–14). Hillsdale, NJ: LEA.

Haplern, D. (1992b). *Sex differences in cognitive abilities,* 2 ed. Hillsdale, NJ: LEA.

Hawkins, D. (1985). The nature of the problem. In M. Apelman, D. Hawkins, & P. Morrison (Eds.). *Critical Barriers Phenomenon in Elementary Science* (pp. 23–47). Grand Forks, ND: North Dakota Study Group on Evaluation.

Lipman, M. (1991). *Thinking in education.* New York: Cambridge University Press.

Mandler, G. (1975). *Mind and emotion.* New York: Wiley.

Nisbett, R., & Ross, L. (1980). *Human inference. Strategies and shortcomings of human judgement.* Englewood Cliffs, NJ: Prentice-Hall.

Office of the Chief Scientist. (1995). *Women in Science, Engineering and Technology.* A discussion paper prepared by the Women in Science, Engineering and Technology Advisory Group. Department of the Prime Minister and Cabinet, Canberra: AGAPS.

Pajares, M.F. (1992). Teachers' beliefs and educational research: Cleaning up a messy construct. *Review of Educational Research,* 62(3): 307–332.

Perry, G., & Rivkin, M. (1992). Teachers and science. *Young Children,* 47(4): 9–16.

Quilter, D., & Harper, E. (1988). Why we didn't like math and why we can't do it. *Educational Researcher,* 30(2): 121–131.

Rivkin, M. (1992). Science is a way of life. *Young Children,* 47(4): 4–9.

Spender, D. (1995). Nattering on the net. Women, power and cyberspace. Toronto: Garamond Press.

Stigler, J., & Baranes, R. (1988). Culture and mathematics learning. In E.Z. Rothkopf (Ed.). *Review of Research in Education 1988* (pp. 253–306). Washington, DC: American Educational Research Association.

Stodosky, S. (1988). *The subject matters.* Chicago: University of Chicago Press.

Tweney, R.D., & Walker, B.J. (1990). Science education and the cognitive psychology of science. In F.B. Jones, & L. Idol (1990), (Eds.). *Dimensions of thinking and cognitive instruction* (pp. 291–310). Hillsdale. NJ: LEA.

Vygotsky, L.S. (1978). *Mind in society. The development of higher psychological processes.* Cambridge, MA: Harvard University Press.

Chapter 26

The Kindergarten Landscape

Isabel M. Doxey

Abstract

In this chapter, the philosophical perspectives of behaviorists, maturationists, and constructivists are used to analyze the curriculum, the family, and the policy contexts of three kindergarten program narratives. The analyses point to an enhanced role for kindergartens in Canada and elsewhere.

Introduction

In this chapter, children's perspectives are used to illustrate components of kindergarten programs and services. Verbal portraits that could have been written by children will address three key components (Corter & Park, 1993):

1. Time—schedules and space organization,
2. People—teachers and parents who are connected to the program,
3. Things—including materials, toys, and equipment that children use.

The three narratives are fictional composites that represent three identified philosophical positions reflected in the nature of the curriculum: maturationist, behaviorist, and constructivist. These narratives also serve as vehicles to present issues related to four ecological perspectives: the nature of children, the family circumstances, the administration, and the policy level.

Mai's Story

My name is Mai. I am so glad that I am old enough now to go to kindergarten. I'm not really four yet, but I will be very soon. I can dress myself.

I can say my phone number. I can print my name. In kindergarten I think I will learn my letters, how to make numbers. I don't need to know about colors because I already know all that.

At home I know how to put my doll's clothes in the suitcase when I am finished playing with her. In my kindergarten there is a place where we can play with dolls. I like to be the mummy and make my doll be the baby and cry when she doesn't want to go to bed, or eat her supper. I like my doll at home better because at school there are only two dolls. At home I have a lot of time to play with my doll. But in kindergarten the teacher only lets us play for a little while and only after we finish our work. Real work the teacher calls it. We are learning to make letters. But I can do it easily and I wish I didn't have to do the letters with the big pencils. I even know how to make S because it is in my sister's name. But I still have to practice before I can play. I never go to the block area because the boys always go there.

I wish we would get some new clothes in the house area, or other things to use to play doctor. Sometimes at home I use one of my mother's old handbags and fill it with all my news, just the way she does. I pretend that I have appointments. But at school we don't have anything to write with in the doll center. We only practice our printing with the big fat pencils and the teacher says we are too young to use pens. She says that we all have to do our printing together so that she can teach us the right way to make letters. I like my own way, and I try to write the letters like my mom does in her little book. If the other girl is in the doll center then I sometimes go to the book area. We have lots of books at school. At home, I like to look at my sister's book and pretend that I can read like she can. At school we only have baby books with pictures and some words. I really can't read my own pretend way with these. I need books with lots and lots of words to do my kind of reading. Today the teacher asked me to sit with her and tell her the names of some colored blocks she had. I knew them all. But she didn't have mauve. I love mauve. At school the teacher only asked me about red, green and blue. Not mauve. My teacher is really nice. When we have play time she doesn't talk to us unless we are too noisy. We just play by ourselves. She sometimes watches and reminds us of the rules, like about getting ready for tidy up time and our snack.

We do snack all together after we tidy up our play things. But sometimes I wish I could just have some juice before I play because I get thirsty. We only can get one cup of juice and then we all have to go to the bathroom. I can really remember all the rules. The teacher doesn't have to tell me what to do like she does with some of the boys.

Mai's Curriculum

Is this an exemplary kindergarten? It could be. As Ashby (1996) notes "a curriculum is a trading post on the cultural boundary between generations, sexes, cultures". He further comments that "curriculum development is necessarily cultural construction work". (p. 13)

Mai's experiences illustrate a curriculum that represents a maturationist philosophy in its organization of time, people, and things (Doxey, 1992). Maturationists view these dimensions through the filter of the child's maturity, or readiness needs. Thus time is scheduled to balance active and quiet activities, with a mid-morning snack and washroom routine because this is what the majority of four-year-old's "need". The teacher sees her role primarily as providing the right environmental match with these needs of the majority of the children and then supporting the children without intervention or interference. Thus she would provide large red pencils, appropriate to the physical coordination readiness of the majority of her four-year-olds.

From a maturationist perspective, these young kindergarten children need preparation. To an exemplary kindergarten teacher this preparation means that instruction is matched to the children's level of learning readiness. Practice in printing letters and numerals, in recognizing colors, could thus ensure competence in these knowledge and skill areas. Time for play is considered necessary for beginning kindergartners. However, it is also important, from this maturationist perspective, to balance work and play times during the day to match the expected attention and concentration level of the majority of these four-year-olds.

Mai's teacher had not had specific training or education in child development. What she knows about children comes from her own personal experiences as a grandmother and her general beliefs about education. Her certification is a BEd degree that endorses her to teach any age group in the elementary school. Before she took the kindergarten assignment she taught Grade 2 in Western Canada, then Grade 1 in a small Ontario town. This is a common background in many parts of the world. It was traditionally believed that teachers could transfer their skills and knowledge about teaching to any grade level. The position that work with young children demanded specialized training and skills was not widely accepted. Early childhood education training now tends to include studies about child development as a foundation for exemplary kindergarten programs (Teacher Education Council Ontario, 1993).

Mai's Family
Mai's family are fortunate to have access to a public kindergarten program. Her parents contribute to education expenses through their taxes rather than paying a regular fee. In Canada, if she attended a private school, her parents would continue to pay taxes, yet would also pay the school fee.

Mai represents close to half-a-million Canadian children between the ages of 4 and 11 who live in female lone-parent families. These children tend to be at increased risk in a range of difficulties compared with children in two-parent families. Although Mai's mother did not complete secondary school, she has had a two-year college education as a mature student. Since a recent study suggests that the mother's level of education was the strongest predictor of a child's vocabulary ability prior to entering school, Mai seems to have had a good start in this area (NLSCY survey, 1997). Mai does not seem to exhibit any of the behavioral warning signs that could be barriers to a child's future educational performance.

Mai's Policy Context
Mai attends a half-day program that is sometimes referred to as junior kindergarten. In Ontario children may enroll and attend if they have their fourth birthday before the end of the calendar year in which they begin school. Junior kindergartens have existed in Ontario since the 1940s. However, they are threatened with extinction. Current government policies and funding decisions have determined that the provision of junior kindergarten programs should be local options and not financed, nor mandated by provincial policies and regulations.

It is still possible for an Ontario School Board to make junior kindergarten programs accessible. There are no regulations prohibiting this. However, as Hayden has noted, sometimes the distributive factor may have a more powerful influence on policy decisions than the regulatory one (Hayden, this volume, chapter 2). In the case of junior kindergartens this is very true. When financing becomes threatened, the will of local elected or administrative officials for such policy initiatives as junior kindergarten diminishes.

Many other provinces in Canada never did offer junior kindergarten programs in the public education system. Consequently access was totally driven by market forces. If the interest, or client base, seemed to be there, private kindergartens proliferated. In Alberta, when early childhood services faced cuts, the number of private kindergartens increased. This is now also happening in parts of Ontario.

As Hayden has noted, policy analyses can involve the review of policy content and the *nonexistence* of policies (Hayden, 1994). In Ontario, directions about curriculum are *nonpolicies*. The only mandated source to guide teacher planning is a new provincial Ministry document, *The Ontario Curriculum*. It defines attainment expectations by the end of the primary division or Grade 3. Currently, in Ontario there are no clear outcomes specified for either the junior or senior kindergartens from the provincial Ministry of Education and Training. Many school boards have, however, developed their own profiles of expected achievements for junior and kindergarten children and supporting materials for teachers. These vary greatly in scope, emphasis on social or cognitive development, and the implications for instructional strategies and materials.

Bo's Story

My name is Bo. I'm in a primary kindergarten. This is not just an ordinary kindergarten. Its called "primary" because I'm getting ready for Grade 1. I go to this kindergarten to learn. My mom says school is not just for fun. I need a foundation. My cousin says I need to get ready for *real* school and that's why I have to go to kindergarten. I don't really *have* to go. But my mom says it's really important and all the other kids I know go to kindergarten. I think I am already ready cause I can print all the letters, can say the alphabet, I know my colors and shapes, I can count to one hundred. I can print all the numbers too. But in my kindergarten I still have to do the lessons. Some of the kids can only print their name, and not other letters. Some make letters backwards. But I can do them all. My mom taught me before I came to school. She bought a program so she could teach me. I wish the teacher knew all that I could do. But she is so busy with lessons. I always get all my worksheets right. I never make the wrong numbers, or make them the wrong way. I can always match the right letter with the right picture. I really like to do worksheets. I am so good at them. At home my mom and I do worksheets. I will teach my little brother when he gets to be two years old. That's when I started to learn letters. I also started to learn Chinese ideograms. But they are really hard. I can only do a few of them. Some days I wish I could just play with my cars, because I know all the names of all the kinds I've got. I can write their names too, but those names are not the same kinds of words that we learn in my kindergarten. Sometimes we paint, but we are only allowed to do that after we finish our lessons and our real work. We go to gym. I wish I could just run around because the space is so big, but in the gym we have to practice. The teacher says we need to learn about fitness, and learn coordination. I don't know what this is. She calls things like walking on the line and skipping "skills". I think I have lots of skills. I don't know why I have to practice, practice all the time and why I can't just play with my cars.

I really hate snack time at school. I don't like cheese and crackers. I don't like to sit so long and wait for my turn. I know how to say please and thank you and sometimes at school I just say pees, pees. Some of the kids laugh but the teacher just thinks it's because I can't pronounce "Please". I can but sometimes I just get really bored and don't want to. Our class is so big. I don't think the teacher knows I like cars. Today we learned about hibernation, about animals sleeping in the winter. I know all about that too because when I went to the zoo with my aunt and cousins we saw one of the bears just all curled up like it was dead. My big cousins are really smart and they told me all about hibernating. In two days my mom comes for an interview. The teacher will tell her the marks that I got on the test. I know the marks were good because I know all about matching letters and pictures and about printing numbers. Maybe my mom will say I don't have to go to school any more and that she can teach me at home. Then I might have time to play with my cars.

Bo's Curriculum

Bo's teacher represents those kindergarten teachers who hold a predominantly behaviorist philosophy about children's behavior and development, the teaching and learning processes, how to organize a program, and the role of instruction. In Bo's kindergarten class, the timetable identifies separate times for the specific subjects of music, gym, mathematics, prereading and preprinting. Many of these times involve direct instruction by the teacher for the whole class.

A behaviorist teacher believes strongly in the emphasis on learning skills, particularly those skills that she feels the children need for the next step of their education. In the case of Bo's teacher, these are skills of auditory and visual discrimination that she believes underpin reading success. This kindergarten teacher also has a sequenced preprinting series of direct instruction lessons. She says that parents like to see how their children are learning to properly form letters of the alphabet and numerals.

The classroom space suits the time scheduling and this teacher's behaviorist philosophy. Bo has his own desk. He has different workbooks for his printing, for reading, for mathematics, and for homework. The printing books have lines so that he can practice making his letters and numerals with the "correct" size and direction.

Bo's teacher takes her instructional responsibilities for his learning most seriously. She plans direct instruction lessons with a focus on skill development. For example, she conducts regular prereading lessons to develop the visual discrimination skills that she believes are precursors for beginning reading. Although much current research provides support for attention to children's socioemotional development (Corter & Park, 1992), Bo's kindergarten teacher seems most pleased when his behavior is compliant and correct. She has clear discipline and management procedures and consistently reminds the children of the rules that she has made. When punishment is required her favorite strategy is to use "time-out".

She also communicates with Bo's parents when required, usually through report cards with test results. She is conscientious about documenting his progress and in sharing the products of his efforts to have his parents understand what and how he is learning. She appreciates their concern about his kindergarten preparation for the "real school" and the expectations of the more formal learning of a Grade 1 classroom. Bo regularly takes his papers home and his parents understand that they have much responsibility for his achievements and must help him complete his homework.

Bo's teacher is satisfied with her curriculum and feels confident that Bo's progress and behavior are within those expected of typical kindergarten children.

Bo's Family

Bo's parents represent that segment of the population in Canada that is attentive to, and concerned most about, their children's school performance. For Bo's parents, report cards are the primary source of information about his school achievements. The report card lets them know that he is "on target". Of course they use this information to also confirm that they are "good parents," conforming to what they perceive as appropriate, albeit middle-class values. They think education is very important. They respect the teacher as a professional and unquestioningly accept her assessment of Bo's school behavior and progress.

Although they do not consider themselves wealthy, they feel that they are comfortable. Their family income is above the average of $54,800 of Canadian families like theirs. Bo's family context determines that he is, thus, better off financially than a child in just about any other of the 174 countries on the United Nations 1996 Human Development Scale.

As a child in a two-parent family, Bo is less likely to display hyperactivity, emotional or conduct disorder, or any social impairment. He is less likely than a child from a lone-parent family to repeat a grade as he moves through the education system in Canada.

Bo's Policy Context

Bo's kindergarten represents a *status quo* position in relation to policy and policy development. Many of the features of his program exemplify policies that have been so thoroughly implemented and accepted that they may be labeled "folk wisdom". These policies frame decisions about

1. the administration and organization of the program,
2. the teacher certification and training,
3. the place of kindergarten in the education/childcare systems.

Bo's kindergarten operates for children to attend for a half-day only. There were not any admission requirements, other than completed immunization. As an Ontario public school kindergarten, his program is totally funded with a combination of provincial grants and funds collected through local property taxes. His class size is determined by the collective agreement that the local elementary school teachers' federation negotiated with the Board of Education and the elected trustees. According to policies of this locally elected Board, he can fail or even repeat his kindergarten experience if the teacher determines that he has not progressed sufficiently in developing those skills determined to be necessary as preparation for admission to Grade 1, or the primary level of the school system.

His teacher is certificated because her education and professional training meet the provincial requirements. As Bo's teacher has been teaching for more than 20 years, she received her certification, an Ontario Teacher's Certificate, before undergraduate degrees were required. At that time, it was also believed completion of a one-year teacher education program was adequate training for teaching any grade or children of any age. Bo's teacher has not always taught kindergarten. She taught grade 5, then grade 2. Her principal recommended that she accept the kindergarten assignment as she had shown her teaching competencies with older grades and thus would be capable of establishing proper management procedures for the kindergarten. The school principal was pleased to approve the teacher's order for the kindergarten level of workbooks of the series used in the Grades 1 and 2 classes of the school. Any knowledge of child development that Bo's teacher has was obtained through her own experiences as a parent or through her own readings. She has taken some university level courses, mainly to improve her salary rather than her practice. Coursework in child development was not considered core knowledge when she undertook her teacher training. She has not completed her degree, nor participated in other professional development coursework.

Her teaching is not supplemented by access to specialist teachers. She teaches her own music and gym classes. She can, however, request assistance from a primary resource teacher or even from one of the translators or social workers who are employees of her school board, but tends not to. She does not have any identified special needs children in her program, although inclusion, or integration, is mandated by provincial authorities.

The education system in the Canadian province where Bo lives does not require compulsory kindergarten attendance. However, it is a policy that local school boards provide access for all children to a kindergarten program one year before this compulsory school age. The purpose is school preparation. While children may socialize and participate in some play activities, the teachers, administrator's and Bo's parents believe that the emphasis must be on the foundation for academics and learning to behave appropriately as a good student.

Carlie's Story

My name is Carlie. I go to kindergarten for the whole day—I even stay for what my mother calls the extended day program: the childcare part. In my kindergarten we are always busy doing projects. Some days I get up early and don't want to eat breakfast because I've got another idea for our new project. You see, I really like hockey and I like to play with my big brothers. I get teased because I'm a girl but I can skate really fast. At school the other day the teacher read a book about the hockey sweater. I'm glad she told us the author so that I can see if he wrote any other books. I think I could ask the next time we go to the school library.

After the story our teacher suggested that we could plan to make the house and block center into an arena with a locker room. Am I ever excited! I asked my brothers if they could lend me their sweaters because the team name is on the sweater and it starts with C, just like my name. My cousin has a hockey sweater with my age—number 5. I want to ask him if I could bring it to school so we could use it in the locker room and pretend to be hockey players when we put on the sweaters. We have to talk all about plays and who will be the offence and the defense. I know about that. When we had a long planning talk about the locker room I said I could bring some sweaters. One of the boys said he could bring a trophy. The teacher said that we could make a big score board to keep track of all the goals and assists. We could put all the names of all the kids in the class on the board, even those girls who only want to play with dolls in the house area. I know the names of two other kids whose names start with C like mine. We could even bring in some pairs of skates and put them on the shelf with price tags and sizes. I said we would need a clock in the locker room so we would know when the periods of the game ended or when the practice should start. I said that I could make one at the art area. I think I could use a big round paper plate. But I'm not sure about how to make the hands go around. Maybe I'll ask Susie to help me. She can't run or walk very fast, like I can so, she doesn't do the same things that I do in the gym. But she could know about making clock hands. The teacher said that she would make some finger paint so that we could put it all over a big sheet of paper and make it look swirly like ice. Someone else is going to make some pretend hockey sticks and pucks. Someone else said she should plan to make pretend skates cause we really couldn't put on skates in the classroom. Two of the kids said they would paint big black skate things that they would cut out and put strings on so we could pretend to skate. I think that's a good idea because some of the kids have never never had skates on.

I just can't wait to get back to my kindergarten tomorrow with some more ideas to talk about in planning time. I'm so glad I go to this kindergarten. I love school. When my kindergarten teacher leaves and the childcare staff arrive, I can still work on my project. My mom really loves my school too. She comes in to work in our class when she gets time. She came two times this year. She looked in my portfolio and saw all the words I had put there that I said I knew. I know about a hundred words already. My teacher says I should become a good reader because I really like stories and I can remember so much about stores. I'm glad that my mom reads to me at home, even though she doesn't read English all that well. She learned to read when she was a little girl in Russia.

I could tell you so much about school, about my friends, about how we plan, about our projects, about my teacher and about when my mother comes. I could also show you all the things I put in my Portfolio. I hope the teacher takes some more pictures of us when we are making the locker room and the arena. I wonder if we should make tickets and have pretend hockey games?

Carlie's Curriculum

Carlie's curriculum represents a predominantly constructivist perspective, based on the theories of Piaget and Vygotsky.

Her day is organized in large blocks of time with minimal transitions. These times do not have separate subject designations, but rather are labeled to indicate the activity of the children. The core block in the morning is labeled *action time*. In the afternoon there is *project time*. The children identify choices, make decisions, and plan with the teacher, sometimes individually, sometimes in a small group.

During these blocks of time the teacher observes and interacts with children as individuals, or in small groups of two or three. She does instruct. However, her instruction is timed to what she observes. In essence, she scaffolds during these interactions, clarifying a situation for a child, offering information as either a clue, probe, or a problem-solving strategy. Sometimes she suggests other people or materials, or sources of information such as books or computer programs to help a child resolve a problem.

The teacher would describe her role as a "facilitator". She feels that she must try to highlight the feature of the child's activity that moves the child to more complex activity, or thinking. Sometimes this highlighting involves suggesting that a child work with another child, or join a small group to hold a conference with the teacher.

The other children in Carlie's class are also her instructors. She will ask them for help, or for collaboration depending on her project. Thus she sometimes may work alone, or with the teacher, or with a few other children. Total class groupings are rare in Carlie's class, although sometimes they have a visitor, or a gym period, or music class, outdoor play, or a library visit as a whole class. Some days there is also a special teacher as Carlie's teacher has planning time. During the extended day or childcare program, other children may attend from other classes so that there is a multiage mix. There will also be other trained educators and assistants with the responsibility for planning and carrying out the extended day or childcare program.

The materials and equipment in Carlie's classroom are very different from those that might be found in either Mai's or Bo's room. At the book corner, for example, there are books that are far too sophisticated for any of the children to read independently. However, they may contain project-related information that the teacher could read for the children. There are also simple books that nearly all of the children can read and understand. These are books that the children may have made themselves. The "Bag book" is but one example. It was a previous class project when all the children brought bags that had words on them. Some of the children put them together to make a "Bag book". They regularly read this together, helping each other with labels that one of the children might forget. They enjoy comparing the letters in their names, or in the labels of the bags that they used. With this description of the book area, one may see that materials in Carlie's kindergarten classroom are varied, multipurpose, of varying degrees of complexity and function. They invite the children to respond as individuals by exploring, comparing, classifying, manipulating, linking to print, observing, and talking about words and ideas. These features illustrate how Carlie's teacher interprets concepts of developmentally appropriate practice (Bredekamp & Willer, 1997) and applies what she understands of the theories of Piaget and Vygotsky.

Although Carlie's first language is English, many of her kindergarten classmates speak a language other than English at home. This linguistically and culturally diverse Kindergarten population is representative of what one might find in many Canadian urban areas. This is a 1990s challenge for the kindergarten landscape: how to provide for this multiculturalism without compromising programming principles that are characteristic of exemplary kindergarten programs (Corter & Park, 1992, Doxey, 1997). According to Katz's classification (1994) this kindergarten represents a quality program.

Carlie's Family

Carlie's mother has a university education and holds an undergraduate and a graduate degree. Although her parents are now separated, they share a duplex so that Carlie sees her father regularly. Both parents take much interest in her education. They share duties of taking her to her Orff music class, and to local cultural locations and events. They believe strongly that they are educating a "whole child" and that the early years are important years.

Carlie does not belong to the one in four children who lives in a Canadian low income family, but rather to the 76.1% of children who live in family circumstances classified as above the median as well as above the low income cut-off. Although her parents might be legally separated, she is not a member of a socioeconomically disadvantaged family. As a current statistical report (NLSCY, 1996) suggests, Carlie belongs to that group of children whose vocabulary and math skills are explainable by the mother and father's level of education and occupation, the household income, and the family composition. Since the mother's level of education has been determined to be the strongest predictor of a child's vocabulary ability prior to entering school, Carlie may be expected to be as well endowed as she is.

Carlie's Policy Context

Carlie's program is only one illustration of how a teacher responds to the policy context in the late 1990s. First of all there is the fact that this kindergarten even exists. With increasingly conservative policies and values in Canadian and other societies, those who advocate for programs and services for young children are having serious struggles. Not only are funding cuts having an impact on these programs, but also there are different and often more demanding curriculum expectations for the children's achievements and progress.

Carlie's teacher is sensitive to the family circumstances of her kindergarten children. This is in response to their own outlook, but also reflects policies of parent involvement in her school. For example, there is now a School Advisory Council that replaces an earlier Home and School Association. Where these exist, these councils are expected to have increasing authority for curriculum and staffing decisions.

Carlie's integrated curriculum and inclusive classroom also match current policy initiatives. In addition, her teacher is expected to undertake more extensive assessments and documentation of Carlie's learning needs and progress according to provincially determined learning outcomes and clearly identified standards of performance criteria. Were Carlie in an upper-primary classroom rather than a Kindergarten she would do required tests with the results compared nationally, even internationally.

Her teacher is a recent graduate of a teacher education program and is in touch with these and other policy and pedagogical changes. The late 1990s is an era of educational change. Caught in the current supply and demand situation that exists, Carlie's teacher belongs to the less than 10% of those from her graduating year who found jobs with school boards in Ontario. After two years as a supply or substitute teacher, and a move to a long-term occasional contract status, she now is in the tenured stream. However, she is expected to keep her professional profile up to date, documenting ways that she has worked toward her own bi-annual "best practice" goals within the context of those of her school board. She has noted the increasing paperwork in her school as accountability becomes a major focus.

In Carlie's story we noted that she attended a childcare program within the school. This is not common, although it is a new initiative in her school district as in others. The childcare staff and kindergarten teachers communicate to reconcile plans, policies and perceptions of children. At present there is not any scheduled time, financial support, or policy mandate to do this.

As a kindergarten child of the late 1990s, Carlie lives in a country that was a supporter of the Declaration of the Rights of the Child. Although her kindergarten landscape undoubtedly could be improved, she is indeed more fortunate than many children living elsewhere in the world. Her program truly does exemplify a developmentally appropriate, exemplary, "best practices" kindergarten.

Conclusion

Which kindergartens are exemplary? Which are endangered? Which are sustainable? Do kindergarten landscapes need redesigning to make them less endangered and more sustainable? Unequivocally yes. There are questions about what to do and how to begin.

Recommendations about these questions may be considered from four aspects:

1. listen to the children,
2. ask the parents,
3. consider the professionals,
4. regularly assess policy.

Listen to the Children

Van Scoy reminds kindergarten educators to pay attention to the four *E*'s: experience, expression, extension, and evaluation when planning the early childhood curriculum. Polito (1993) offers teachers the advice that they should make note of, and plan for, interactions between the children's play and their work. Ashby's (1996) directive about the power and role of culture can be taken into account when educators listen to the children and try to be sensitive to the cultural and linguistic diversity in the child population of the kindergarten. Katz (1994) suggests that it is the bottom-up perspective, or the children's perspective, that is a crucial one for determining the quality of any program.

Ask the Parents

The expectations of parents for the outcomes of the kindergarten program can provide the policymaker and the educator with some direction. Many parents are committed advocates for their own child's program. They can be helped to organize for quality programs for *all*, not just some, children. The message is that kindergarten teachers should carefully consider the message they are communicating about the role and value of the kindergarten program. They can ally themselves with parents and provide the necessary information about the criteria and characteristics of exemplary programs or best practices for early childhood education. Policymakers can be influenced by the parent clients as taxpayers to carefully consider the issues around full-day programs—more individualized instruction, the quality and expertise of the teachers, and the cost-effectiveness of the kindergarten program from a prevention rather than a remediation perspective (Valpy, 1997). If 98% of parents (Corter & Park, 1992) claim to desire more academic focus in the kindergarten program, policymakers should use this information as only one piece of the puzzle when creating or modifying policy and funding formulas.

Consider the Professionals

What should be the degree of influence on policies of the research and theoretical literature about kindergarten landscapes? Kindergarten teachers, their associations, parents, and concerned taxpayers need direction and support to be advocates for sustaining exemplary early childhood programs. Policymakers should be urged to make research based decisions. To do this they need information about program access and cost-effectiveness. Much research, for example, has suggested that teachers' informal, day-to-day assessments of children's socializing, problem-solving abilities and academic potentials are quite accurate in comparison with the reliability and predictability of normed tests. Research (Corter & Park, 1992) has provided data for decisions about class sizes, materials, groupings for positive teacher-child interactions, and teacher training and certification requirements for exemplary kindergarten programs. Research has also documented the need for philosophical and program coordination between childcare and kindergarten.

Regularly Assess Policy

As policies are dynamic not static, they need be regularly assessed to determine whether or not they are facilitative toward access to kindergarten programs, the curriculum outcomes, and toward the certification of teachers. Policies at all levels of all governments can be restrictive rather than enabling of initiatives, improvement, or change generally. The greatest challenge for the kindergarten landscapes has been identified by Kagan (1994) as making schools ready for children.

Glaser (1978) reminds us that kindergartens are really for children first and that children should not be expected to sacrifice their culture for school success. Indeed, this is the essence of the "children first" assumption of the United Nations Declaration of the Rights of the Child.

Are exemplary kindergarten environments sustainable? With improved marketing, leadership, and advocacy from early childhood educators, the answer must be absolutely—Yes!

References

Ashby, G. (1996). Culture and the Early Childhood Curriculum in Australia. *Early Child Development and Care* 123: 127–141.

Bredekamp, S., & Willer, B. (1997). *Developmentally Appropriate Practice*. (Revised Edition.) Washington, DC: NAE YC.

Corter, C., & Park, N. (1993). *What Makes Exemplary Kindergartens Effective?* Research Report, Ontario Ministry of Education: Queen's Park.

Doxey, I. (1992). Childcare and Education: Canadian Dimensions. Nelson: Toronto, Ontario.

Doxey, I. (March, 1997). *Exemplary Kindergartens*—address to Waterloo Region Roman Catholic School Board. Waterloo, Ontario.

Hayden, J. (1994). Half full or half empty? Children's services and the missing bits. In E. Mellor & K. Coombe (Eds.), *Issues in Early Childhood Services: Australian Perspectives.* (pp. 11–25). New York: WCB.

Kagan, S. (November 1994). Readying Schools for Young Children: Polemics and Priorities. *Phi Delta Kappan:* November: 226–233.

Katz, L. (November 1994). Perspectives on the Quality of Early Childhood Programs. *Phi Delta Kappan*: 200–205.

McLean, S. V., Hass, N., & Butler, B. (1994). Kindergarten curriculum: Enrichment and impoverishment. *Early Child Development and Care* 101: 7–12.

NLSCY (Summer 1997). Growing Up in Canada: A Detailed Portrait of Children and Young People. Research Report. *Interaction Vol. 11* (2): 31–34.

Polito, T. (1996). How play and work are organized in a kindergarten classroom. In *Journal of Research in Childhood Education 9(1)*: 47–57.

Valpy, M. (February, 1997). But what about childcare? In *Toronto Star*. February 17, p. 6.

Van Scoy, I. (Fall, 1995). Trading the 3R's for the 4E's: Transforming Curriculum. *Childhood Education* 72(1): 19–26.

The Way Forward

Chapter 27

British Columbia's Ministry for Children and Families: A Case Study in Progress

Alan R. Pence
Allison Benner

Abstract

In the period 1995–1997 the Government of British Columbia, in response to major concerns regarding the Province's ability to effectively protect children in their care, undertook to restructure and consolidate services to children and families within one new Ministry for Children and Families. The proposed thrust of the new ministry toward community-based early intervention and prevention provides the opportunity for a reconceptualization of early childhood services that better supports the well-being of children, families, and communities across British Columbia. As the Ministry is still relatively young in its development, it is not yet possible to determine the success of the reforms undertaken. In this chapter, distributional and constitutional factors that could enhance or limit the new ministry's potential to achieve its goals are discussed.

Introduction

On September 26, 1996, the Premier of British Columbia announced the formation of a new Ministry for Children and Families that would bring together child and family programs previously delivered by five different ministries of the provincial government. The new ministry included not only the consolidation of services within one ministry, but also a new regional planning and delivery system to promote integrated service delivery and more opportunities for parents and communities to shape services. The new ministry was also directed to develop and implement a province-wide strategy for early intervention and prevention.

The creation of the Ministry for Children and Families was the culmination of an extensive review process that began with an investigation into the death of a young child at the hands of his mother (Gove, 1995) and ended with the government-commissioned response to the Gove Report, *British Columbia's Child, Youth and Family Serving System—Recommendations for Change* (Morton, 1996). Both reports identified the need for an integrated, coordinated, child-centered system to meet the needs of children and families in British Columbia.

The three defining approaches of the new ministry—early support and prevention, better integration of services, and the greater involvement of families and communities in shaping services— all have the potential to foster an early childhood service system that better meets the needs of children and families, and childcare services may provide a particularly strong foundation for the development of such a system, as they reach the greatest number of families. The majority of the new ministry's programs are targeted to children and families "at risk". While such programs may benefit individual families (and by extension, society), they have little potential to engage whole communities in creating a culture that values children and families—and that, ultimately, is what is necessary to assist children and families "at risk". Despite childcare's strong potential to strengthen children, families and communities—both as an entry point to other services and as a vehicle for community and social development—a number of factors constrain its potential within the new ministry. These factors include the vulnerability of childcare programs within the new ministry, attitudes toward childcare, and a narrow conception of the nature and purpose of childcare services within the new ministry and society as a whole. These factors are discussed below with a view to illuminating the landscape of early childhood services, and of suggesting new possibilities for childcare to strengthen children, families and communities.

Childcare in British Columbia

On January 1, 1997, responsibility for childcare programs and services was transferred from the Ministry of Women's Equality to the new Ministry for Children and Families. Depending on how childcare is seen in the new ministry, this transfer has the potential to strengthen or weaken childcare for families, childcare providers, and communities across British Columbia.

Within the Ministry of Women's Equality, childcare was the single largest program area, accounting for over 80% of the ministry's budget in 1995–1996. In contrast, childcare programs are only a small part of the range of child and family programs within the Ministry for Children and Families, accounting for approximately 14% of the ministry's budget for 1997–1998. There is, therefore, the risk that childcare will be "lost" in such a large ministry, particularly one where media attention and the majority of programs are focused on "at risk" families experiencing a crisis.

Childcare has received focused attention from the British Columbia government only within the past five years, a factor that increases its vulnerability in the new ministry. Despite a substantial investment of new money in childcare (over $100 million since 1992) and the creation of a range of new programs and services, the provincial government has yet to articulate or implement a consistent, comprehensive vision for childcare. The current complement of programs and services, while supporting a continuum of childcare choices: such as licensed and license-not-required, center-based and family-based, nonprofit and commercial, does so in a piecemeal fashion, rather than as part of an overall strategy for strengthening the childcare system. The provincial government's failure to clarify its vision for childcare reflects a widespread ambivalence among policymakers and society-at-large about the role of childcare in the lives of children, families and communities.

Childcare in the Lives of Children, Families, and Communities

Changes in the labor force, in family structure, and in the demographics over the past three decades have generated a dramatic increase in the need for childcare in British Columbia. Single-parent families now account for approximately 20% of families in the province. Over two-thirds of women with children under the age of six participate in the labor force and the majority of two-parent families require two incomes to maintain an adequate standard of living (Statistics Canada, 1995). These and other factors, such as the increasing diversity of families and the prevalence of part-time work and atypical work schedules, have affected the demand for childcare and the types of childcare required. Data from the Canadian National Childcare Study, collected in 1988 (Lero, Pence, Shields, Brockman, & Goelman, 1992), indicate that, at that time, more than 75% of children in British Columbia between the ages of birth and six were receiving some form of nonparental childcare and approximately 50% had two or more arrangements weekly (Pence, 1992); assuredly the percentage of children receiving care has increased since that time.

In response to the increased demand for childcare, governments and communities have responded with a range of programs and services to meet the childcare needs of families. However, despite the fact that childcare is an established part of contemporary life, and despite evidence in support of quality childcare, policymakers and the public alike continue to have doubts about the appropriateness of childcare services for young children. There remains a persistent attitude that childcare, far from mitigating risk factors, may itself constitute a risk factor. Fragmented funding and delivery systems across Canada and the absence of a national or provincial childcare policy are but the most obvious expressions of this ambivalence, resulting in a "nonsystem" of childcare in most Canadian provinces, British Columbia included (Pence, 1993). Such ambivalence limits the potential for childcare policies and programs to play as strong a role as they could in strengthening the lives of children, families, and communities. This factor has a particular bearing on the potential of the new Ministry for Children and Families to meet its mandate.

The Importance of Quality Childcare
A significant number of children in British Columbia may be at particular risk of neglect during the preschool years when they are in the greatest need of support if they are to realize their future potential as individuals and as citizens. Canadian and international childcare research confirms that, while high-quality childcare can enhance children's development, low-quality childcare may have harmful effects. Children from high-resource families are often able to compensate for the effects of poor quality care, but children from socially and economically disadvantaged families are less likely to have access to experiences that could provide such protective buffers (Goelman & Pence, 1988).

Research evidence consistently supports the finding that high-quality childcare services do not have a negative impact on children's development (Lamb & Sternberg, 1990; McGurk, Caplan, Hennessey, & Moss, 1993). Indeed, in Sweden children commencing childcare during their first year of life outperform home-care-only children on a range of measures at ages 8 and 13 (Andersson, 1989, 1992). The impact of high-quality care on high-risk children is even more dramatic. For example, the American High/Scope Perry Preschool longitudinal study, comparing at age 27 children who participated in a quality preschool program with children who had not, has estimated the returns to the preschool program as $7.16 for every $1.00 invested, based on reduced delinquency, substance misuse, and school dropout rates, as well as increased labor force participation (Schweinhart, Barnes, & Weikart, 1993).

When viewed through this lens, childcare becomes much more than "care-giving". In its broadest conceptualization, it refers to the diversity of contexts where the majority of young children in contemporary society spend most of their time, when not with their families. As such, it is the context where the majority of children are cared for during that time of their lives when they are most sensitive to the presence or absence of factors that shape their physical, social, emotional, and intellectual development, for better or worse, for their entire lives. An issue of this importance warrants the engagement of the entire community in a dialogue about quality childcare, and more generally, about what we as a society want for our children. In the absence of such a dialogue, childcare's potential is co-opted by a variety of limiting discourses.

Childcare: Taking a Broader View

Childcare's potential to shape the lives of children, families, and communities makes it essential that it be framed broadly enough to contain, rather than be contained by, shifts in public opinion and changes of government. As noted by Moss:

> The term "childcare" is problematic, both conceptually and in practice... If "childcare" is used specifically in relation to services, it is important to recognize that it is used as part of a very specific discourse. The "childcare for working parents" discourse is used by groups primarily interested in labor market, gender equality and welfare benefits issues; the main concept here is of services delivering a commodity (care) to a consumer (the parent or employer). But there are other discourses about services for young children. The "nursery education (or kindergarten) for over 3s" discourse is used by groups primarily interested in education and child development, while the "day care for children in need" discourse is used by groups primarily interested in child protection and the prevention of family breakdown: both of these discourses conceptualize services as a means for delivering a program or intervention. All three of these discourses take a narrow view of the role of services for young children, focusing on a particular need (for care or education or support) and a particular group (working parents or children aged over three or children at risk in social work terms) (Moss, 1997, p. 27).

Within the Ministry of Women's Equality, childcare was conceptualized partially as a support to women, who continue to assume primary responsibility for childcare in our society. More broadly, childcare was viewed as a critical support to the government's strategy to strengthen the economy:

> By investing in childcare, the BC government is helping parents participate in education and training and get the jobs they need to support their families... Better childcare means healthier families and communities—and a stronger

economy as British Columbians approach the 21ˢᵗ century. (Childcare: Choices at Work, Ministry of Women's Equality, 1994).

Within the context Moss outlines above, the Ministry of Women's Equality framed its childcare programs within the first discourse, that of "childcare for working parents"—as Moss points out, a narrow discourse. Given the impetus for the creation of the Ministry for Children and Families (the death of a young child at the hands of his mother), there is the risk that childcare will be framed in a different, but equally narrow discourse, that of "day care for children in need". However, as Moss points out:

> There is a fourth discourse, which starts from the needs of young children and their families and attempts to take a holistic view of these needs, recognizing them to be varied and inter-dependent. This discourse of "early childhood services" conceptualizes these services as institutions of cultural, social and economic significance, community resources that should be multi-functional to meet a variety of needs including care, education, socialization, health and family support, and that should be available to all families irrespective of parents' employment status. The discourse recognizes that early childhood services are an important part of the economic and social infrastructure, and as such meet important employment and social welfare goals. It rejects the concepts of services as businesses supplying a product to a consumer or as a means to deliver an intervention to a targeted group; the early childhood service serves multiple purposes for a variety of constituencies, and serves collective as well as individual ends (Moss, 1997, p. 28).

Moss's discussion is part of a larger international undertaking led by Peter Moss, based at the University of London, and Alan Pence, based at the University of Victoria. Moss and Pence edited an international volume, *Valuing Quality in Early Childhood Services: New Approaches to Defining Quality* (1994), that pointed the way toward a more inclusionary and community involving understanding of childcare. They have been joined by Gunilla Dahlberg of the University of Stockholm in authoring a second volume (Dahlberg, Moss, and Pence, 1999) that provides a reconceptualization of childcare as the basis for an inclusionary society which, as Moss notes, would serve "collective as well as individual needs".

Compartmentalization

A central tenet of Moss, Pence, and Dahlberg's current work is that the care of young children has been narrowly compartmentalized into a set of discrete and separate services, each of which follows an inwardly focused understanding of the role of childcare in the lives of children, families, and communities. For example, most early childhood educators receive extensive training in what should happen inside a program, but virtually no information on children and programs in a societal context. Indeed, in many cases, childcare programs fail to connect meaningfully even with the families of the children they serve (Larner & Phillips, 1994). The result is a landscape of programs, facilities, and services that lacks a vision of the common good, an idea of the total world of the child, or an appreciation of the importance of such linkages for the emotional well-being of children. This landscape is so pervasive as to be practically invisible. However, by exposing ourselves to other landscapes, we may come to a clearer vision of our own, and of how to transform it.

The Landscape of Reggio Emilia

A community in which childcare appears to have achieved an optimum level of integration and inclusion is the northern Italian city of Reggio Emilia. The early childhood programs of Reggio Emilia have achieved international recognition, primarily for the creativity of their programs and through the impact of *The 1,000 Languages of Children,* an international travelling exhibition of art produced by the children from the Reggio programs. The art, centers, and curriculum of the Reggio programs have captured the attention and imagination of early childhood educators across North America. Programs that "look like" and produce materials "like Reggio" have proliferated. Such commitment and emulation are in many respects laudatory; however, from the perspective of this chapter, it is not the trees but the forest that is of greatest interest. Taking this broader view, the relevant question becomes: What context has produced this exciting ecosystem of programs and activities?

That question led the lead author of this chapter (Pence) to undertake his own visit to Reggio Emilia, not only to view the programs of Reggio, but to spend time attempting to understand the region of Emilia Romagna and other regions of Italy. In this regard, Harvard University economist Robert Putnam's award-winning book, *Making Democracy Work—Care Traditions in Modern Italy* (1993), provides insights not generally found in the early childhood literature. Based on a detailed longitudinal study of six diverse regions of Italy, Putnam concluded that there is a powerful connection between the richness and diversity of informal social interaction, government performance, and societal and economic dynamism.

Putnam's empirical data rang true to Pence's impressionistic sense of Reggio Emilia, Emilia Romagna, northern Italy, and Italy more broadly. What struck Pence in his visit and related discussion about Reggio were not so much the "products" of Reggio—its curriculum and programs, for example, as impressive as they were—but its "processes": dialogues within and between programs; engagement in discussions regarding historical traditions of pedagogy and childhood; and children and programs with a vibrant physical presence in the broader community. Rebecca New's description of community involvement in Reggio Emilia's childcare programs highlights these processes:

> Throughout the school year, parents, teachers, and members of the larger community meet to discuss the challenges, opportunities, and controversies associated with their municipally-funded program. As a result of such meetings, adults in the community remain well-informed about the potentials of children and the benefits of participating in an educational context that provides the resources and the respect that children deserve. In Reggio Emilia, the concept of civic participation is interpreted as both privilege and responsibility, and thus becomes both a means and an end (New, 1997, p. 11).

The example of Reggio Emilia suggests that a supportive ecology is central to child, family, and community well-being. Without a supportive ecology, children and families will not thrive no matter how many dollars are directed to individual programs. With a supportive ecology, the creativity of locally developed childcare programs like Reggio's is possible; and adequate funding and meaningful policies and legislation are likely to follow, given the high degree of public support and involvement in the programs. The key to a supportive ecology is: "doing with", not "doing to"; creating links, not walls; engaging in dialogue; and focusing on strengths, assets, and the shared good.

In developing its regionally based child and family service system, the Ministry for Children and Families has the opportunity to promote a supportive ecology. Creating such a system in British Columbia will, however, be a major challenge. As John McKnight and others have pointed out (Kretzman & McKnight, 1993; Adams & Nelson, 1995), this has not been the history of health and social services in North America. Deeply ingrained practices will not change until their underlying paradigms are identified and a commitment to transformation is made. The experience of early childhood services in Majority World or "developing" countries serves as an interesting contrast to the North American experience.

Early Childhood Services in Majority World Countries

The work underway by Moss, Pence, and Dahlberg represents an emerging current of thought in early childhood services—one that sees as central the contextualization of services for children and families, and one which follows an inclusionary philosophy of involvement, dialogue, and shared decision making. That direction finds support in a second emerging literature, that of Early Childhood Care and Development (ECCD) in Majority World or "developing" countries (the term "early childhood care and development" is more typically found in this literature than "early childhood education or childcare").

Within the Ministry for Children and Families, as is the case across North America and in many countries in the western world, the primary challenge is to transform a highly specialized, compartmentalized system of community social services into one that includes parents, families, and communities in the planning, development, and delivery of services. In most Majority World countries, the challenge is quite different: to ensure that, in the process of development, such specialization and compartmentalization do not evolve in the first place, and to maintain an inclusionary, community-based process of capacity building. As such, many of the ideas and writings that emerge from Majority World ECCD are also helpful to the rebuilding efforts of governments and service providers in the West.

The Majority World literature on young children was, for much of the post-World War II period, focused on child survival as opposed to child development. In the 1990s, however, a new direction for early childhood discussions was hailed by Robert Myers in *The Twelve Who Survive*. The title refers to the greatly increased proportion of children in the Majority World who are surviving their early years, largely as the result of extensive efforts in the fields of child health. Myers argued that with such a dramatic change in survival rates, the world community must now turn its attention to the *quality* of survival. To this end, programs for early childhood care and development were deemed a key component to promote child well-being.

Myers and other key individuals associated with the development of Majority World childcare were keenly aware of the resource restrictions most communities face in the developing world and the need to ensure that programs draw from and complement the existing strengths within communities. The history of Majority World development efforts is replete with examples of external technology and expertise having little or no sustainable potential. Clearly, if programs for young children are to be sustained by communities, the communities must be actively involved and invested in their development. More so than in most western contexts, it was clear that the role of the ECCD specialists was to facilitate, support, and promote early childhood programs—not to provide prescriptive plans and recipes.

The facilitator role that is clearly required in the Majority World context is one that must be learned in developed countries as well. As ever more governments realize the need for community involvement in decision making, planning, and provision of services, the need for an understanding of facilitative processes becomes even greater. The need for human service professionals who can support and promote processes and networks at the local level is one of the key challenges facing the new Ministry for Children and Families.

Childcare in the Ministry for Children and Families: The Next Steps

The ground-breaking vision of the Ministry for Children and Families is consistent with an international, emerging literature on early childhood services that places children at the center of communities' promotion of future societal well-being. As the ministry continues its decentralization process, with each of the 20 regions becoming responsible for the conceptualization and structure of child and family services, it is important that the achievements to date in British Columbia's childcare system be maintained and promoted and that an appropriate philosophy and vision be adopted within the regions to further the objectives of the ministry.

Over the past five years, British Columbia has been seen as a leader across the country in the development of childcare services. Through new dollars for childcare, particularly the Childcare Strategic Initiative, the Province has been able to launch a number of innovative projects that address key issues of accessibility and inclusion. Three initiatives that may provide a particularly useful foundation for the integration and inclusion of childcare programs within the lives of families and communities are Supported Childcare, One-Stop Access Centers, and Childcare Resource and Referral programs.

Supported Childcare, launched in 1994, provides for a phased-in transition to the integration of children with special needs into regular childcare settings. Supported Childcare explicitly embraces the vision and philosophy of inclusion; as such, it represents a significant movement from the segregation of particular, targeted groups of children from the broader community of children. The initiative supports families, caregivers, and other community service providers to work together in meeting the needs of individual children, for the ultimate benefit of the entire community.

Within Supported Childcare, children considered "at risk" because of social and economic disadvantage may be considered "children with additional support needs", along with physically and mentally challenged children. Families, caregivers, and community service providers could learn much from the Supported Childcare model in meeting the needs of these children and recognizing their well-being as critically important to the health of whole communities. Quality childcare may be seen as an important way of supporting these children.

The provincial government funds 34 Childcare Resource and Referral programs, which provide training, support, information, and referral services to parents and childcare providers in 140 communities across the province. The Childcare Resource and Referral programs are an excellent example of community infrastructure that can be used to mobilize parents, caregivers, and other community service providers to work in partnership to strengthen services for children and families.

Through the Childcare Strategic Initiative (a four-year, federal-provincial program launched in 1995), projects are already under way to build on the potential of Childcare Resource and Referral programs to serve as a foundation for service integration and community partnerships. For example, the provincial government has worked with communities to create four One-Stop Access Centers that bring childcare resource and referral services, childcare licensing and subsidies under one roof. As well, many of the innovative research projects undertaken at Childcare Resource and Referral agencies through the Childcare Strategic Initiative provide examples of communities working together to develop approaches to childcare services that are responsive to local needs. It is critical that such "indigenous" seeds of activity be studied and shared broadly. Childcare and early childhood services represent one of the most accessible and potentially powerful entry points for a more integrated and holistic approach to better serving and supporting children, families, and communities.

The accomplishments highlighted above are examples of childcare programs and initiatives that complement the vision of the Ministry for Children and Families, and which could serve as parts of a foundation to extend it even further. However, the greatest challenge in making that vision a reality, given its significant departure from the philosophy and practice of service provision that has dominated the western world for at least 50 years, is to foster a new way of seeing and behaving. This challenge was noted when the ministry was created:

> At the bureaucratic level, leadership in the new Ministry must reflect and entrench a fundamentally new approach to serving children, youth and their fami-

lies. It must: have vision and be able to communicate that vision clearly and often to members of the organization and communities; be opportunity-focused not problem-focused; [and] seek and initiate needed changes rather than relying on the status quo (Morton, 1996, p. 23).

Amid the pressures of developing a new ministry and a new system while meeting the increasing demand for measurable outcomes from the public, the media, and politicians, central and regional staff may be tempted to formulate narrow, easily quantifiable objectives and to protect themselves by adherence to rigid bureaucratic protocols. Such an approach would, however, seriously undermine the ministry's potential. Indeed, the ministry's ability to sustain practices that support the realization of its vision of "children, youth and families living in supportive communities that enable them to achieve physical, intellectual, emotional, social, economic and spiritual well-being" (Ministry for Children and Families, 1997) is precisely the ability to take a road less traveled, guided by some commonly shared principles, a strong sense of direction, and the experience of fellow travelers in government and communities. The stories of others who have attempted similar journeys (e.g., Reggio Emilia) may be instructive or inspiring, but they cannot serve as blueprints or models to be "applied" to British Columbia.

This sense of uncertainty is not something most trained professionals, in governments or communities, are comfortable with: it requires stepping out of one's area of expertise, risking exposure, and seeking the guidance of others, all of which run counter to the tenets of western professionalism. Yet venturing into the unknown is precisely what is necessary to foster partnerships between governments and communities, between service providers and "clients" (Adams & Nelson, 1995). Over the coming years, the challenge of maintaining a sense of direction and shared purpose amid such potentially disorienting circumstances is one that ministry staff, community service providers, children, and families will face together as the Ministry for Children and Families develops.

Conclusion

The Ministry for Children and Families envisions "a child centered, integrated approach that promotes and protects the healthy development of children and youth" (Morton, 1996, p. 17). To meet this goal, children and families "need a single point of access into the child and youth serving system" (Ibid., p. 20).

Childcare and early childhood services represent one of the most accessible and potentially powerful entry points for a more integrated and holistic approach to better serving and supporting children, families, and communities. A substantial body of research demonstrates that quality childcare benefits children, and may be of particular benefit to children "at risk". As such, quality childcare has the potential to support the overall objective of the ministry, as well as its particular focus on early support and prevention. Quality care, when coupled with an inclusionary philosophy, has the multifold benefit of not only supporting the present and future well-being of children, but the well-being of families and society as well. No other program area within the new ministry has the potential to meet the needs of the majority of children and families at the community level, while at the same time addressing the needs of children experiencing significant risk factors.

Because of their inclusive focus, early childhood services may be conceived as the center of the range of programs and services within the new ministry. The philosophy and regional structure of the new ministry signal a move toward a more integrated, community-centered approach to service delivery. Emerging literature in western and Majority World countries supports this direction for early childhood services. By linking with progressive initiatives in Canada and internationally, the Ministry for Children and Families has the potential to achieve the vision of communities that are supportive of children, families, and future societal well-being. Both distributional factors, such as the continued availability of adequate funding for childcare and constitutional factors, such as the ministry's ability to engage families, service providers, and community members in the process of change, are interdependent and critical to the success of the ministry's reforms.

References

Adams, P., & Nelson, K. (1995). *Reinventing human services: Community- and family-centered practice.* New York: Aldine de Gruyter.

Andersson, B.E. (1989). Effects of public day care: A longitudinal study. In *Child Development, 60*: 57–66.

Andersson, B.E. (1992). Effects of day care on cognitive and socio-emotional competence of thirteen year old Swedish school children. In *Child Development, 63*: 20–36.

Dahlberg, G., Moss, P. & Pence, A. (1999). *Beyond Quality in Early Childhood Education and Care: Postmodern Perspectives.* London: Falmer Press.

Goelman, H., & Pence, A.R. (1988). Children in three types of day care: Daily experiences, quality of care and developmental outcomes. In *Early Child Development and Care, 33*: 67–76.

Gove, T.J. (1995). *Report of the Gove inquiry into child protection. Volume 2.* Victoria, BC: Queen's Printer for British Columbia.

Kretzman, J., & McKnight, J. (1993). *Building community from the inside out.* Chicago, IL: ACTA Publications.

Lamb, M., & Sternberg, K. (1990). Do we really know how day care affects children? In *Journal of Applied Developmental Psychology, 11*: 351–379.

Larner, M., & Phillips, D. (1994). Defining and valuing quality as a parent. In P. Moss and A. Pence (Eds.). *Valuing Quality in Early Childhood Services.* (pp. 43–60). London: Paul Chapman Publishing Ltd.

Lero, D.S., Pence, A., Shields, S., Brockman, L., & Goelman, H. (1992). *Canadian national childcare study. Introductory report.* Ottawa, ON: Statistics Canada, Health and Welfare Canada.

McGurk, H., Caplan, M., Hennessey, E., & Moss, P. (1993). Controversy, theory and social context in contemporary day care research. In *Journal of Child Psychology and Psychiatry, 34,* No. 1: 3–23.

Ministry for Children and Families. (1997). *Strategy: Healthy beginnings—healthy lives.* Victoria, BC: Author.

Ministry of Women's Equality. (1994). *Childcare: Choices at work.* Victoria, BC: Queen's Printer for British Columbia.

Morton, C. (1996). *British Columbia's child, youth and family serving system. Recommendations for change.* Victoria, BC: Queen's Printer for British Columbia.

Moss, P. (1997). Early childhood services in Europe. In *Policy Options,* 18(l): 27–30.

Moss, P., & Pence, A.R. (1994). *Valuing quality in early childhood services: New approaches to defining quality.* New York and London: Teachers College Press and Paul Chapman Publishers.

Myers, R. (1992). *The twelve who survive: Strengthening early childhood development in the Third World.* London: Routledge.

New, R. (1997). Reggio Emilia's commitment to children and community: A reconceptualization of quality and DAP. In *Canadian Children,* Spring 1997: 7–12.

Pence, A. (Ed.). (1992). *Canadian childcare in context: Perspectives from the provinces and territories.* Ottawa, ON: Statistics Canada, Health and Welfare Canada.

Pence, A. (1993). Canada. In M. Cochran (Ed.), *International Handbook of Childcare Policies and Programs.* Westport, CT and London: Greenwood Press.

Putnam, R. (1993). *Making democracy work: Civic traditions in modern Italy,* Princeton, NJ: Princeton University Press.

Schweinhart, L., Barnes, H., & Weikart, D. (1993). *Significant benefits: The High/Scope Perry Preschool Study through age 2–7.* Ypsilanti, MI: The High/Scope Press.

Statistics Canada (1995). *Women in Canada. A statistical report.* Ottawa: Minister of Industry.

Afterword

Chapter 28

Early Childhood Education: An Empowering Force for the Twenty-First Century?

Donna S. Lero

While each Canadian province and territory hosts a tangle of early childhood education and childcare programs, few children and families have access to the services they need (Friendly & Oloman, this volume).

The concept that early childhood education is a benefit for children—a way of ensuring that *all* children have access to positive experiences during their formative years—is not a consideration on the current Australian political or social agenda (Hayden, 1997, p. 45).

Despite considerable advantages, early childhood services are in a critical state and at a critical stage. The services are fragmented, inflexible, incoherent and full of inequalities, unable to meet the changing and varied needs of families (Moss & Penn, 1996, p. vii, reflecting on early childhood services in the UK).

Many Americans are disturbed by the inadequate programs in which young children spend long days; they are realizing that more coordination, higher standards, and increased intentionality are needed to achieve the quality programs that young children, their families, and the country need (Kagan & Cohen, 1996, p. 310).

These excerpts describe a common pattern among some of the wealthiest countries on the planet. Each quote reflects the results of a lack of systemic planning and policy development and a lack of funding and political will that has resulted in uncoordinated programs of variable quality; programs that fail to support parents' efforts to raise healthy, competent children. This fact that has profound significance, not only for children and families, but for the greater public good. Surely, these are not intended outcomes; most certainly, dramatic and systemic change and more rational, effective policies are required.

New policies, however, must not only deal with the *old* problems we already recognize; they must also affirm a collective responsibility for all children as a first principle—a step that would naturally lead to a rethinking of other policy issues that affect children and their life prospects that extends far beyond the field of early childhood education. Developing a consensus on this principle as a first step and working purposefully to transform current early childhood policies and services will require building on our existing knowledge base and working with others who share our common purpose in ways that could have far-reaching effects.

As Moss (1997) reports, there are at least four alternative discourses on early childhood services. Each of these reflects a different primary purpose to be served by childcare policies and programs, and leads to different implications about why and how the state might be involved in providing public funding for early childhood programs. Three of the four major discourses appear repeatedly. They are the *childcare for working parents* discourse; the *day care for children in need* (or welfare) discourse; and the *nursery education (or kindergarten) for over 3s* discourse.

Discourse No. 1: Childcare for Working Parents
The focus on childcare needs of working parents has been fuelled by the dramatic changes that have occurred in mothers' participation in the labor force in most industrialized countries since the late 1970s or early 1980s. In Canada, for example, more than two thirds of mothers with children under six years were in the paid labor force in 1997, and 64% of mothers with a child under three years of age were employed or actively looking for work. An additional small, but important segment of mothers with young children, particularly single mothers, require early childhood care while they complete or continue their education or participate in job training programs to become more employable. We should note that while policy statements may refer to working *parents*, in reality most childcare is assumed to be required as a substitute or supplement for *maternal* care. Economists have confirmed that difficulties in childcare arrangements and in affording childcare typically have a more profound impact on women's participation in the labor force, and the stress they experience combining work and family responsibilities; and that these effects are visible across a range of incomes and occupations (Cleveland & Krashinsky, 1998).

While the quality of service delivery is always recognized as important, in the context of being framed as a support to employment, childcare is seen largely as a necessary service to meet the economic needs of parents and their employers and as a crucial tool for supporting women's economic equality. From this standpoint, discussions about the supply and cost of suitable, reliable early childhood care, that is available at the times when parents are working, reflect the concept of childcare services as a *commodity*.

Within this framework, the need for mechanisms to offset the cost of childcare for working parents and to expand the supply of places is a major consideration. Within a market framework, efforts to make childcare more affordable are addressed through a combination of fee subsidies for low-income parents and tax deductions or credits for middle and upper income families, with smaller amounts of public funds allocated directly to services in the form of various grants to offset operating expenses or to ensure that, for example, children with special needs can be included. In some countries, employers may be involved either as managers of, or contributors to, employee benefit plans that ease childcare costs or, much less commonly, as hosts of on-site childcare programs.

In contrast to France and Sweden, where all employers contribute to a national pool for funding childcare programs that have almost universal coverage, relatively few employers in Canada or the UK have any direct involvement in funding childcare services. In Australia, tax incentives are meant to encourage employers to be more actively involved in off-setting costs of childcare for their employees and/or encouraging the development of workplace-supported childcare as part of that country's expansionary phase—but the incentives are minimal—and have not been very successful. In the U.S., relatively few employers (usually large corporations) have sustained any ongoing involvement in service provision, although many enable employees to access pre-tax dollars in daycare savings accounts to which employers may also contribute. More recently, the American Business Collaboration, a consortium of large employers, has become more directly involved in providing funds to increase the supply and quality of care available in selected communities that include many of their corporations' employees. However, true corporate-community collaborations are rare. In most cases, employers who are involved to any degree in "dependent care services" do so with a primary interest on the effects on their company's bottom line—e.g., through reductions in absenteeism, work-family stress, and role interference that affect productivity. It is fair to say that the discourse on working parents' needs and the interest in developing an adequate early childhood care industry to service those needs reflects a view of children as, perhaps, necessary inconveniences to the "real" (productive) world of adult work.

As a side note, there is a secondary underlying discourse on the extent to which mothers of young children are experiencing undue stress caused by carrying a double workload and the extent to which mothers working outside the home and using childcare is harmful to children. This underlying discourse reflects the ambivalence many people still feel about changing gender roles, often leading to neo-conservative assertions that women with young children should be at home, and that public funds, rather than being used to expand nonparental childcare services, should be shifted to tax cuts or credits to reward/support (married) mothers who opt to stay home. While such policy suggestions are often accompanied by substantial rhetoric about individual choice and personal (parental) responsibility, by posing the public policy response as a shift to move funding away from the development and maintenance of affordable, high-quality services, neo-conservative policies typically reduce women's choices (Teghtsoonian, 1993). Moreover, such suggestions ignore women's increasingly important role as income earners in their families and deflect attention from discussions of a range of policy instruments, including paid parental leave, that could lead to more harmonious means to integrate work and family responsibilities across the life span.

Discourse No. 2: Services for Children in Need

Services for "children in need" (more recently "children at risk") have a long history in most countries, and in both Canada and the U.S. this motive has served as the main vehicle for providing federal and state funding to programs delivered outside the school system. A recent history of early childhood services in Canada (Prochner, 1999) recounts the development of programs from the 1830s onward which included many programs for poor children run by church groups and charitable organizations. Eventually *free kindergartens* that served immigrant populations and many children of the working poor became an integral part of social reform efforts, including the establishment of public education systems.

Since the mid 1960s early childhood programs for disadvantaged children have attracted substantial amounts of public funds. In Canada, the Canada Assistance Plan (CAP), which served as the major cost-sharing instrument on which current childcare programs are based, provided a means to channel public funds into programs for young children in families "in need" or "likely to be in need". CAP funding, in particular, has been used for fee subsidies for children in low-income families, largely for parents who are working or studying, whose eligibility is determined either through income or means testing. Children from middle- and upper-income families also use these regulated services, with parents paying the full fee.

Research suggests that many children who would be eligible for a subsidized space are not accommodated within the limited supply of regulated childcare settings, either because all subsidy dollars in their province/community are limited, or because there are no "empty" eligible spaces in their neighborhood to which a subsidy can be applied (Friendly, 1994). With no sliding fee scale geared to family income or the number of children needing care, parents in modest and middle income families who do not qualify for a fee subsidy have the "choice" of paying a relatively hefty fee for regulated care ($340–$450/month for 3–4 year-olds).

Since the replacement of CAP by a reduced block fund (CHST) that also includes the federal contribution to provincial health costs and expenditures for postsecondary education programs and social welfare benefits, childcare has not fared well. Each provincial/territorial government, faced with significant pressures to reduce deficits and debt, has limited its direct support for early childhood programs. There have been cuts to, or the elimination of, the operating grants that provided stable program funding to centers and a redirection of this important component of direct funding to centers into fee subsidies paid to parents, ostensibly with the intention of providing greater access to services for children in need. Ironically, the destabilization of childcare programs appears to be leading to higher fees being charged by centers to offset the reduction in operating grants, as well as reduced service availability in communities if centers close or reduce their intake of younger children. Research in progress also indicates that funding cuts are affecting centers' capacities to include children with special needs (Lero, Irwin, & Brophy, in progress).

Ironically, while current high-quality early childhood programs that already serve vulnerable children are experiencing funding cuts, there is increased interest in developing separate initiatives to provide primary prevention and intervention programs for children at risk. In at least two Canadian provinces, significant initiatives that include home visiting and parenting supports have been launched to reduce the likelihood of child abuse and neglect without recognizing the complementary family support role that community-based early childhood programs have, especially if they are integrated with other community services.

Recently in the U.S.A., policies related to welfare provision changed dramatically. Time limits and work requirements were imposed for the receipt of welfare benefits. Social service programs are designed to move recipients (and their children) out of public welfare rolls as quickly as possible. In the concomitant rush to accommodate many more poor children in childcare to support welfare to work initiatives, early childhood advocates worry about reductions in quality standards, exemptions from licensing requirements and the pressure to serve many more troubled and stressed families quickly without adequate supports. Meanwhile welfare recipients are being urged to take positions as early childhood care providers. This could mean that children are increasingly likely to be in settings staffed by workers with limited training, resources, or commitment to promoting the development of children in their care (Gnezda, 1996). One cannot help but observe that while early childhood programs for the poor enjoy substantial public funding, even that funding is insufficient to meet the needs of many families. As well, separate service streams for early childhood for welfare purposes and for programs for other children result in continuing segregation by class and race in many communities, are expensive, and inevitably result in less sustainable, poorer programs over the longer term. These are some of the reasons why Skocpol (1991) has consistently argued *against* targeted programs for poor children or those at risk.

Discourse No. 3: Nursery Education for Over Threes
The third discourse Moss refers to is the discourse on nursery education for over threes. It comes closer to a universal interest in children's education and development that could reflect a broader, more holistic approach. Moss notes that the movement to universal, publicly funded provision of early childhood services for children aged 3–6 years is "one of the most widespread trends in the European Union" (Moss, 1997). Universal coverage for over threes has already been achieved in Belgium, France, and Italy, with universal provision as a stated policy objective in Denmark, Finland, Germany, Spain, and Sweden. The driving force for this development is an appreciation of the educational benefits derived from these services and an increasing emphasis on ensuring school readiness. Thus, public funds are being invested in the early education of all children, regardless of parents' work status or income. The disadvantage of this approach is the obverse of its strength. It ignores both the need to offer full-day programs of comparable quality to accommodate children whose parents work full time, and the need to extend services beyond an early education mandate to address the broader range of family and community needs for economic, social, and instrumental support. While there is an intention to provide a high-quality service on a universal basis, this approach fragments the focus across the full age range of 0–6 years,

leaving the under threes vulnerable to poor quality and unstable arrangements. It also runs the risk of focusing primarily on traditional educational approaches for children, rather than expanding the programs to address a broader range of child, family, and community concerns. Given the increasing numbers of children in families that are vulnerable to poverty, who are experiencing difficult transitions in their family lives, and who are far more diverse in cultural and linguistic background, newer, more holistic models are required to support children's development.

Currently, interest in extending the school system downwards to serve younger children is also a model that is being pursued in several areas as an approach to promote school readiness, and/or as part of a broader family policy initiative. While publicly funded kindergarten for the year before Grade 1 is widely available in OECD nations, the new approach would include children as young as three years of age. It appears that states moving in this direction are giving little if any consideration to how such services might be operated in a more integrated manner with existing and new community-based programs. Research indicates that the effort to integrate school-based junior kindergarten and kindergarten programs with day care and to reconcile vastly different salary scales and cultures once the two systems are in place is formidable.

Discourse No. 4: Multifunctional Resources

In their book, *Transforming Nursery Education*, Moss and Penn make a strong case for converting the limited nursery education approach that is prevalent in the U.K., and that exists alongside other public and private services, into a single, holistic, multi-function early childhood service for children 0–6 years of age, that has broader ties to parental and community needs. In so doing, they come closest to an argument in line with a fourth discourse—one that Moss calls a discourse of early childhood services that "conceptualizes these services as institutions of cultural, social and economic significance—community resources that should be multifunctional to meet a variety of needs including care, education socialization, health and family support that should be available to all children and families". This discourse recognizes the importance of early childhood services that meet employment and social welfare goals, but extend beyond them to meet multiple purposes for a variety of families, serving collective as well as individual ends. Moss further states that, like schooling or health, such holistic services can only be provided through substantial public investment.

This fourth discourse is one that probably finds sympathy with many readers of this volume who have struggled with incoherent, limited, fragmented, and underfunded approaches to meeting the needs of children and families in current programs. As a discourse on early childhood services, it is also a discourse on children generally and embodies a values framework that, while recognizing that children are primarily a parental responsibility, affirms that children are also our shared responsibility.

This belief is rooted in a moral and compassionate obligation to *all* children as citizens and recognizes the importance of collective efforts to contribute to each child's optimal development for the collective benefits that accrue in return. In effect, this view unites our interest in investing not only in the development of *children's human capital* (their future knowledge, skills, and competencies that presumably will be manifested in positive individual outcomes and a healthy economy), but also in *our own social capital* (the vitality we generate in developing and maintaining social cohesion through shared values and collective, mutual and personal engagement with others in ways that are mutually supportive).

Such a perspective is a far cry from one that considers children individually or collectively as a social problem or as an economic or social liability. It is also one that applies more broadly, leading inevitably to the consideration of other policy areas that unfairly limit children's life prospects: issues of income security; child support payment systems; affordable housing; and medical, educational, and social supports for families of children with disabilities, for example. The point is that policies related to the provision and quality of early childhood services are themselves reflections of broader policies and perspectives related to children, and potentially can confirm our collective ties to them through intergenerational relationships and mutual obligations.

The prevailing discourse about early childhood education and about children generally that is dominant at one time or another, and the degree to which various governments commit funds and invest in national programs to support young children (such as via direct public funding versus tax credits or vouchers; through extending the school mandate downwards or developing whole new community-based systems to serve young children and their parents) reflect differences in ideology, values, labor market press, popular consensus, and political support. Increasingly, governments are less willing and able to develop and fund massive new social programs at the national or state level. They are, however, open to realistic proposals that could involve national, state/provincial, and local governments as partners, perhaps in collaboration with employers and community/professional organizations and with parents in ways that allow each player to make a sound contribution in keeping with their level of expertise/accepted mandate. This more diversified, shared approach to understanding social needs and developing coherent long-term strategies to achieve desired outcomes provides those of us who wish to participate with the opportunity to do so. But it is a time-consuming, demanding, long-term process that requires serious dedication, openness to alternative points of view, and willingness to seek and build on consensus where it can be found.

Moving Forward: Taking the Gauntlet

It is evident that the 1990s have been a time of momentous change. Political and economic shifts, new demographic and social patterns, international agreements on trade and investments, and new technologies are changing the very structure and pace of our daily lives. There is far more economic insecurity, and a significant potential for increasing income inequality and polarization. This could reduce our willingness to participate in and support social programs that depend on pooled funding sources and a collective sense of ownership. At the same time, in public opinion polls in Canada, for example, there is consistent support for programs that reduce the adverse impacts of child and family poverty and contribute to the healthy development and well-being of children and families. There is also a clear sense that current approaches are not working; that governments alone cannot solve these problems; and that a broadly based, holistic approach to support children and families is needed. These views are strong ones on which to build, and the general willingness on many people's part to engage in a "rethinking" of how we can do better is a positive foundation. Recognition of these points is currently helping to facilitate significant steps toward formulating a multipronged *National Children's Agenda*—such as are beginning to be discussed in Canada, Australia, New Zealand, and elsewhere.

How then to move forward? No doubt, many readers of this volume have been engaged in efforts to change current programs, structures, and/or processes within individual early childhood programs, educational institutions, communities, or organizations. Some have been involved at the political level as well. In each of these home organizations and in our past experiences we have seen what factors work to produce positive change and what the impediments are to that process.

We know, for example, that a first step is one of problem recognition—of understanding that things are not going well or that our efforts are not having the desired results. In that early stage, we typically need to confirm what the exact nature of "the problem" is and how others view it. We may need to document what is and is not happening and determine what specifically needs to be changed. This is what Hayden referred to in her list of constitutional questions in chapter 2.

Understanding how things can be done differently requires examination of alternatives and generally requires seeking new information. We may read about other approaches/programs, consult with colleagues, collect information from various stakeholders, bring in outsiders, and do some research. In some cases, that is sufficient to understand what changes might be helpful, and if the problem is one that we are personally involved in, we might go ahead and try something new. In more complex circumstances, doing something differently, especially if it is costly or requires multiple other changes and "buy-in" from others, is a much larger process. In those cases, more extensive documentation, discussions with others, openness to alternative approaches, and consensus building will be required. As many of the case studies in this volume show us, there have been successes along the way. Creating and facilitating systemic change requires both doing our own homework and engaging others who have a major stake in the process or outcome in ways that allow them to provide input and make a contribution. Leadership is required, as is consensus-building.

The purpose of this volume has been to present examples (case studies) of the process that we, in the early childhood field, can use, either as springboards for our own efforts, or as models that might be adapted at a local or larger level.

My suggestion is that readers use this information as starting points for further debate and discussion and that they commit to doing so over a period of time in a structured way. A significant advantage and tool that we now have at our disposal is electronic media for sharing discussion papers, posting material on websites, and conversing with each other—even across state and international boundaries. Conferences provide another vehicle for this purpose.

There is no doubt that we, who care about the future of early childhood education, both as a profession and as a way to make a positive contribution in the lives of children, families, and communities, face many challenges. But we also have many tools at our disposal: a solid and enlarging base of research and conceptual knowledge to draw upon; a maturing field that includes significant journals and publications; considerable practice wisdom; and the means, dedication, and vision to engage in an empowering process of social change.

In their work with community groups, researchers at Cornell University have defined empowerment as "an intentional, ongoing process centered in the local community, involving mutual respect, critical reflection, caring and group participation . . . through which people lacking an equal share of valued resources gain greater access to and control over these resources" (Cochran, 1988). Perhaps a re-evaluation of early childhood policies can, indeed, be an empowering force for the twenty-first century.

References

Cleveland, G., & Krashinsky, M. (1998). *The benefits and costs of good childcare.* Toronto: Childcare Resource & Research Unit, University of Toronto.

Cochran, M. (1988). Parental empowerment in family matters: Lessons learned from a research program. In D. R. Powell (Ed.). Parent Education as Early Childhood Intervention: Emerging Directions in Theory, Research and Practice. Volume 3 in *Annual Advances in Applied Developmental Psychology.* Norwood: Ablex.

Friendly, M. (1994). *Childcare policy in Canada: Putting the pieces together.* Don Mills, Ontario: Addison Wesley Ltd.

Hayden, J. (1997). Our mission for the next millennium. In *Children: Commodity or Investment or. . .?* Proceedings of the Crèche and Kindergarten Association of Queensland Early Childhood Conference, Brisbane: C & K.

Gnezda, M.T. (November 1996). Welfare reform: Personal responsibilities and opportunities for early childhood advocates. *Young Children*: 55–58.

Kagan, S.L., & Cohen N.E. (1996). A vision for a quality early care and education system. In S.L. Kagan & N.E. Cohen (Eds.), *Reinventing Early Care and Education: A Vision for a Quality System.* San Francisco: Jossey-Bass Publishers.

Lero, D. S., Irwin, S.H., & Brophy, K. (research in progress). Caregivers' attitudes and experiences regarding inclusion of children with special needs in childcare programs—A longitudinal study.

Moss, P. (1997). Early childhood services in Europe. *Policy Options,* 18, (1): 27–30.

Moss, P., & Penn, H. (1996). *Transforming Nursery Education.* London: Paul Chapman Publishing Ltd.

Prochner, L. (1999). Childcare and kindergarten in Canada, 1828–1966. In L. Prochner, & N. Howe (Eds.), *Early Childhood Care and Education in Canada: Past, Present and Future.* Vancouver, BC: UBC Press.

Skocpol, T. (1991). Targeting within universalism: Politically viable policies to combat poverty in the United States. In C. Jencks, & P. Peterson (Eds.), *The Urban Underclass*. Washington, DC: The Brookings Institution.

Teghtsoonian, K. (1993). Neo-conservative ideology and opposition to federal regulation of childcare services in the United States and Canada. *Canadian Journal of Political Science*, 26 (1): 97–128.

Glossary of Terms

Accreditation The Quality Improvement and Accreditation System (QIAS) is administered by an Australian government agency, the National Childcare Accreditation Council. In order to receive federal government financial support, day care centers must undergo both an internal and external review to establish if they meet the 52 determining principles of quality care. The system also addresses "contributing" factors such as working conditions, job satisfaction, wages, training, experience, and stability of day care staff.

Arbitration The Australian industrial relations system of compulsory conciliation and arbitration is a process whereby disputes between employers and trade unions are settled either by agreement (conciliation) or arbitrated upon by a third party—an industrial tribunal. A dual system of industrial regulation tribunals operate in both federal and state jurisdictions; hence each Australian state has its own industrial relations machinery that functions parallel to the federal machinery. The legal instrument that settles disputes is called an award (see Industrial Awards).

Board of Teacher Registration The Board of Teacher Registration is a state government agency in Australia that provides for the registration of teachers and also determines the qualifications required for registration.

Childcare Resource and Referral Programs This term is used in British Columbia and refers to community-based programs where parents, childcare providers, and community members can access childcare training, support, and information and referral services. The British Columbia government funds 34 such programs, which provide services to families and childcare providers in 140 communities across the province.

Childcare Strategic Initiative This is the four-year federal-provincial agreement (1995–1999) between the governments of Canada and British Columbia to develop, test, and evaluate innovative ways of delivering childcare services. The objectives of the Childcare Strategic Initiative are to improve the accessibility, affordability, and quality of childcare services for children and families and to ensure a more responsive, effective, efficient, and inclusive system for childcare in the province.

Day Care This term refers to center-based day care or "long-day care" operations that operate for at least eight hours a day, five days a week, 48 weeks of the year, and provide childcare services for 0–5-year-old children.

Early Childhood This term refers to the first seven or eight years of life during which the child will have achieved a significant amount of all necessary learning, especially those attitudes, motives and dispositions regarded as essential for later success.

Early Childhood Education This term is generally taken to indicate a planned and developmentally appropriate institutional environment for children under the age of about eight years. Thus it concerns values and styles of pedagogy that overlap the domains of care, kindergarten, and elementary/primary school.

Early Childhood Professional In this book early childhood professional refers to individuals with specialized training, but not necessarily solely those with tertiary training in early childhood education. Any teacher, health worker, advocate, policy analyst, researcher, and/or administrator whose focus is upon the development and/or delivery of services for children aged 0–8 years old could be an "early childhood professional". Professionals in the field of early childhood education, as in other fields, are those who have demonstrated, through concentrated study and years of practice, a commitment to the area; who subscribe to a common set of principles; and who perceive themselves to be emissaries of their field.

English Foundation Schools These are run either by education foundations in Hong Kong to provide schooling leading to international qualifications, or are private schools run mainly for expatriate children, offering a curriculum similar to that of their country of origin.

ICRW This is the International Center for Research on Women, a non-government research and development Organization based in Washington DC. Information on their research and publications can be found on the worldwide website at www.icrw.org

Industrial Awards Awards are legally enforceable minimum wages and conditions of employment for most employees in Australia. Awards are determined by the relevant industrial tribunal, a quasi-legal authority, during the process of arbitration.

OECD This is the Organization for Economic Cooperation and Development. The offices are based in Paris and Washington. It is an influential advisory organization drawing upon funds from its 29 member countries (basically the richest 29 countries in the world). Its economic reports and indices are particularly powerful and influential, but it produces international surveys on aspects of education and social affairs as well.

OMEP This is the *Organization Mondiale pour l'Education Prescolaire* (World Organization for Early Childhood Education).

One-Stop Access Centers These are locations where parents, childcare providers, and community members can get information and assistance on licensing, childcare subsidies, and childcare choices in their communities (currently operating in British Columbia).

Play This is the primary vehicle of young children's learning. Play takes place almost from birth and through play children imitate, model, and develop intellectually, physically, emotionally, socially, and creatively.

QIAS See Accreditation

Senate Employment, Education, and Training Reference Committee This is a federal government committee established in 1995 to report to the Senate with regard to the experience of Australian children up to the age of seven. The Committee examined research bearing on the capacity to learn, the impact of early childhood education on later school success, the role of parents as early educators, initiatives, interventions, and relationships between early childhood services and school education.

Supported Childcare This initiative was launched in British Columbia in 1994 to integrate children who need extra support into "mainstream" childcare settings. The principles of Supported Childcare are inclusion, family-centered care, community-based service, individual planning, and shared responsibility.

TAFE College Technical and Further Education Colleges throughout Australia provide education and training courses for school leavers and adults seeking to gain trades skills and qualifications. Early childhood students can take diploma level courses to prepare them for work in childcare settings. Recently TAFE programs are being referred to as "tertiary" education, a term previously used exclusively for university education.

UNICEF This is United Nations International Children's Emergency Fund. Supported by funds from the United Nations and from donations, it carries out important relief and survey work all over the world and is based in New York.

The Contributors

Allison Benner is a research and policy consultant, specializing in services to children and youth, and gender issues.

Judith Burton lectures in Child and Family Studies at Griffith University. She is completing a Doctor of Philosophy on the topic of workplace relations and teaching dilemmas in childcare.

Trevor Cairney is Professor of Education and Pro Vice-Chancellor, Research, at the University of Western Sydney, Nepean, Australia. He has written seven books and over 150 papers in the field of literacy and has presented the findings of this work at over 100 conferences worldwide. He is a past President of the Australian Literacy Educators' Association, and Director of the New South Wales Children's Literacy and ESL Research Network.

Patricia Canning is a developmental psychologist and Professor in the Faculty of Education, Memorial University of Newfoundland. She has worked and published in the areas of day care, social policy, special education, and the effects of unemployment and economic uncertainty on children and families.

Margaret Carr trained as a kindergarten teacher and has been working in teacher education for the past 12 years. Her current position is Chairperson, Department of Early Childhood Studies, University of Waikato, New Zealand. Margaret is a joint director of the Early Childhood Curriculum Project (with Professor Helen May).

Loraine Corrie is Senior Lecturer at Edith Cowan University. Her current research interests include assessing quality in early childhood teaching and young children with challenging behaviors.

Isabel Doxey has been a Professor at Ryerson Polytechnical University, Toronto, for 20 years. Her contributions to research, curriculum, and policy development regarding early childhood are well recognized nationally and internationally. Her publications include the book *Childcare and Education: Canadian Dimensions* (1990).

Marjory Ebbeck is Professor of Early Childhood Education and works in the deLissa Institute of Early Childhood and Family Studies, South Australia. Marjory has published widely in the area of early childhood curriculum, home school community relations, and sociocultural contexts and is consultant to a number of countries on policy development and teacher education.

Alison Elliott is Associate Professor in Early Childhood Education at the University of Western Sydney, Nepean. She has had a lengthy career as a teacher, researcher, academic, and policymaker in early childhood education. Alison is the editor of *Every Child* and author of numerous publications about children's development and learning.

Evelyn Ferguson is Associate Professor of Social Work at the University of Manitoba. Her research interests focus on child day care policy, particularly parent preferences and involvement. Her areas of interest are women and social policy and feminist social work practice.

Martha Friendly is the Coordinator of the Childcare Resource and Research Unit at the Center for Urban and Community Studies, University of Toronto, and Adjunct Professor at the Urban Center. She has written many reports and articles on childcare policy and a book, *Childcare Policy in Canada: Putting the Pieces Together* (1994).

Philip Gammage trained and taught as an early years teacher, then studied psychology. He is Emeritus Professor and former Dean of Education at Nottingham University and has just completed a period as President of the British Association of Early Childhood Education. He is a consultant for OECD (in Early Childhood Education) and currently holds the Foundation deLissa Chair in Early Childhood, University of South Australia.

Vicki Greive is a Lecturer in the School of Educational and Social Inquiry, Early Childhood Studies at Edith Cowan University, Western Australia. Vicki is a moderator for the Childcare Quality Improvement and

Accreditation System and has a particular interest in crosscultural issues and promoting acceptance of diversity.

Jacqueline Hayden has researched and worked in the field of early childhood education in the British West Indies, Canada, the U.S., Australia, New Zealand, and Africa and has published widely on comparative social and policy issues in early childhood education. Jacqueline is Director of the Master of Teaching (Early Childhood) program at the University of Western Sydney, Nepean, Australia. Her publications include the book *Management of Early Childhood Services* (1996).

Richard Johnson is a former preschool teacher who now teaches at the University of Hawaii at Manoa, and is the Graduate Chair of the Department of Teacher Education & Curriculum Studies. His upcoming book *Hands Off: The Disappearance of Touch in the Care of Children* is being published by Peter Lang.

Donna Lero is an Associate Professor in the Department of Family Studies at the University of Guelph in Ontario, Canada, where she teaches courses in child and family poverty and social policy. Donna was Director of the Canadian National Childcare Study and is currently involved in two other major studies of childcare programs in Canada.

Mary Lyon is Professor and Chairperson of the Department of Child & Youth Study at Mount Saint Vincent University, Nova Scotia. Areas of research in which she has published include social policy, childcare quality, childcare training, policy, and services for children with disabilities and their families and the development of language and play in young children with hearing and language disabilities.

Michael Lyons is a Lecturer in the School of Industrial Relations, Griffith University. He has degrees in politics and public policy and in industrial relations and labor law. His doctoral research examines the employment relations of long day care in Australia.

Carmel Maloney is a Lecturer in the School of Educational and Social Inquiry at Edith Cowan University, Western Australia. Currently she is the Chairperson of the Early Childhood Program Committee. Her research interests include young children's learning and early childhood pedagogy.

Helen May is Professor of Early Childhood Teacher Education, Institute for Early Childhood, Victoria University and Wellington College of Education, New Zealand. She is joint director of the Early Childhood Curriculum Project (with Margaret Carr).

Margaret McKim is Director of the Infant and Preschool Mental Health Clinic and an associate professor in the Clinical Psychology Program at the University of Saskatchewan. She has been working with families with young children for more than 20 years and has written extensively on early family development and intervention.

Anne Meade is Director of the New Zealand Council for Educational Research. Prior to this position she was Senior Lecturer in Education at Victoria University of Wellington, with special responsibility for early childhood education courses. Her extensive publications include the books *The Children Can Choose* (1985) and *Thinking Children* (1995).

Elizabeth Mellor was an Associate Professor at Monash University with long-standing responsibilities for the early childhood program. She recently completed a two-year appointment as Principal Lecturer at the Hong Kong Institute of Education and is an Honorary Research Associate of the Center for Applied Studies in Early Childhood and Consultant to the Hong Kong Institute of Education.

Linda Newman works in Early Childhood Education and Early Intervention at University of Western Sydney, Nepean. She is past President of the New South Wales Early Childhood Practicum Council.

Mab Oloman was Director of Childcare Services at the University of British Columbia from 1982. She has worked for the British Columbia provincial government for several years and is responsible for the Childcare Resource and Information Services at Westcoast Childcare Resource Center, Vancouver, Canada.

Alan Pence is Professor at the School of Child and Youth Care, University of Victoria, British Columbia. He is internationally recognized for his extensive publications in the field of early childhood care and education research.

Andrea Petrie is Senior Lecturer in Child and Family Studies at Griffith University. She has over 25 years of experience in the early childhood/children's services field, specializing in the areas of early childhood and sociology.

The Contributors

Susan Prentice is Assistant Professor of Sociology at the University of Manitoba. She specializes in historical and contemporary analysis of childcare and family issues. From 1993–1996, she held the Margaret Laurence Chair in Women's Studies; she is currently the Manitoba representative to the Canadian Childcare Advocacy Association.

Bridie Raban holds the Mooroolbeek Chair of Early Childhood Education at the University of Melbourne. She has taught young children for 13 years before taking up an academic career in the U.K. at the universities of Bristol, Reading, Oxford, and Warwick where she was Professor of Primary Education. She is the author of over 200 publications in the field of language and literacy development.

Tracey Simpson is Lecturer in Early Childhood Education, School of Teacher Education, Charles Sturt University, Australia and has worked in a variety of roles and early childhood services over a period of 20 years in both metropolitan and rural areas of New South Wales.

Collette Tayler is Professor of Early Childhood Education at Queensland University of Technology, Australia. She is a Fellow of the Australian College of Education and has served as a National Vice-President of the Australian Early Childhood Association.

Christine Ure is a Senior Lecturer in the Department of Early Childhood Studies at the University of Melbourne. Her primary research interest is in the area of transition to school and children's early progress in the school program.

Ann Veale is Head of School of the deLissa Institute of Early Childhood and Family Studies at the University of South Australia. Ann has had teaching experience with young children in New Zealand and Australia. Her publications are in the field of teacher development, art education and art development.

Jan White is Senior Lecturer and Director of Early Childhood Education, School of Teacher Education, Charles Sturt University, Australia.

Rethinking Childhood

JOE L. KINCHELOE & JANICE A. JIPSON, *General Editors*

A revolution is occurring regarding the study of childhood. Traditional notions of child development are under attack, as are the methods by which children are studied. At the same time, the nature of childhood itself is changing as children gain access to information once reserved for adults only. Technological innovations, media, and electronic information have narrowed the distinction between adults and children, forcing educators to rethink the world of schooling in this new context.

This series of textbooks and monographs encourages scholarship in all of these areas, eliciting critical investigations in developmental psychology, early childhood education, multicultural education, and cultural studies of childhood.

Proposals and manuscripts may be sent to the general editors:

> Joe L. Kincheloe
> 637 W. Foster Avenue
> State College, PA 16801
>
> *or*
>
> Janice A. Jipson
> 219 Pease Court
> Janesville, WI 53545

To order other books in this series, please contact our Customer Service Department at:

> (800) 770-LANG (within the U.S.)
> (212) 647-7706 (outside the U.S.)
> (212) 647-7707 FAX

Or browse online by series at:
> www.peterlang.com